# The Contested Territory of Architectural Theory



This book brings together a diverse group of theoreticians to explore architectural theory as a discipline, assessing its condition and relevance to contemporary practice.

Offering critical assessment in the face of major social and environmental issues of today, 17 original contributions address the relevance of architectural theory in the contemporary world from various perspectives, including but not limited to: politics, gender, representation, race, environmental crisis, and history.

The chapters are grouped into two distinct sections: the first section explores various historical perspectives on architectural theory, mapping theory's historiographical turn and its emergence and decline from the 1960s to the present; the second offers alternative visions and new directions for architectural theory, incorporating feminist and human rights perspectives, and addressing contemporary issues such as Artificial Intelligence and the Age of Acceleration. This edited collection features contributions from renowned scholars as well as emergent voices, with a Foreword by David Leatherbarrow.

This book will be of great interest to graduate and upper-level students of architecture, as well as academics and practicing architects.

**Elie G. Haddad** is Professor of Architecture at the Lebanese American University, where he is currently Dean of the School of Architecture and Design. Haddad completed his PhD studies at the University of Pennsylvania in 1998 with a dissertation on Henry van de Velde. His research focuses on architectural theory, urbanism, and modern architecture. In 2014, Haddad co-edited a survey on contemporary architecture and is in the process of finalizing a new volume titled *Modern Architecture in a Post-Modern Era* (forthcoming). In parallel to his academic activities, Haddad was recently elected as President of the Association of Arab Architects.

# The Contested Territory of Architectural Theory

Edited by
Elie G. Haddad

Foreword by
David Leatherbarrow

LONDON AND NEW YORK

Cover image: Restoring the Ruins, Salam Omar el Ansari (2002)

First published 2023
by Routledge
4 Park Square, Milton Park, Abingdon, Oxon OX14 4RN

and by Routledge
605 Third Avenue, New York, NY 10158

*Routledge is an imprint of the Taylor & Francis Group, an informa business*



*British Library Cataloguing-in-Publication Data*
A catalogue record for this book is available from the British Library

*Library of Congress Cataloging-in-Publication Data*
Names: Haddad, Elie, editor.
Title: The contested territory of architectural theory / edited by Elie Haddad.
Description: New York : Routledge, 2023. | Includes bibliographical references and index.
Identifiers: LCCN 2022018331 | ISBN 9781032274751 (hardback) | ISBN 9781032274720 (paperback) | ISBN 9781003292999 (ebook)
Subjects: LCSH: Architecture—Philosophy.
Classification: LCC NA2500 .C615 2023 | DDC 720.1—dc23/eng/20220718
LC record available at https://lccn.loc.gov/2022018331

ISBN: 978-1-032-27475-1 (hbk)
ISBN: 978-1-032-27472-0 (pbk)
ISBN: 978-1-003-29299-9 (ebk)

DOI: 10.4324/9781003292999

Typeset in Bembo
by codeMantra

# Contents

# Figures

# Contributors

**Esra Akcan** is Professor of Architecture at Cornell University. Her awards include those from the Getty, CCA, Clark, Graham, UIC, American Academy, and Institute for Advanced Studies in Berlin and at Harvard University. She is the author of *Landfill Istanbul* (2004), *Architecture in Translation* (2012), *Open Architecture* (2018), and *Abolish Human Bans* (2022).

**Joseph Bedford** is Associate Professor of History and Theory at Virginia Tech. He holds a PhD from Princeton University, architecture degrees from Cambridge University and Cooper Union, and is the founding editor of *Attention: The Audio Journal for Architecture* and *The Architecture Exchange*, a platform for theoretical exchange in architecture.

**Nathaniel Coleman** is Reader in History and Theory of Architecture at Newcastle University, UK. He leads design studios and theory seminars, concentrating on the limits and possibilities of the neo-avant-gardes. His books include *Materials and Meaning in Architecture: Essays on the Bodily Experience of Buildings* (2020), *Lefebvre for Architects* (Routledge, 2015), *Utopias and Architecture* (Routledge, 2005), and as editor, *Imagining and Making the World: Reconsidering Architecture and Utopia* (2011).

**Stefano Corbo** is an Italian architect and educator. He holds a PhD and an MArch II in Advanced Architectural Design from UPM-ETSAM Madrid. Over the last years he taught at several academic institutions in the United States, Europe, the Middle East, and China. In 2022 Corbo joined the Faculty of Architecture and the Built Environment at TU Delft.

**Charles L. Davis II** is Associate Professor of architectural history and criticism at the University of Texas at Austin. His academic research excavates the role of racial identity and race thinking in architectural history and contemporary design culture. Davis is the author of *Building Character: The Racial Politics of Modern Architectural Style* and co-editor of *Race and Modern Architecture: A Critical History from the Enlightenment to the Present.*

**Penelope Dean** is Professor of Architecture at the University of Illinois at Chicago, where she teaches architectural theory, history, and design.

She is founding editor of *Flat Out*, an independent print magazine based in Chicago.

**Macarena de la Vega de León** is an architect and holds a PhD in Architectural History. She is an honorary fellow with the Australian Centre for Architectural History, Urban and Cultural Heritage (ACAHUCH) at the University of Melbourne and serves on the Editorial Board of the Society of Architectural Historians, Australia and New Zealand (SAHANZ).

**Elie G. Haddad** is Professor of Architecture at the Lebanese American University. He is the dean of the School of Architecture & Design since 2012. Among his publications is the co-edited architectural survey *A Critical History of Contemporary Architecture* (Ashgate 2014), and *Modern Architecture in a Post-Modern Era* (Forthcoming).

**Lidia Klein** is an Assistant Professor in Architectural History at the School of Architecture, University of North Carolina at Charlotte, specializing in global contemporary architecture. She earned her PhD in 2018 from Duke University. She also earned a PhD from the University of Warsaw in Poland in 2013.

**Kasper Lægring** is a theorist of architecture and the arts and is currently a New Carlsberg Foundation Postdoctoral Fellow in Art History at Aarhus University. He holds degrees in Architecture (PhD, Royal Danish Academy of Fine Arts, School of Architecture; MS, University of Pennsylvania) and Art History (Mag.art., University of Copenhagen).

**Andrew Leach** is Professor of Architecture at the University of Sydney School of Architecture, Design and Planning, where he teaches history of architecture and codirects the Histories of Architecture and Built Environments group.

**Neil Leach** is a Professor at FIU, Tongji, and EGS. He has previously taught at the AA, Harvard GSD, Columbia GSAPP, Cornell, SCI-Arc, IaaC and DIA. He has published over 40 books on architectural theory and digital design. He is a co-founder of DigitalFUTURES, and an academician within the Academy of Europe.

**Francesco Marullo** is an architect and theorist interested in the relationships between labor, space, production, and the forms of life they entail. He holds a PhD in History and Theory of Architecture from the Delft Institute of Technology and is currently Assistant Professor at the University of Illinois at Chicago.

**Giacomo Pala** is a designer and researcher in the fields of architectural theory and design. He is currently research assistant at the Institute of Architecture Theory at the University of Innsbruck, while pursuing a PhD with Peter Trummer at the same university.

**Véronique Patteeuw** is an architect, critic, and researcher based in Brussels. She is maître de conférence (Associate Professor) at the Ecole Nationale Supérieure d'Architecture et du Paysage de Lille and visiting professor in architecture theory at KU Leuven and at ENAC-EPFL Lausanne.

**Jane Rendell** is Professor of Critical Spatial Practice at the Bartlett School of Architecture, UCL. She is author of *The Pursuit of Pleasure* (2002), *Art and Architecture* (2006), *Site-Writing* (2010), and *The Architecture of Psychoanalysis* (2017), and co-editor of books such as *Gender, Space, Architecture* (1999), and *Critical Architecture* (2007).

**Claudio Sgarbi** is a practicing architect and an educator. His research focuses on the ethics, image, and role of the architect. Sgarbi teaches visual imagination at the Marangoni School of Design and is Adjunct Research Professor at Carleton University lecturing in the PhD Program in Architecture and advising doctoral students.

**Léa-Catherine Szacka** is an architect, critic, and researcher based in Manchester and Paris. She is Associate Professor in Architectural Studies at the University of Manchester and visiting tutor at the Berlage Center for Advanced Studies in Architecture and Urban Design.

# Acknowledgments

This book grew out of some questions that I had about the condition of architectural theory today, and that I thought would be best answered by soliciting a diversity of opinions on this topic. Some of us began our studies during the period of efflorescence of architectural theory in the 1980s and 1990s, to witness thereafter its relative decline or, as some would say, its co-option in the service of specific contemporary practices. At the turn of the new century, architectural theory became a 'contested territory' where in some cases anything goes, while in other cases its whole purpose was put into question and in line with many 'ends,' its end was proclaimed.

In addressing this 'contested territory,' I have thought to open the debate to a large group of colleagues who have been engaged with these issues, including new voices that bring in a fresh perspective. From this collection, one can gather that not only is theory not dead, but it has sprouted in multiple directions. The various chapters presented in this collection do testify to one thing: the continuing importance and relevance of theory in architecture. It remains to be seen whether its relevance would find once again its right place within architectural education where in many instances, the 'professional' requirements have led to its downgrade in the curriculum. And while other disciplines have reduced their 'liberal arts' component, which constituted one of the foundations of theoretical reflection, architecture appears like the last bastion among professional programs where such questions that go beyond the narrow disciplinary limits continue to elicit interest and to provide a fertile ground for theoretical reflection.

I would like to thank all the participants in this project for their contributions and for delivering their essays under the difficult circumstances that have gripped the whole world over the past three years. I would like to express my thanks to David Leatherbarrow for contributing an insightful foreword to this collection of essays and to the editors at Routledge for supporting this project.

Finally, I wish to dedicate this book to the scholars and faculty in architecture schools around the world, who still uphold the necessity of critical thought in the face of leveling discourses that aim at reducing our discipline to a purely operative system, geared toward the satisfaction of individual desires in a what has become a 'society of the spectacle,' as Guy Debord predicted, more than five decades ago.

# Foreword

*David Leatherbarrow*

## Fighting for Life

Provocation as much as description seems intended in this collection's title. Taking up the challenge, it seems reasonable to ask what is being disputed on this contested ground? The implied and obvious answer is architectural theories, which is to say bodies of ideas prepared for advance and defense, having been drafted into service by authors in possession of insights into the discipline—how architecture comes into being, makes sense, is related to practices in other fields, and so on. Still another combat zone, however, might be the terrain of methods, no less a battlefield these days, on the wide plains of which some architects equip themselves with data, "big" today, no doubt bigger tomorrow, others the methods of the social sciences, and still others the procedures of building criticism or textual analysis. Only an out-of-date and presumptuous sense of common purpose would allow one to assume an easy congeniality of approaches, for ours is a time when every theorist, or each group of them, issues or follows a different set of orders.

Yet, a basic premise of any territorial dispute is that opponents must have at least some common interests if they are to enter into combat, otherwise there would be nothing to contend for. Presumably, that common concern in this case is the field of architecture itself, composed of knowledge and know-how, of ideas and skills, maybe also the designed or built works that result from the combination of these two. Opposed stances might advance or attack theories of construction (for example, the superior merits of manual, industrial, or digital techniques), or of configuration (Euclidian vs. non-Euclidian geometries), or contextuality (intensification of or divergence from pre-existing conditions), and so on.

But today the territory in dispute far exceeds the ostensible borders of the discipline. Chapters in this book, especially its second part, variously draw resources from theories of computation (parametric and robotic techniques and instruments), feminism, evolutionary biology, philosophy, politics, race studies, and still other domains of inquiry. In fact, any quick survey of recent writing will show that in much of the past decade's theorizing, architecture as built—even as designed—is treated rather parenthetically, addressed by implication only, as if it were someone else's proper concern or simply uninteresting. Commonly debated instead are the strengths of ideas and methods that originated outside the field and have been conscripted into theory campaigns because of their pertinence, quality, or status. Today few doubt that designers and professors must squarely face the world's urgent challenges of environmental crisis and social injustice, hence the turn toward theories developed in the ecological and political sciences, for example, and their application to the description and design of buildings, streets, and urban settings. And there are many other arguments and approaches that have currency today. A more complete list would include subjects as diverse as post-colonial studies, post-humanism, heritage preservation, materials science, neuroscience, and artificial intelligence, followed by still more themes and associated styles of thought. The terrain through which today's architectural theory travels has become very wide indeed. Surely expansion of this kind—both topical and methodological—enriches the field, as it does in this book. Of course, the borrowing also begs the question of what architecture can contribute to the urgencies we all feel, and what it can offer theorists in engineering, politics, or philosophy who need reinforcements in the construction of their responses to the current crises.

When, by contrast, the theoretical turn is not out- but inward, self-consciously confining itself within architecture's disciplinary precinct, prompted perhaps by a sense of intellectual or professional responsibility, or maybe just a love for architecture, it is writings not buildings that generally attract the attention of theorists, ideas for and against other ideas about what is essential in this particular form of practice. Hence, the familiar and frequent turn to the long history of architectural theories from the time of Greco-Roman antiquity to the present. More and more today, however, consideration is being given to the writings and transcribed oral traditions of 'non-Western' architectures, as they developed or disappeared in widely dispersed nations, languages, or indigenous cultures. On this front, itself very broad, theorists often take up arms for or against sibling subjects, architectural history, for example, or building technology, in any one of its many divisions. Part I of this book presents a good sampling of the current dilation of disciplinary theory.

While our apparent disinterest in built work may be surprising, the tendency to theorize and historicize theories themselves should not be dispiriting, for self-reflexivity is neither new nor uncommon in intellectual work. In neighboring fields, philosophy, for example, there is hardly a thinker one can name who hasn't reflected on the nature of philosophy itself, often contesting, sometimes amplifying the arguments of predecessors. Theories like things define themselves through opposition: "a thing without oppositions *ipso facto* does not exist."[1] The same role for contesting an inheritance can be found in anthropology and art history, as well as many other fields. As they accumulate, these disputes contribute to the formation of institutions of thought, which might be characterized as the subsoil of a discipline's contested territory. No less common are conflicts between contemporaries, one countering another or the inheritance, for institutions remain relevant only if they remake themselves in response to new challenges. Of course, public debates are variously antagonistic, ranging from peevish complaints to rather more combative confrontations. Among philosophers, again, debates rarely amount to more than testy skirmishes. Despite all the excited anticipation, the encounter between Cassirer and Heidegger in Davos, for example, was rather glancing, the protagonists mostly talking past one another, like ships passing in the night. Derrida and Gadamer in Paris were slightly more engaged, but the event seems to have been largely deflating.

Still, in view of the fact that contestation often animates the life of theory, it seems reasonable to ask if there might not be something essentially antagonistic about it, both today and in the past, that the terrain of theory is perforce adversarial, with pens handled like swords, infantry-propositions on the march, essays conquering new territories, and so on; in short, theory and theoretical projects proposed and recognized as architecture's *avant garde*. Were support for such a premise needed, we could, perhaps, turn to one of the great historians and combat and sport, Johan Huizinga, who observed "All knowledge—and this includes philosophy—is polemical by nature."[2] For such a thesis to be workable, we would need to rethink the commonly assumed disengagement and passivity of reflection; it would need to be reimagined as a way of getting something done, effectively, a form of *practice*. The architectural vanguard would thus be expected to issue declarations, recruit partisans, and lead movements, steps taken in a world-building campaign or crusade, albeit one that was probably self-commissioned. Le Corbusier titled one of his less well-known books *Croisade, ou le crepuscule des academies* (1933). The reverse thesis is no less interesting, and perhaps even more challenging: seeing the practitioner, at least in part, as something of a theorist, equipped with a questioning pencil and penetrating eyes, even those of the professional who is deeply entrenched in practical concerns. I suspect that few readers of this book will find it easy to name any architect we take seriously today who did not sit back now and then and wonder what might make sense in the light of given circumstances, unpropitious as they may have been or seem today. Isn't that wonder, and the pain of unknowing that prompts it, both essential in creative work and the heartbeat of non-trivial thought? If so, theoretical reflection wouldn't be a matter of choice in architecture, but of necessity or inevitability, despite any claims to the contrary. Troops marshaled on *the contested territory* would then include both intellectuals and practitioners, in disagreement no doubt, but occupying the same ground, improbable as that alignment and close proximity appear today. Many, many names (from whom I've learned much) come to mind: in the post-war period Aldo van Eyck, Fumihiko Maki, or José Luis Sert, for example; more recently, Álvaro Siza, Kengo Kuma, or Raphael Moneo. Surely talk of the end of theory is ill-considered and rash when one recalls its permanent residency in the questioning that is native to culturally productive design.

The history of education and its institutions would seem to fortify the thesis about *dispute* at theory's core. There is an exceedingly long-lived heritage of *contest* in academia, from its early days in ancient Greece (gymnastic exercises in the morning and rhetorical persuasion in the afternoon at Plato's Academy and Aristotle's Lyceum, for example), through the following centuries of *dialectic* in western monasticism and the proto-universities of the cathedral schools, into the period when *dispute-developed-thought* took the form of scholarly *polemic* in the renaissance academies (Ficino's most famously), and then to the time of hot *debates* on the respective merits of ancient or modern learning (in the Royal Academies in Paris and London), followed by the institutionalization of the *interrogative/argumentative spirit* in European colleges and modern universities, the adversarial traditions of which survive to this day in somewhat threadbare garments, such as *viva voce* doctoral disputations, or the courtroom-styled back and forth that enlivens design project *juries* in architecture schools, characterized by on-the-spot and spontaneous responses to unanticipated questions.

This brief chronicle illustrates both periods and kinds of contestation. Does it also show the history of *theorizing*? Do these several chapters narrate kinds of encounter we could see as generative? Might dispute not *result from* encounter, but *reestablish* the positions it assumes had already been secured, as if stances weren't maintained in dialogue but renovated? If so, the contested territory would be not only martial but correspondingly agricultural. In the early days of the story, contestation was indeed productive. Individuals were strengthened, social bonds were reinforced, and cultural memories were enlivened through conflict. The engagement or reciprocity of contestants assumed commonality, as I said at the outset. A sense of shared concern is also apparent. Antinomy needn't be hardened polarity in all such encounters, hence the distinction between *agonism* and *anti-agonism* (*antagonism*). Nietzsche observed that *agon* was a key concept in ancient Greek thought. The *agora* was a site of disputatious encounters in law courts, theaters, and festivals. What's more, *Agones*, the periodic festive games, were not only competitive, but celebratory, which is to say, recalling and imitating the ways the world works. Ant*agon*ism, in its modern, more militant sense, preserves the adversarial dimension of ancient conflict or contest—prot*agon*ist vs ant*agon*ist—but tends to abbreviate its generative or world-building dimensions. Controversy sometimes leads to a parting of ways, but other times to agreement, on the battle or sports field, in the court room, or design project review. Not all adversaries are enemies, conflict can be constructive.

The key question for practitioners and professors who step onto this battlefield today would be whether theoretical positions aren't simply *defended* but *developed* in conflictual encounters. I understand this premise requires rethinking the assumptions about sole authorship and firm conviction that we tend to associate with theory today. For what it's worth, myth lends this thesis some support: one of Ares' three great loves was Persephone, which is to say, the personification of war was strongly attracted to images of seasonal change, particularly the coming of spring, when winter's forces were in retreat, and the blossoming of vegetation had begun to show its strength and purpose. In consideration of modern art, one might think of a few improbable blades of grass emerging from post-war scorched earth, as portrayed in the bleak landscapes of Anselm Kiefer. The developmental thesis would mean that intellectual territories obtain definition through border conflict. For this to be the case, one would need to allow two senses of battle: on the one hand would be assaults intended to bring something barren or doubtful to its end (typified by the denunciations that are so common in *avant garde* theory), on the other struggles that endeavor to bring a more fruitful alternative into being. These two kinds of conflict might be conveniently distinguished as fighting *against* and fighting *for*. In philosophical terms, the first would be a hermeneutics of suspicion or critique that proceeds through deconstruction or demystification, and the second one of recollection or reconceptualization that advances understanding through translation and re-articulation. Most of the theorists considered in the chapters that follow can be listed under either of these headings—Tafuri under the first, for example, Rykwert the second. Adopting this book's *agonistic* orientation, I propose calling this second practice *fighting for life*, the life of ideas, of course, but also of the discipline, and more largely, the existence that architectural practice endeavors to accommodate and represent.[3]

There is a tacit premise in arguments for *thinking-with-and-against-others,* or *thinking-in-public* ("without a banister" as Hannah Arendt said): that theory at its best—when it is creative, persuasive, and relevant—is not something one keeps in a back pocket, ready for future applications, like well-practiced procedures or techniques, but something that hasn't yet left the workbench, still needs some reshaping, through one's own work of course, but also the labors of others that have their effect through encounters that were initially oppositional. Along this line of argument, better understanding results from battle-tested thought. One of the pleasures of reading this book is the discovery of the several ways these theorists develop their understanding in confrontation with opposed positions.

Given today's widespread and deeply felt need to act in response to all manner of injustices that trouble our world, concern with theory—yet another book on the subject—might seem at first glance to be untimely, misguided, and even irresponsible. At worst, it could be viewed as mere indulgence, at best, a form of service to practice; certainly not legitimate as an end in itself. But what if we have no choice in the matter, as I've already suggested; what if there is no way of doing architecture without invoking theory, intentionally or not; that action and reflection are no less inseparable than one's self and shadow on a bright day? My principal aim in these introductory observations is to remind readers of the life of theory within architecture itself, even architectural practice. This reminder is not meant to compromise theory's relative autonomy as one of the discipline's basic subjects, nor to subordinate its alliances with nearby fields, the thematic and methodological expansion to which I referred earlier, only to revisit the terrain that could well be architectural theory's native domain.

For centuries, architects have reminded themselves that knowledge in their field is hybrid in its make-up, composed of practice and theory in equal measures. The truism has been repeated so often that one feels disinclined to give it more thought. Assumed in the commonplace is the sharp distinction of the two terms and the kinds of knowledge they signify. According to the Western tradition's oldest source, the architect's well-rounded course of training, the famous *encyclios disciplina*, is *the child of practice and theory.* Centuries later, at the end of the modern professional's long apprenticeship, the re-worked portrait included both practical know-how and a requirement for insight into *the highest and most noble disciplines.* Enlightenment essayists commonly distinguished attention to *necessities* from dedication to both *taste and principles of order,* as evident in nature. Likewise, in a late summary of Beaux Arts instruction on the elements and theory of architecture, architects were instructed to give equal weight to the *artistic and scientific* sides of the discipline. In a very unlikely place to find advocacy for both sides of the equation, a mid-twentieth-century account of the scope of total architecture paired *skills and method* with *spiritual and scientific understanding.* And when a post-war or late modern architect coupled *rule* and *law,* the ancient distinction between matters that alternately addressed *method* and *basic order* was reinterpreted one more time. Heirs to this history (the premises of Vitruvius, Alberti, Laugier, Guadet, Gropius, and Kahn—key players in the institution of architectural thought I mentioned earlier), it is hard for us to imagine that matters could be, may well have been, quite otherwise. Tacit assumptions have their force today, as do institutionalized vocations and professional affiliations. Most of us who address matters of theory, as distinct from practice, are at home in institutions that give durable form to precisely this separation. Generally speaking, teachers who practice architecture professionally instruct in design, those who don't teach theory. In many schools, it would be outrageous for non-practicing professors to teach design, no less extreme for practitioners to give courses on theory.

But could the relationship be understood differently, not quite so dogmatically nor so categorically? Might these two, practice and theory, be sharply distinguished in analytical thought only, indivisible when architects are at work, at least alternately required and mutually informative? If so, might we then reconceptualize both the contest and terrain of theory, imagine it occupied by both professors and professionals, each struggling with comparable measures of experience and uncertainty? With its different contestants jointly engaged, architectural theory, I believe, would then be ready for confrontations with not only the earlier theories it inherits, but also challenges from extra-architectural forces.

To make any headway with the question concerning *theory internal to practice,* one would first have to provisionally bracket their customary polarization, categorical as we assume it to be. The divide is not, I'm confident, one that can be simply wished away. It can be, however, temporarily put out of play. When it is, a pair of reciprocal relationships comes into focus. In the first instance, theory inside practice is apparent in its typical manifestations: a designer's doubts, questions, or wonderings about the continued merits of what had been developed in the past, with this or that element or in one or another location, reservations motivated by the precedent's inadequacy perhaps, leading to imaginings of what might be done otherwise in future, possibly with something newly envisaged, but still pertinent to both the time and place of the current project. In the second case, theory is a set of premises that are taken for granted and tacitly understood as principles that guide or rule over practice, principles of rational building, for example, or of cultural and environmental sustainability, and so on. Here confidence takes the place of questioning, and theory is understood as something one has rather than something one seeks.

To take the next step, let's circle back for a moment to the antagonism with which we began, the contested territory this book studies and shows. But instead of imagining two or several theories in dispute, let's start with their source, an architect (designer or author) with unblinkered eyes and a pencil-fisted hand. But let's not assume the opponent against whom the stand is taken to be another theorist or practitioner. Let's risk the premise that the subject matter of theory is not another theory, but the world targeted by architectural action. What sort of object might test the mettle of the ideas one seeks to advance; what type of figure might offer the art of building genuine and productive resistance? I'd say that the truly formidable opponent, the one that would make engagement worthwhile, is the adversary with a comparable stance, strength of conviction, and line of attack. The eyes of such an opponent could, of course, be those of another theorist, but more interesting, I think, would be those of a built work, or still more so, those of some particular dimension of the world, world in a cultural or philosophical, not planetary sense.

On this point, a question came to my mind as I was reading the studies in this book: doesn't theory really come to life when it works out its stance in confrontation with thinkers, works, and worlds that press themselves forward against it with such force that it must redefine its position, ceding some ground perhaps in order to secure some other terrain? Better thought, on this account, is animated by dispute and actualized through dialogue, which is to say quickened by confrontation and creative when contested.

Perhaps combative experience isn't the only guide here; equally good, I suspect, is the experience of play, which is in most instances comparably adversarial, but often pleasurable, sometimes even joyful, characteristics that do not immediately come to mind when one thinks about combat. Might not theory or what I prefer to call theoretical reflection come to life in the *interplay* between an architect's sense of possibilities and the counter-theses of another position, in and of the world? Creative work in both theory and theoretical projects would then require not only a willingness to play with, but be played by a theme, purpose, or place, rather like a sailboat turning into choppy waters, or a kite dancing with the wind. The world looking back at an argument or project would thus give rise to reassessments of preliminary theses. Theoretical insight, on this premise, would result from a gradual dispossession of certainty, or, in positive terms, the discovery of positions that survive the challenges that typify dispute. In this arena, the eyes of the opponent (text, object, or world) would be perceived as a corresponding source of architectural sense.

Let me rephrase these suggestions as a few related questions that elaborate the profile of theory's productive opponent.

What if theory results from an intensification of prosaic involvements in the world as given, the seemingly intractable challenges mentioned earlier, of course, but also more prosaic conditions? Institutions of thought, I've said, would provide orientation for taking part in such a contest. Might theoretical "seeing" at its core require participation in the lived entanglements that make thinking again every architect's recurring task and responsibility? Were this the case, the disengagement we generally assume to be its prerequisite would be replaced by involvement, leading not to the dawn of clarity, but daylong uncertainties, provisionally eased through projects and propositions. Could it be that theory in and of architecture takes up residence in territories that are perforce ill-defined or indeterminate? If so, theory's optic would then seek to discover hollows and harbors in landscapes that shelter overlooked content and unforeseen possibilities.

## Notes

1 Charles Sanders Pierce, *Collected Papers*, edited by Charles Hartshorne, Paul Weiss, and A. W. Burke, vol. 1 (Cambridge, MA: Harvard, 1931), 457.

2 Johan Huizinga, *Homo Ludens: A Study of the Play Element in Culture* (Boston, MA: Beacon Press, 1955), 156.

3 Three books have guided this observation and, in fact, whole study: Walter Ong, *Fighting for Life* (Ithaca, NY: Cornell University Press, 1981), a title that seemed perfectly apt for what is argued here, Georg Simmel, *A View of Life* (Chicago, IL: The University of Chicago Press, 2010), and Hans Jonas, *The Phenomena of Life* (New York: Harper Row, 1966). On the matter of *agon*, I've benefitted from Wendy Pullan, "Agon in Urban Conflict: Some Possibilities," in *Phenomenologies of the City*, edited by Henriette Steiner and Maximilian Sternberg (Farnham, Surrey: Ashgate, 2015), 213–224.

# Part I

# Historical Perspectives on Architectural Theory

# 1 What ever Became of Architectural Theory?

*Elie G. Haddad*

In the view of several critics and theoreticians, the past few decades have witnessed the eclipse of theoretical discourse, a discourse that expanded in the 1980s and 1990s on a flurry of ideas and movements drawing on philosophy and literary criticism, to cultural studies and aesthetics. According to some of these critics, the eclipse of theory is due to nothing less than the actual concretization of the post-modern condition, which led to the withdrawal of all issues that relate to social and political concerns, toward an acceptance of the status quo, i.e. the condition of late-capitalism, where all that is solid actually melts into air. The increasing role of media, the surrender to new digital technologies in communication and representation, and the espousal of the methods of the marketplace had their impact on the current condition and accordingly signaled the eclipse of theory.[1] This argument has found some echoes in the emergence of various notions of the 'end': the end of history, the end of architecture, the end of theory.[2]

Before we get to the period of its assumed decline, it is important to highlight some of the highpoints of the renaissance of 'critical thinking' in architecture. In *Restructuring Architectural Theory*, published in 1988, Catherine Ingraham and Marco Diani produced one of the typical collections of that 'golden period' of theory, celebrating architecture's fateful and complex relationship with philosophy and linguistics, stretching from the mid-1960s until the mid-1990s. In their introduction, drawing on Jacques Derrida, they asserted that architecture derives its authority from the power granted it by philosophy, and not through its internal principles of materiality, technique, or aesthetics. Architecture finds itself in this 'construct' embedded or dissolved within political, social, linguistic, and philosophical systems. While denying the possibility of an autonomous architectural language, the authors stressed the infiltration of history, literary theory, and philosophy into architecture as part of its long heritage, despite being latent or repressed for a long time. For Ingraham and Diani, the project of deconstruction provided one of the major points of demarcation between the old practices and the new ones, where the 'radical critique of structure' creates a desire for the same practices that it deems as repressive.

DOI: 10.4324/9781003292999-2

One of the first major compilations of theoretical texts, edited by K. Michael Hays, set the year 1968 as a major milestone from which contemporary theory started to develop in different directions, from the discussion of built works to the debates on historicism and rationalism, to the assimilation of theory within larger 'cultural' constructs that transformed the architectural discourse, bringing into it the various strands of Marxism, structuralism, semiotics, and psychoanalysis.[3] The period in question, from 1968 to 1993, provided a rich assortment of competing ideas, from Marxism to Phenomenology, revealing the diversity of tendencies that sought to provide alternative maps for architectural interventions. Hays noted the evolution of architectural theory to a level where it began to operate a 'displacement' of philosophical problems in favor of attention to distinctly architectural ideas, through 'an attempt to dismantle the whole machinery of master texts, methods and applications, putting in its place concepts and codes that interpret, disrupt, and transform one another'.[4] In a typical attitude that epitomized that period, he celebrated the diversity of texts that were part of his collection, without commitment to any particular tendency or movement, confessing to the pleasures and limitations of theoretical work, caught as it is within the web of consumerist culture of which it is at times critical while partaking of its benefits. In a series of essays on the "Troubles in Theory", Anthony Vidler also referred to the period 'around 1968' as an important marker in the development of theory, not due to the revolutionary atmosphere as some had asserted, but rather due to the fact that architecture became a subject of interest to philosophers, linguists, and social scientists. The failure of governments to address the post-war social problems opened the way for intellectuals like Althusser, Lefebvre, and others to critique architecture as one component of the 'ideological state apparatus'.[5]

From another perspective, Harry Francis Mallgrave and Christina Contandriopoulos also identified the year 1968 as a key marker in the development of modern theory, whereby the social and political unrest that overtook many European and American cities triggered a radical change of perspective in architectural circles. Theory began to overtly address philosophical and social concerns, from structuralism to phenomenology to post-structuralism. For Mallgrave and Contandriopoulos, this marked the beginning of a 'postmodern' era that would recede by the beginning of the 1990s, giving way to a fascination with the new technological and digital tools that expanded architecture on a global scale.[6] In their anthology, the two editors divided the scope of their collected texts into several sections, one of which was aptly labeled as "The End of Theory?" with a speculative question mark. In this section, the two authors defined the main agent of change in architectural discourse that constituted a challenge to the prevailing theoretical trends since the 1960s, as coming from the 'new pragmatism' which appeared on the scene with the emerging Dutch practices, spearheaded by Rem Koolhaas and evolving with other figures like UN Studio and

MVRDV. Koolhaas's brand of theoretical analysis, which appeared first with his *Delirious New York*, and continued to evolve and to materialize into a new form of practice, avoided the complex associations and presented itself as a pragmatic, 'research'-oriented approach to the analysis of the urban and sub-urban conditions. This research-oriented theoretical discourse would avoid any confrontations with the political-economic order, be it in China or in the main centers of capitalism, but would rather seek accommodations with the neo-liberal order. Sanford Kwinter was one of the first to wage a critical counter-response to these propositions, which he branded as manifestations of a 'neoconservative fundamentalism', operating in close association with a neo-capitalist system that has surrendered society to the market forces.[7] Yet in his critique, Kwinter spared Koolhaas to focus on his progenies, accusing them of poorly assimilating the original reference, lacking its complexity and vision.

In her introduction to one of the latest anthologies to appear on the scene, A. Krysta Sykes drew a comprehensive picture of the condition of theory by the end of the first decade of the twenty-first century, summarizing the main sources of attack against architectural theory, or perhaps the theoretical construct of the 1960–2000 period, as a three-pronged attack: first, from the techno-managerial side, represented by figures like Michael Speaks and Alejandro Zaero-Polo, second from a post-critical front advocated by Somol and Whiting, and last by the neo-pragmatists represented by a number of young architects, among whom the Dutch architects figure prominently, in a sense corroborating the earlier diagnosis of Mallgrave and Constandriopoulos. The "critical tendency" of that period was thus exacerbated by the emergence of new technologies that catapulted certain architects, like Frank Gehry and Zaha Hadid to the position of global stars, with their spectacular buildings, once only the subject of fantasies by German Expressionists, now realized through innovative materials and building techniques. Sykes appropriately codified "Theory" as referred to by Nesbitt and Hays to denote a specific movement that began in the 1960s, and which drew heavily on different fields from philosophy, to linguistics, psychology, and anthropology, while attempting to claim for architecture its own territory. The pluralistic manifestations of architectural theory in that period were also a reflection of the post-modern movement that accommodated various tendencies under the label of theory.[8]

A survey of architectural theories since the Renaissance does indeed give credence to the claims that a different kind of architectural theory emerged on the architectural scene, beginning with the momentous 1960s which witnessed a widespread movement of contestation of what had been established as the normative ideology of Modern Architecture. Architectural theories, since the times of Alberti and Palladio, were concerned with setting the proper framework, or establishing a general paradigm for the realization of works that conformed with the principles of Classical architecture.

The debate evolved later, especially in the eighteenth century, centering on the opposition between various strands of Classicism, and what some upheld to be the appropriate style for a 'Christianized' Europe, i.e. Gothic. This debate evolved in different ways, leading one architectural theoretician to pose the existential question: "In what style should we build?"[9], at a time when the foundations of Classicism and Gothic were being subjected to a new intruder: the engineering-driven iron and steel structures. One can safely state that until the middle of the nineteenth century, architecture developed in a rather autonomous sphere, whereby the discussions centered on the appropriate styles and types, without going beyond the discipline proper, or aiming to address issues related to the social or political orders. By the middle of the nineteenth century, the impact of industrialization extended the scope of architectural theories to address the urban dimension, and through that extended to socio-political issues, which nevertheless remained in the background of those debates.[10]

The nineteenth century provided a fertile ground for the development of another source of inspiration for architects. The idea of an 'organic' architecture appeared then in the writings of Viollet Le Duc, John Ruskin, and Patrick Geddes, among others. In their different ways, these thinkers advocated an architecture that would draw from Nature by adapting its structural and functional principles, which were also being studied under the emerging sciences. This continued in the twentieth century with new protagonists, namely Lewis Mumford and Frank Lloyd Wright, and later on, the Italian Bruno Zevi. The general concept underlying this 'idea' is that Nature, in her 'natural' processes of growth and evolution provides a sourcebook and model for all forms, avoiding the artificial and misconstrued historicist imitations. This new source of inspiration signaled an early attempt to look beyond the confines of architecture, taking cues from the natural sciences. The natural analogy would resurface again later at the end of the twentieth century, with the studies of Greg Lynn and the new wave of digital architecture.

From this historical overview, which centers on a Western background, one can note that the twentieth century evolved its own set of theoretical directions, from Mumford's social studies to Sigfried Giedion's attempt to anchor the new tradition within a space-time conception that synthesizes aesthetic and scientific concepts, to the structuralist and semiotic studies of the 1960s and 1970s, and reaching a highpoint with the deconstructionist theories of the 1990s, before the red flags of a theoretical decline were raised. In examining the development of architectural theory over the past decades, I will focus on a few moments and figures that crystallize major turning points, starting with the enigmatic figure of Manfredo Tafuri, and concluding with the recent propositions of Patrick Schumacher. This survey cannot, by definition, be comprehensive and all-inclusive, and certain important markers in the development of theoretical thought, such as phenomenology and the discourse on the body that preoccupied much of the 1990s until today, would merit a separate study by itself.

## The First Wave: Theory as Radical Criticism

It is no coincidence that the name of Manfredo Tafuri appears frequently in any surveys and discussions about architectural theory. For many critics, Tafuri represents the central figure in the theoretical landscape of the twentieth century, especially if one looks at it from a wider cultural perspective that goes beyond the confines of architecture.[11] Tafuri emerged on the architectural scene during the 1960s in a post-war European context still searching for its lost political and cultural role in the world. He appeared within a movement around Ludovico Quaroni and Ernesto Rogers, which attempted to establish a new role for architecture and architectural criticism at a time of political crisis.[12] His early work reflected his wide scope of interests and his comprehensive vision of architecture across history, from the study of the Renaissance and Mannerist architecture, to urban planning in Italy and culminating with Modern architecture. These studies appeared as the prelude to the later urban studies, especially the important collective work on Vienna.[13]

Ideas, informed by the complex layers of philosophy, politics, aesthetics, and social sciences, formed a central element in the Tafurian edifice, although they always appear in a precarious condition as temporary scaffolds within which architecture is scrutinized, at times probing deep into the "thing-in-itself" to uncover its myths or to celebrate its rare moments of epiphany measured on a historical scale, while at other times examining the scaffolding itself in its relation to the edifice, dismantling it and re-erecting alternative scaffolds in the process.[14]

In his seminal work, *Teorie e storia dell' architettura,* Tafuri laid out his theoretical framework, which would not change much in its structural form over the years, while the issues under scrutiny would vary, as well as his assessments of major movements or architects. The main problem that this work proposed to examine was the relationship between Modern architecture and history, going back all the way to the origins of what he diagnosed as the 'crisis of the object' in the eighteenth century. One of the characteristic features of the Tafurian method is its ability to move across different periods with the swiftness of a magician, calling out in the process a number of sources from Hegel and Nietzsche to Benjamin, Adorno, and Foucault. Tafuri surveyed Modern architecture, identifying its main figures and their role within the modernist project, later diagnosing the desperate attempts of the 'avant-garde' to deal with the 'crisis', which he referred to as the problematic relation between architecture and capitalism. Tafuri looked at all these approaches to deal with the crisis with the same suspicion, seeing in all of them only futile attempts that do not fundamentally address the core of the problem.[15]

In 1973 Tafuri published his second theoretical work, *Progetto e utopia,* which examined architecture in relation to capitalist development, and which is considered by most scholars as the most reflective of Tafuri's critical position of architecture from a Marxist perspective. Yet in this study Tafuri did not go to the root of capitalist development as it manifested itself in the re-organization of capital, the concentration of new industries in or around urban centers, and the consequent restructuring of the city into workers' settlements and bourgeois neighborhoods, as he had done in his earlier studies; but rather directed his investigation toward aesthetic problems, as evidenced by his reading of Piranesi's imaginative prisons, which would later be counter-balanced by the symbolic valuation of Mies's paradigmatic 'silence'.[16] Tafuri re-affirmed the contemporary city as the locus of the modern crisis, which it had to contend with as it attempted to redefine its new order. The ultimate confrontation with 'modernity' would develop at the beginning of the twentieth century, with the various Avant Garde movements, reduced to an opposition between two directions: on the one hand, those who affirmed the validity of intellectual work within the reality of industrialization, on the other those who claimed the position of autonomy or 'pure ideology'. Tafuri pointed out the inevitable assimilation of the former under the capitalist system whereas the latter took the form of a false consciousness, reflecting back on the same reality they tried to escape.[17] This radical position seems to imply no way out, and betrays Tafuri's debt to the *Frankfurt School*, and especially to one of its important figures, Theodor Adorno.[18] Adorno's critical positions toward contemporary 'culture', in general, were exemplary of this radical refusal to accept the ideological premises of Modernism. The greatest critique of Tafuri's position came from another Marxist, Fredric Jameson, outlining the inherent nihilism of the Tafurian project, namely his rejection of the Modernist project, under the pretext that no substantial change can occur under capitalism before a total and systematic transformation. One is tempted, according to Jameson, to read in Tafuri's rejectionist stance, the dialectical opposite of the post-modernist complacent free-play, as two sides of a double-bind.[19] In retrospect, one would also be tempted to read in Schumacher's advocacy of free-play and the dissolution of architecture within the neo-liberal economic framework, the absolute dialectical opposite of Tafuri's project.

## The Second Wave: Theory of/within Practice

If Tafuri betrayed throughout his work a radical Marxist position under which the analysis of architectural developments could not take precedence over the larger economic and political system in which they are inscribed, the adventures of theory were not limited by his imposing figure over the cultural climate of the 1970s and 1980s. Soon, a new wave of theoretical tendencies would spread, especially in the American context where, as Francois Cusset demonstrated in his illuminating study, the impact of a specifically "French Theory" on the 1980s and 1990s, spreading across various disciplines from cultural to gender studies, and from art to architecture, would become felt across academic circles.[20] Building upon the similar experiences in the art world which turned to the theories of Barthes, Baudrillard, and Foucault, to find a way out of the constraints of a Modernism in crisis, the architectural intelligentsia found in Derrida and his deconstructionist approach a way to liberate architecture from its ideological constraints, bringing it within the realm of a post-humanist and post-structuralist discourse. The attempt to apply French theoretical thought to architecture constituted, according to Cusset, the 'theoretical vogue' of the 1990s, which failed nevertheless to renew with the political project of Modernism while giving architects an experience of the limits of their discipline, whether in terms of unrealized projects, of buildings as texts, or open questions resulting from the new technologies.[21] Nevertheless, this period witnessed an abundance of theoretical events, publications, and debates that emerged after the MoMA exhibition on "Deconstructivist Architecture" (1988), which was unprecedented in the field.[22]

This post-structuralist vogue swept through the theoretical field of the 1990s, with Peter Eisenman as one of its most illustrious representatives. Despite the museographic trend of bringing together diverse figures to constitute a 'movement', it was evident that few architects branded as 'deconstructivist' were actually as theoretically invested as Eisenman in this new project. Eisenman was influenced by the writings of Derrida, and before that, by the structuralist studies of Noam Chomsky. This can be seen in the gradual transformation of Eisenman from a 'structuralist' phase of experiments on the House series, to the House El-Even Odd which, by its play on words as well as its play on its own rules of syntax, already expressed a shift in his work, a process which continued in the later projects, animated by a continuous exchange and at one time a collaboration with the philosopher of Deconstruction, Jacques Derrida. The theoretical manifestation of this position appeared in a series of writings after 1980. These writings moved from the investigations of the architectural 'sign' as exemplified in the House studies to a post-structuralist phase which started around 1982 with "The Representations of Doubt: At the Sign of the Sign"[23] and the seminal essay "The End of the Classical, the End of the Beginning, the End of the End".[24] The publications by Eisenman during this phase also reflected this radical shift, with *Fin d'Ou T Hou S*[25] a collection of loose-plate drawings that document the last project of the House series, elevating the architectural document to the level of a rare and precious manuscript. A year later, another publication came out under the title *Moving Arrows, Eros and Other Errors,* this time printed on transparent sheets, featuring the Romeo and Juliet project designed for Verona.[26] Eisenman thus began to re-orient his work, after the series of experiments on the House series (1967–1975), toward a form of 'artificial excavation' which sought to uncover latent or hidden signs in the territory, to be subsequently subverted and turned against the original site of operation. These artificial excavations would take place in a number of 'charged' urban sites, from Canareggio (1978) to Berlin (1980), to other less historically laden sites such as Long Beach in California (1986).[27]

The title of Eisenman's seminal essay "The End of the Classical, the End of the Beginning, the End of the End", bears a striking similarity to Derrida's title for a chapter in *De la grammatologie,*[28] although in this case he acknowledged his debt to Franco Rella who published an article in the same issue of *Casabella* in which Eisenman's winning project for the Wexner Center in Ohio was featured.[29] In this essay, building on Foucault's concept of *epistemes*, Baudrillard's concept of *simulation*, and Derrida's notion of the *trace*, Eisenman set for himself the task of critically exposing architecture as a humanist discipline founded on the *logocentric* discourses of the Renaissance. Following Foucault, he defined the Classical as an *episteme*, a continuous period where a dominant form of knowledge reigned and marked by the three "fictions" of Representation, Reason, and History. The architect appropriated Derrida's notion of the trace, in an attempt to overcome the predicament of architecture as an activity rooted in physical, functional, or representational purposes, in order to wage an attack on its foundational certainties: origin, function, and history. These 'certainties' constituted the foundations of a classical metaphysics of architecture, in which the representation of a fixed set of ideas edify a complete 'body' of architecture, whether Classical or Modern. Instead, he proposed an architecture which would negate these various 'fictions' through operations in which the architect would take the role of a de-cipherer, bringing to light hidden fragments, repressed meanings, or traces of other significations, transforming the site of each project into a palimpsest which would generate new fictions, multiple histories, and narratives.[30] This transformation in Eisenman's work, from a practice focused on a study of 'syntax' to one which resorts to strategies of 'decomposition'[31] that would transform architectural projects into 'texts', started well before the attempted collaboration that brought together Derrida and Eisenman.[32]

The later phase in Eisenman's deconstructionist project was marked by a collaboration with Jacques Derrida, at the suggestion of Bernard Tschumi, on a section of the Parc de la Villette in Paris. This unrealized project was documented in a series of transcripts that appeared in book form as *Chora L Works,* idiosyncratic in its title as well as in its form,[33] as the grid of the proposal actually punctures the written text and renders the operation of reading a difficult exercise, in addition to the reversal of the traditional book organization, by relegating the introduction to the center of the book, among other features.[34] This work also revealed the limits of translating philosophical concepts into architecture, as the architect struggled to give forms to a discourse that does not always lend itself to formal translation. This collaboration was followed by a period of active exchange with Derrida over two years[35] culminating in a final exchange in which the philosopher posed a series of unsettling questions to the architect, putting into question his whole deconstructionist experiment in architecture.[36]

A different approach to theoretical work appeared at the same time with Rem Koolhaas, whose efforts were geared toward putting ideas in practice and avoiding the ideological traps of historians like Tafuri and architects like Eisenman. Koolhaas's project, while utopian in some of its aspects, did not attempt to tie this utopia to any larger social or political ideals. His analysis of New York city as a phenomenon of the twentieth century in *Delirious New*

*York*, looked at it from the perspective of an objective, although sympathetic, observer. Koolhaas's theoretical venture fell in line with what Tafuri termed as 'operative criticism', i.e. destined to corroborate or justify the practice that the architect would later engage in. From the analysis of the city as a site of congestion, to the notion of Bigness as a new opportunity for an architecture of the future, to the subsequent investment in targeted 'research' that crosses disciplinary lines, overlaying urban analyses with economics and politics in graphically stimulating essays, Koolhaas charted new paths for architectural theory that sometimes lapsed into visually seductive presentations that missed to address the crucial questions being raised, only surfing their surface.

If *Delirious New York* constituted a "retroactive manifesto", in the words of its author, destined to rehabilitate the Metropolis in all its complexities and contradictions as the site of architectural entrepreneurship that eschews questions of style, privileging instead innovative responses to real-life challenges including latent psychological desires; then *S, M, L, XL,* in its biblical format (perhaps the first architectural book to take this form after the great compendia of ornaments of the nineteenth century) concretized the mature position of Koolhaas as a theoretician in practice, i.e. as an architect who does not privilege ideas over formal experiments, but rather sees the two as acting in-sync to generate new projects that overthrow the status quo. As some critics noted, *S, M, L, XL* ushered a new form of architectural publication, soon emulated by others, not only in terms of its large format but in its juxtaposition of architectural drawings, images and collages with newspaper clips, statistical data, and tangential information that is supposed to expand the reader's perception of the architectural condition in the context of globalization.[37] Yet beyond the question of its 'representation', it is the concepts themselves that Koolhaas propagated throughout his career that have affected the way we perceive and respond to crucial architectural problems. One of the major issues is the question of planning within a global economy, with Koolhaas responding by celebrating the virtues of the unplanned, the unpredictable, and the mutating, as in *Generic City*. In a sense, Koolhaas reversed the traditional 'rational' project of Modernism, by seeking to find strategic solutions through a surrender to the economic (and consequently the political) forces at play.[38] As Anna Kligmann perceptively noted, Koolhaas's approach may be compared to the work of Duchamp and Warhol in the art world, where their focus on the everyday, the banal, the reproducible, and the generic destabilized artistic practice, and caused a complete reversal of such notions as the authentic and the beautiful. As she noted, Koolhaas avoided the complications of a 'critical' practice by espousing commercialism, all the while adopting certain key aspects of popular culture as in the celebration of cheap materials, the acceptance of the marginal and the banal, the generic and the 'found objects'. Similar to Duchamp's subversion of art by adopting the ready-made or the found-object, exhibited and re-admitted into the artistic sphere, Koolhaas elevates the generic to the level of an architectural 'original'.[39]

## The Third Wave: The Digital Turn

The impact of digital technologies on architecture has been overwhelming, leading some critics to posit this development as the major reason for the demise of architectural theory, specifically that type of theory which evolved between 1968 and 2000. Yet this digital turn also attempted, at its beginnings, to base itself on a philosophical conceptual edifice. The early forms of digital architecture resorted to Gilles Deleuze's concept of the Fold, metaphorically drawing on it in order to give legitimacy to the new architecture. Deleuze's concept of 'smooth and striated' spaces in *A Thousand Plateaus* was picked up by the architectural circles as a way out of Derrida's complex and convoluted constructs, and as a shift from linguistic-based design to considerations of geometrical nature.[40] Greg Lynn was one of the earliest proponents of a digital approach to architecture. His theoretical proposition proceeded from a reflection on Wittkower's analysis of Palladian Classicism to a discussion of D'Arcy Thompson's study on the growth of natural organisms, in what amounts to an effort to anchor this latest trend within a historical continuity of architectural theory. This formal transformation had as one of its primary objectives, to free form from its submission to strict geometry, effecting a return to the 'organic', which would succeed this time in emancipating architectural forms from a static to a dynamic condition characteristic of all living organisms. The new direction in architecture adopted the Deleuzian concept of the 'fold', which the philosopher referred to as an illustration of a historical period, the Baroque, and not as an architectural style per se. But the association with the Baroque, added to the metaphor of the 'fold', served well to veer architectural practice away from both the post-modernist nostalgia of the 1980s as well as the Deconstructivist discourse of the 1990s.[41]

In a significant development, the influential and trend-setting periodical Architectural Design [AD] devoted several issues to this new 'paradigm shift' in architecture.[42] The crusade for a digital architecture, later under the label of "Parametricism", found its most able promoter in the figure of Patrick Schumacher who deployed an arsenal of theoretical ideas, laying down the foundations of what he termed the style to replace all styles.[43] Schumacher, whose background in philosophy added a substantial dimension to his arsenal, was the main protagonist of the transformation of Zaha Hadid's practice from a constructivist-inspired tectonic approach, to fluid and smooth forms, emblematic of this new wave. In his ambitious drive to set the practice on a theoretical foundation, he also proposed a comprehensive system that would encompass all previous theories of architecture. Drawing on the work of the German sociologist Niklas Luhmann, and applying his theory of social systems to architecture, Schumacher proposed in a two-volume compendium of Biblical form a 'complete theory of architecture as a system of communication'.[44] In marked contrast with previous theories that drew on Deleuze in a superficial manner, he projected a more elaborate system that drew on major thinkers, from Kant to Deleuze, including Hegel, Marx, Simmel, Benjamin,

Adorno, Derrida, and others, and culminating with Luhmann. Yet, in his all-englobing totalitarian system, the chapter dedicated to the 'Societal Function of Architecture', which probably remains one of the primary concerns of the architectural discourse today, was reduced to a simplistic, even naïve axiom: "[...] architecture's unique function is the provision of spaces that *frame* communication. The societal function of architecture is thus to order and adapt society via the continuous provision and innovation of the built environment as a system of frames".

This reduction of architecture to mere communication would conveniently serve the next step of justifying the unmitigated drive toward innovation and the elaboration of new formal geometries. Thus, Parametricism emerges out of this dialectical process as '*the style to end all styles*', and as one of the great or 'epochal' styles that would succeed Modernism; with Zaha Hadid and Patrick Schumacher as its apostles. The architect gave the Masterplan for a business park in Singapore as one example of this 'auto-poetic' architecture, where the integration of various field forces leads, in his own words, to a 'monumental synthesis'. Yet in this proposal, significant issues, among which the social dimension and the historical context, have been completely ignored or overlooked, leading to the construction of a new post-modern subjectivity that hinges on 'communication' theory, at the service of 'global capital'.[45] One reply to Schumacher's position may be found in an earlier statement by Zaha Hadid herself, in her intervention at the symposium on 'The End of Architecture'. In a very perceptive analysis of the condition of architecture at the beginnings of the 1990s, Hadid offered a premonitory response, rejecting both the allusion to 'autonomy' as well as the escape into 'fashion' as potential answers to the architectural dilemma. Hadid then deplored the economic conditions that turn architects into either docile technicians or experimental star-architects, arguing instead for an architecture of social purpose:

> Architecture for architecture's sake cannot be the solution, cannot be the antidote to fashion; only a social purpose to architecture, publicly formulated, can be such an antidote. There can be no great architecture without a social program. A visionary architecture has to take part in a political vision, and its reality presupposes a political process which puts a new architecture on the agenda and thus transforms the profession into a movement with new aims and inspirations.[46]

Yet Schumacher did not relent in his pursuit of liberating architecture from its formal and political shackles. In another one of his essays, he posited 'freedom' as an essential objective from the early days of Modernism, and advocated a more radical privatization "beyond neo-liberalism towards anarcho-capitalism, further empowering individual freedoms and market rationality while disempowering political processes".[47] Such a move has been rendered feasible, according to Schumacher, through the potentials of the digital revolution and its capacity to generate solutions that respond more efficiently to the changing demands of a market economy. This translates into what he defines as the 'soft order', i.e. an informational spatial order, in opposition to the 'hard order' that traditionally defined architecture. As an illustration of this soft order, Schumacher gave the example of the Sberbank Technopark in Moscow, a project that supposedly orders the life-process in the office complex through a typology of 'communicative situations' defined by the settings that privilege communicative interactions. In the second volume of his theoretical treatise, Schumacher addressed the contentious relationship between architecture and politics, dismissing the calls for a 'political architecture' as a nostalgic lament that harks back to revolutionary periods, ignoring the reality of contemporary practice. While re-affirming the necessity for architectural theory, he selectively defined its primary function as the 'compensation for the lost certainty of tradition' with the underlying purpose of 'producing innovations', implying the 'production of new statements and possibly the elaboration of new concepts'.[48]

## Theory and Criticism: An Open Question

The theoretical discourse in architecture over the past five decades was quite rich in its ramifications, spilling beyond the limits of the discipline itself and its one-time obsession with autonomy, and crossing over other disciplines from the humanities to the social sciences and the natural sciences. This richness testifies to the importance of architecture as a liberal discipline par excellence, liberal in the sense of rejecting dogmatic positions and open to question its own foundations. The liberalism of architectural discourse can also be attested to by its opening up, recently, to questions of race, gender, and colonialism. The hypothesis of the demise of theory, as discussed at the beginning of this essay may be countered by its continuing currency in academic and professional circles, as evidenced in a recent flurry of titles that purport to examine the very question of its continued relevance.[49] Although the time of large compendia, in the form of anthologies, seems to be behind us, recent publications, even those that are generated from conference proceedings, testify to a renewed interest in investigating the ramifications of architectural practice, whether in philosophical, economic, political, or social terms. In a timely essay that addressed both the necessity of criticism in architecture, as well as the positive aspects of what has been so far largely a matter of glitz and formal play, i.e. the parametric paradigm, Michael Sorkin advocated taking advantage of the potentials of machine-enabled design to develop an environmentally responsive architecture. Sorkin concluded:

> The challenge for criticism is not simply to acknowledge the political but to struggle to infuse the practice of architecture with the means for understanding and incorporating progressive social values, including ever-expanding rights for comfort and desire.[50]

A renewed interest as well in the economic and political ramifications of architectural practice has translated into a series of publications that explore these issues in contemporary practice. Paradoxically, the figure of Tafuri, which loomed large in the theoretical landscape of the 1970s and 1980s has recently resurfaced in these architectural discussions, in a way indicating the importance of criticality, and the role that architectural theory would be called upon in contesting the dominant socio-economic system, and where issues of greater significance than 'formal play' would be once again brought to the table.[51] It is within such larger frameworks that theory may continue to play an essential role in architectural education and praxis.

## Notes

1 K. Michael Hays, for one, stated that the decline of theory can be witnessed in the rise and fall of critical journals during the 1980s–1990s, such as *Oppositions,* founded in New York city by Peter Eisenman. The journal lasted from 1973 to 1984 but was followed up by Assemblage (1997-2001). On the European continent, two critical journals were also short lived: Daidalos (1981-2000) and 9H (1980-1995). Yet, despite this argument, critical journals did not disappear altogether, and the relay was taken by Grey Room (2001–) and LOG (2003–), both of which continue to be published.

2 In parallel to the political scientist Francis Fukuyama's popularization of the notion of the 'End', through his polemical book *The End of History and the Last Man* (1992) in which he argued that humanity had reached the end of history, after the collapse of the Soviet Union and the triumph of Liberal Democracy, some architects and critics also adopted this notion in their writings. Noteworthy in this respect is the symposium organized by Peter Noever at the Austrian Museum of Applied Arts in Vienna in June 1992 at which a number of prominent architects were invited. The proceedings were published in a book titled The End of Architecture? published by Prestel (1993).

Deborah Hauptmann explored also the issue of the end of theory in her essay: "Repositioning; the after(s) and the end(s) of theory," in *This Thing Called Theory,* T. Stoppani, G. Ponzo, & G. Themistokleous, eds. Routledge, 2017 (89–95).

3 K. Michael Hays. *Architecture Theory since 1968.* MIT Press, 2000.

4 K. Michael Hays. *Introduction to Architecture Theory since 1968.* MIT Press, 2000 (x–xv).

5 See Anthony Vidler's series of four essays in *The Architectural Review,* titled "Troubles in theory" (Sep. 21, 2011, Dec. 20, 2011, July 24, 2012 and April 10, 2013).

6 See Harry Francis Mallgrave and Christina Contandriopoulos. *Architectural Theory, Volume II: An Anthology from 1871 to 2005.* Blackwell, 2008.

7 Sanford Kwinter. "FFE: Le Trahison des Clercs (and other Travesties of the Modern)," in *ANY: Architecture New York 24.* Anyone Corporation, 1999 (62)

8 A. Krysta Sykes. *Constructing a New Agenda: Architectural Theory 1993–2009.* Princeton Architectural Press, 2010.

9 Heinrich Huebsch. *In welchem Style sollen wir bauen?* Karlsruhe: Müller, 1828. Translated into English as *In What Style Should We Build?* Getty/University of Chicago Press, 1992.

10 William Morris is the most prominent advocate of a socialist approach to design work, in general, including architecture. His novel *News from Nowhere* tackled several issues related to the problems caused by industrialization, and fused romance with moral lessons and political positions.

11 A prolific writer with a large number of books and essays to his credit, translated into all major languages, Manfredo Tafuri (1935–1994) has not ceased from preoccupying the architectural scene. Following his death, Casabella published a dedicated commemorative issue on Tafuri. Casabella 619–620, 1995. Later, a number of studies tackled the complex legacy of Tafuri. See Andrew Leach's *Manfredo Tafuri: Choosing History*. A&S Books, 2009; Cynthia Davidson's *ANY:25/26: Being Manfredo Tafuri*, 2000; Pier Vittorio Aureli's "Recontextualizing Tafuri's Citique of Ideology" in Log #18, Winter 2010 (89–100); and Marco Biraghi's *Project of Crisis: Manfredo Tafuri and Contemporary Architecture*. MIT, 2013. As one example among many, K. Michael Hays' anthology started with Tafuri's article "Toward a Critique of Architectural Ideology". Another example of Tafuri's continuing presence in the architectural discourse, a recent collection of essays edited by T. Stoppani, et al. (op.cit.) featured under the first section, three of the four essays that revolved around Tafuri. See especially Marco de Michelis's "Manfredo Tafuri and the death of architecture" (9–20), Sergio Figueiredo's "Theories and history of architecture (museums)" (21–32) as well as Michael Chapman's "Architecture and the neo avant-garde" (147–156).

12 For more on Tafuri's background see the essay by Giorgio Ciucci: "The formative years", in *Casabella 619–620*. Electa, 1995 (13–25).

13 Manfredo Tafuri, *Vienna Rossa*. Milano: Electa, 1980. Translated into French as *Vienne La Rouge: La Politique Immobiliere de la Vienne Socialiste 1919–1933*. Bruxelles: Mardaga, 1981. This work was never translated into English.

14 Most scholars agree on the seminal importance of this work by Tafuri, the first to examine architecture in its broad theoretical dimension. Anthony Vidler, for one, described it as a 'cathartic work'. See Anthony Vidler. *Histories of the Immediate Present*. MIT, 2008 (168–169).

15 Manfredo Tafuri, *Theories and History of Architecture*. Manhattan, NY: Harper & Row, 1980 (32)

16 Manfredo Tafuri. *Progetto e utopia*. Bari: Laterza, 1973.

17 In his third major work, *The Sphere and the Labyrinth*, Tafuri brought together in one collection a number of essays that addressed a variety of topics, spanning three centuries. The introduction to this work, carrying the emblematic title of "The Historical Project" laid out a new vision for writing history, which built upon a method that Tafuri had already mastered. The main references for this new 'construction' were Marx, Nietzsche and Foucault, who provided the necessary foundation for dismissing other approaches to historiography, as in the simplistic recourse to semiotic studies, to hermeneutics or even to typological studies.

18 Fredric Jameson was the first critic to make this comparison between Tafuri and Adorno. In his introduction to *The Sphere and the Labyrinth*, Tafuri in fact referred to Adorno, quoting a passage from his *Aesthetic Theory*, in his discussion of the artwork aura. *The Sphere and the Labyrinth*, op.cit. (21).

19 Fredric Jameson. "Architecture and the critique of ideology," in *Architecture Criticism Ideology*, ed. Joan Ockman. Princeton Architectural Press, 1985 (51–87).

20 Francois Cusset. *French Theory: Foucault, Derrida, Deleuze & Cie et les mutations de la vie intellectuelle aux Etats-Unis*. Paris: La Decouverte, 2003.

21 Cusset, op. cit.

22 See Michael Chapman's "Architecture and the neo avant-garde" (147–156), in Stoppani, et al. eds (op. cit.).

23 Peter Eisenman, "The representations of doubt: At the sign of the sign," *Rassegna* 9 (March 1982), reprinted in *Eisenman Inside Out: Selected Writings 1963–1988*. New Haven: Yale University Press, 2004 (143–151).

24 Peter Eisenman, "The end of the classical, the end of the beginning, the end of the end," *Perspecta* 21 (1984): 154–172; reprinted in *Eisenman Inside Out*, 152–168.

25 Peter Eisenman, *Fin d'Ou T Hou S*. London: Architectural Association, 1985.
26 Peter Eisenman, *Moving Arrows, Eros and Other Errors: An Architecture of Absence*. London: Architectural Association, 1986.
27 *Cities of Artificial Excavation* appeared in 1994 and covered projects that date from 1978 to 1988. Incidentally, the Wexner Center for the Arts, which is a major work in this group, (completed in 1989) was not included in this collection.
28 Derrida titled his chapter "The end of the book and the beginning of writing."
29 Franco Rella, "Tempo della fine e tempo dell' inizio" (The age of the end and the age of the beginning), *Casabella* 498–9 (January/February 1984): 106–108.
30 Eisenman, "Misreading," in *Houses of Cards*. Oxford: Oxford University Press, 1987 (167).
31 The term used by Eisenman at that time was "decomposition." Later "deconstruction" would supplement decomposition in some of the discussions of his work.
32 Jeffrey Kipnis commented that this particular project came at a time when Eisenman's pursuit of the 'elusive' goal of structuralism was faced with doubts, and as he started his readings of Derrida. See Kipnis, op. cit., 15–21.
33 The previous works of Eisenman had exhibited equally word-playful titles. See above.
34 Jeffrey Kipnis and Thomas Leeser, eds. *Chora L Works: Jacques Derrida and Peter Eisenman*. New York: Monacelli, 1997.
35 From September 17, 1985 to October 27, 1987.
36 Jacques Derrida, "Letter to Peter Eisenman [October 1989]," in *Chora L Works*, ibid. (161–165).
37 Gabriele Mastrigli, "The last bastion of architecture," in *Log*, Winter/Spring 2006, No. 7. New York: Anyone Corporation (33–41).
38 See Esra Akcan's analysis of "The generic city: Retroactive manifestoes for global cities of the twenty-first century," *Perspecta*, 41 (2008): 144–152.
39 Anna Klingmann, "The meaningless popularity of Rem Koolhaas," *Thresholds*, 29 (Winter 2005): 74–80.
40 As Douglas Spencer noted:

> Where Deleuzism in architecture originally undertook, then, to establish its autonomy from the linguistically oriented concerns of poststructuralism, it subsequently sought to distance itself too, as part of its affirmation of the new – indeed, affirmation of affirmation – from any obligation to engage with *critique*. Through its alliance with the 'post-critical' position emerging, around the same time, in US architectural discourse – marked by the publication of Robert Somol and Sarah Whiting's now near-canonical 'Notes Around the Doppler Effect and Other Moods of Modernism' in the journal of *Perspecta* in 2002 – it articulated its opposition to critique as a matter both extrinsic to the 'proper' concerns of architecture, and as a counterproductive form of 'negativity'.

See: "Architectural Deleuzism: Neoliberal Space, Control and the 'Univer-City," *Radical Philosophy* Jul/Aug 2011.

41 Antoine Picon (2010) "Continuity, complexity,and emergence: What is the real for digital designers?", *Perspecta*, 42 pp. 147-157 in an essay on this topic, explained this obsession with complexity:

> Complexity, often equated with non-linearity, is among the key characteristics of the systems these designers are interested in. In most of these systems, complexity goes with the property of emergence. Michael Hensel, Achim Menges, and Michael Weinstock define emergence as "an explanation of how

> natural systems have evolved and maintained themselves, and a set of models and processes for the creation of artificial systems that are designed to produce forms" [...] Emergence appears all the more enticing in that it seems profoundly non-contingent.

42 This was further reaffirmed in a special issue of AD, guest edited by Patrick Schumacher, and titled *Parametricism 2.0,* which came out with the explicit objective of resuscitating a declining interest in the new movement.

43 The role that such reviews like AD played in the promotion of the new style was well attested to by the main advocate of the movement, Patrick Schumacher who declared:

> Within this increasingly hostile environment, AD is not only Parametricism's most important communication platform, but indeed its last high-powered bastion where it maintains a strong (if not dominant) presence. Its many dedicated issues have been Parametricism's organs for theoretical debate and project exposition.
>
> (Schumacher, 2016, p. 9)

44 Schumacher (2011–2012).

45 As confirmation of the latent neo-liberal position of Parametricism, Schumacher declared in one of his most controversial statements his opposition to all forms of social welfare, calling for the scrapping of social housing, removal of urban regulations, and even for the privatization of public spaces. Speaking at the World Architecture festival in Berlin in August of 2016, the architect presented an eight-point manifesto in which he advocated foreign investment and gentrification as a way to progress and to resolve the housing affordability crisis. This unequivocal attack on urban planning and social welfare may be one of the factors behind the 'fall from grace' that the movement witnessed in recent years (Frearson, A. 2016). For a critique of Schumacher's approach see Manuel Schwartzberg's "The technocratization of the space of appearance," *Azimuth*, I (2) (2013): 97–109.

46 Zaha Hadid. "Another beginning," *The End of Architecture?* ibid. (25–28).

47 Patrick Schumacher, "Freedom via soft order – architecture as a foil for social self-organisation," in *Architectural Design: Architecture & Freedom*. Owen Hopkins, ed. London: Wiley, 2018.

48 See Chapters 9 and 10 of Patrick Schumacher. *The Autopoeisis of Architecture.* Vol. II. Wiley, 2012. In his survey of architectural theory, Schumacher identifies three 'treatises' that played a key role in the development of architectural autopoiesis, leading to his own treatise. These are Alberti's *De re aedificatoria,* Durand's *Precis* of 1802–1805, and Le Corbusier's *Vers une architecture* of 1923.

49 See Theresa Stoppani et al., eds., *This Thing called Theory*. Routledge, 2016; James Graham, ed. *2000+: The Urgencies of Architectural Theory*. New York: Columbia, 2015; and Bruno Marchand, et al., eds, *Où va la théorie de l'architecture?* Matieres 16, EPFL, 2020.

50 Michael Sorkin, "Critical measure: Why criticism matters," *The Architectural Review,* 28 (2014): 91–99.

51 See, for example, Douglas Spencer. *The Architecture of Neo-Liberalism*. Bloomsbury, 2016; and Nadir Lahiji, ed., *The Political Unconscious of Architecture: Re-Opening Jameson's Narrative.* London: Ashgate, 2011.

# 2 Architecture's Historiographical Turn

*Andrew Leach*

The decades spanning from the 1960s to the 1990s witnessed the advent of a form of architectural theory that was institutionally self-sustaining: an intellectual practice enacted in books, journals, exhibitions and paper architecture of various forms, becoming increasingly self-referential over time. With its anchors in the American, British and European metropoles, its reach beyond architecture's historical centres was uneven. Among its various camps, it cohered around shared references in literature and philosophy. Despite its divergent objectives and many tensions, the theoretical production of these years displayed a common density of expression and intensity of ambition that was mobilised by its principal interlocutors in an era of unprecedented global travel and amplified publishing.

This chapter will explore the historiography of architecture (that is, the production and practice of history—literally, history writing) over these decades, considering how forms of historiography served as a dimension of architectural theory and how the study of architectural history was, in turn, shaped by the intellectual gains of the theory moment. This essay locates a growing preoccupation in the 1980s and 1990s with the mechanisms of architectural historiography itself as something at the intersection of (a) that field's attention to the self-reflective disciplinarity of art history in these same decades; and (b) the work done by architectural theory to weaken the façades of architecture's institutions, for which the history of architecture (or a form thereof) had been conditionally claimed since around the start of the 1960s.[1] The intellectual freedoms secured by the writing and discourse of the later decades of the twentieth century established new roles and limits for architectural history into the following century, while at the same time presenting the tools needed to define architectural theory's own historical contingencies.

## Architectural History and the Theory Moment

Architecture's "theory moment" followed an enquiry into questions of meaning, power, authorship and representation that positioned new modes of discourse against established forms of historical analysis and prescriptive theory—theory, that is, in the "old sense," aligned with the classical treatises.[2]

DOI: 10.4324/9781003292999-3

The authors of this work aligned themselves with countercurrents, margins and the suppressed forms of knowledge that could be activated by a world of progressive, indeed revolutionary ideas—another canon, of course, but not seen as such by those who established it. The questions put to architecture by figures like Stanford Anderson, Diana Agrest, George Baird, Alan Colqhoun, Peter Eisenman, Kurt W. Forster, Kenneth Frampton, Mary McLeod, Denise Scott Brown, Jorge Silvetti, Ignasi de Solà-Morales, Manfredo Tafuri, Bernard Tschumi, Anthony Vidler or Colin Rowe (to recall, for instance, some names from the pages of *Oppositions*—one of the most influential vehicles of architecture's theory moment) revolved around the production and apprehension of how architecture and its significance were produced and sustained. These figures, and many others besides, parsed architecture's stakes in the modern age, as a product and vehicle of modernity. They took up the language and questions of thinkers of the Frankfurt School, scholars of French structuralism or (Heideggerian) existentialism, and the intellectuals whose work they extended, turning those questions time and again towards architecture. The literature of this architectural theory was, consequently, in no small way a processing of architecture's history in new terms, and an advancement of practices shaping the representation and activation of the past in a postmodern present.[3]

The discourses captured by architectural theory's institutions (the prominent schools, presses, journals and events) thus fostered a form of history writing, especially of the modern movement, or of modernity writ large, that was read against the grain of a "traditional" architectural history. It expanded boundaries, upset hierarchies, and recalibrated a stable of essential architects and unavoidable works.[4] This coincided with new forms of scholarship in architectural history around the world, which in turn informed an increasingly defensible disciplinarity for the architectural historian as a figure *within* (and not simply *concerned with*) architecture, forged in the discourse of architectural theory as a *theorised* history of architecture. Manfredo Tafuri's *Teorie e storia dell'architettura* (1968, Engl. ed. 1980) captured this project in its formation: against what new knowledge, what methods, can architecture test its artistic and intellectual ambitions?[5] Bound up in this "project" was a systematic reassessment of modernism, wherein the relationship between historical assessment and the architect's projective stance had been most explicitly problematised. Schools of architecture, as the principal institutions of architectural discourse, took all manner of positions towards history in these decades. Across the 1980s and 1990s, though, a theorised history, focussed on modernity as the historical landscape of contemporary architecture, including and activating its philosophical underpinnings, became near hegemonic.[6] Architecture was hardly alone in accommodating "theory" in this way. It pervaded the humanities and arts, and figured in all the fields informing how history was done in architecture, like social and intellectual history, industrial archaeology, cultural geography and the history of art (in which the history of architecture kept one foot).

## Architectural Historiography at the End of the Century

The premise of *Teorie e storia*—as clarified in the preface to that book's second, 1970, edition—was to account for what architecture had been, as an institution, from the fifteenth century until that moment. Its efficacy in demonstrating enduring themes, preoccupations and assumptions as to what architecture was and how it could be apprehended fuelled a significant period of reflection on architecture as a form of cultural and intellectual production.[7] Tafuri argued that architectural history was not a passive practice within architectural culture (merely maintaining a record of the past) but had a critical, even political role as a point of resistance against an easy uptake of the authority of the past in present-day practice. The task of history was to complexify the record of the past and to make it more difficult to abstract, to make the path out of a history held together by evolving forms of historicity more resistant. The tools offered by theory at the end of the 1960s fostered that project of complexification. By the end of the 1990s, the production of theory itself needed to be problematised along lines that had been established by theory itself. In this, historiography (and, more nebulously, criticism, as a not-"theory" form of theory) emerged as a tool in the place once assumed by theory, through the historicisation of ideas and institutions, big and small.

The disciplinary auto-analysis undertaken by Tafuri in the 1960s reanimated in the 1980s and 1990s a long-established discussion on how and why the study of history operated within architecture. Consider the meeting of the Association of Collegiate Schools of Architecture at Cranbrook in 1964, published as *The History, Theory and Criticism of Architecture*, in which numerous figures of late modernism took a stance on these terms and the practices for which they stood; or Bruno Zevi's *Architettura e storiografia* (1974), which restated ideas that had been decades in the making, and had likewise explored the correlation between what one could, and ought to know, of the past and how one could know it.[8] Each served as provocations without casting a clear shadow, and were ripe to be picked up and explored across the last decades of the century. For its imbrications with the theorisation of language, politics, art and economics, Tafuri's own book extended this enquiry with a structure and ambition unmatched elsewhere—and largely overshadowed it. For much of the theory moment, *Teorie e storia* offered a lesson for how to do theoretical architectural history. By the end of the century, it came to be read more and more as a meditation on the historicity of historiography, and hence, again, as a reflection on the historian's tools and tasks within architecture.

Tafuri's own work was highly selective as to its references and narrative, but a number of new studies published in the 1980s and 1990s—including books by Jennifer Bloomer, Beatriz Colomina and Catherine Ingraham—broke open architecture's historiological mechanics in the spirit of his book.[9] Even so, a categorical ambiguity persisted such that a work cast as "theory" may have been undertaken in a mode of historiography that was heavily inflected by the realm of ideas. Arguably, much of what was called "architectural theory" in the twentieth-century's last decades would now be called "architectural history," its authors once theorists (as the aforementioned writers were), now historians and critics.

This body of scholarship and debate—history/theory—intersected with two other emerging discourses in the disciplinary history of historiographical practices, each asking what it had meant to study and write the history of architecture across the same mid-twentieth-century decades in which theorists had openly located themselves in counterpoint to historians.

Within architecture, this evolving library included works (each developed out of doctoral dissertations) by Sokratis Georgiadis on the life and works of CIAM stalwart Sigfried Giedion; Hilde Heynen on the modernity of architectural knowledge (including the production of modern architectural historiography) and Panayotis Tournikiotis on modernist practices in the historiography of architecture.[10] Together, these titles formed pillars for the study of modern architecture's relationship with history and historians, and through them, modern architecture's history. Cast as intellectual histories or biographies, they overlapped with the most historiographically astute studies of architectural theory, such as Joseph Rykwert's *First Moderns* (1981); Vidler's *Architectural Uncanny* (1992); Frampton's *Studies in Tectonic Culture* (1995) or Françoise Choay's *La règle et le modèle* (1996).[11] The methodological conclusions of each book were consistent and clear: rhetoric aside, architecture's structural reliance on historical knowledge (as argued by Tafuri) had never diminished. The forms and practices mediating that knowledge, though, had changed over time and continued to do so.

This body of work intersected with another produced since the early 1980s. Already at the start of the decade, David Watkins' *The Rise of Architectural History* (1980), the UMI edition of Joan Hart's dissertation on Heinrich Wölfflin (1981) and the special issue of *Architectural Design* "On the Methodology of Architectural History," edited by Demitri Porphyrios (1981), had explored the methodological underpinnings of architectural history.[12] At the end of the 1990s, a special issue of the *Journal of the Society of Architectural Historians* (1999), edited by Eve Blau, took the millennial moment to historicise the intellectual and institutional mechanisms of a discipline that had, in the United States, fostered professionalisation for half a century.[13] Iain Borden and Jane Rendell likewise captured the import of the British critical theory tradition for architectural history in their edited collection *InterSections*, published in 2000; as did Dana Arnold in her study of the intersection of architectural and social historiography.[14] In these studies architectural history at once remained a specialisation within the history of art (wherein architecture comprised a medium alongside other media) and extended naturally from architecture itself, its books and articles capturing the patrimony of the contemporary architect, or the material of architectural heritage.[15]

Such studies lent methodological weight to initiatives like the Getty programme, led by Harry Francis Mallgrave, of translating the key volumes of modern architecture such as editions of writing by Herman Muthesius, Otto Wagner and the authors of the central European debate on style (much of which had not yet been translated into English, and hence not entered the Anglo-American discourse) that demonstrated modernism's operations within rather than against history.[16] History was written back into a modern(-ist) architecture that had rhetorically rejected this dimension of architecture, showing history's operations as more complex than had been demonstrated in the decades in which postmodern historicism was exercised without restraint.

A third discourse to take form at the end of architecture's theory moment—the tail end of a span lasting from the 1960s to the 1990s—was explicitly concerned with the interpretation of architecture in the history of art, where anthologies like *Art History's History* (1995), edited by Eric Fernie, and *The Art of Art History* (1998), edited by Donald Preziosi—oriented towards graduate students, and hence the task of disciplinary professionalisation—located architectural history in the institutional gains of that field, less its sister than its aunt.[17] These anthologies recalled that the problems posed by founding figures like Jacob Burckhardt or Heinrich Wölfflin arguably found greatest clarity in the art of building. They built, too, on a disciplinary self-awareness that was already embedded in the scholarship of ancient, medieval and early modern architecture within the history of art, but which could be explicitly encountered in events like the 1960 conference, staged at Rome's Accademia dei Lincei, on the subject of *Manierismo, barocco, rococò*, or the 1961 CIHA conference session on "Recent Concepts of Mannerism," or the issues of the *Journal of Aesthetics and Art Criticism* published in the 1940s and 1950s on the baroque in the arts.[18]

The greater attention given around the turn of the century to the mechanics of historiographical production, the institutions and figures through which architectural history acquired and maintained disciplinary identity, and the renewed importance of architectural history within architecture's academic culture owes something to each of these strands of investigation. The importance of the gains of architecture's theory moment within them lies in the centrality that this work would enjoy for architecture in the years after theory lost its postmodern sheen. Without the work that had been done by theory since the 1960s, the investigations and accommodations made within architecture from the end of the 1990s could not have occurred.

## Architecture in History

Across the 1990s, the distinct discourses described above increasingly intersected around the question of architecture's intellectual and institutional histories. One body of work was concerned first and foremost with the question of method in the history of art as a matter of advanced disciplinary training and methodological self-consciousness, although it took up the preoccupations of intellectual history itself and its interdisciplinary imperatives (Figure 2.1). On what bases could works of architecture (as artworks) be

*Figure 2.1* Clip/Stamp/Fold 2: The Radical Architecture of Little Magazines 196X–197X. Installation view, 2007. Photograph by Michel Legendre © CCA.

drawn together within historical narratives? How could meaning be found and figured in architecture (or any other art form)? How did the questions driving interpretation in time and fomenting relationships across time arrive? And how did the world of architecture's ideas—the substance of its disciplinarity—relate to the world of ideas as such?

Especially insofar as they shed light on tensions that remained in play in architectural culture at the end of the twentieth century, those studies *of* history that were more concerned with the activation of ideas through the study of the past (intellectualisation through historiography) formed a newly inscribed line from which new histories of architecture could be written, and in which the study of the work of history itself, in architecture, could serve architectural culture. This, arguably, had been the function of the forms of historiography that had been embedded in architectural theory up to this time.

Those investigations naturally extended into and beyond the 1990s. Processing those figures concerned with history but vital to architectural theory were books like Nigel Whiteley's critical biography of Reyner Banham (*Historian of the Immediate Future*, 2003), Vidler's doctoral dissertation on Emil Kaufmann, Colin Rowe, Banham and Tafuri (*Histories of the Immediate Present*, published in 2008) and studies by Marco Biraghi and myself on Tafuri (respectively, published in 2005 and 2007)—alongside a wide range of theses and dissertations. These works all pondered the question of history's proper place in the architectural culture of the twentieth century, and by implication the current century, through the privileged figure of the historian who was no longer claimed for architectural theory.[19] The methodological enquiry of Heynen, Tournikiotis and many others who took up Tafuri's invitation to see that the complicity of the historiography of modern architecture with modern architecture's project was hardly a monument around which the field now had to negotiate. It complemented other new lines of research and scholarship opened up by this same moment, into colonialism and race, political and economic conditions of architectural production, gender and sexuality, modes of representation and their interpretation, technology, pedagogy and so on.[20]

Alongside these, though, another common effort took root at the intersection of the historiography of modern architectural culture and the long-standing demands of art history to process disciplinary legacies through the production of new work. This was, again, but on new terms, the exploration of the relationship between historical practices and historical subjects—in a long twentieth century, but now engaged with the full array of subjects that had been studied over that time. This served to expand the alignment once assertively defended by architectural theory of an *architectural* history most properly concerned with the modern era to incorporate timespans and geographies beyond what could be encountered in the pages of *Oppositions*.

One of the direct consequences of this stream of scholarship and debate has been the interrogation of architectural history as a discipline—not only with a view to what the field has been, until now, but also the tools and limits that shape the work that lies ahead. It is difficult to divorce the current preoccupations in architectural history with questions of social justice, historiographical artifice, "minor" and "unpedigreed" architectures, and the global; from the discourse that forced open architecture's doors and rattled its every seemingly stable element across the 1970s, 1980s and 1990s. As such, contemporary architectural history responds to an expanded concept of architecture informed by the theory moment.[21] And it has done so gradually, in the absence of radical moves, as a recalibration of language, style, subjects considered and authorities claimed. It retains a foothold in the world of architects, monumental buildings and the media and mechanics of architecture and construction; taking the problems of representation and power as givens; while pondering with fresh eyes the major issues of colonialism and imperialism both historical and contemporary; systems of finance and security; governance; information management and communication.

The theory moment located architecture both as a subject (in new terms) and a manner of thinking, evidenced by theory itself. This historiographical turn it variously prompted or ushered in pursued the intellectual history of architecture as a project that was attentive to three consequences, in particular: first, that the study of architectural historiography offered new kinds of cross-sectional analysis through the history of architecture, substantiated not in architects and buildings, but through their historical representation; second, that this study acted to remove the certainty that had accrued through use around the terms, frames and devices of historical analysis, introducing a new degree of provisionality into the language of architectural history itself; and third, a new degree of disciplinary maturity in the history of architecture such that it demanded its own reflective practices akin to those it saw in the history of art. In borrowing tools and drawing methodological lessons from the history of art, the historiography of architecture came to extend the theory project—by leaving its overt ambitions behind.

## Notes

1 This observation is explored in Johan Lagae, Marc Schoonderbeek, Tom Avermaete and Andrew Leach, eds., *Positions: Shared Territories in Historiography and Practice*, special issue, Oase 69 (2006).

2 Architecture's "theory moment" reflects the developments in the humanities described in Ian Hunter, "The History of Theory," *Critical Inquiry* 33, no. 1 (2006): 78–112; and Terry Eagleton, *After Theory* (London: Basic, 2004). That this categorisation is itself tentative, however useful, is demonstrated in the exchange between Frederick Jameson, "How Not to Historicize Theory"; and Ian Hunter, "Talking about My Generation," both in *Critical Inquiry* 34, no. 3 (2008): 563–582 and 583–600, resp. On the prescriptive theoretical tradition, see Hanno-Walter Kruft, *A History of Architectural Theory from Vitruvius to the Present* (New York: Princeton Architectural Press, 1994). On the "theory" of the theory moment in architecture, see Anthony Vidler's six-part article series "Troubles in Theory" in the *Architectural Review* (2011–14), at https://www.architectural-review.com/author/anthony-vidler/. Vidler considers theory's trajectory from 1945 to 2000.

3 The authorship of this literature overlaps significantly with that of the journals *Oppositions* and *Assemblage*, and *Perspecta* as their testing ground; in Britain, with the trajectory of Academy Editions by Andreas Papadakis and the associated arc (1970s–1990s) of *Architectural Design*; and with a discursive generation each of *L'architecture d'aujourd'hui*, *Casabella* and the like.

4 Its canonisation is discussed in Sylvia Lavin, "Theory into History; Or, the Will to Anthology," *Journal of the Society of Architectural Historians* 58, no. 3 (1999): 494–499. Lavin argues that the proliferation of "theory" anthologies in the 1990s established a new institutional ground-plane. She invokes Joan Ockman, ed., *Architecture Culture 1943–1968: A Documentary Anthology* (New York: Columbia Book of Architecture/Rizzoli, 1993); K. Michael Hays, ed., *Architectural Theory since 1968* (Cambridge, MA: MIT Press, 1998); Neil Leach, ed., *Rethinking Architecture: A Reader in Cultural Theory* (London: Routledge, 1997); and Kate Nesbitt, ed., *Theorizing a New Agenda for Architecture: An Anthology of Architectural Theory* (New York: Princeton Architectural Press, 1996). See, too, Mitchell Schwartzer, "History and Theory in Architectural Periodicals: Assembling Oppositions," *Journal of the Society of Architectural Historians* 58, no. 3 (September 1999): 342–348.

5 Manfredo Tafuri, *Teorie e storia dell'architettura* (Bari: Laterza, 1968); Engl. ed. *Theories and History of Architecture*, trans. Giorgio Verrecchia (London: Granada, 1980).

6 Joan Ockman reflected on that development in American schools in "Slashed," *History/Theory*, special issue, *e-flux* (2017), https://www.e-flux.com/architecture/-history-theory/159236/slashed/. See also the introduction by Sebastiaan Loosen, Rajesh Heynickx and Hilde Heynen to *Conditioning Architectural Theory, 1960s-1990s* (Leuven: Leuven University Press, 2020), 9–28.

7 Consider the mobility of ideas described in Jean-Louis Cohen, *La coupure entre architectes et intellectuels, ou les enseignements de l'italophile* (1984, Brussels: Mardaga, 2015), 137–166.

8 Marcus Whiffen, ed., *The History, Theory and Criticism of Architecture: Papers from the 1964 AIA-ACSA Teacher Seminar* (Cambridge, MA: MIT Press, 1966); Bruno Zevi, *Architetture e storiografia. Le matrice antiche del linguaggio modern* (Turin: Einaudi, 1974).

9 Teresa Stoppani writes of such books as *Architecture and the Text: The (S)crypts of Joyce and Piranesi*, by Jennifer Bloomer (New Haven, CT: Yale University Press, 1993); *Privacy and Publicity: Modern Architecture as Mass Media*, by Beatriz Colomina (Cambridge, MA: MIT Press, 1994); and *Architecture and the Burdens of Linearity*, by Catherine Ingraham (New Haven, CT: Yale University Press, 1998); in "Unfinished Business: The Historical Project after Manfredo Tafuri," in *Critical Architecture*, ed. Jane Rendell, Jonathan Hill, Mark Dorrian and Murray Fraser (London: Routledge, 2007), 22–30. "Historiology" is an archaic term, but a more accurate word for the study of history's methods and practices than historiography.

10 Sokratis Georgiadis, *Sigfried Giedion: An Intellectual Biography* (Edinburgh: Edinburgh University Press, 1993); Panayotis Tournikiotis, *The Historiography of Modern Architecture* (Cambridge, MA: MIT Press, 1999); Hilde Heynen, *Modern Architecture: A Critique* (Cambridge, MA: MIT Press, 1999). Their doctorates were completed, respectively, in 1986 (ETH), 1988 (Paris VIII), and 1988 (Leuven).

11 Joseph Rykwert, *The First Moderns: The Architects of the Eighteenth Century* (Cambridge, MA: MIT Press, 1981); Anthony Vidler, *The Architectural Uncanny: Essays in the Modern Unhomely* (Cambridge, MA: MIT Press, 1992); Kenneth Frampton, *Studies in Tectonic Culture: The Poetics of Construction in Nineteenth and Twentieth Century Architecture* (Cambridge, MA: MIT Press, 1995), or Françoise Choay's *La règle et le modèle. Sur la théorie de l'architecture et du urbanisme* (Paris: Seuil, 1996—later published in English by MIT Press).

12 David Watkins, *The Rise of Architectural History* (London: Architectural Press, 1980); Joan Hart, "Heinrich Wölfflin: An Intellectual Biography" (PhD diss., University of California Berkeley, 1981); Demitri Porphyrios, ed., "On the Methodology of Architectural History," special issue, *Architectural Design* 51, nos. 6–7 (1981).

13 Eve Blau, "Architectural History 1999/2000," special issue, *Journal of the Society of Architectural Historians* 58, no. 3 (1999).

14 Iain Borden and Jane Rendell, eds., *Intersections: Architectural Histories and Critical Theories* (London: Routledge, 2000); Dana Arnold, *Reading Architectural History* (London: Routledge, 2002).

15 Themes I have myself explored in *What Is Architectural History?* (Cambridge: Polity, 2010), and for which the present essay could well serve as an alternate final chapter.

16 Herman Muthesius, *Style-Architecture and Building-Art: Transformations of Architecture in the Nineteenth Century and Its Present Condition*, trans. Stanford Anderson (Santa Monica, CA: Getty Research Institute, 1995); Otto Wagner, *Modern Architecture: A Guidebook for His Students to This Field of Art*, trans. Harry Francis Mallgrave (Santa Monica, CA: Getty Research Institute, 1988); Herman Hübsch, et al., *In What Style Should We Build? The German Debate on Architectural Style*, trans. Wolfgang Hermann (Santa Monica, CA: Getty Research Institute, 1992).

17 Eric Fernie, *Art History and its Methods* (London: Phaidon, 1995); Donald Preziosi, *The Art of Art History: A Critical Anthology* (Oxford: Oxford University Press, 1998).

18 *Manierismo, barocco, rococò. Concetti e termini* (Rome: Accademia dei Lincei, 1962); Ernst Gombrich, section ed., "Recent Concepts of Mannerism," in *The*

*Renaissance and Mannerism*, vol. 2, *Studies in Western Art: Acts of the Twentieth International Congress of the History of Art* (Princeton, NJ: Princeton University Press, 1963), 163–255. This distinction was explored in the contribution by Maarten Delbeke and Andrew Leach ("Problem? No Problem") to the roundtable "Pre-Modern Architecture and the Shift of Historiography," Fourth International Meeting of the European Architectural History Network, Dublin, June 2016.

19 Nigel Whiteley, *Reyner Banham: Historian of the Immediate Future* (Cambridge, MA: MIT Press, 2002); Anthony Vidler, *Histories of the Immediate Present: Inventing Architectural Modernism* (Cambridge, MA: MIT Press, 2008); Marco Biraghi, *Progetto di crisi. Manfredo Tafuri e l'architettura contemporaneo* (Milan: Christian Marinotti, 2005); Andrew Leach, *Manfredo Tafuri: Choosing History* (Ghent: A&S Books, 2007).

20 This library is, by now, too large to list off, but prominent English-language publishers with whom a significant number the titles implied by this observation include the University of Minnesota Press and Pittsburgh University Press.

21 See the ABE Journal at http://journals.openedition.org/abe/. Among the collective projects of Aggregate, see *Governing by Design: Architecture, Economy, and Politics in the Twentieth Century* (Pittburgh, PA: University of Pittsburgh Press, 2012); and *Writing Architectural History: Evidence and Narrative in the Twenty-First Century* (Pittburgh, PA: University of Pittsburgh Press, 2021); and Meredith TenHoor and Jonathan Massey, eds., "Black Lives Matter," http://we-aggregate.org/project/black-lives-matter. I also refer to Mark Jarzombek, Vikramaditya Prakash and Francis D.K. Ching, *A Global History of Architecture* (Hoboken, NJ: John Wiley & Sons, 2010).

# 3 Erase the Traces! History and Destruction in Brecht, Benjamin, and Tafuri

*Francesco Marullo*

Destruction is hard to deal with, as it tends to expose the crises and contradictions occurring everywhere without concealing the violence of their transformative processes. Conflictual, divisive, and allegedly more controversial than its counterpart, destruction is a constituent trait of the human-animal, which capitalism progressively turned into a driving force. Lacking a specific environment, humans spread across the planet as an invasive and endangering species, extracting resources, colonizing lands, and drastically altering ecosystems to survive, forcing them to the brink of collapse, as clearly manifested by the environmental catastrophes of the past year.

At the same time, destruction uses negation to widen the possibility for developing other ways to expend energy, improve connections, and grow potential. It is both historical and generative: it never occurs in a vacuum but operates with contexts and precedents to be analyzed, dismantled, modified, overturned, or reframed, preparing the ground for something to happen. In this sense, perhaps, it would be possible to rethink destruction as a method for questioning and undoing what has been done so far, conjecturing other ways of dwelling in the world, retooling the instruments of profit for different purposes and kill the 'live monster that is fruitful and multiplies'.[1]

A significant example of such an attempt can be found in Bertolt Brecht and Walter Benjamin's writings of the 1930s, who used the notion of destruction to redefine the role of history and the mission of the new intellectual within the modern relations of production: themes that affected Manfredo Tafuri's early work and still have large relevance in the current architectural debate (Figure 3.1).

## Part One

In his notes, Walter Benjamin recalls a "truly unusual afternoon" spent in the south of France with his dear friend Bertolt Brecht discussing two alternative modes of dwelling.[2] Brecht begins distinguishing those who settle down and conform space to their living necessities from those who minimize their belongings and do not leave traces behind. To Brecht, the former is a 'sympathetic' dweller, who shapes the environment in an ordered and

DOI: 10.4324/9781003292999-4

*Figure 3.1* Jeff Wall, *The Destroyed Room*, 1978. Transparency in lightbox, 159.0 × 229.0 cm. Courtesy of the artist.

compliant arrangement legitimized by the stability of boundaries, possessions, and furniture.[3] The latter is a nomadic dweller, who inhabits the world as a temporary guest, constantly renegotiating her relationships with the context and setting up a place like a stage with just the bare essentials.

Developing Brecht's polar opposition, Benjamin recognizes how modern dwellers often become a function of the very objects they own and the habits they perform. An excess of comforts produces the *étui*-men, who are victims of their necessities and desires, stiffened by mechanized routines and 'encased' in their domestic interiors. Conversely, nomads seem able to readjust their identities to the circumstances through ephemeral habits and constellations of references, relying on the idea of *using* the world's resources rather than owning them.[4]

Without fixed habits or objects, to dwell as a temporary visitor is to choose to be *house*-less but not *home*-less: to live in a voluntary state of exile, at once embedded and withdrawn from reality, acknowledging the responsibility of every action while rejecting harmful commitments and endorsing empowering connections.[5] Such an estranged mode of inhabiting the world is entirely rational, as it implies a meticulous selection and elimination of whatever is unnecessary to provide the broader possibility of movement and adaptation, reimagining destruction as a creative process for getting rid of consolidated customs and reinventing how to dwell within an overly saturated system of exchange.

Undoubtedly influenced by their personal experiences after the decade of mixed excitement and despair, misery and industrialization between World War I and the 1929 crisis, Brecht and Benjamin attempted to reverse the uprootedness and overstimulation of modern living into presuppositions for freedom and political awakening. Instead of soothing the dominating techniques of production—mechanization and automation, acceleration of work rhythms and efficiency, scientific management and capillary infrastructure, information sharing, and logistics—they looked for ways to harness and convert them into instruments of mass emancipation.

Long before his conversation with Benjamin, Brecht contemplated the nomadic character seeking to escape the bourgeois subjectivity and societal norms in several theatrical and literary works. For example, in his collection of poems titled *Lesebuch für Städtebewohner* (*Handbook for city-dwellers*, 1926–1927), he recommends the absolute anonymity and discretion of the fugitive as an ultimate form of resistance against the overstimulation and control of the modern metropolis:

> Erase the traces!
> Whatever you say, don't say it twice.
> If you find your ideas in anyone else, disown them.
> The man who hasn't signed anything, who has left no picture.
> Who was not there, who said nothing: How can they catch him?
> Erase the traces![6]

Brecht's verses and the conversation on dwelling would later resurface in Benjamin's short essays—most notably *Der destruktive Charakter* (The Destructive Character, 1931) and *Erfahrung und Armut* (Experience and Poverty, 1933)—where the *étui*-man, who lives comfortably surrounded by objects and velvet interiors, is opposed to a *destructive character*, which obliterates everything, even the traces of its destruction. "The destructive character knows only one watchword: make room. And only one activity: clearing away"—writes Benjamin—

> The destructive character is the enemy of the *étui-man*. The *étui-man* looks for comfort, and the case is its quintessence. The inside of the case is the velvet-lined trace that he has imprinted in the world (...) The destructive character sees no image hovering before him. He has few needs, and the least of them is to know what will replace what has been destroyed. (...) First of all, for a moment at least, empty space —the place where the thing stood or the victim lived. Someone is sure to be found who needs this space without occupying it.[7]

Destruction is a mutation process rather than a simple annihilation of the past. It unveils the structures and foundations of reality to understand and reset its functioning with different principles. As Friedrich Engels warned in his *Housing Question*, a revolutionary movement should eliminate the very foundations of the system of oppression rather than improve its superficial consequences or mitigate its exploitative apparatuses. A calibrated destruction would interrupt the alleged linearity of progress imposed through centuries of capitalist domination against those who passively accept the established practices and ideological frames governing their lives without questioning neither the reasons nor their roles within such a large-scale mechanism.

The will to make room and get rid of consolidated forms and accrued values would turn the annihilating logic of capitalism against itself. In *Experience and Poverty,* Benjamin advocates for a new kind of barbarism against the reactionary and plush attitude of the dominant classes:

> For what does poverty of experience do for the barbarian? It forces him to start from scratch; to make a new start; to make a little go a long way; to begin with a little and build up further, looking neither left nor right. Among the great creative spirits, there have always been *the inexorable ones* who begin by clearing a tabula rasa. They need a drawing table; they were constructors.[8]

Here the tabula-rasa does not stand for a material strategy of eviction, substitution, or reuse, but as the crude operation of reason to deduce a different world view from the anomalies of the established socio-economic framework: to make 'a little go a long way' (*aus Wenigem heraus zu konstruieren*) from the visceral spirits of the modern metropolis. Indeed, among the 'inexorable ones' were the coeval projects of Hannes Meyer's Co-op Zimmer, Ludwig Hilberseimer's Citybebaung, Mies van der Rohe's office buildings, and Le Corbusier's Dom-Ino system. These architectures accelerated and radicalized the rational principles of the new metropolis to suggest the possibility of a life beyond ownership, liberated from the obligations and constraining comforts of society as well as from the fetters of individuality, stable limits, and assigned roles, somehow anticipating the increasing flexibility, pervasiveness and indeterminacy of the architecture of advanced capitalism. "The modern style of building, whatever else may be said of it"—writes Benjamin meditating on Brecht's verses in *Erase the Traces,* and returning to the conversation about dwelling—

> has now created rooms in which it is hard to leave such traces (this is why glass and metal have become so important) and which make it almost impossible to acquire habits in the first place. This is why the rooms are empty and often adjustable at will.[9]

Glass, steel, and concrete frames dematerialized traditional forms of construction, reducing architecture to a slender and porous structure able to flaunt any form of life activity without obstructing the multiplication of exchanges: a *typical plan*.[10]

Nevertheless, beyond the spatial correspondence of the destructive character with modern architecture is a liminal temporal dimension and a highly precarious form of living:

> The destructive character sees nothing permanent. But for this very reason he sees ways everywhere. Where others encounter walls or mountains, there, too, he sees a way. But because he sees a way everywhere, he has to clear things from it everywhere. Not always by brute force; sometimes by the most refined. Because he sees ways everywhere, he always stands at a crossroads.[11]

A paradigm for this new unstable subjectivity was certainly Bertolt Brecht's alter-ego and protagonist of his first play *Baal*: hobo and storyteller, lumberjack and poet, wandering across cities and countryside with no expectations of what the next will bring. By owning nothing but his capacity to work, yet cynically refusing to participate in the wicked logic of exchange, Baal is pure untamed potential, not ascribable to any function within a system characterized by the total commodification of human relations. His actions and words exceed any moral or ethical requirement, working within and against the eternal presentness of capitalist production. To Benjamin, Brecht fabricates the revolutionary intellectual precisely from this mixture of poverty, nastiness, and genius of outcast figures such as Baal: the asocial trump who opportunistically accepts the violence of class struggle, dismantling dogmas and eternal truths, disproving the authority of origins and the simplification of overarching narratives through his barbarian mode of dwelling in the world.[12]

Baal/the destructive character does not erase tradition but questions its principles and exposes its limits: making it practicable rather than uncritically preserving it, manifesting "the consciousness of historical man, whose deepest emotion is an insuperable mistrust of the course of things and a readiness at all times to recognize that everything can go wrong."[13] Unafraid of tearing apart worn-out ideas and embracing the desert of the unknown, these barbarians *historicize* reality, by first recognizing their position within the current production system, for then exposing the ideological mystifications embedded in its material and immaterial expressions—from buildings and cities, monuments and infrastructure, to words and images, habits, and behaviors: using Manfredo Tafuri's words, for the destructive character "there is no criticism, but only history."[14]

## Part Two

Brecht and Benjamin's essays profoundly influenced *Teorie e Storia,* the first major theoretical work of the Italian architecture historian Manfredo Tafuri, written between 1966 and 1968 before becoming head of the Istituto di Storia dell'Architettura (ISA) in Venice. The book attempted to redefine the role of historian in architecture, at the time of social disorders and economic prosperity, when the discipline was 'rotten to the core'—trapped between a sclerotized academia and the student movements, large urban plans and real-estate speculations, exalted rationalisms and visionary projects, typological researches and the postmodern proliferation of images and pastiches. "This moment of great openness ranged across the whole political field, calling everything into question"—Tafuri recounts in a lengthy interview with Luisa Passerini—

> But calling everything into question meant that our role was *pars destruens*. I mean to say that the task of the intellectual was *pars destruens*. You must bear in mind here that the influence of Walter Benjamin was very strong, especially from 1966. We even read works that hadn't been translated into Italian, like *The Destructive Character*.[15]

Against those who instrumentalized history to liberate architectural forms from their contexts and material conditions, Tafuri remarked that history is not just the 'past,' nor a malleable material that can be easily shaped according to different molds of the present. These operative manipulations risk degenerating history into fetishisms or personal appropriations, flattening the heterogeneity of its material, casting holistic perspectives over a variety of languages and sources while limiting their capacity to problematize and criticize the present. Instead, the historian should investigate how architecture and architectural knowledge are produced, multiplying and exacerbating questions rather than offering grand narratives, evaluating how architecture responds to the broader different socio-economic conditions to delineate possible margins for freedom, creativity, and development.[16]

History would then appear as a dynamic battlefield rather than a collection of linear trajectories traced a-posteriori by the dominating classes: a motley field of conflicting emergences more than a uniform sequence of facts floating in a 'homogeneous empty time.'[17] "Rather than turning to the past as a sort of fertile ground, rich in abandoned mines to be successively rediscovered, finding in them anticipations of modern problems, or as a slightly hermetic maze for amazing trips leading to a more or less miraculous catch"—writes Tafuri in the introduction to *Teorie e Storia*—"we must get used to seeing history as a continuous *contestation of the present,* even as a threat, to the tranquilizing myths wherein the anxieties and doubts of modern architects, find peace."[18] As there are neither solutions nor straight paths but only contradictions, interruptions, and different starting points, the task is to dismantle any attempt to establish unique lines of cause-effects or definitive origins, searching for crises instead of syntheses.

In particular, the first chapter of *Teorie e Storia* proves that Brecht and Benjamin's destructive character was not just an episodic expression of the 1920s and 1930s avant-garde movements but a constituting trait of the Western humanist culture that emerged with the rise of capitalism in mid-Quattrocento Florence and the projects of Filippo Brunelleschi and Leon Battista Alberti. Translating the lesson of classical antiquities into a new linguistic code,

Brunelleschi and Alberti forerun the 'inexorable ones,' radically transforming the conception of space and the production of architectural knowledge, ultimately differentiating 'Architecture' from the building practice, the architectural project from the mere execution, and architectural theory from history as such. Brunelleschi, by realizing an archipelago of autonomous objects within the cramped medieval fabric of Florence which reinterpreted the principles of Roman Imperial architecture through rigorous geometrical structures, from the Foundling Hospital to the Old Sacristy in San Lorenzo, from the dome of Santa Maria del Fiore to the inner modular frame and the undulating perimeter of Santo Spirito. Alberti, by philologically systematizing the fragmentary notions and building practices inherited from Vitruvius into a coherent theoretical treatise of architecture—*De Re Architectura Libri Decem*—without renouncing to undermine its apodeictic assumptions through the linguistic pluralism of his design, from the Tempio Malatestiano and Santa Maria Novella to the Rucellai Palace, San Sebastiano, and Sant'Andrea.[19]

If modernity connotes the emergence of an acute auto-criticism and self-reflective research, when architecture begins to examine its language, formal logic, and organizational processes, then modernity for Tafuri begins with Alberti and Brunelleschi. Their projects broke away from the medieval traditions, offering the architect a higher professional and intellectual role within society, the authorship over the design process, and the control over the construction site. They both attempted to make history communicable and experienceable, not to consolidate it into traditions but for problematizing the present and undermining its established values: their anti-historicism paradoxically became "the symbol of authentic historic continuity."[20]

Nevertheless, while Brunelleschi and Alberti's projects were still able to "*actualize* historical values as a transformation of mythical time into present time, of archaic meanings into revolutionary messages, of 'words' into civil actions," it has become increasingly difficult for architecture to extrapolate knowledge from the past without considerably reshaping its discourses or succumbing to the merciless imperatives of production.[21] The chapter unfolds the modern 'eclipse' of the Western architectural history through a selection of paradigmatic precedents across a 500-year long parabola, moving from Brunelleschi and Alberti to the contaminations of Raphael and Serlio, the bricolages of Borromini, the tormented fragments of Piranesi, the scientific excavations of the Enlightenment, up to the ruptures of Dada and De Stijl, Malevich and Mies, Le Corbusier and Hilberseimer, Rossi and Stirling, Hejduk and Eisenman, among others. And yet, by suspending historical time, these different projects of modernity lay bare how architecture fabricates and dismantles ideologies to fill the expanding gap between history and representation, form and the power relations to which it complies, program and social contexts, construction and economic frames.[22]

Modernity is a dissecting table, but not everyone can operate these drastic cuts. Paraphrasing Benjamin's *The Work of Art in the Age of Mechanical*

*Reproduction*, Tafuri distinguishes the *surgeons*—fully engaged with the principles and technologies of the new forms of production, while trying to unveil their inner mechanisms—from the *magicians*—who are instead interested in the new forms of art but unwilling to participate in their processes—leaving apart the *indecisi*, or those unable to take any position.[23] The destructive character is a surgeon, who does not create better or more beautiful forms, nor evokes the nostalgia of those long gone but, as Brecht suggested, historicizes 'the bad new ones' even at the cost of destroying those once considered sacred and inestimable. Concepts, artworks, or architectural forms should be dismissed when no longer valid, once their aura is exhausted, perhaps '-re-functioning' some of their properties if still useful for meaningful new assemblages, otherwise destroyed.

To better elucidate the destructive attitude, Tafuri reports a passage from Brecht's *Dreigroschenprozess* (The *Threepenny Lawsuit*): a lucid analysis about the culture industry, cognitive labor and immaterial modes of production, which also underpinned Benjamin's *Work of* Art:

> If the concept of 'work of art' can no longer be applied to the thing that emerges once the work is transformed into a commodity, we have to eliminate this concept with cautious care but without fear, lest we liquidate the function of the very thing as well. For it has to go through this phase without mental reservation, and not as a noncommittal deviation from the straight path; rather, what happens here with the work of art will change it fundamentally and erase its past to such an extent that should the old concept be taken up again — and it will, why not? — it will no longer stir any memory of the thing it once designated.[24]

Brecht revolutionized the traditional forms of theatrical representation—based on eternal human values, universal passions, and the empathic involvement of the audience—creating a pedagogic experience that does not captivate but rather estranges its spectators, inducing them to actively question what occurs on the stage. Rearranging all sorts of literature material, from troubadour ballads, poems, and sport magazines to biblical texts, detective stories, Brecht created an *epic* theatre: not an entertaining pastime or a report of events, but the objective analysis of facts; not passive escapism but an experience of collective awakening.[25]

The purpose of the epic theater was *to interrupt,* to destroy the linearity of facts into a montage of episodes and gestures, scientifically dissecting the characters and their gestures as on an anatomical table, leaving the play open to interpretation. As for his sympathetic/nomadic dweller, Brecht deploys estrangement to short-circuits any vicarious reception of reality, automatic repetitions and habits, defamiliarizing words, ideas, images, and gestures to polarize the attention of the spectators, stimulating alertness and awareness instead of feelings, encouraging them to think about their roles within society while figuring out the events happening on stage.[26]

Tafuri was interested in the particular open fruition of Brecht's plays, whose 'consumption' aimed to a state of awareness and collective understanding beyond the optical-tactile experience without offering any definitive solution.[27] Similarly, the subversive character of an architectural artifact would depend on its capacity to conceptually and spatially stimulate its users, more than by seduction through the exuberance or absoluteness of its forms, leaving leeway for a critical apprehension of the whole context and its complex stratifications.

"A photograph of a Krupp factory or the AEG"—writes Brecht in another illuminating passage of his *Dreigroschenprozess*—"says practically nothing about these institutions. Reality itself has shifted into the realm of the functional. The reification of human relationships, such as the factory, no longer betrays anything about these relationships."[28] In such a world without any stable reference point, where it is difficult to hold on to a common ground or definite notions, where everything turns into a hieroglyph or a performative flux, historicization and estrangement become a viable strategy to swerve from the spectacle and reconstruct the mechanisms behind its farce. To look at the world from an estranged point of view is to rediscover and reinvent it, to render it at a sharper resolution: it is not a fugue from reality but rather a total immersion in it.

## Part Three

Last autumn, following the brutality of George Floyd's death, numerous statues were toppled on both sides of the Atlantic. The destruction of these monuments was neither the expression of an iconoclastic fury nor the displacement of collective memory but a conscious act of rewriting history to raise awareness and bring about social justice. Their removal underlines how historical narratives are never innocent, warning against other forms of colonialism, racism, and segregation still haunting our society. Most importantly, these statues witness a much more tectonic reassessment of the whole notion of history, considered as never before as a litmus test for the present rather than a mere repository of dead forms, buildings, monuments, or significant events to remember.

The urge to constantly reinterpret and revise how to look at the past is not just an intellectual exercise but a political challenge to construct a different understanding of what surrounds us. And architecture is a vital means for such a historical examination, framing every human activity on earth like no other form of knowledge and crystallizing how we imagine, inhabit, or modify the world around us in concrete and immaterial form. Not by chance, the role of history in architecture always generated intense debates among scholars, practitioners, artists, curators, and independent researchers, as witnessed by the biennales and triennials of the past decades, from *The Presence of the Past* to the more recent *Elements of Architecture* and *Make New History*.[29]

This is nothing new. As we have seen in other moments of crisis—when reference points, consolidated positions, political representation, economic stability, and building opportunities seem to sway—in an impetus of self-criticism, architecture often seeks to analyze, dismantle and update its disciplinary foundations through an active confrontation with the past: wandering backward while searching for other ways to continue forward. Indeed, such an increased historical awareness induces positive effects within the discipline, expanding the field of research, accelerating the dissemination of knowledge and circulation of references, multiplying archives and resources, creating institutions and platforms for discussion. Nonetheless, resorting to historical material as a "horizon, open and accessible, with multiple entry and exit points, where the old and the new are in a cyclical relationship, or where the old becomes new when viewed through contemporary knowledge," could be a strategy to reduce the distance between history and practice bypassing the intimidations of theory and move straight to the project, but at the risk of aestheticizing or oversimplifying the architectural discourse.

Unfortunately, the chasm between most architectural practices and the considerable challenges of the present has been relentlessly widening, limiting the efficacy of history as critical support. While democracies and political representation are waning, inequalities erupting, and our impact over the planet reaching the point of non-return, architecture seems unable to produce a valid response, something more than a silent reverence or ironic commentary on the system it has contributed to creating. Numerous firms keep basking in the stylistic use of idiosyncrasies and formal jokes without any intention to translate these complexities and contradictions into different ideas of space, use, or subjectivity. Others attempt to contrast the world's non-referential nature through the rigor of form and the ingenious definition of boundaries. Some create complex forms with sophisticated structural ambivalences and unstable equilibriums. A few compose boulders and natural elements to reproduce 'primitive' arrangements, like an uncontaminated playground. Others do not believe in communication beyond those able to speak it, praising either a superior indifference or ordinary dumbness. A smaller group seeks to redeem its sins by serving basic living necessities and making goodwill gestures, while the majority tries to survive from one client to the next, with the ambition of reinventing something or donating beauty to the mundane.

However, not all is lost. The decline of public commissions, urban competitions, and long-term planning, worsened by the pandemic's dramatic effects of distancing and isolation, forced architects to finally 'rediscover' the pleasures and discontents of domestic space as the quintessential spatial and political instrument to construct the coming community. Reimagining how to live together, ensuring equal rights and a basic income for all, sharing spaces, objects, infrastructures, and resources beyond traditional social bonds, exchange values, or the trite distinction between public and private, with the aims of developing solidarity, integration, and cooperation among different living forms, is now the most urgent mission to avoid the self-extinction of our (endangering) species and safeguarding the conditions for its survival.

When architecture no longer makes a difference in a world exacerbated by differences, it is time to unlearn what we know and reevaluate how we produce architecture within old and new cultural institutions. It is time to get back to history again. After being relegated within specialized research and philological studies in archives, museums, or academic departments for too long, architectural history prominently manifests all its potential of liberation through knowledge institutions, offering ground for new theoretical discourses and design speculation to expand the discipline's horizons. Survey courses, theory seminars, and doctoral programs have been restructured to foster equity, justice, diversity, and inclusion, debunking the domination of Western canons, decolonizing curricula, and reconsidering the educational purposes toward the future concerns.

Architecture history cannot just be a sclerotic collection of references and models, comparative studies, and typological analyses supplied to architects for better situating their designs. It forges a critical attitude, the capacity to challenge the very principles and methods of the discipline, not taking anything for granted but understanding the built environment as a continuous construction for which we are all responsible, and reading architecture beyond its drawings, relativizing its objects within its constituent conditions. Above all, it teaches us not to be afraid of destroying for beginning again, estranging ourselves from the limited perspective of our individual positions, being open to contradictions, learning to observe through foreign eyes and embracing otherness in all its forms.

As Brecht, Benjamin, and Tafuri made clear through their work, history gets eclipsed when we are deprived of the capacity to imagine alternatives to the status quo. If, for centuries, we have been considering architecture as construction, exalting its coming to being without acknowledging the detrimental effects and negative externalities, perhaps it is now time to rethink the project of destruction, accepting the responsibilities of collapse and, starting from these ruins, to reinvent how to dwell within the world and the principles of coexistence between humans and non-humans.[30]

## Notes

1 Karl Marx, *Capital: A Critique of Political Economy*, Vol. 1, Moscow: Progress Publishers, 1887: 163.

2 Walter Benjamin, *Selected Writings*, Vol. 2, Part 2, 1931–1934, Cambridge, MA: The Belknap Press of Harvard University Press, 1999: 479–480.

3 Brecht invents the adjective *mitahmend,* composed by *mitfühlen* to "sympathize" and *nachahmen,* "to imitate."

4 Benjamin refined this comparison in other works, as in *The Arcades Project*:

> The primal form of all dwelling is not a house but a case. This bears the imprint of its dweller. Taken to an extreme the dwelling becomes a case. More than any other age, the nineteenth century felt a longing for dwelling. It thought of dwelling as an *étui* and tucked the individual and all his belongings so far into it that it reminds one of the inside of a bow of compasses in which

> the instrument together with all its accessories is sheeted in deep, usually violet-colored velvet cavities.

Walter Benjamin, *The Arcades Project*, trans. Howard Eiland and Kevin McLaughlin, Cambridge, MA: Belknap Press, 2002: 220–221. Concerning Brecht's influence on Benjamin see, Ermudt Wisitzla, *Walter Benjamin and Bertolt Brecht. The Story of a Friendship*, New Haven, CT and London: Yale University Press, 2009.

5 We allude here to Reyner Banham's essay "A Home Is Not a House," *Art in America*, vol. 53 no. 2 (1965): 70–79; and to Chloe Zhao's recent film *Nomadland,* awarded an Oscar and Gold Lion in 2020, adapted from Jessica Bruder, *Nomadland: Surviving America in the Twenty-First Century*, New York: W. W. Norton & Company, 2017.

6 Bertolt Brecht, "Ten Poems from a Reader for Those who Live in Cities," in *Bertolt Brecht, Poems 1936–1951*, John Willet and Ralph Manheim (Eds.). London: Methuen, 131. Also see Walter Benjamin's "Commentaries on Poems by Brecht," in *Understanding Brecht*, London and New York: Verso Books, 1988: 59–64.

7 Walter Benjamin, "The Destructive Character," in *Selected Writings,* Vol. 2, Part 2, 1931–1934, Cambridge, MA: The Belknap Press of Harvard University Press, 1999: 541–542.

8 Walter Benjamin, "Experience and Poverty," in *Selected Writings*, Vol. 2, Part 2, 1931–1934, Cambridge, MA: The Belknap Press of Harvard University Press, 1999: 732 (emphasis mine).

9 Walter Benjamin, "Juan-les-Pins, May 5, in the Morning. May-June 1931," in *Selected Writings*, Vol. 2, Part 2, 1931–1934: 473. See also Detlef Mertins, "The Enticing and Threatening Face of Prehistory: Walter Benjamin and the Utopia of Glass," *Assemblage*, vol. 29 (1996): 6–23; and Pier Vittorio Aureli, "The Theology of Tabula Rasa: Walter Benjamin and Architecture in the Age of Precarity," *Log*, vol. 27 (Winter/Spring 2013): 111–127.

10 Rem Koolhaas, 'Typical Plan,' in *S, M, L, XL*, Rem Koolhaas and Bruce Mau (Eds.), New York: The Monacelli Press, 1995: 334–353; and Francesco Marullo, *Typical Plan. The Architecture of Labour and the Space of Production*, Ph.D. Dissertation, TUDelft, 2014.

11 Walter Benjamin, "The Destructive Character": 542.

12 Walter Benjamin, "Bert Brecht," in *Selected Writings*, Walter Benjamin (Ed.), Vol. 2, Part 1, 1927–1930: 365–371.

13 Walter Benjamin, "The Destructive Character": 541–542.

14 "There is no such thing as criticism, there is only history. What usually is passed off as criticism, the things you find in architecture magazines, is produced by architects, who frankly are bad historians. As for your concern far what should be the subject of criticism, let me propose that history is not about objects, but instead is about men, about human civilization. What should interest the historian are the cycles of architectural activity and the problem of how a work of architecture fits in its own time. To do otherwise is to impose one's own way of seeing on architectural history. What is essential to understanding architecture is the mentality, the mental structure of any given period. The historian's task is to recreate the intellectual context of a work." Manfredo Tafuri, "There Is No Criticism, Only History," interview by Richard Ingersoll, in *Design Book Review*, vol. 9 (Spring 1986): 8–11; republished in *Casabella*, vol. 619–620 (1995): 96–99.

15 Tafuri confesses to Passerini also his profound debt to Bertolt Brecht: "Two things I remember about the time when I was writing *Teorie e Storia*: First, Giorgio Strehler organized a very important recital with Milva at the Eliseo in Rome around 1967, *I, Berthold Brecht.* I remember admiring Brecht's technical strength and intelligence: "Io Bertolt Brecht, venuto dai deserti d'asfalto." He had been

a key figure for us because of his commitment and his importance as a poet." Luisa Passerini, Manfredo Tafuri and Denise L. Bratton, "History as Project: An Interview with Manfredo Tafuri," *Being Manfredo Tafuri, ANY: Architecture,* vol. 25/26 (2000): 10–70. On Tafuri and Brecht, see Hélène Lipstadt and Harvey Mendelsohn, "Philosophy, History, and Autobiography: Manfredo Tafuri and the 'Unsurpassed Lesson' of Le Corbusier," *Assemblage*, vol. 22 (1993): 58–103; and Panayotis Tournikiotis, *The Historiography of Modern Architecture*, Cambridge, MA: The MIT Press: 193–219.

16 Manfredo Tafuri, "There Is No Criticism, Only History," *Casabella*, vol. 619–620 (1995): 96–97.

17 Walter Benjamin, "Theses on the Philosophy of History," in *Illuminations*, Hannah Arendt (Ed.), London: Collins/Fontana Books, 1973: 255–266.

18 Manfredo Tafuri, *Theories and History of Architecture*, London: Granada, 1980: 233 (emphasis in the original).

19 Manfredo Tafuri, *Theories and History*: 17.

20 Manfredo Tafuri, *Theories and History*: 30.

21 Manfredo Tafuri, *Theories and History*: 14–15. See also "The Historical Project," in *The Sphere and the Labyrinth. Avant-Gardes and Architecture from Piranesi to the 1970s*, Cambridge and London: The MIT Press, 1987: 16.

22 On the notion of crisis in Tafuri, see Marco Biraghi, *Project of Crisis: Manfredo Tafuri and Contemporary Architecture,* Cambridge, MA: The MIT Press, 2013.

23 Andrew Leach, *Choosing History: A Study of Manfredo Tafuri's Theorisation of Architectural History and Architectural History Research*, PhD Dissertation, Ghent University, 2006: 91–113.

24 Bertolt Brecht, "The Threepenny Lawsuit," in *Bertolt Brecht on Film and Radio*, Marc Silberman (Ed.), London: Methuen, 2000: 194, and Walter Benjamin, "The Work of Art in the Age of Mechanical Reproduction," in *Illuminations*, Hannah Arendt (Ed.), New York: Schocken Book, 1968: 246. About the re-appropriation of mass-communication instruments see Bertolt Brecht, "The Radio as a Communication Apparatus," in *Bertolt Brecht on Film and Radio*, Marc Silberman (Ed.), London: Bloomsbury (2007): 41–46, and Francesco Marullo, "Ocean Flights and Crashed Planes. A Reading of Brecht's Two Learning Plays," in *Counter-Signals*, Vol. 2, Jack Henri Fisher (Ed.), Chicago, IL: Other Forms (2017): 84–91.

25 "Epic theatre, by contrast, incessantly derives a lively and productive consciousness from the fact that it is theatre. This consciousness enables it to treat elements of reality as though it were setting up an experiment, with the 'conditions' at the end of the experiment, not at the beginning. Thus they are not brought closer to the spectator but distanced from him. When he recognizes them as real conditions it is not, as in naturalistic theatre, with complacency, but with astonishment. This astonishment is the means whereby epic theatre, in a hard, pure way, revives a Socratic praxis. In one who is astonished, interest is born: interest in its primordial form." Walter Benjamin, "What Is Epic Theatre. First Version," in *Understanding Brecht*, London: Verso, 1983: 2–5.

26 Walter Benjamin, "Bert Brecht" (Radio talk broadcast by Frankfurter Rundfunk, June 1930) in Walter Benjamin, *Selected Writings*, Vol. 2, Part 1, 1927–1930, Cambridge, MA: The Belknap Press of Harvard University Press, 1999: 366. For a general account on the Epic Theatre see chapter 13 "The Modern Theatre is the Epic Theatre," chapter 24 "Alienation Effects in Chinese Acting", chapter 29 "The Street Scene," and chapter 31 "Short Description of a New Technique of Acting which Produces an Alienation Effect" in Bertolt Brecht, *Brecht on Theatre*, John Willet (Ed.), New York: Hill and Wang, 1964: 33-42; 91-99; 121-129; 136-140.

27 Tafuri considered Brecht's plays 'open-works' as Umberto Eco theorized in his 1962 essay *Opera Aperta*: when the author deliberately leaves the arrangement and development of some constituents of a work to the public or to chance. Brecht's

epic theater did not attempt to deliver a positive message or draw conclusions. Instead, it encouraged the audience to discuss and find out interpretations, considering the world as an object to be deciphered:

> Here the work is 'open' in the same sense that a debate is 'open.' A solution is seen as desirable and is actually anticipated, but it must come from the collective enterprise of the audience. In this case, the 'openness' is converted into an instrument of revolutionary pedagogics.

See Umberto Eco, *The Open Work*, trans. Anna Cacogni, Cambridge, MA: Harvard University Press, 1989: 11.

28 Bertolt Brecht, "The Threepenny Lawsuit," in *Bertolt Brecht on Film and Radio*, Marc Silberman (Ed.), London: Methuen, 2000: 164–165. The non-representability of capitalism resonates also in Tafuri:

> The theoretical knot that must be confronted is how to construct a history that, after having upset and shattered the apparent compactness of the real, after having shifted the ideological barriers that hide the complexity of the strategies of domination, arrives at the heart of those strategies—arrives, that is, at their modes of production. But here we note the existence of a further difficulty: modes of production, isolated in themselves, *neither explain nor determine*. They themselves are anticipated, delayed, or traversed by ideological currents. Once a system of power is isolated, its genealogy cannot be offered as a universe complete in itself. The analysis must go further; it must make the previously isolated fragments collide with each other; it must dispute the limits it has set up.

See Manfredo Tafuri, "The Historical Project," in *The Sphere and the Labyrinth. Avant-Gardes and Architecture from Piranesi to the 1970s*, Cambridge, MA and London: The MIT Press, 1987: 10.

29 "From the First Biennial to the Second and Back Again," interview by Sarah Herda, Co-Artistic Director of the inaugural 2015 Chicago Architecture Biennial, with 2017 Artistic Directors Mark Lee and Sharon Johnston, in *Make New History. 2017 Chicago Architecture Biennial*, Mark Lee, Sharon Johnston, Sarah Hearne, and Letizia Garzoli (Eds.), Baden: Lars Müller Publishers, 2017: 19–27. Among the vast debate on history, see the recent online essay collection curated by e-flux Architecture, accessible at https://www.e-flux.com/architecture/-history-theory/, but also Timothy Hyde, "Is Architectural History Getting Any Bigger?," *arq: Architectural Research Quarterly*, vol. 21, no. 4 (2017): 347–350; Sylvia Lavin, "Theory into History; Or, the Will to Anthology," *Journal of the Society of Architectural Historians*, vol. 58, no. 3 (1999): 494–499; Sylvia Lavin, "The Uses and Abuses of Theory," *Progressive Architecture*, vol. 08 (1990) 113–114, 179; Daniel Sherer, "The Architectural Project and the Historical Project: Tensions, Analogies, Discontinuities," *Log*, vol. 31 (2014): 115–113.

30 "Today, too, hope for a new world rests on faith in violent fractures, the jump into the dark, the adventure accepted without reserves: if this were not the case we should resign ourselves to seeing our capacity for action and understanding slumber in the evasive celebration of the past." Manfredo Tafuri, *Theories and History*, 150. See also, Mark Fisher, *Capitalist Realism: Is There No Alternative?* London: Zero Books, 2009.

# 4 The End of Theory and the Division between History and Design

*Joseph Bedford*

The "theory moment" in architecture in the 1970s and 1980s is often viewed, crudely, as that moment when French post-structuralist ideas entered the field of architecture and led to a transformation of architectural forms.[1] "Theory" in the sense of "French Theory," as the intellectual historian Francois Cusset describes it, meant a trans-disciplinary mode of thought that liberated itself from philosophy; that was incubated in the fields of semiology, linguistics, anthropology and literature; and that transcended those disciplinary boundaries and spread throughout many university departments from the 1960s to the 1980s.[2] At the time, the spread of these ideas was claimed to be subversive. As Sylvere Lotringer, the editor of *Semiotext(e)* and the figure who perhaps played the largest role in its transatlantic "importation," put it, theory was understood as containing a "politics in language." It promised to "scuttle discursive modes" of language that operated as a "command system."[3]

For the past quarter century, architects have been discussing the decline of this "theory moment," making numerous critical arguments about the apparent ultimate ineffectualness of French post-structuralist ideas within architecture, or the lack of a need for them in the first place, or their irrelevance to the subsequent complexities of the global situation.[4] As so many voices cried: "Theory never really belonged in architecture;" "Theory never really addressed architecture's specific material practice;" "Theory was only ever illustrated metaphorically by form;" "Theory was always from the outside and never from within;" and "The world has become too complex for theory," etc. Yet, much of this debate assumed that what really constituted the theory moment was precisely the novelty of ideas, the promise of their effects, and their failure to deliver.

In what follows, I will sketch an alternative argument that might account for the theory moment in different terms. It is less concerned with the ideas themselves, the politics claimed on their behalf, the way they were applied in architecture, and the judgement of their success or failure. Rather it is concerned with the institutional conditions of architectural education, and, in particular, the relationship between history and design within schools of architecture in the last half century and the curricular changes brought about in the same period as a means to manifest this new relationship.

DOI: 10.4324/9781003292999-5

The theory moment, in the end, might be more usefully understood as an effect of these underlying academic transformations within schools of architecture in which the domain of history within the curriculum was expanded to include the realms of theory and criticism as part of a newly enlarged nexus called "history, theory and criticism" (or simply "HTC" for short). This expansion was crucial to the forging of a relationship of mutual influence between the more scholarly domain of history and the more creative and speculative domain of design; one which gave birth to a critical public sphere within schools of architecture and, with this, a form of design that functioned in close proximity to the culture of this critical public sphere, as in itself a form of design-based historical and theoretical criticism.

In this view, the term "theory" as a keyword used to describe this historical moment from the late 1960s to the late 1980s is best understood as the name for a particular culture within schools of architecture in which historical understanding, theoretical speculation, and a critical attitude worked together to guide, inform, and elevate design to a more rigorous, intellectual and critical level. This culture ultimately owed more to a particular desire among architectural educators to link the realms of scholarship and design creativity within schools of architecture than it did to the particular effects of this or that theoretical "import."

These changes brought into being new kinds of educators who viewed the relationship between history and design differently than those of the modernists generation immediately preceding them, and who understood the function of history as crucially guiding, shaping, and improving architectural design, serving a theoretical and critical role in transforming the profession.

Today, the expanded disciplinary domain of "history, theory, and criticism" that was forged in the 1960s has begun to come apart. HTC is still the official title of many course and program descriptions in schools of architecture around the world. A cursory internet search returns at least 24 schools spread across the United States, Europe, Asia and Australia that use the formulation of HTC in their course catalogues and syllabi today.[5] Yet, in many of the leading institutions in which HTC first emerged, it has been shrinking back to the domain of history alone, and many educators in architecture today, place ever greater emphasis upon the vocation of the historian as being independent from theorization or critical engagement.

Architectural history's newfound will to autonomy, is perhaps best expressed by Reinhold Martin when he writes the following: "Despite its institutional location in schools of architecture and in departments of art history, the history of architecture—or "architectural" history—is, as I conceive it, of a piece with historical scholarship in general."[6] Rather than history *for architects*, Martin writes of doing "history with architecture."[7] He also writes of reversing the formula that was developed in the late 1960s in which several educators asked what the uses of history are for architecture, to ask instead what the uses of architecture are for history. In Martin's words: "Rather than confine architectural history (and theory) to the humdrum task of servicing a sclerotic profession, then, we might consider reversing the order."[8] From Martin's perspective the leading edge of the field of architectural history should seek to place the architectural profession in the service of the work of writing history.

At this moment in the third decade of the twenty-first century, when architectural historians in schools of architecture aspire to distance themselves from the culture of design and the architectural profession, we might look back to the 1960s to a moment in which the opposite arguments prevailed, and remind ourselves once more why a new type of architectural historian came into being within schools of architecture in the first place. We might remind ourselves at this historical juncture, that is, about why schools of architecture were ever dissatisfied with a prevailing split between scholars and designers within their ranks, and reflect upon how the "theory moment" was a product of institutional responses to these dissatisfactions.

We can do so by returning, yet again, to the Cranbrook AIA-ACSA Teachers Seminar on "The History, Theory and Criticism of Architecture" in June 1964 and its relationship to the founding of the MIT HTC doctoral program shortly afterwards, and to the parallel and related events taking place at Princeton University and Essex University.[9]

## "History, Theory and Criticism" and the Rise of the "Historian-Architect"

In 1964 a number of architectural historians including among them Sybil Maholy-Nagy, Stanford Anderson, Colin Rowe, Bruno Zevi, Steven Jacobs, Reynor Banham and Peter Collins, gathered at that years AIA-ACSA teachers conference held annually in Cranbrook. These seminars first began in 1956 and had taken different topics in earlier years, from the theme of city planning to the role of psychology and sociology in education. The theme of the teaching seminar in 1964 was the relationship between the role of the architectural historian and studio design education in schools of architecture and the conference proceedings published the following year took the title of "History, Theory and Criticism." As John Harwood has argued, this event can be seen as an origin point of History, Theory and Criticism as a triadic nexus within architectural education. Though, where Harwood focuses more upon its implications for historiographical methods, what follows focuses on implications for curricula arrangements within architecture.[10]

As Harwood argues, Millon was the organizer of the seminar, and played a central role in the selection of its participants, many of whom were drawn from his orbit, especially at MIT where he had been appointed as an assistant professor in 1960. Buford Pickens was Millon's former teacher. Serge Chermayeff taught briefly at MIT. Marcus Whiffen, who edited the Cranbrook seminar proceedings, taught the history survey course at MIT in 1953 and remained associated with the school into the 1980s. Stanford Anderson was, as Millon had been earlier, a doctoral student under Rudolf Wittkower in the history of art department at Columbia (completed in 1968) and had been appointed alongside Millon at MIT the previous year. Bruno Zevi was likely invited because Millon had encountered his work on a stay in Italy and taken his position on the relation between history and design very seriously, responding to it critically in print.[11] And similarly, Reyner Banham was likely invited because Anderson had encountered his work on a stay in London and had also responded to his work critically in a lecture at the Architectural Association.[12]

Given that the HTC doctoral program at MIT, officially founded in 1974, was instrumental in the institutionalization of doctoral studies in architecture as a specific field of history, theory and criticism as opposed to building sciences or urban planning, and as opposed to doctoral studies in architecture within art history, and given that the intentions behind this institutionalization spoke then, and still speak now, to a set of larger issues regarding the relationship between scholarship and design, it is useful to trace back these intentions and see their connections to the larger discussions on the matter staged at Cranbrook.

The wider context for the discussions staged at Cranbrook was the by then fairly widespread sentiment in the late 1950s and early 1960s that the rejection of tradition by numerous protagonists of the modern movement in architecture had been problematic first because it led subsequent generations in the 1950s (such as Philip Johnson and figures labelled under the banner of "Neo-Liberty") to return somewhat naïvely to historicism, though second, and more importantly, because it had led to a built environment that was conceived in a scientistic and instrumental manner, and was as a result hostile to human nature.[13] As Sibyl Moholy-Nagy (Figure 4.1) put it:

> the preponderance of repetitive box shapes of impermanent materials and construction … never rose above a subtractive purism, incapable of replacing the eliminated historical appeal with a new aesthetics. This

*Figure 4.1* *The History, Theory and Criticism of Architecture AIA-ACSA Teacher Seminar, Cranbrook*, 1964 (Front Right: Sibyl Moholy-Nagy. Photograph Buford Pickens).

> so-called new architecture has created a featureless environment of handcrafted machine products, belonging neither to architecture as art nor to architecture as technology, neither to history nor to the future. The failure of the International Style to stimulate either the creative imagination of the architect, *or* provide identification for the client, *or* answer to the need for historical consciousness in cityscapes was the immediate cause for the reanimation of the historical corpse.[14]

The symptomatic culprit for Moholy-Nagy, as for many others at the seminar, was Walter Gropius who had eliminated history teaching at the Bauhaus and had placed it in the later years at Harvard.[15] The consequence of these curricula changes, which had been repeated across several other schools from the 1920s to the 1960s, had been to exacerbate the modernist divorce between history and design in institutional terms.[16] If history was taught in schools, it was taught only briefly, only by visiting faculty, and only by art historians who it was claimed did not always understand architectural design and therefore what it might have to teach or learn from history. As Moholy-Nagy put it, art historians tended to offer little more than iconographic documentation of styles.

While Stanford Anderson, Bruno Zevi, Peter Collins and Stephen Jacob alike all advocated for strengthening the relationship between history and design, based on a similar diagnosis of the problem as that put forward by Moholy-Nagy, it was Stephen Jacobs (Figure 4.2) who advanced the clearest educational response to the problem, advocating explicitly for the creation of a new kind of architectural educator; one who would be able to synthesize

*Figure 4.2 The History, Theory and Criticism of Architecture AIA-ACSA Teacher Seminar, Cranbrook*, 1964 (Left: Reyner Banham, Right: Stephen Jacobs).

the orientation of the historian towards scholarly academic work with the orientation of the architect towards creative production engaged with the wider social world.[17] One can see how the idea of developing doctoral-level architectural history within the school of architecture was in the air in the early 1960s. It was so partly as a result of the boom in the university research economy which put pressure upon architecture schools to enhance their own position within the research university in terms of what might constitute its research program. But it was so also as a result of the desire to redefine this more advanced research program in order to defend a humanistic view of architecture, protecting architecture from further absorption within the general scientific research economy.

While Stephen Jacob argued at Cranbrook that architects tended to have "a lamentable lack of scholarly dedication ....,"[18] he also argued, in equally critical terms, that art historians were ill-equipped to teach architectural history in professional schools because, as he put it, they tended to "be consumer rather than producer oriented, to emphasize the what at the expense of the how, and perhaps to misunderstand the why."[19] Art historians occupied the role of teaching history to architects in modern architectural education because of the long-standing inclusion of architecture within their academic domain, and in the late 1950s, with the presence of German émigré art historians such as Rudolf Wittkower at Columbia and Erwin Panofsky at Princeton, the architectural history emerging out of art history programs was of an advanced nature in terms of their philosophical and cultural interpretations of architectural form.[20] Art history in this mould habitually demonstrated a practiced degree of disciplinary autonomy from the production of art, however. That it did, has much to do with the fact that in the German context, art history emerged precisely within the larger field of cultural history rather than within art schools and academies. And in the British Courtauld tradition, art history also emerged within the context of responding primarily to the exigencies of dating, attribution, and valuation demanded by the art market, also ensuring its distance from creative training within art schools. As a result, art historians did not commonly view their task as theorizing and guiding contemporary practice, neither for art nor for architecture, even if many of them were highly sympathetic to design and had some partial experiences of design.

In place of this polarized condition between the academic art historian and the lamentably non-scholarly architect, Jacobs advocated for the creation of a figure he called the "hybrid historian-architect," someone who would have, in his words "sympathy for architecture's creative, intellectual, and technical problems, as well as the usual understanding of its meanings, forms and social character."[21] Jacobs advocated also for the development of graduate-level education in order to foster the training of such hybrid historian-architects. It would be a graduate education that would "make available to the professional schools qualified, creative, and productive architectural historians able to make a contribution of high scholarly caliber to the local educational scene."[22] By "local educational scene," Jacobs meant something like the scene of the professional school, with studio-based design training at its heart. As such the new hybrid figure, partly scholarly and partly creative, would have a dual allegiance. They would aim to contribute both to the scholarly domain demanded by the vocation of historical practice as well as the creative domain of studio, and ultimately, through the latter, to the future of architectural practice.

In advancing the case for the dual allegiance of the historian-architect towards both scholarship and creative practice, several of the contributors at the Cranbrook conference also outlined positions on the importance of viewing the practice of history in the context of architectural design education as simultaneously a practice of theory and a practice of criticism. As Bruno Zevi put it, "you cannot have history without a theoretical approach and without critical involvement."[23]

Discussion of the conjunction of history with "theory" was perhaps the least agreed upon matter at the Cranbrook seminar. As one attendee put it bluntly, "No one has really stated what theory is." Some argued that theory was synonymous with the writings of architects; some argued that it was a set of concepts or philosophies involved in design decision-making; some that it was a set of principles that relate the form of a building to wider social, economic and technological conditions surrounding its creation.[24] Jacobs shared the opinion, echoing John Summerson, that no theory of architecture existed as a final "valid statement of principles,"[25] but that it must be taught in historical terms through a presentation of a dialectical sequence of ideas that circulated around architecture and among architects—something that he thought necessarily fell to the historian to undertake, even if it was not necessarily or naturally part of the historian's assumed vocation. Yet despite the relative lack of consensus, few participants disagreed with the central location of theory in the expanded conjunction of "history, theory and criticism" and some positively advocated for the relationship between history and theory in which at the very least, one could assume that history inevitably always facilitated theoretical reflection and, even if theoretical reflection could never be finalized, history always served to stimulate the architects thoughts about what a working definition of theory might be. For Peter Collins, for example, history could "provide the basis of speculation about architectural theory,"[26] and for Buford Pickens, an "intelligent use of historical knowledge" could provide, at least, "a solid basis for working theory."[27]

The relation of history to criticism was a much clearer matter among several of the participants, above all, Peter Collins and Bruno Zevi. Collins, for example, argued that the historian in the school of architecture had a duty to demonstrate critical judgement in the process of conveying historical knowledge to the student, and by doing so they would convey to the student that "every architect is morally bound to criticize (and design critically)..."[28] This critical judgement was of course partly that of the historian, but he insisted it should not be based simply upon "personal emotions" (à la Vincent Scully) but upon "principals" about the common methods and reasons by which any design is undertaken within its own historical context.

*Figure 4.3 The History, Theory and Criticism of Architecture AIA-ACSA Teacher Seminar, Cranbrook*, 1964 (Centre: Bruno Zevi. Photograph Buford Pickens).

For Bruno Zevi (Figure 4.3), the value of bringing history close to the design studio, to the point of teaching history directly in studio, had the benefit of creating a critical form of design. "We have to find a system of teaching design with a historical method, so as to achieve a complete coherence, almost a fusion between history courses and design courses," and "If history uses the instruments of design, the reverse is also true: Design is going to use the instruments of history and criticism more and more."[29] And As Zevi put it in 1957, history "must serve to create better architects, not only specialized historians of art. The study of history creates a critical consciousness whose usefulness can be checked at the drawing table better than in the library."[30]

## Beyond Cranbrook

The Cranbrook seminar captured the larger winds of the late 1960s, both at MIT, Essex University and Princeton University where a similar range of curricular changes were taking place. At MIT, Millon and Anderson played major roles in expanding and institutionalizing HTC within the curriculum and, in the process of doing so, attempting to define the rationale for this expansion and institutionalization. In 1966, they established a Bachelors-level HTC major, which enabled them to hire two specialized faculty to support these new classes: two doctoral trained art historians, Wayne V. Anderson and Rosalind Krauss—trained at Columbia and Harvard, respectively. By 1971, they had prepared a proposal for a new PhD program in History, Theory and Criticism, which was eventually approved in 1974.[31] After Krauss's and Millon's departures in 1972 and 1973, respectively, two additional professors were hired to support the program, Dolores Hayden and Donald Preziosi, followed by David Friedman in 1978. Thus by 1978, MIT had expanded and institutionalized HTC within the curriculum with a core of four dedicated HTC faculty.

Harwoods interpretation of these events are historically rigorous and insightful, yet they overemphasized the distance which he claimed the MIT HTC programs founders sought to establish between history and design by foregrounding Millon's own critical views of Zevi's position on the subject and linking Millon's views to those put forward by Manfredo Tafuri in *Theories and History of Architecture*—a book that began with critical commentary on the discussion at Cranbrook.[32] It is quite true that the young Millon of 1960 was critical of Zevi's position, and rejected the claim that the purpose of history in a school of architecture was to "fashion better architects"[33] or be a "vitamin to invest ... design with new vigor"[34] and that, in order to do this, the historian must use history to convey truths to the student and be interpreted according to the present situation faced by the architect. For Millon, history's purpose for the student architect was far more general and humanistic, in the way that it aided "the maturation process of an individual"[35] and the way that it helped the student "learn something about themselves and others as human beings" helping them to discriminate between the "valid" and the "vacuous."[36] Not only was Millon's view of the effects of history upon the student architect more modest, he also claimed that it was better suited to the nature of historical method itself, because history could not be rendered in such a final and dogmatic form as Zevi proposed as there were "many different 'true' histories."[37] If one had to answer for the historian's engagement with the present, Millon argued, it was sufficient to simply emphasize how this engagement with the present was already built into the work of history itself; that "historians, in their process of selection, organization and presentation, interpret the past."[38]

In focusing upon Millon's own early position and its alignment with Tafuri, Harwood underplays the facts that these views were put forward while Millon was still a doctoral candidate, and not yet an assistant professor in a school of architecture, that there is no evidence of Millon's views being strongly advanced or supported by anyone at the Cranbrook seminar and that, by 1971 Millon might have reconsidered his position after the events at Cranbrook, CASE, and his experience teaching in an architecture school and advocating for the place of a new HTC program precisely within the context of a professional school.[39] What comes across far more clearly in the proposal documents is the alignment between the arguments made in support of the new HTC program at MIT and the arguments advanced at Cranbrook by Zevi, Jacobs, Collins, and Moholy-Nagy. For example, Millon and Anderson's proposal argues that historians already teaching in the architecture school at MIT were "committed to a close association between their efforts and the school as a whole;" that they believe that "studio-oriented contemporary art historical studies have a creative role to play;" and that "a critical and theoretical grasp of history shares a natural and mutual growth with the criticism which is the core of the design studio."[40] None of these statements strike the reader as evidence of the proposers of the new program advocating for the autonomy or at least scholarly distance of history from design. Indeed, reflecting back on his role in founding the new HTC program at MIT many years later, Anderson also made it clear that the development of history and theory was intended to "influence" design. As he put it, the "intention" of the new program, was "to remain in contact with, and to influence … [the] design, and production of our cultural realm and our environment."[41]

In addition, these remarks clearly outline the expansion of the historian's practice to include criticism and theory, that criticism in history cultivates criticism in design, and that theory in the various ways it might be understood, as "an examination of the scientific basis for theoretical positions," as the study of "current views about the sources and growth of knowledge in the field," or as the analysis of "current and earlier conceptual thought" about the environment, would all be central to the conception of the new HTC program.[42]

Furthermore, in Anderson's view, the program was designed specifically to train the next generation of Jacob's "historian-architects" who would differ from their own generation in combining training as architects with historical training as scholars, and for the reason that such a combination would be mutually beneficial to both architectural practice and historical scholarship. As Anderson put it, the new historian-architects would benefit from their professional training not simply because it would give them the technical competence needed to understand what they were looking at, but because their "prior training as [an] architect," "provided a mentality more open to speculation."[43]

One can also look beyond Cranbrook to the United Kingdom in the same years where, following the RIBA Oxford Conference in 1958 whose recommendations advocated for the increase in the scholarly requirements of the profession as well as for the growth of new graduate studies, new independent graduate-level courses in architectural history and theory began to be established for the first time.[44] Similarly to the situation within the United States, graduate courses had first begun in more technical fields such as building sciences and urban planning, and were now being developed in humanities fields, such as history and theory. The first such course of its kind in Britain, if not the world, was the new masters-level program in the History and Theory of Architecture at Essex University created by Joseph Rykwert in 1968, and in line with the developments so far outlined, Rykwert too emphasized the need to conceive of history as critical history, and the need for a new kind of historical training by and for architects.[45]

Rykwert, himself a practicing architect trained at the Bartlett School of Architecture and the Architectural Association, shared a similar concern to that voiced by Stephen Jacobs at Cranbrook about the kind of architectural history that was presently being taught in architecture schools largely by art historians. In 1974, in the context of outlining his methodological approach, Rykwert attacked art history for being unconcerned with the contemporary situation and with contemporary cultural production.[46] And as he put it caustically several years later the art historian in a school of architecture was like "a eunuch in a brothel." They "know who does it with whom, how many times, which way, and in which room; but what he can't understand is why they want to do it in the first place."[47]

Like Jacobs before him, and in agreement with Anderson, Rykwert advocated for a closer link between the work of the historian and the concerns of the architect. As he put it a couple of years after the Essex Course closed: "the history of architecture done by architects is important … because we as architects know how we proceed when we are on the drawing board, and how we make decisions, that we can understand certain decisions of past architects."[48] It was with this view in mind that Rykwert made clear in his promotional material for his Essex course, that the course was *for architects*, and *not* for historians, and that it imagined that architects might take the course and then continue on in their professional education towards practice: "The scheme will provide a course of instruction in architectural theory included primarily for those who have acquaintance with current practice in industrial design and architecture rather than specifically for historians."[49]

We can note here the ease with which Rykwert's course description shifted to describe his course as simply a course in "architectural theory." His own seminar, titled "Theoretical Literature of Architecture Before 1800," addressed a history of architectural writing from Vitruvius to Laugier, and his co-teacher on the course, Dalibor Vesely, taught a course titled "The Phenomenology and Psychology of Perception: Their implications for Methods of Design" that was exclusively focused on the philosophical interpretation of contemporary design, giving significant weight to the role of theory in historical work. And in regards to the role of criticism, we can note Rykwert's own personal advocacy of a mode of history that he referred to as "critical" and his discussion of what he considered to be the critical histories of Johann Joachim Winckelmann (whom Rykwert described as advocating for an art that was better than in his own day); Jacob Burckhardt (whose history he saw as a form of social criticism); Giovanni Morelli (whose history Rykwert thought was clearly politically motivated); and Gottfried Semper (whom Rykwert praised for offering a vision that ran "counter to the practice of his day").[50]

## Princeton University 1966–1980

The case of Princeton University is especially helpful in allowing the reader to observe how these ideas had consequences in the reorganization of the curriculum and the creation of new links between spaces of teaching inside a particular architecture school. If the events at Princeton paralleled those at MIT, it is likely because Kenneth Frampton and Anthony Vidler at Princeton and Henry Millon and Stanford Anderson at MIT had been brought together to discuss the relationship between history and design in the context of Peter Eisenman's CASE meetings in 1964 and because they remained collaborators through the early development of the Institute of Architecture and Urban Studies (IAUS) between 1967 and 1972. We can recall here that the editorial statement of the second issue of the Institute's journal, *Oppositions*, also attached itself to the new triadic arrangement of HTC, and internalized this triad in its division of three subject areas.[51]

Robert Geddes was in the midst of completing a report on the state of architectural education in 1966 when he took the position of Dean of the School of Architecture at Princeton.[52] Like the Cranbrook symposium two years earlier, Geddes's report also advocated for the elaboration of history, theory, and criticism within schools of architecture. It articulated the view that HTC was to serve a critical function in rethinking contemporary architectural design practice and how it might surpass the limitations of the present situation. Geddes's report, for example, argued that students "should be able to formulate a concept of a better environment beyond present day constraints,"[53] and that education should enable "the development of a set of values" and crucially values that should be developed even if they "cannot be fulfilled unless society undergoes significant structural changes."[54] Here, again, lay a clear statement of the critical role that theory—in Geddes's terms concepts and values—was to play in architectural education. Architects should seek to imagine a better approach and a better world that went beyond the present to such a degree that bringing that world into being may require structural change. To facilitate students in coming to such a view of a structurally transformed world, the report recommended that "the student should have a basic grounding in the widest possible range of knowledge ... a command of the vocabulary and conceptual framework of many fields, and ... a large varied diet of reading."[55]

Geddes was also inspired by the precedent of Leslie Martin's headship of the department of architecture at Cambridge University where Martin had championed the alignment between research and design.[56] For Martin, research was did only mean the scientific research premised on the application of mathematical modelling to various design problems such as lighting, occupancy scheduling, and floor area allocation, but also historical research. He was a rare example in the 1960s of a practicing architect with a PhD in architectural history, and he insisted at Cambridge that history in the school be taught not by the art historians in the art history department next door, but by the architectural faculty. As a result, history courses at Cambridge were taught by trained architects such as Martin himself, Colin St John Wilson, Peter Eisenman, and Colin Rowe.[57]

In his role as the new dean at Princeton, Geddes then undertook curricular changes that appear to closely follow the prescriptions of his own report as well as the precedent of Martin's Cambridge. He established a set of courses the following year titled "Values, Concepts and Methods" (VCM) courses and hired a number of new teachers, who we might now see as perfect examples of Jacob's new hybrid historian-architect, to teach design studios as well as to teach graduate-level history and theory courses. These courses certainly widened the diet of reading of the students and created a space in which values that stood in sharp contrast to the present day could be fostered, creating a space in which the archival and interpretative attitudes of historical research could be fused with the speculative attitudes inherent to practice.[58]

Geddes hired a range of young faculty—including Kenneth Frampton, Anthony Vidler, Alan Colquhoun, Gunter Nitschke, Robert Maxwell, Thomas Schumacher, Diana Agrest, Mario Gandelsonas and Demitri Porphyrios to teach these VCM courses and to do so alongside their teaching in the design studio. The range of books found on the syllabi of these various faculty shows the widening scope of their seminar courses; expanding to include philosophy, critical theory, religious studies, anthropology, semiology, ethnography, sociology, psychology and aesthetics. Exemplary of the range of texts that appeared on the syllabi of these VCM courses include readings from Karl Marx, Friedrich Engels, György Lukács, Walter Benjamin, Martin Buber, Raymond Williams, Hannah Arendt, Herbert Marcuse, Mircea Eliade, Jacques Ellul, Ernst Cassirer, Johan Huizinga and Christian Norberg-Schulz. And exemplary of the plurality of positions entertained by these courses is one particular course in Spring 1971–1972 co-taught by the young architectural historian, Anthony Vidler, that surveyed a set of theoretical material under five topic areas: (1) Architecture and Survival, (2) Architecture and Phenomenology, (3) Architecture and Communication, (4) Architecture and Behaviour, (5) Architecture and Social Action (Figure 4.4).

The Princeton VCM courses in the 1970s were not yet as scholarly and historical as later courses later labelled as "history, theory and criticism" would become. They have, instead, the flavour of a non-specialist willingness to mix fields common to the undisciplined autodidact. They often combined such readings and topics in continental philosophy with drawing or design assignments, or building analyses and were actively experimental, confronting architectural design with theoretical frameworks and vice versa. They preceded by two decades the emergence of what would become the typical "introduction to theory" courses that would be established in many schools of architecture by the end of the 1980s, and which, along with the anthologies that serviced them, have been taken as a marker of the triumph and thus consequently the subsequent death of the image of theory under the sign of French Theory.[59] These so-called "introductory theory courses" as they continue to exist today, by virtue of the fact that they often package theory into limited one-off educational smorgasbords separated from studio, might also be seen furthermore as a sign of a subsequent curricular compartmentalization that played a role in fraying the knot of history, theory, and criticism and divorcing it from design in the last quarter century.[60] Yet here, in the early 1970s, one can observe a distinct interlinking of these fields and a kind of explicitly non-specialized approach to each that enabled their synthesis in a fruitful creative nexus.

Kenneth Frampton is one particularly exemplary case of Jacob's new hybrid architect-historian (Figure 4.5). Kenneth Frampton began his career at

**Outline:**

| | | |
|---|---|---|
| Architecture and Survival | Seminar 1. | Buckminster Fuller, the Myth of Technological Super Think.<br>Text: Fuller, "Utopia or Oblivion"<br>Project: Manhattan Dome, in Jenks, "Architecture 2000" |
| | Seminar 2. | Paolo Soleri, Arcology or Ecotecture?<br>Text: Soleri, Arcology<br>Project: Babel 1,2,3 (in above) |
| Architecture and Phenomenology | Seminar 3. | Experience, Space and the Microcosm<br>Introduction to the Phenomenology of Shelter<br>Text: Bachelard: "The Poetics of Space pp. VII - 73,<br>(Minkowski) Handout<br>Projects: Corbusier's Mother's House, Geneva<br>FL. Wright Martin House<br>Falling Water |
| | Seminar 4. | Man, Space, and the Macrocosm<br>Text: M. Eliade, Cosmos and History<br>A. Rapoport, "Australian Aborigines and the Definition of Place."<br>(handout) |
| Architecture and Communication | Seminar 5. | Semiological Esoterica<br>Text: Eisenman, "Conceptual Architecture"<br>Project: Eisenman House |
| | Seminar 6. | Semantic Dimension<br>Text: M. Gandelsonas - "Who is this Man Eisenman - Graves"<br>Project: Graves, Suiederman House |
| Architecture and Behavior | Seminar 7. | Dimensions of Personal Space<br>(to be announced) |
| | Seminar 8. | Community and Privacy<br>Text: I. Goffman, Behavior in Public Places<br>Project: Alexander, Mole City |
| Architecture and Social Action | Seminar 9. | Advocacy or Control<br>Text: Davidoff - (to be announced) |
| | Seminar 10. | Politics of Spatial Experience<br>Text: Henri Lefebvre, "Daily Life in the Modern World"<br>or AD, Beaux Arts Issue, Sept. 1971<br>Architecture vs Politics,<br>Battle of Les Halles<br>Project: Covent Garden Caros Up.,<br>AD July '71 |

*Figure 4.4 ARC 302: Values Concepts and Methods II*, Spring 1971–1972 (Fraker and Vidler).

*Figure 4.5* Kenneth Frampton at Princeton circa 1963–1972.

Princeton teaching studio first, which he did continuously between 1963 and 1967. Having practiced in England with Douglas Stevens and Partners, he was invited by Geddes to teach graduate studios. Once he was promoted to the rank of assistant professor in Fall of 1967, Geddes asked him to also teach HTC courses such as "Historical Development of Urban Form" in Spring 1968, and "Architectural Analysis and Theory." He taught his first VCM course in Fall 1968, shortly after Geddes introduced them, being one of the first faculty to do so. In his VCM course of 1968, he asked his students to read one book, Christian Norberg-Schulz's *Intentions in Architecture* and to apply its theoretical framework to the analysis of one building, Le Corbusier's Unite d'habitation. Frampton wrote in the syllabus that "The result of Western Humanism has been the mutual propagation of architecture and architectural theory; both theory and practice being interdependent."[61] The aim of the course, he declared was "to criticize a given work through the agency of an independent architectural theory and in turn to criticize this theory through the agency of a particular work.[62]

Anthony Vidler is a second example of Jacob's hybrid historian-architect, who had an almost parallel trajectory to that of Frampton. Having graduated from Leslie Martin's school of architecture at Cambridge University in 1965,

Vidler began his career immediately at Princeton University co-teaching a design studio with Peter Eisenman. Vidler then began to combine this role in studio with precepting for lecture courses and, in Fall 1968, he began to deliver occasional lectures in the VCM courses. In Spring 1968, he began teaching his own graduate-level history and theory seminar that complimented Frampton's "Architectural Analysis and Theory" course.

The graduate history and theory seminars that Frampton and Vidler taught concurrently between 1968 and 1972 sought to offer histories of architecture that also claimed an engaged position within the contemporary political situation; particularly by tracing back the socialist legacy of modernism to nineteenth-century socialist traditions. Where Vidler emphasized a French utopian tradition from Ledoux through Fourier to Le Corbusier, Frampton emphasized an English socialist tradition from the Gothic Revival of Ruskin and Morris through Germany to Soviet architecture and back to the housing projects of Soviet émigré Berthold Lubetkin.[63] While the two men shared an interest in socialism as central to the formulation of their own critical positions as historians and educators, they each drew from different bodies of literature as a theoretical basis for their work, with Vidler reading principally in French post-structuralism and Frampton reading primarily in German phenomenology and the Critical Theory of the Frankfurt School.

Despite the differences between them, their common critical stance in their teaching was clearly indicated by common keywords such as "crisis," "technology," "alienation," "control," "consumption," "commodity," "kitsch" and "bourgeois," placed within the titles of their lectures.[64] Like many young men in their thirties in the late 1960s, their critical stance can also be seen as linked to their own personal relationship to the political climate of the moment. Frampton discussed the actions of the "revolutionary students" in Paris, for example, in his syllabus in 1969 and linked their actions to the larger "tradition of the city as the setting and the object of political revolution"[65] and Vidler was active in the student unrest on campus in 1970 when Princeton University went on strike to protest the United States's invasion of Cambodia.

In the same years, Robert Geddes asked Frampton and Vidler to help revise the existing PhD program in architecture at Princeton, which they did between 1966 and 1972.[66] As Vidler has recalled, echoing the similar intentions of Rykwert in the 1960s, the program was "*for architects*, as opposed to art historians. To be entered into the doctoral program you had to be trained *as an architect* or an urbanist. You could not come with a simple degree in art history."[67] And as Vidler put it, describing his role in founding the PhD program at Princeton "… in Princeton, we observed two basic principles: all teachers had to have a diploma in architecture and all teachers had to teach both design and a theoretical subject. Kenneth Frampton, Alan Colquhoun, myself and others all taught architectural design as intellectuals looking at our discipline from a simultaneously theoretical, historical and design perspective."[68]

Frampton and Vidler can be seen as exemplary of the type of historian that Jacobs, Zevi, Collins, Rykwert, Anderson and Geddes imagined when they spoke of the need for a historian in schools of architecture with "sympathy for architecture's creative, intellectual, and technical problems," who sought to develop "a critical apparatus for discussion of crucial issues," who looked to develop "theoretical positions," who were "open to speculation," who saw the architect as "bound to criticize (and design critically)," who saw design as increasingly moving towards the "use of the instruments of history and criticism," who saw the growth of critical methods in history as moving hand in hand with the "criticism in design studio" and who offered a history "*for architecture*" rather than specifically for historians.

Kenneth Frampton, in particular, was to develop his book titled *Modern Architecture: A Critical History*, in the context of his history teaching begun at Princeton. The archives at Princeton University contain long manuscripts of writing on such topics as the Soviet Architecture written and shared with his students and which formulated the basis of his later manuscript. In his introduction to that book, published in 1980, Frampton specifically marked his debts to the Frankfurt School of Critical Theory in order to account for his use of the phrase "critical history" at that moment. In his paper, "History, Theory and Criticism: Operative Writing in a Post-Modern Period" delivered at the 76th ACSA Annual Meeting in 1988, Frampton elaborated further on these remarks, suggesting that, in contrast to Manfredo Tafuri, who chided historians such as Zevi for allowing theory and criticism to distort their histories, he was happy to describe his book as "operative criticism" because of his own rejection of the radical position of the historical avant-garde, of which he claimed Adorno and Horkeimer's *Dialectic of Enlightenment* had taught him to recognize its "instrumental and self-alienating dimensions."[69]

Tafuri had resisted what he labelled as operative criticism, precisely because he believed that the notion of the historian as intellectual guide to design foreclosed the revolutionary possibilities both of historical objectivity and design praxis alike. Tafuri's sympathy for Gropius's decision to separate history from design, indicates his underlying ongoing sympathy for revolutionary breaks as the only true historical gesture. As he put it, the modern movement was already "rooted in it [history], because of its anti-historicism."[70] That is, Tafuri as a literal card-carrying communist party member of 1968 held out hope for a true historical event to come and thus refused the hubris that the historian of the present knew enough to judge and act. In Tafuri's estimation, rigorous historical work that refused any ideological closure in the present, and thus refused the moment of criticism, was the mirror image of avant-garde practice. Both held open the door to a genuine transcendent break from the present situation.

Where for Tafuri, the conception of the historian in the school of architecture as a kind of resident theorist or critic that might lead architectural design practice in a critical direction, sacrificed the radical potential of independent historical work and the independent work of design, for Frampton, the radical divorce of history from design was symptomatic of the avant-garde's self-alienating instrumentality, whose utopian millenarian conception of time annulled communicative participation in the present. As Frampton argued his case in 1988, "the ideal of an absolutely objective, factual history is an illusion"[71] as "everything bathes in ideology."[72] He understood the critical moment in his own historical writing as its foregrounding of "ideological intent" and "ideological position[s]" in an effort to unmask current mythologies. Drawing upon Raymond Geuss's interpretation of the Frankfurt School, he clarified that this is how he understood critical theory as "aim[ing] at … making agents aware of hidden coercion, thereby freeing them from that coercion."[73]

Yet recognizing one's immersion in an ideological field, did not lead simply to the logic of might is right. Rather, in line with Stanford Anderson's arguments presented at the Cranbrook seminar, the confirmation of one's critical approach was gained through "the moral and cultural efficacy of its critical judgment in the realization of common goals or in its resistance to a common threat."[74] That is, one did not have to presume to know the truth of history in order to act critically to guide the present. One could act under a pragmatic, and in the end scientific, Popperian, proceduralism of conjecture and refutation in an iterative process; as Frampton put it, "a continuous self-reflexive, cyclical" practice.[75]

Above all, the work of history, theory and criticism for Frampton was to be seen as significant less in terms of its validation in ever more accurate historical writing, but in its ability to enable the positing of "the architectural institution as a site of critical practice" in which "criticism, debate, conception, realization, transformation and counter critique succeed one another, in an unending ebb and flow."[76] In this, the historian in the school of architecture was to work to create a kind of critical public sphere that informs and supports a critical practice. As he concluded: "Today, instead of the avantgarde, we have to reassert the resistant value of a self-reflexive critical culture that spans from critique to practice and back again without a break."[77] It is because of this continued focus on criticism in equal measure to history throughout his career, that we find Kenneth Frampton, alongside Joseph Rykwert and Bruno Zevi, as a member of the International Committee of Architectural Critics (CICA) in the 1980s.

## Conclusion

It should be clear from this review of some familiar moments that lay at the origin of the recent institutional history of the field that many leading educators, historians, and architects in the late 1960s once considered too great a separation between the scholarly vocation of the historian and the creative practical vocation of the architect to be problematic for the field of architectural education and the training of historically sensitive, theoretically informed, and critically engaged practitioners. Indeed, we must note at this point that the fact that they did so was crucial to the entire cycle of academic expansion of the field of history, theory and criticism inside schools of architecture in the last half century, with the growth of masters and doctoral programs in this area.

We might agree with Tafuri about the value of rigorous historical methods, just as we might agree with Leopold Von Ranke in his debate with Georg Wilhelm Friedrich Hegel.[78] As a practice, history writing is surely improved by the desire to keep its distance from present day politics which might seek to cook the books or reduce history to present concerns alone and ultimately to distort the facts. But the question of the value of rigorous historical method is not the only thing that is at stake in the relationship between history and design in the school of architecture. What is also at stake is the best way to train architects and the best way to create an educational environment which advances a critical culture and critical practice. The presence of the historian inside the school of architecture, let us recall, was never originally the result of the idea that rigorous historical methods were in themselves of direct value to architectural practice. The same likely goes for the professional fields of medicine or law, which might explain why historians of those fields tend not to be a central feature of schools of law or schools of medicine, but that, like historians of art or science, they are more likely to be found inside departments of history.

The presence of the historian inside institutions of architectural education is itself somewhat historically contingent. It is due firstly to the fact that architects have long claimed, at least since Vitruvius, that knowing history was central to their work, and even more so during the eighteenth century and nineteenth century emergence of historicism in its different forms at the moment when schools of architecture were being established as modern full-time institutions. It is due secondly to the fact that history became institutionally stable as a scholarly field. That there is no "department of theory" or "departments of criticism" inside a modern university, speaks to the difficulty in institutionalizing such practices as disciplines, for understandable reasons.

Yet, once history took its place inside architectural education and gained an established role within an otherwise practically oriented, creative, and professional domain, it could be, and was, expanded into the broader nexus of history, theory and criticism. One can view theory and criticism as having been grafted on to contingent presence of history, as a convenient location to give them some kind of stable curricula home, and without their willing acceptance by history, they are prone to disappear from the curriculum. It is this more recent rejection of the functions of theory and criticism by historians in schools of architecture, that can be taken as furnishing an alternative and perhaps better account of what happened to theory, and to the theory moment.

What was at stake in the expansion of history into HTC in the 1960s, and its institutionalization in close proximity to design inside schools of architecture, was precisely the way that theory and criticism began to play their role in fostering a critical culture and public sphere within the school, and a critical intentionality within architectural design. The new historian-architects of this generation were not simply scholars-in-residence, but functioned as the moral conscience of the school and the profession, serving as analysts and diagnosticians of the historical situation, and intellectual guides for practice.

Today, the events of the past half century seem to have come full-circle to return to something like the situation of the early 1960s in which art historians taught designers about things in the past but never fully engaged or seemed primarily concerned with the possibilities, potentials and transformations of future architectural practice. Much of this transformation might simply be a function of the manner in which today's professors of history, theory and criticism are torn between two competing poles: on the one hand, the design school, whose many aspiring architects ultimately are the reason for the employment of so many architectural historians, and on the other hand, the university, not just their own particular university but the university as a collective noun, and the scholarly discourse of history that they are a part of and which ultimately they rely upon to evaluate and certify scholarly merit. A more detailed explanation of this tension and a more elaborate account of the course of this return will have to wait for another occasion, but for now it is sufficient to simply document the difference between the current aspirations of historians, at least that represented by Reinhold Martin, though arguably adopted by many of his students and protégés within schools of architecture today, and the generation of historians that began the cycle of growth in the field that led to this present moment.

## Notes

1 For a standard narrative regarding this moment, marked at its height by the engagement between architect the French deconstructionist Jacques Derrida see Harry Francis Mallgrave, "The Gilded Age of Theory," in *Introduction to Architectural Theory: 1968 to the Present* (London: Blackwell, 2005), 123–131.

2 François Cusset, "Theory (Madness of): From structure to Rhizome, Transdisciplinarity in French Thought," *Radical Philosophy* 167 (2011): 24–30.

3 "In short, what French Theory brought to America was a politics in *language*, famously borrowed from Bakhtin and so many others. Politics in language means the scuttling of any discursive mode that refuses to account for its "implicit presuppositions," its despotic significations turning language into a command system that keeps saving representation despite the latter's ceaseless dissolution—books, newspapers, radio, TV, Internet: each plays the role of simplifying." Sylvere Lotringer and Sande Cohen, *French Theory in America* (London: Routledge, 2001), 5.

4 For these arguments, see: Michael Speaks, "It's Out There…the Formal Limits of the American Avant-Garde," *Architectural Design Profile* 133 (1998): 31; Stan Allen Untitled Article, *Assemblage* 41 (2000): 8; Stan Allen, Contribution to "Things in the Making" Conference, Museum of Modern Art, New York, November 2000, cited in Pauline Lefebvre, "What Difference Could Pragmatism Have Made? From Architectural Effects to Architecture's Consequences," *Footprint* 20 (2017): 27; Michael Speaks, "Theory Was Interesting… but Now We Have Work-No

Hope No Fear," *Architectural Research Quarterly* 6, 3 (2002): 211; Robert Somol and Sarah Whiting, "Notes around the Doppler Effect and Other Moods of Modernism," *Perspecta* 33 (2002): 72–77.

5 A brief list of schools of architecture using this convention of "history, theory, and criticism" today in their course and program descriptions, include: MIT, Princeton University, Yale University, Arizona State, IIT, New York Institute of Technology, Georgia Tech, KU Leuven, Université catholique de Louvain, Edinburgh University, University of Wisconsin, University of Houston, University College London, University of Cincinnati, The University of Queensland, Monash University, Massachusetts College of Art and Design, Florida International University, The Academy of Fine Arts in Vienna, Kyoto University, University of Sydney, Sepuluh Nopember Institute of Technology, Amherst College, and Bilkent University.

6 Reinhold Martin, *Knowledge Worlds: Media, Materiality and the Making of the Modern University* (New York: Columbia University Press, 2021), x–xi.

7 Martin, *Knowledge Worlds*, xi.

8 Reinhold Martin, "On the Uses and Disadvantages of Architecture for History," *History/Theory* e-flux Architecture.

9 Other discussions of the Cranbrook seminar and its relation to MIT include: John Harwood, "How Useful? The Stakes of Architectural History, Theory and Criticism at MIT, 1945–1976," in Arindam Dutta, ed., *A Second Modernism: MIT, Architecture, and the 'Techno-Social' Moment* (Cambridge, MA: MIT Press), 106–143 and Ole W. Fischer, "Institutionalized Critique? On the Re(birth) of Architectural Theory after Modernism: ETH and MIT Compared," in Sebastiaan Loosen, Rajesh Heynickx, Hilde Heynen, eds., *The Figure of Knowledge: Conditioning Architectural Theory, 1960s–1990s* (Leuven: KU Leuven Press, 2020), 145–160.

10 Harwood, "How Useful?".

11 Millon's "History of Architecture: How Useful?" *AIA Journal* 34, 6 (1960): 23–25, was a critical response to Bruno Zevi's "La Storia Dell'Architettura per gli architetti moderni" *L'Architettura, cronache e Storia* 3, 23 (1957): 292–293.

12 Stanford Anderson's "Architecture and Tradition That Isn't 'Trad, Dad,'" was first presented as a lecture at the Architectural Association, in response to Reynor Banham's "Coventry Cathedral—strictly Trad, Dad," *New Statesman* 63 (1962): 768–768. Anderson's paper was represented at the Cranbrook conference and published in its proceedings.

13 This wider context of discussion can be traced through Zevi's "La Storia Dell'Architettura per gli architetti moderni" and Millon's "History of Architecture: How Useful?", as well as Nikolaus Pevsner, "Modern Architecture and the Historian, or the Return of Historicism," in *Journal of the Royal Institute of British Architects*, 48 (1961): 230–240.

14 Sibyl Moholy-Nagy, "The Canon of Architectural History," in Marcus Whiffen, ed., *The History Theory and Criticism of Architecture* (Cambridge, MA: MIT Press, 1965), 40.

15 On Walter Gropius's treatment of history within the curriculum as Dean at Harvard University's Graduate School of Design, see Mark Swenarton, "The Role of Architectural History in Architectural Education," *Architectural History* 30 (1987): 206–207.

16 On the decline of architectural history teaching within the curriculum in the United States from 10.8% in 1920 to 8.8% of the curriculum in 1960, see, J.A Chewing, "The Teaching of Architectural History during the Advent of Modernism, 1920s–1950s," *Studies in the History of Art* 35 (1990): 101–110.

17 As Ole W. Fischer argues, the same proposition had been discussed during the CASE meetings organized by Peter Eisenman and which brought together figures

such as Kenneth Frampton, Henry Millon and Stanford Anderson that same year, though Fischer's source for this claim are not given. Fischer, "Institutionalized Critique?," 152.

18 Stephen Jacob, "History: An Orientation for the Architect," in Marcus Whiffen, ed., *The History Theory and Criticism of Architecture* (Cambridge, MA: MIT Press, 1965), 59.
19 Jacob, "History: An Orientation," 59.
20 On the relationship between architectural history and art history see Alina A. Payne, "Architectural History and the History of Art: A Suspended Dialogue," in *Journal of the Society of Architectural Historians* 58, 3 (1999): 292–299.
21 Jacob, "History: An Orientation," 60.
22 Jacob, "History: An Orientation," 60.
23 Bruno Zevi, "History as a Method of Teaching Architecture," in Marcus Whiffen, ed., *History, Theory, and Criticism of Architecture* (Cambridge, MA: MIT Press, 1965), 17.
24 For all these participant and audience remarks on theory see the extracts of the proceedings published as "History, Theory and Criticism: The 1964 AIA-ACSA Teacher Seminar," *Journal of Architectural Education* 19 (1964): pp1-12.
25 Jacob, "History: An Orientation," 51.
26 Peter Collins, "The Interrelated Roles of History, Theory and Criticism in the Process of Architecture," in Marcus Whiffen, ed., *History, Theory, and Criticism of Architecture* (Cambridge, MA: MIT Press, 1965), 5.
27 Buford Pickens, "Forward," in Marcus Whiffen, ed., *The History Theory and Criticism of Architecture* (Cambridge, MA: MIT Press, 1965), vi.
28 Collins, "The Interrelated Roles," 8.
29 Zevi, "History as Method," 17–18.
30 Zevi, "La Storia Dell'Architettura per gli architetti moderni" translated by Millon in "History of Architecture: How Useful?" and cited by Harwood, in ""How Useful?," 122.
31 John Harwood dates this proposal to Spring of 1971. Henry Millon and Stanford Anderson. "Proposal for a Ph.D Program in History, Theory and Criticism of Art, Architecture and Urban Form," Spring 1971 n p., MIT Institute Archives. Series VII. Departments 1965–85. Box 175, Folder Department of Architecture and Planning, 1969–76, 2/4.
32 First published in Italian as Manfredo Tafuri, *Teorie E Storia Dell' Architettura* (Bari: Laterza, 1968) and translated into English as Manfredo Tafuri, *Theories and History of Architecture* (New York: Icon, 1981).
33 Millon in "History of Architecture: How Useful?," 24.
34 Millon in "History of Architecture: How Useful?," 24.
35 Millon in "History of Architecture: How Useful?," 24.
36 Millon in "History of Architecture: How Useful?," 25.
37 Millon in "History of Architecture: How Useful?," 24.
38 Millon in "History of Architecture: How Useful?," 24.
39 As Harwood points out, however, Millon did assist Albert Bush-Brown teaching his history course at MIT in 1956. Harwood, in "How Useful?," 119.
40 Millon and Anderson, "Proposal for a Ph.D Program in History," Unpaginated.
41 Stanford Anderson, "HTC at MIT: Architectural History in Schools of Architecture," in Claus, Sylvia, Dalibor Vesely, and Werner Oechslin, eds., *Architektur Weiterdenken: Werner Oechslin Zum 60 Geburtstag* (Zürich: gta, 2004): 330–339. Anderson, "HTC at MIT," 333.
42 Anderson, "HTC at MIT," 333.
43 Stanford Anderson, "Architectural History in Schools of Architecture," *Journal of the Society of Architectural Historians* 58, 3 (1999/2000): 282–290, [284–285].

44 Leslie Martin, "RIBA Conference on Architectural Education," *The Architects' Journal* 12, 3299 (1958): 775.

45 As Rykwert wrote in 1966 when describing his proposed course, "As far as I know, we will be the only university school of architecture in Great Britain offering such a course." Letter from Joseph Rykwert to John Entenza at the Graham Foundation dated 15th November 1966. Special Collection, Albert Sloman Library, Essex University. And as a newspaper advert for the course at the time put it, "There is at present no mastership course of this nature being offered at any school of architecture or university elsewhere." See newspaper clipping dated between 1966 and 1968 in Special Collection, Albert Sloman Library, Essex University.

46 Joseph Rykwert, "Art as Things Seen," *The Times Literary Supplement* 3768 (Friday, May 24, 1974): 547.

47 Joseph Rykwert, "A Healthy Mind in a Healthy Body," in John E. Hancock, ed., *History in, of, and for Architecture: Papers from a Symposium* (Cincinnati: School of Architecture and Interior Design, University of Cincinnati, 1981), 45.

48 Rykwert, "A Healthy Mind," 45.

49 As he went on, "In view of the standard five-year period required by most schools of architecture, the course may be taken either as an intercalated year from an architectural school or on completion of either an architecture, design or engineering course" Essex Course Prospectus. "Graduate Scheme of study in the History and Theory of Architecture leading to the degree of Master," The University of Essex: School of Comparative Studies, Department of Art (1970–1971) Special Collection University of Essex Archives.

50 Rykwert, "Art as Things Seen," 547.

51 As the final editorial statement put it:

> the criticism of constructed projects as vehicles of ideas; the revision of the past as a means of determining the necessary relationships existing between constructed form and social values; the definition of a spectrum of theoretical discourses that link ideology and the constructed form.
>
> *Oppositions 2* (January, 1974).

52 Robert Geddes and Bernard Spring, *A Study of Education for Environmental Design: The "Princeton Report"* (Washington, DC: American Institute of Architects, December, 1967).

53 Geddes and Spring, *"Princeton Report,"* 9–10.

54 Geddes and Spring, *"Princeton Report,"* 9–10.

55 Geddes and Spring, *"Princeton Report,"* 9–10.

56 Robert Geddes, Interview with the author, Princeton, New Jersey, June 4 2011.

57 Anthony Vidler, "Histories of Architecture: Then and Now: Theory and Practice in the Anthropocene," Lecture presented at the Autonomous University of Lisbon, March 23, 2022, https://youtu.be/VbnTLJed-T4.

58 As the first introductory course in the VCM sequence at Princeton, ARC 102 in 1969–1970, described its aim: "This course is based on the premise that the two major objectives of education are: first, to provide definite knowledge and second, to give a sense of the value of things that help in the formulation of sound judgement." See ARC 102: Shellman, Course Binder Fall 1969–1970, Princeton University School of Architecture, Archives.

59 Sylvia Lavin, "Theory into History; Or, the Will to Anthology." *Journal of the Society of Architectural Historians* 58, 3 (1999): 494–499.

60 Joseph Bedford, "Schooling Theory," in *Theory's Curriculum* (AE Press, 2022), pp. 25–33.

61 Kenneth Frampton, Syllabus, Fall 1968. Princeton University Archives.

62 Frampton, Syllabus, Fall 1968.
63 After Frampton left Princeton University for Columbia University in 1972, Vidler began to develop courses that addressed *both* French and English traditions of socialism in respect to histories of architecture and the city.
64 Examples of their lectures include: "Technology and the Dissolution of the City" (Frampton), "The Pathology of the Nineteenth Century City, 1844–1850" (Vidler), "Bourgeois Consumption and the Generation of Kitsch" (Frampton), "The Commodity and Historical Stasis" (Vidler), "Neo-Capitalism and the Alienation of the Architect" (Frampton), "The Environment as an Agent of Social Control" (Vidler), and "The Third World and the Crisis of Number" (Frampton).
65 Kenneth Frampton, Syllabus, ARC 520, Spring 1969. Princeton University School of Architecture Archives.
66 Vidler, "Histories of Architecture."
67 Vidler, "Histories of Architecture."
68 Anthony Vidler, Interview with Panos Mantziaras in *Mise en œuvre de la réforme LMD dans les écoles d'architecture* (Paris: BRAUP, March 2004), 17. (Translated by the author).
69 Kenneth Frampton, "History, Theory and Criticism: Operative Writing in a Post-Modern Period," in *Who Designs America: A Selection of Papers Presented at the 76th Annual Meeting of the Association of Collegiate Schools of Architecture* (ACSA, 1988), 20.
70 Tafuri, *Theories and History of Architecture*, 64.
71 Frampton, "History, Theory and Criticism," 17.
72 Frampton, "History, Theory and Criticism," 17.
73 Frampton, "History, Theory and Criticism," 21.
74 Frampton, "History, Theory and Criticism," 21.
75 Frampton, "History, Theory and Criticism," 21.
76 Frampton, "History, Theory and Criticism," 21.
77 Frampton, "History, Theory and Criticism," 21.
78 See Helen P. Liebel, "The Enlightenment and the Rise of Historicism in German Thought," *Eighteenth-Century Studies* 4 (4) (1971), 359–385 and Katherina Kinzel, "Method and Meaning: Ranke and Droysen on the Historian's Disciplinary Ethos," in *History and Theory* 59, 1 (2020): 22–41.

# 5 Rehabilitating Operative Criticism

## The Return of Theory against Entrepreneurialism

*Nathaniel Coleman*

### Giedion, Modernity and the Production of Architecture

Despite claims to the contrary, in the age of neoliberal consensus, theoretical reflection represents a commercial liability for auteur and conventional architectural practices alike.[1] Most architects learn this through direct experience, first in architecture school, then as apprentices, employees, and finally, most pronounced and ostensibly painfully, as firm directors or principals, as reflection is successively squeezed out by the economic imperatives of production. Traditionally cast in-between art and science (irrational and rational simultaneously), architecture today rests between business and fashion, which architect and theorist Adolf Loos was already aware of by the early years of the twentieth century.[2] Unsurprisingly, in the world of spectacle taking shape during the post-World War II years – arriving at its definitive Neoliberal form between the 1970s and 1990s, encouraged by Reagan and Thatcher, reports of the end of architectural theory have gained traction, largely on account of the appealing commercial benefits non-reflection promises.[3]

By nature reflective, theory represents an obstacle to the unfettered productivism of anti-theoretical entrepreneurialism, from banal practices to the so-called neo-avant-gardes. Deriving from the Greek *theōros* (spectator), *theōria* (contemplation, speculation, viewing) and *thea* (a view), theory looks beyond present limitations, toward the not-yet of future possibilities. However, as commonly used, theory connotes the supposed limits of the possible, anesthetized by presumptions of unfeasibility. Accordingly, since architects believe history only remembers them if they build, theoretical speculation is overwritten by imagined certainties, in line with the monotonous sway of the building industry.[4] Arguably, the limited, largely negative, perceptions of theory that dominate education (high or low-end) and practice (auteur or banal) are a consequence of perpetually weakening conceptions of architecture as a discipline, in favor of the dominance of (commercial) practice. Largely dissociated from its own disciplinary knowledge (as a practical necessity in an age of populist consensus and capitalist production), theory as sets of principles (in)forming architectural imaginaries and practices dissolves into

DOI: 10.4324/9781003292999-6

shorthand for the antithesis of building; affirmed and denigrated as preoccupied with that which does not happen.

In much the way formalism and stylistic postmodernism were touted as correctives to the putatively utopian aspirations of orthodox modernism, entrepreneurialism has emerged as an apparent corrective to the supposed cul-de-sac of theory.[5] Within architecture, three notable boosters of entrepreneurialism stand out: Michael Speaks, who asserted 'Theory was interesting ... but now we have work'; Rem Koolhaas, for promoting opportunism as having the capacity to supposedly radically overload the dominant system. Likewise, his assertion that 'Utopia [...] is the dirty secret of all architecture' promotes retreat from social imaginaries, ostensibly to escape complicity with its 'more or less serious crimes', conventionally attributed to orthodox (European) modernism.[6] And Patrik Schumacher, a champion of (architectural) neoliberalism who urges architecture's full alignment with global capitalism, as apparently necessary for returning architecture to itself, by setting aside nearly all problems other than form.[7]

No doubt, entrepreneurialism is seductive, carrying with it the whiff and promise of conventional (mainstream) success, concomitant with renewed purpose and (exchange) value for architects. For the Left, Capitalism's impressive entrepreneurialism and creative destruction has proven irresistible. For the Right, it is the natural order of things. No wonder auteur architects longing for association with the fine arts compulsively recast entrepreneurialism as insurgent.

Yet, because theory is speculative in a philosophical sense, while entrepreneurialism is speculative in a commercial sense, the latter is limited to capitalizing on discoveries, whereas the former makes discoveries by reaching beyond the limits of the present. The first pushes against the given, the second is opportunistic. As such, entrepreneurialism necessarily neutralizes theory, as if justified by unimaginative readings of Engels' *Socialism: Utopian and Scientific*, which places systemic transformation beyond incremental improvement, foreclosing on any possible block-by-block (building-by-building) accrual of utopian surplus. Thereby, looking beyond dominant conditions is in equal measure cast as harbingers of failure and impossibility. Hence, Speaks', Koolhaas' and Schumacher's imperative is to recast entrepreneurialism as vanguard (as against opportunism), to make a virtue of active conformity.[8]

By denouncing – rather than extolling – the virtues of acting against (or upon history) through piecemeal change, *scientific histories* side-line the operative utopian imaginaries of theory, leaving little room for disruptive theoretics, ostensibly revealing entrepreneurialism as the only viable option, and as truth. Consequently, altering the fate of architectural theory begins with acknowledging the entrepreneurial turn as enervating. In the event, recovering architectural theory is an open question, unresolved by claims or appearances.

To make a start, Sigfried Giedion's (1888–1968) so-called operative history and criticism is reintroduced, in tandem with the reinvigorating role utopian imaginaries promise for architectural theory. As by definition operative,

Utopia articulates models for reasoning through architecture's alienation from theory (and itself). Giedion's double position between materialism and idealism is his thought's primary virtue. His inherently dialectical approach hints at how architecture might escape its servility to the building industry, neo-avant-garde and putatively authentic practices alike (while banal practices are simply extrapolations of the building industry). When viewed within a utopian frame, the focus of Giedion's operative history and criticism is redirected from his cheerleading specific forms of modernist architecture toward his neglected ideas about social purpose, as architectural and urban questions. Giedion's operativeness is utopian, precisely because it is operative. In his thinking, the relationship between project and future, for theory and practice, is ever present, introduced here as a prerequisite for rescuing moribund architectural history/theory/criticism from enfeebling turns toward vapid formalism, aligned with opportunistic entrepreneurialism. In an observation adroitly summarizing the contours of Giedion's method, Benjamin asserts: 'Bear in mind that commentary on a reality (such as we are writing here) calls for a method completely different from that required by commentary on a text'.[9] For Giedion, this reality is architecture as building, past, present and future.

Giedion engaged in concrete materialist analyses proximate with Lefebvre's Marxian interpretation of the production of space. Like Lefebvre, his project was also idealist (Hegelian), but he was not a technological determinist. Walter Benjamin's esteem of Giedion's *Building in France, Building in Iron, Building in Ferroconcrete* (1928) and its influence on Benjamin's Arcades project encourage more nuanced readings of Giedion.[10] Confirming his admiration for Giedion's book in a letter to him, Benjamin wrote the following:

> I am studying in your book [...] the difference between radical conviction and radical knowledge that refreshes the heart. You possess the latter, and therefore you are able to illuminate, or rather to uncover, the tradition by observing the present. Hence the nobility of your work, which I admire most, next to its radicalism.[11]

Inevitably, Giedion was far more complex than the unsophisticated 'operative critic' Manfredo Tafuri (1935–1994) made him out to be. The benefit of countering common presumptions that Giedion's insights are of little value because operative resides in revealing operativeness as the linchpin of creative invention. Giedion's reputation as an operative historian does not preclude his also being a figure worthy of study. Indeed, positioning him as simultaneously materialist and idealist begins to expose the enduringly elusive constitutively utopian dimensions of his project, as countercurrents to the anti-theoretical entrepreneurialism presently dominating architecture.

Getting a sense of Giedion's understanding of the relation between the production of reality and the production of space, and of architecture as manifestations of both, involves reconsideration of his dialectical method as a form of historical materialism. His relative position *vis-à-vis* Hegelian idealism and Marxian historical materialism is the counterdistinctive value of his alternative to the ambitions of post-theoretical entrepreneurialism. Charting the difference between the fuzzy mysticism that unsympathetic readers identify in Giedion's writing (psychic and formal unity / an eternal present) and his concrete engagement with the relation between modes of production and the production of reality allows a Giedion for our times to emerge; a Giedion engaged in elaborating on a pragmatic utopian project, imagining *concrete* utopias, rather than *abstract* ones, bound up with cyclical relations between individual change and systemic transformation.[12]

## Historical Materialism

According to Marx, Historical Materialism is defined as a 'conception of history' dependent on the 'ability to expound the real process of production, starting out from the material production of life itself, and to comprehend the form of intercourse connected with this and created by this mode of production [...]'. Importantly, the processes of production, including 'the material production of life' are key. Concentrating on modes of production, from micro to macro scale, makes it possible to produce accurate accounts of the ebb and flow of human events. According to Marx, modes of production are 'the basis of all history', including the production of architecture and space, which preoccupied Giedion, Lefebvre, and Tafuri, but which Marx gave little consideration. Marx explained the difference between historical materialism and an idealistic view of history as the difference between remaining 'on the real ground of history', rather than measuring periods of history against their accordance with certain ideas. For Marx, historical materialism 'does not explain practice from the idea but explains the formation of ideas from material practice'. For him, 'not criticism but revolution is the driving force of history, also of religion, of philosophy and all other types of theory'.[13]

In terms of architectural production, including reconciling form and content, structure and surface, historical materialism begins with 'material practice', as the source of ideas, rather than the obverse. In this regard, making makes meaning – the direction of travel is from the concrete to the abstract – even if material is empty in itself, with its value determined by what is done with it.[14] The basis of reality resides in socially constructed practices, informed by dominant modes of production. Analogously, concrete utopian perspectives derive transformative ideas from existing material practices, reshaping existing reality into the revolutionary driving force of history. Modes of production are simultaneously sources of conformity, and potentially also sites of resistance and transformation. Making and use (material reality) establish a ground of possibility, beyond representation and exchange (abstract ideals). Accordingly, no matter the autonomy desires of (neo-avant-garde) architects, architecture is ever in the building, never just in the drawing, project or theory: the burden of use is inescapable, and modes of production, from drawing table to construction site, are central.[15]

Instaurating new practices or modes of production is inevitably limited: only 'the practical overthrow of the actual social relations which gave rise to' specific modes of practice and phenomena can transform the conditions and results of practices.[16] Resolving problems, including disaggregation of exterior surface and form from internal structure and services, is a matter of consciousness, shaped by modes of production, rather than a simple matter of education or will. Visual, verbal, or textual pronouncements alone cannot alter stubborn historical conditions. Likewise, 'the impotence of corporate capital to generate a socially cohesive environment' is a matter of consciousness, a byproduct of material (and spatial) practices that makes corporate capital viable, while ensuring its (re)production.[17] So long as spatial practices and modes of production are dominated by state capitalist and corporate imaginaries, claims to having produced the 'new' are self-deceiving and empty. Formal differences and radical claims merely mask intractable conformity with the way things are and how they are done. Yet, while Marx emphasizes predetermination (amplified by Tafuri), it is by no means absolute:

> [Historical materialism] shows that history does not end by being resolved into "self-consciousness as spirit of the spirit", but that in it at each stage there is found a material result: a sum of productive forces, [...] which, on the one hand, is indeed modified by the new generation, but also on the other prescribes for it its conditions of life and gives it a definite development, a special character. It shows that circumstances make men just as much as men make circumstances.[18]

Marx's articulation of the tensions between the present as prescribed by the past and as also independent of it is more nuanced than Tafuri's assertions of total closure. If 'circumstances make men just as much as men make circumstances', the future is at least partly unwritten. But change, the delineation and accomplishment of alternatives, requires cognizance of the degree to which social relations establish the boundaries of possibility, which makes production the landscape of concrete reality, and a primary concern of theory.

Although systemic transformation cannot be forced, slowly shape-shifting awareness prepares a ground for it. As Lefebvre observed, to change life and society, space must first be changed.[19] Even if far off in the distance, or beyond the horizon, acting upon history – including by changing space – is the motive force of Utopia: to alter history's shape by making the future into a project, guided by counterfactual utopian imaginaries. Like Giedion's history and design propositions, in its intentions, Utopia is operative, despite never being fully realized. While realization of the new, fulfilling hope and the installation of Utopia may be doomed to failure, this need not necessarily translate into resigned passivity in the face of history. Likewise, non-fulfillment does not defeat concrete considerations of future possibilities. Without a project – of the sort operativeness permits – reportage and repetition must dominate.

## Giedion and Spirit

Giedion presents a problem for postmodern architects, shaped by Tafuri's denouncing him as an 'operative critic', reflection on his project stalls at the edge of his seemingly naïve boosterism. Intriguingly, although K. Michael Hays largely follows Tafuri's conclusions regarding Giedion's history, he observes:

> Giedion's effort was to chart the commerce between inner and outer reality – especially the impact of mechanization on what he conceived as our unchanging humanity, on the stability of the individual psyche — and to project new means of reconciliation. As such, his interpretative method can precisely and properly be reasserted as *mediation*.[20]

Hays continues, quoting Fredric Jameson, who describes 'Mediation' as 'the classical dialectical term for the establishment of relationships between, say, the formal analysis of a work of art and its social ground, or between the internal dynamics of the political state and its economic base'.[21] Understood in this way, 'Mediation' reveals artifacts, including architecture and urban space, as expressions of the foundations out of which they emerge: 'Thus, state power is seen as the mere expression of the economic system that underlies it [...]; culture is seen as the expression of the underlying political, juridical and economic instances, and so forth'.[22]

Accordingly, human artifacts and their consequent affects are socially produced, shaped by the dominant that dominates. Jameson describes 'the analysis of mediations' as aiming 'to demonstrate what is not evident in the appearance of things, but rather their underlying reality namely that *the same* essence is at work in the specific languages of culture as in the relations of production', which aligns with Marx in one direction and Lefebvre's heretical Marxism in the other: modes of production are crucial.[23] Continuing, Jameson asserts:

> Mediations are thus a device of the analyst, whereby the fragmentation and autonomization, the compartmentalization and specialization of the various regions of social life (the separation, in other words, of the ideological from the political, the religious from the economic, the gap between daily life and the practice of the academic disciplines) is at least locally overcome on the occasion of a particular analysis.[24]

However, as Hays notes, it is just this aspect of Giedion's project – 'to make connections among the seemingly disparate phenomena of social life generally' – that opens him to the charge of being far too conciliatory in the face of social life and space fragmented by capitalist modes of production. Worse still, he promoted a specific sort of architectural production as a teleology – supposedly leading toward social renewal, which in its exaggerated (consumed) forms mirrored the splintering Giedion imagined the work he preferred could overcome. His historical narrative is likewise denounced for ignoring architects who ostensibly attempted to subvert prevailing conditions, even through intensification, or who are situated outside of his limited parameters. The most rigid readings of Giedion cast him as an uncritical conformist, who was little more than a promoter of the architectural and urban dominant of post-World War II orthodox modernism. The picture of him that emerges portrays him as aligned with the culture of consumer of capitalism, despite his casting such apparently homologous work as liberating and progressive, as shorthand for (mostly empty) promises of freedom.[25]

According to Hays, by presuming a non-alienated subject at that the very moment 'when reification was penetrating into the very core of personal experience, leaving no vestiges of non-alienated reality as its reciprocal or opposing notion', Giedion's ungrounded optimism – encompassing his operative history/theory practices – is ostensibly revealed as complicitous, militating for a certain approach, rather than benefitting from adequately analyzing the myriad possible approaches in play at the time, especially ones attempting to subvert the status quo.[26] As such, Giedion's most famous work, *Space, Time, and Architecture: The Growth of A New Tradition* (1941), when read at all, is read as a species of woefully naïve operative history, rehearsing a post-hoc instrumental teleology in which architectural goals are presented as a function of their ends. In particular, laudable aims, especially social renewal, are confirmed by work (inevitably) achieved along a straight line of history. However, Giedion's critics challenge the supposed achievement of renewal he applauds, nullified by his reference to work putatively and paradoxically in lockstep with the dominant alienated conditions it supposedly overcomes.

## A New Tradition?

For Giedion, the nascent new tradition he identified and indexed, comprising select works produced by a limited grouping of architects, mostly members of CIAM (*Congrès Internationaux d'Architecture Moderne*), for which he was secretary-general from its 1928 founding until 1956, was ostensibly a faithful reflection of the spirit of the age. Even if true, the works Giedion esteemed have, through time, become muddled together with buildings he might well have responded to with ambivalence. If the post-World War II success of modernist architecture paralleled its exhaustion, the dominant trend was toward the production of state capitalist and state socialist space (as Lefebvre observed), dominated by an increasingly fictitious socialism in one direction and dubious conflations of corporate sensibilities with freedom in the other. Giedion had neither in mind. Before its institutionalization as propagator of arid rationality, suited to corporate and state imagery, the *Congrès* (CIAM) took shape in response to disqualification of Le Corbusier's League of Nations competition entry (despite his being the most inventive of post-Baroque architects); its end came with the emergence of the heretical Team X.[27]

Ultimately, Giedion's thought runs closer to Le Corbusier's irrationalism and the enriching relativity and anthropological turn of Aldo van Eyck, than to the currents of mainstream modernism.[28] He is closer to that *other* modern (outlined by van Eyck), not the one doggedly faithful to the Enlightenment, myths of objective natural sciences, or the bad social science of bureaucratic rationality. Instead, it is a kind of critical-modernity, of augmentation rather than reduction. Conceptualizing the modern beyond techno- and natural sciences resists the administered world, and does so informed by the insights of Marx, Freud, Surrealism, and the Frankfurt School, including Adorno, Benjamin, and Bloch. Beyond his boosterism, Giedion is closer to van Eyck's 'authentic avant-garde' conception than to International Style complacency (as formulated by Johnson, Hitchcock, and Barr), the commercial turn of the Bauhaus, of Gropius in the USA, or SOM (Skidmore Owings and Merrill).[29] If Giedion has a charge to answer, it is for not more robustly resisting conventional conflations of the International Style, the Bauhaus, and CIAM that continue to take shape in historical and architectural imaginaries. Giedion's thinking was of a different order than either Gropius' (1883–1969) or Johnson's (1906–2005), no matter how much they trod shared establishment territories.[30]

## Entrepreneurial Pleasures?

While Giedion has been largely rejected, the legacies of Gropius and Johnson endure, in the diagrammatic and extruded architecture of banal practice in one direction and in the entrepreneurial neo-avant-garde in another (even if cancel culture seems finally to be catching up with Johnson—perhaps his cronies are next).[31] Indeed, Gropius and Johnson are the godfathers of prevailing present-day architecture (mundane and auteur alike), not Giedion, whose project was re-enchanting the world, by overcoming limiting Enlightenment imaginaries, informing conceptualizations of how the pseudo-radical guises of formalism and the neo-avant-garde might be outrun.

As generally transparent reflections of ideological and utopian exhaustion, the disappointments of post-World War II orthodox modernism mirrors intensified divisions of labor, paralleling desperate efforts to rescue some substance for building, architecture and the city, history, theory, and criticism. Disaggregated, each component of the discipline goes its own way, on behalf of self-interest and autonomy fantasies, without the noble sense of obligation Tafuri imagined. While architecture builds the city of spectacle, theory is almost entirely deprived of meaningful work, beyond reinforcing autonomy delusions, or extolling reproduction. In contradistinction to most subsequent architectural historians, Giedion's mode of doing history, theory, and criticism comes closest to architectural invention, precisely because enchantingly operational.

If Giedion fused his architectural and urban preferences with pronouncements of inevitability, his commitment sets him apart from vapid formalism and opportunistic entrepreneurialism. If, as Tafuri observed, 'the crisis of modern architecture is [...] a crisis of the ideological function of architecture', and the Left's postwar failure is attributable to its lack of a project, Giedion furnishes a rejoinder to both.[32] Solipsistic neo-avant-garde formalism (that followed denunciations of Giedion, which Tafuri initially extolled as bravely embracing alienation as all encompassing, only to later reject it as empty) has metamorphosed into the dominant entrepreneurial spirit, whose adherents labor at transmuting conformity into radicality (perhaps to assuage a bad conscience).[33]

## Tafuri's Giedion

Summarizing dominant views on Giedion inherited from Tafuri, Hays asserts that the 'architectural objects' Giedion ostensibly extols as providing 'visual symbols for the integral psychological self' are best understood as distorting and overly deterministic, or less charitably as complicitous (with state socialism and state capitalism alike).[34] By pronouncing disaggregating spatial practices and forms as unifying, albeit dynamic, Giedion ostensibly provides cover for the dissolution of social life. But this view of Giedion's project is paradoxically reactionary, inasmuch as, according to Jameson, 'The realm of separation, of fragmentation, of the explosion of codes and the multiplicity of disciplines is merely a reality in appearance [...] of our daily life and existential experience in late capitalism'.[35]

Jameson's reflections on total closure are Lefebvrean, not Tafurian; more importantly, they show up tout court rejections of Giedion as absolutist totalizing positions that invariably misconstrue his assertions and preferences as closed. In contrast, going further than Jameson, Lefebvre's anti-systematizing approach encourages more open readings of the sort developed here. According to him, while fragmentation of everyday life under capitalism (and dominating systems generally) irrefutably affects communities, labor, space, life, in all their dimensions, the more 'directly lived' experiences he was preoccupied with are perennial; nascent amidst the negative conditions of a bureaucratically rational modernity projected as absolute. Alternate futures persist as imaginable, even against the worst conditions, because the extremes deployed to make them appear eternal are sure indications of fragility and eventual collapse, as against the total closure Tafuri perceived.[36]

Echoing Lefebvre, Giedion championed prefigurative settings where other ways of being could take shape, including renewed social life and reemergent belonging. His imaginaries encompass 'built homecoming' (akin to van

Eyck), or the notion of 'homeland' (as conceptualized by Ernst Bloch). Like theirs, Giedion's figures are dialectical, made out of alternatives to alienation that do not presume recovery of any lost objects of wholeness. The configurative settings he imagined are more polemical than conciliatory (akin to the concepts of Hope and Utopia for Bloch and Adorno).[37]

Unquestioning rejection of Giedion's utopian project (for more directly lived and experienced renewed social life, prefigured by settings for its appearance) is naïve in its default conformism, oblivious to his nuanced realism about prospects for realization. Uncritical embrace of Giedion's utopianism would be equally illogical. However, without Utopia, architecture, including architectural theory (as formulations of the discipline's responses to its own problematics), is bereft of a project. Without a utopian project (hope, not blueprints), architecture must make-do with either caricatured claims to art (autonomy) or technicity (banal practice).

As the supposed great achievement of postmodernism and its entrepreneurial neo-avant-garde offspring, overcoming Utopia deprived architecture of suitable pragmatics for articulating which places are best (for whatever use), or how they might be manifested. Into the void of purposelessness, entrepreneurialism enters without resistance, undercover of real-world-like solutions, portrayed as simultaneously sensible (unsentimental) and radical (avant-garde), but mostly vapid, reproductive, and conformist. Echoing Lefebvre's conviction that alternative (better) ways of being perpetually hide within the hegemonic spaces of capitalism, Jameson asserts that Tafuri's resolute rejection of 'operative criticism' (including Giedion), is at best premature, thereby putting the lie to assertions of total closure. Jameson observes, 'the constitutive relationship between Tafuri's possibility of constructing dialectical history' depends on 'his systemic refusal of what, in *Theories and History of Architecture*, is called operative criticism', which is 'most strikingly employed in classical works like Giedion's *Space, Time and Architecture*'. Closely following Tafuri, Jameson states that operative criticism 'reads the past selectively and places an illusory historical analysis, the *appearance* of some "objective" historical narrative, in the service of what is in reality an architectural *manifesto*, the "normative" projection of some new style'.[38]

Jameson's incisive overview captures the substance of persisting negative evaluations of Giedion's historical narratives. However, what if the supposedly negative attributes of operativeness actually articulate enduring alternatives to theory's sacrifice on the altar of entrepreneurialism. In point of fact, is it really possible to imagine *any* history, theory, or criticism that is not at least partly operative, does not have an agenda, and which does not argue for something as against something else. Indeed, nowhere is this operative character more evident *than in illusions of an objective (scientific) history, extolling the virtues of* passivity and inaction on behalf of unprejudiced description (including Tafuri's use of Gideion as a foil). At his most extreme, Tafuri idealizes reportage of just the facts. Moreover, objective histories are paradoxically operative, in much the way entrepreneurial anti-theory is as theoretical as it is ideological. The shared tendency that separates them from Giedion is a diagnostic propensity, largely excluding the prognostic. From a utopian angle, history is pointless if it encompasses no project beyond description, and is wanting theoretically, no matter how perceptive.

Tafuri's 'stoic renunciation of action and of value' undergirds his narrative of total closure, but according to Jameson, this is ultimately less 'a formal necessity of the generic structure of his text' than 'an "opinion" or a "position" in its own right [...] the vehicle for a whole set of ideological messages': in short, operative.[39] In its vocation for acting upon history on behalf of hope (desire, transformation), the prognostic virtues of Utopia nascent in Giedion's project are unashamedly 'operative', in contradistinction to entrepreneurialism's self-serving claims to objectivity. Deprived of 'operative criticism', architectural invention and disciplinary recovery of architecture's social vocation – beyond exterior decoration (or formal play) – are unimaginable. Despite Tafuri's derisive description of Giedion's *Space, Time and Architecture* as 'history for architects' – pronouncing its unscholarly failings – artistic imaginaries thrive on different food than academic ones.

Where Tafuri saw 'total closure', Lefebvre sought out 'cracks'. Moreover, Giedion's capacity for seeing future possibility in intersections of past and present, between thought and feeling, and in a coexistence of form and content, amongst myriad other reconcilable dualities, presumes tensions – fissures – rather than totalities, which makes it timely for returning architectural theory to itself. Overcoming unproductive oppositions by intensifying the tensions between them, counters the estranging divisions necessary for capitalism's survival, along with its oxygenating handmaidens: entrepreneurialism, and Left declarations of its totality.

## Lefebvre and Giedion

Any effort to recuperate Giedion must engage with Lefebvre's authoritative appraisal. In *The Production of Space,* Lefebvre's project was to write a history of space, by expanding Marxism to include accounts of the city and urbanization more generally, primarily as spatializations of state capitalism (and state socialism), while resisting tendencies toward system building. In *Production,* he acknowledges that 'The first initiative taken towards the development of a history of space was Siegfried Giedeon's'. According to Lefebvre, although

> Giedion kept his distance from practice [he] worked out the theoretical object of any such history in some detail; he put space, and not some creative genius, not the "spirit of the times", and not even technological progress, at the centre of history as he conceived it.[40]

Lefebvre applauded this precisely because the 'spatial practices of a society secretes that society's space', which are in turn shaped by the dominant modes of production during any given period.[41] Analogously, for Giedion, architectural developments are fundamentally transformations in spatial conceptions, largely independent of any individual architect. While this understanding of architecture's evolution (and of space) is intriguing, even correct – insofar as it links architectural expression directly to a prevailing spatial consciousness – the source of that consciousness remains largely unarticulated, escaping explicit verbalizations, whereas modes of production, and the spatial practices they shape, are more concretely observable.

Despite acknowledging Giedion's importance, Lefebvre's had significant reservations. In particular, he took issue with the 'three successive periods' of spatial development posited by Giedion: the first, identified with Ancient Egypt and Greece emphasizes the *exterior*, the second, identified with Ancient Rome emphasizes the *interior*, and the third, identified with the present, attempts to unify *interior* and *exterior* (dynamically).[42] According to Lefebvre, with this periodization, 'Giedion succeeds [...] only in inverting the reality of social space'.[43] As a corrective, Lefebvre literally turns Giedion's interpretation of Ancient Roman spatialization inside out: 'The fact is that the Pantheon, as an image of the world or *mundus*, is an opening to the light; the *imago mundi*, the interior hemisphere or dome, symbolizes this exterior'.[44] Where Giedion observes literal interiority in the enclosing form of arches, domes, and spheres, Lefebvre reads it figuratively, as reaching outward, as embracing the whole of the known world, as Roman, as *exteriorizing* Rome.

Lefebvre similarly inverts Giedion's reading of Greek architecture: the 'Greek temple, [...] encloses a sacred and consecrated space, the space of a localized divinity and of a divine locality, and the political centre of the city'.[45] According to Lefebvre, the source of Giedion's 'confusion is to be found in an initial error [...], echoes of which occur throughout his work: he posits a pre-existing space – Euclidean space – in which all human emotions and expectations proceed to invest themselves and make themselves tangible'.[46] For Lefebvre, this is evidence of 'a naïve oscillation between the geometrical and the spiritualistic'.[47] Conceptualizing space as Euclidean, argues Lefebvre, posits it as 'pre-existing' and thus as permanent and essential, but also as empty, as a void to be filled. In contradistinction, his conviction is that space is continuously shaped, or re-imagined (produced), within a given condition, specific to the culture out of which it emerges, as representations of its dominant modes of production, spatial practices, and the governing power that dominates. Whereas, by contrast, traditional space, according to Lefebvre, is embedded culturally, because not yet produced, in the more abstract modern sense. However, recuperating lived space entails intensifying tensions between *produced space* and *culturally embedded space*, to reveal cracks through which it can be recovered.

In short, Lefebvre argues that certain 'operative' histories obfuscate – introducing and propagating confusion – rather than clarifying developments.[48]

For him, a central problem Giedion could not overcome was an inability to 'separate the history he was developing [of space] from the history of art and architecture'.[49] The former emphasizes tensions between production and use (the concrete), the latter concentrates on the abstract and the visual. Art may be things seen, but architecture is settings lived.

If use gives space value and renders it social, adherents of the autonomy project in architecture – often selfsame with architectural entrepreneurs – lament use as architecture's inescapable burden, going so far on occasion to imagine freedom from it as the source architecture's redemption. Lefebvre, however, reminds us that it is only possible to evaluate architectural or urban settings by way of use. He asks: 'how could a constructed space subjugate or repel otherwise than through *use*?'[50]

Although Giedion's contribution to 'the development of a history of space is undeniable', in Lefebvre's estimation, his project comes up short, because he 'did not tackle the tasks that still await the history of space proper', including showing 'up the growing ascendancy of the abstract and the visual, as well as the internal connection between them'. In doing this, historians of space could begin

> to expose the genesis and meaning of the "logic of the visual" – that is, to expose the *strategy* implied in such a "logic" in light of the fact that any particular "logic" of this kind is always merely a deceptive name for a strategy.[51]

While Giedion was arguably more of an 'historian of space' than Lefebvre allows, purveyors of entrepreneurial neo-avant-gardes, including architects obsessed with autonomy – who posit that architecture is in the drawing, while asserting that building is something lesser, fallen, or irrelevant – could not be more distant; their's is the 'logic of the visual'.[52] Since architects are involved in the production of space, the conventions of art history or connoisseurship do not suit them. As such, the general neglect of 'use' (not program, function, or type), as a crucial indicator, and test, of architectural significance, propagates confusion about the (practical and theoretical) tasks of architecture, which only abstraction and an overemphasis on the visual (formalism, exchange, autonomy myths) could justify.

As Lefebvre contends, the neglect of use is less some accident of modernity than a specific product of the 'internal connection' between 'the abstract and the visual', which he deems a 'strategy' that remains concealed from view in its guise as 'the logic of the visual'. The predominance of conceptualizing architecture as 'abstract' and 'visual' does not simply obscure the importance of 'use'; it establishes architecture as empty; anathema to Giedion, but a core principle of the entrepreneurial neo-avant-garde. And, as Lefebvre shows, special pleading aside for such a view as revolutionary, architecture as abstract and visual, and thus as empty, is coincident with the spread of global (neoliberal) space as the mirror of its consciousness, whether blandly planar, or interestingly dynamic. It is on this basis that he singles out the Bauhaus (as distinct from either Giedion or CIAM) for special reprobation:

> When it comes to the question of what the Bauhaus's audacity produced in the long run, one is obliged to answer: the worldwide, homogeneous and monotonous architecture of the state, whether capitalist or socialist.
>
> How and why did this happen? If there is such a thing as the history of space, if space may indeed be said to be specified on the basis of historical periods, societies, modes of production and relations of production, then there is such a thing as a space characteristic of capitalism [...]. It is certainly arguable that the writings and works of the Bauhaus [...] outlined, formulated and helped realize that particular space – the fact that the Bauhaus sought to be and proclaimed itself to be revolutionary notwithstanding.[53]

## Conclusion

In light of the above, perhaps Giedion's most serious shortcoming was hubris, demonstrated by his uncritical promotion of modernist architecture as CIAM secretary, inasmuch as it is coterminous with the Bauhaus. But his most significant contribution is his assertion that the task of architecture is, or ought to be, as Adorno affirmed, the production of 'Architecture worthy of human beings', only possible when architects think 'better of [human beings] than they actually are'.[54] Giedion surely concurred but was acutely aware of just how difficult accomplishing this would be:

> Social disorder was delivered to us as an inheritance from the Industrial Revolution. To restore order to this unbalanced world, we must alter its social conditions. But history shows us that this is not sufficient. It would be a fundamental mistake to believe that socio-political change would itself cause today's maladjusted man, the product of a [more than] century-long rupture between thinking and feeling to disappear. Unintegrated people are today multiplying everywhere.[55]

Giedion recognized the 'division of labor' as 'one of our central problems', which brings him close to Marx and Lefebvre, and to utopian socialist thinkers more generally: 'Though [the] integration of labor is undoubtedly desirable, it would not be enough, for it would only be the treatment of a single symptom'.[56] The problem according to Giedion, then, is one of consciousness, but where he differs from Lefebvre is in locating the sources of consciousness. It is fair to say that for Lefebvre, space produces consciousness as much as it is a production of it. However, it is spatial practices, as expressions of modes of production, that produces the frame within which consciousness takes shape. This is why the 'theory of moments' is so important for Lefebvre.[57] Alternatives can be grasped on the far horizon of the possible in the cracks of the status quo, where apparent oppositions confound boundaries. Analogously, Giedion observed:

> At the base of everything is the individual man. It is he who must be integrated – integrated in his inner nature, without being brutalized [by mechanization, technology, homogeneous and monotonous architecture, or the division of labor], so that his emotional and intellectual outlets will no longer be kept apart [...]. To bring this fact into consciousness and to try to overcome it is closely connected with the outstanding task of our period: to humanize – that is, to reabsorb emotionally – what has been created by the spirit.[58]

Since the 1960s, mainstream and neo-avant-garde architecture has turned away from such tasks as just too difficult to deal with, or even as irrelevant; sure to persist as intractable, so long as architecture is a minor adjunct of the building industry of limited relevance, or is conceived of as primarily a problem of abstraction or visuality; of exchange, rather than of use.[59] The result is products, rather than works, in Lefebvre's terms. But the persistent inadequacy of the built environment – synonymous with industrial and post-industrial productions of space on a global scale – necessitates something else. As Giedion recognized, 'All talk about organizing and planning is in vain unless we first create again the whole man, unfractured in his methods of thinking and feeling'.[60] Therefrom, more directly lived social spaces might arise with origins traceable to a pre-capitalist past. But how consciousness is shifted, or raised, outwits cultural mainstreams. Inevitably, architectural education, and the practices it supplies (commercial or otherwise), remains largely satisfied with persisting as overwhelmingly reproductive (conservatively hidebound to self-servingly limiting conceptions of practice, profession, and the discipline).

Giedion was intensely aware of the conundrum of consciousness but underplayed it in his role as CIAM Secretary. However, his discussion of Le Corbusier in *Space, Time, and Architecture* highlights consciousness, as do the two volumes of his *Eternal Present*.[61] The past may well be a *foreign county*, but that does not negate its persistence, including as suggestive of alternatives to capitalist production, marked by the abstraction, formalism, visual emphasis, and concentration on exchange of the entrepreneurial neo-avant-garde and banal practice alike, as against use, or the production of space for people thought to be better than they are, rather than worse.

Theory looks ahead and beyond – toward the not yet, revealing culture as something achieved always in the future, though rooted in the past. Akin to Lefebvre, Giedion was intensely aware of this, which his concept of the eternal present encompasses, alongside Lefebvre's romanticism and concrete utopianism. Antithetically, the entrepreneurial neo-avant-garde inhabits the present full-stop, aligned with the cycles of fashion, perpetually going out of date, rather than the long duration of culture and human experience, grounded in the body, shared across time and space, which use continuously appropriates and renews.[62]

## Notes

1 David Letherbarrow, 'Introduction', *Roots of Architectural Invention*, New York: Cambridge University Press, 1993, pp. 1–6; Michael Speaks, 'Theory Was Interesting … but Now We Have Work', *arq*, Vol. 6, No. 3 (2002), pp. 209–212. Michael Speaks, 'After Theory', *Architectural Record*, June 2005, pp. 73–75; George Baird, 'Criticality and Its Discontents', *Harvard Design Magazine*, No. 21 (Fall 2004/Winter 2005), pp. 1–6.

2 Adolf Loos, 'To Our Young Architects' (1898); 'On Thrift' (1924), in *On Architecture*, Michael Mitchell (trans.), Riverside, CA: Ariadne Press, 2002, pp. 29–30, 178–183.

3 Mary McLeod, 'Architecture and Politics in the Reagan Era: From Postmodernism to Deconstructivism', *Assemblage*, No. 8 (1989), pp. 22–59; Felicity D. Scott, 'On Architecture under Capitalism', *Grey Room*, No. 6 (Winter, 2002), pp. 44–65; George Baird, 'Criticality and Its Discontents'; Nathaniel Coleman, *Utopias and Architecture*, London: Routledge, 2005, pp. 63–87, 88–112; Douglas Spencer, *The Architecture of Neoliberalism: How Contemporary Architecture Became an Instrument of Control and Compliance*, London: Bloomsbury, 2016.

4 See Iman Ansari, 'Eisenman's Evolution: Architecture, Syntax, and New Subjectivity', *The Architectural Review*, 26 April 2013, in which Eisenman is quoted as saying:

> Manfredo Tafuri once said something very important to me. He said, "Peter, if you don't build no one will take your ideas seriously. You have to build because ideas that are not built are simply ideas that are not built." Architecture involves seeing whether those ideas can withstand the attack of building, of people, of time, of function, etc. Tafuri said history will not be interested in your work if you haven't built anything. I think that's absolutely correct. If I had built nothing, you and I wouldn't be talking now.

See also, Eisenman, 'Fame as the Avatar of History', *Perspecta*, Vol. 37, Famous (2005), pp. 164–171. And: Letherbarrow, *Roots of Architectural Invention*, pp. 1–6.

5 Colin Rowe and his students, alongside Philip Johnson, were crucial in manifesting these developments. See, Robert Venturi, *Complexity and Contradiction in Architecture*, New York: Museum of Modern Art, 1966; Johnson, *Writings*, New York: Oxford University Press, 1979; Rowe and Koetter, *Collage City*, Cambridge, MA: MIT Press, 1979; Colin Rowe, 'Introduction', *Five Architects*, New York: Oxford University Press, 1975, pp. 3–7; Tafuri, *The Sphere and the Labyrinth* (1980), Pelligrino d'Acierno (trans.), Cambridge, MA: MIT Press, 1987; Kazys Varnelis, *The Spectacle of the Innocent Eye: Vision, Cynical Reason, and The Discipline of Architecture in Postwar America*, Ithaca, NY: A Cornell University Dissertation, 1994; Robert Somol, Editor, *Autonomy and Ideology: Postioning an Avant-garde in America*, New York: Monacelli Press, 1997; Eisenman, *The Formal Basis of Modern Architecture* (1963), Zurich: Lars Müller Publishers, 2006; Coleman, *Utopias and Architecture*; Coleman, *Lefebvre for Architects*; Coleman, *Materials and Meaning in Architecture: Essays on the Bodily Experience of Buildings*, London: Bloomsbury, 2020.

6 Koolhaas, 'Utopia Station', in Rem Koolhaas, Editor, *Content*, Köln and London: Taschen, 2004, p. 393.
7 For Speaks, see: 'Theory Was Interesting … but Now We Have Work'; Koolhaas, 'Utopia Station'; Katrina Heron, 'From Bauhaus to Koolhaas', Interview with Rem Koolhaas, *WIRED*, 07.01.1996. Available online at: https://www.wired.com/1996/07/koolhaas/. Also, Rem Koolhaas, 'Whatever Happened to Urbanism', in OMA, Rem Koolhaas and Bruce Mau, Editors, *S, M, L, XL*, New York: Monacelli Press, 1995, pp. 959–971. And: Rem Koolhaas, *Conversations with Students* (1991), Architecture at Rice 30, 2nd Edition, New York: Princeton Architectural Press, 1996. For Schumacher, see: Patrik Schumacher, "The Autopoeisis of Architecture," in *LATENT UTOPIAS - Experiments within Contemporary Architecture*, Vienna/New York: Springer Verlag, 2002. Also: Schumacher, "On Parametricism: Georgina Day interviews Patrik Schumacher" (2012), available at http://www.patrikschumacher. com/Texts/On%20Parametricism_.html. See also: Coleman, 'Utopia beyond Amelioration', *Boundaries*, Vol. 8 (2013), pp. 4–11; and Coleman, 'The Myth of Autonomy', *Architecture/Philosophy*, Vol. 01, No. 02 (2015), pp. 157–178.
8 Fredric Jameson, 'Is Space Political?', in C. Davidson, Editor, *Anyplace*, Cambridge MA: MIT Press, 1995, pp. 191–205, thematises this problematic.
9 Walter Benjamin, 'First Sketches', *The Arcades Project*, Howard Eiland and Kevin McLaughlin (Trans.), Cambridge, MA: Harvard University Press, 1999, p. 858.
10 For the Benjamin-Giedion connection, see, Socrates Georgiadis, 'Introduction', in Sigfried Giedion, Editor, *Building in France, Building in Iron, Building in FerroConcrete (1928)*, Santa Monica, CA: The Getty Center, 1995, pp. 1–78. Also, Benjamin, *The Arcades Project*, 1999.
11 Benjamin, Letter to Giedion (15 December 1929), reprinted in, Socrates Georgiadis, 'Introduction', in Sigfried Giedion, Editor, *Building in France, Building in Iron, Building in FerroConcrete (1928)*, Santa Monica, CA: The Getty Center, 1995, p. 53.
12 See Ruth Levitas, 'Educated Hope: Ernst Bloch on Abstract and Concrete Utopia', *Utopian Studies*, Vol. 01, No. 02 (1990), pp. 13–26. Also, David Haney, 'Spaces of Resistance and Compromise the Concrete Utopia Realized', in Coleman, Editor, *Imagining and Making the World: Reconsidering Architecture and Utopia*, Ralahine Utopian Studies, Vol. 8, Oxford and Bern: Peter Lang, 2011, pp. 223–236; Coleman, *Lefebvre for Architects*; Ernst Bloch, *The Utopian Function of Art and Literature, Selected Essays*, Zipes and Mecklenburg (trans.), Cambridge, MA: MIT Press, 1988. Henri Lefebvre, *The Production of Space* [1974], Nicholson-Smith (trans.), Oxford: Blackwell, 1991.
13 Karl Marx, *The German Ideology*, 'Chapter 2: Civil Society and the Conception of History', available online at: https://www.marxists.org/glossary/terms/h/i.htm, Accessed 13 September 2021.
14 Coleman, *Materials and Meaning*.
15 Ibid. See also, references to K. Michael Hays and the autonomy project, *Utopias and Architecture*, pp. 22–23; p. 298, note 29; and p. 315, note 2. See also: Coleman, 'The Myth of Autonomy'; Coleman, *Utopias and Architecture*; and Ansari, 'Eisenman's Evolution'; and Coleman, *Materials and Meaning*.
16 Marx, *The German Ideology*. See also, Lefebvre, *The Production of Space*; and Coleman, *Materials and Meaning*.
17 Joseph Rykwert, *The Seduction of Place: The History and Future of the City*, New York: Vintage Books, 2002, p. 227
18 Marx, *The German Ideology*.
19 Lefebvre, *The Production of Space*, pp. 59, 190.

20 Hays, *Modernism and the Posthumanist Subject: The Architecture of Hannes Meyer and Ludwig Hilberseimer*, Cambridge, MA: MIT Press, 1995, p. 19.
21 Jameson, *Political Unconscious: Narrative as a Socially Symbolic Act* (1981), London: Routledge, 2002, p. 24.
22 Ibid.
23 Ibid.
24 Ibid., p. 25.
25 For considerations of Giedion, in addition to the references already indicated, see: Tafuri, *Theories and Histories of Architecture* (1976), Verrecchia (trans.), London: Granada, 1980, pp. 148–167; Joseph Rykwert, 'Siegfried Giedion and the Notion of Style', *The Burlington Magazine*, Vol. 96, No. 613 (April, 1954), pp. 123–124; Spiro Kostof, 'Architecture, You and Him: The Mark of Sigfried Giedion', *Daedalus*, Vol. 105, No. 1 (Winter, 1976), In Praise of Books (Winter, 1976), pp. 189–204; Hilde Heyne, *Architecture and Modernity: A Critique*, Cambridge, MA: MIT Press, 1999; Arthur P. Molella, 'Science Moderne: Sigfried Giedion's Space, Time and Architecture and Mechanization Takes Command', *Technology and Culture*, Vol. 43, No. 2 (2002), pp. 374–389; Douglas Tallack, 'Siegfried Giedion, Modernism and American Material Culture', *Journal of American Studies*, 28 (1994), pp. 2, 149–167; Norm Friesen, 'Anonymous Historiography: A Metaphorology of the Constellation in Benjamin, Giedion and McLuhan', and Michael Darroch, 'Giedion and Explorations: Confluences of Space and Media in Toronto School Theorization', in Norm Friesen, Editor, *Media Transatlantic: Developments in Media and Communication Studies between North American and German-speaking Europe*, Switzerland: Springer, 2016, pp. 51–61, 63–87; Reto Geiser, *Giedion in America*, Zurich: ETH/gta Verlag, 2018.
26 Hays, *Modernism and the Posthumanist Subject*, p. 20.
27 Frampton, *Le Corbusier*, London: Thames & Hudson, 2001, pp. 83–85; Siegfried Giedion, *Space, Time and Architecture*, pp. 696–697. See also Coleman, *Materials and Meaning*; Coleman, *Lefebvre for Architects*; and Coleman, *Utopias and Architecture*.
28 See: Giedion, *Space, Time and Architecture*; James Stirling, 'Ronchamp: Le Corbusier's Chapel and the Crisis of Rationalism' (1956), reprinted in *In the Footsteps of Le Corbusier*, C. Palazzolo and R. Vio, Editors, New York: Rizzoli, 1991, pp. 214–221; John Summerson, 'Architecture, Painting and Le Corbusier', in John Summerson, Editor, *Heravenly Mansions and other Essays on Architecture*, New York: W. W. Norton, 1963; Alexander Gorlin, 'The Ghost in the Machine: Surrealism in the Work of Le Corbusier', *Perspecta*, Vol. 18 (1982), pp. 50–65; Stanislaus von Moos, *Le Corbusier Elements of a Synthesis, Revised and Expanded*, Rotterdam: 010 Publishers, 2009, pp. 246–249; Francis Strauven, *Aldo van Eyck: The Shape of Relativity*, Amsterdam: Architectura & Natura, 1998; Aldo van Eyck, *Writings*, 2 Volumes, Vincent Ligtelijn and Francis Strauven, Editors, Amsterdam: SUN Publishers, 2008; Frampton, 'The Other Le Corbusier: Primitive Form and the Linear City' (1987), in *Frampton, Labour, Work and Architecture, Collected Essays on Architecture and Design*, London: Phaidon: 2002, pp. 219–225. Also, Coleman, *Utopias and Architecture*.
29 Coleman, *Materials and Meaning*; and Coleman, *Utopias and Architecture*.
30 Ibid.; also Coleman, *Lefebvre for Architects*.
31 See, Klaus Herdeg, *The Decorated Diagram: Harvard Architecture and the Failure of the Bauhaus Legacy*, Cambridge, MA: MIT Press, 1983. On cancelling Johnson, see: https://www.dezeen.com/2020/12/10/philip-johnson-racism-harvard-gsd-name-removal/; https://www.architecturaldigest.com/story/artists-are-calling-on-moma-to-remove-philip-johnsons-name; https://www.instagram.com/

johnsonstudygroup/?hl=en; https://news.artnet.com/art-world/harvard-philip-johnson-1929592.

32 Tafuri, *Architecture and Utopia: Design and Capitalist Development* (1973), Barbara Luigia La Penta (trans.), Cambridge, MA: MIT Press, 1976, p. 181.
33 See, Coleman, 'The Myth of Autonomy'; and Coleman, *Utopias and Architecture.*
34 Hays, *Modernism and the Posthumanist Subject*, 1995, p. 20.
35 Jameson, *Political Unconscious*, (1981), 2002, p. 40.
36 Lefebvre, *The Production of Space*, (1974), 1991, pp. 10–11.
37 See van Eyck, "Labyrinthian Clarity', *Forum*, (July 1967), p. 51, and 'Steps Toward a Configurative Discipline', *Forum 3* (August 1962), pp. 81–93, reprinted in Aldo van Eyck, *Writings, Vol. 1: The Child, the City and the Artist; Vol. 2: Collected Articles and Other Writings 1947–1998*, respectively, pp. 472–3, 327–343. See also, Ernst Bloch and Theodore Adorno, 'Something's Missing', in Ernst Bloch, *The Utopian Function of Art and Literature: Selected Essays*, Jack Zipes and Frank Mecklenburg (Trans.), Cambridge, MA: MIT Press, 1998, pp. 1–17; Ernst Bloch, *The Principle of Hope, 3 Vols.*, Stephen Plaice, Paul Knight and Neville Plaice (Trans.), Cambridge, MA: MIT Press, 1995; Theodore Adorno, *Aesthetic Theory*, Robert Hullot-Kentor (Trans.). London: Continuum, 1997; Theodore Adorno, *Negative Dialectics*, E. B. Ashton (trans.), London: Routledge, 1973; and Theodore Adorno, 'Functionalism Today', Jane O. Newman and John H. Smith (Trans.), *Oppositions*, No. 17 (Summer 1979), pp. 30–41. See also, Coleman, *Materials and Meaning*, and Coleman, *Utopias and Architecture.*
38 Jameson, 'Architecture and the Critique of Ideology', in Joan Ockman, Editor, *Architecture Criticism Ideology*, Princeton, NJ: Princeton Architectural Press, 1985, p. 65. See also, Tafuri, *Theories and Histories*, pp. 141–170.
39 Ibid.
40 Lefebvre, *The Production of Space*, p. 126.
41 Ibid., p. 38.
42 Ibid., p. 126.
43 Ibid., p. 127.
44 Ibid.
45 Ibid.
46 Ibid.
47 Ibid.
48 Ibid., pp. 127–28.
49 Ibid., p. 127.
50 Ibid., p. 128.
51 Ibid.
52 See, Ansari, 'Eisenman's Evolution'.
53 Lefebvre, *The Production of Space*, p. 126.
54 Adorno, 'Functionalism Today', p. 38.
55 Giedion, *Space, Time and Architecture*, pp. 879–80.
56 Ibid., p. 880.
57 Lefebvre, 'The Inventory', *La Somme et las reste*, Paris: Méridiens Klincksieck, 1989 [1959], pp. 642–55, reprinted in Lefebvre, *Key Writings*, Stuart Elden, Elizabeth Lebas and Eleonor Kofman, Editors, London: Continuum, 2003, pp. 166–176; Lefebvre, 'The Theory of Moments', *Critique of Everyday Life, Volume II* (1961), John More (Trans.), London: Verso, 2002, pp. 340–358.
58 Giedion, *Space, Time and Architecture*, pp. 880.
59 For more on this shift, see, Coleman, *Utopias and Architecture*, 2005, pp. 88–112; Coleman, 'Building Dystopia', *Revista MORUS – Utopia e Renascimento*, No. 4 (2007), pp. 181–92; Coleman, 'Utopia and Modern Architecture?', *Architectural Research Quarterly*, Vol. 16, No. 04 (2012), pp. 339–348; Coleman, '"Building in

Empty Spaces": Is Architecture a "Degenerate Utopia"?'; *The Journal of Architecture*, Vol. 18, No. 02 (2013), pp. 135–166; Coleman, 'The Problematic of Architecture and Utopia', *Utopian Studies*, Special Issue: Utopia and Architecture, Vol. 25, No. 01 (2014), pp. 1–22; Coleman, 'Can Architecture Really Do Nothing? Lefebvre, Bloch, and Jameson on Utopia', in D. Bell and B. Zacka, Editors, *Political Theory and Architecture*, London: Bloomsbury, 2020, pp. 217–234.

60 Ibid.

61 Coleman, *Utopias and Architecture*.

62 Coleman, *Materials and Meaning*.

# 6 Building without End

## The Travails of *Archè* and *Téchne*

*Claudio Sgarbi*

Notwithstanding everything which has been done and written to unravel the meaning of architecture and the architect, much remains to be figured out in a multicultural context open to diversities, minorities, oppressed and violated cultures and entities. This must include some radical approach to the legitimacy in the use and imposition of the noun "architecture" and the profession of the "architect", to social groups and cultures that might be alien to them[1] or might have already been polluted and manipulated by their colonization.[2]

Could these words (architecture and the architect) be avoided or even abandoned and forgotten? Many colleagues feel uncomfortable to use the epithet "architect" and the appellative "architecture".

Do these words have a meaning? Do they make sense? The significance to continue to insist on using them must be discussed. This is why theory exists.

### Theory

Theory, in the archaic Greek meaning of the word,[3] is the capacity to share a dignifying life with difficult questions that might not have any answers.[4] Those answers that do not exist are the paramount reason to practice theory: to share the enigmas that leave no alternatives.[5] For sure this does not mean that we have to invent problems and enigmas for the sake of overcomplicating life.[6]

There are questions without answers that are worthy and useful to be raised and discussed. This is the role of philosophy.

We practice philosophy in every single moment of our life.[7] To think is not an option: either we do it or we live through the thoughts of others. Either we think or we are thought about. Philosophy formulates as well as possible many relevant questions that do not have answers. This formulation of questions a community cares for is the ideal space of theory. Questions that do not have answers are the truth of philosophy.

This kind of questioning (philosophy calls it "critique"), that might seem irrelevant, is the substratum of the human necessity of artifice.[8]

All the disciplines that deal with the limits of reason, that raise doubts, questions, problems and all that which keeps being unknown, difficult or impossible to understand, are relevant for theory.

DOI: 10.4324/9781003292999-7

Architecture and the architect have always relied on the work of philosophers.[9] Indeed, they may be words "invented" by philosophers. Philosophers are still fully committed to their meanings[10] and particularly to the meanings of technique.[11]

For many architects this might be vane and totally irrelevant. This faith into the absolute irrelevance of this "thinking thought"[12] constitutes the logic of a radical way of thinking by denial. To insist on the irrelevance and futility of theory, to complain about its confusion, to give up on debates, books and lectures, seminars and the common enigmas of everyday life, to maintain that it is a privilege that we cannot afford, to deny the necessity of fiction, is our way of dealing with theory by means of exclusion.

Theory is simply the necessity to live with the questions that this human condition raises. Philosophy is the questioning.

To be an architect does not mean to be willing to build buildings at any cost: architects are those who try, as best as they can, to master the principles (archi-/arché) of the technique of building (-tecture/téchne). This is what the words architecture and the architect evoke: "the arcane of technique".[13]

## *Archè* and *Téchne*

The words "architecture and the architect" express the travails of two Greek words: *arché* and *téchne*. Their travails demand the permanent enactment of philosophy.

The difference between *archi* and *archè* and between *tekton* and *téchne* must be overlooked here.[14] *Archè* and *téchne* are complex ideas, substantial enough to ground this discussion around the permanence of a theory of architecture.

*Archè* is the research of a principle that allows us to try to comprehend all the phenomena of the world, that is their *archai*.[15] The *archè* is that which stands still while everything appears to be in a constant flux, always becoming something different. *Archè* is not something that happened at the origin or beginning of time: it is eternally[16] happening and it is the kernel of the apparent contradiction between permanence and change. Greek philosophy presents it as a fundamental, that is, an ontological, contradiction. That which is arcane is not the polarity (between one and the other) but the unity of the contradictions that is definitively permanent. We might call it ancestrality[17]; the ancestrality of the art of building: the art of building with or without us – indifferent, in the face of our being-not-being. The archi- is the one that tries to know how to master, to deal with the recurring arcane.

*Téchne*, which we may translate as "technique",[18] is the acting and making, the thinking and doing of everything according to the logic of instrumentality. Technique is spread into everything that is human: to be human means to be indissolubly bond to technique.

We are often totally absorbed by our technique and try to avoid thinking about its arcane character. Indeed, technique is the highest form of human rationality that sets forth a radical belief: it justifies the creation and the happening of things without an end, as when we say "art for art's sake". Technique – when it's free from any constrictions – has only one aim: its self-empowerment, without an end. Any technique drifts into its own "autopoiesis". Every technique aims to be self-sufficient and follows the logic of its own discipline.[19] This is precisely the problem of technique.

Technicians force the imagination in a panorama of means without end. The uninhibited abuse of technique has found in some philosophies of life its most loyal partners. Technique has provided even philosophy with an extremely efficient way to deny the relevance of the research of its arcane.

Are we human artificers aware of this? At this moment in the history of humanity, when something called "Anthropocene" appears as a spectre on the scene, when ecological collapse and catastrophic conditions permeate our ideas of civilization, questioning is not just a "piety of thought",[20] it is the commitment to the thinking thought: an active process of thinking as end for a community of people who care about it.

## Architecture and the Architect

*Nomen omen*[21]: a name is a premonition like a forewarning that has always been around even if we don't notice it. An omen could be a gift or a curse.

Any word has an atmosphere and lives through its use,[22] abuse, misuse and usure. A word has a trajectory (that is the Italian meaning of the word "sense", *senso* as direction).

It would be important to remain as faithful as possible to all the enigmas that the words architecture and the architect can still evoke. It's not a matter of being obsessed with etymology.[23] Architecture more than any word is a wording: be aware of the arcane of technique! That is an open call to those enigmas that constantly insist to be as such, notwithstanding all the reasoning that we can afford to unravel their obscurity. Many of them are unmasked, others are not. To learn to live with these recurring enigmas is the role of theory.

"Architecture is not an object". Is it a thing?[24] Which came first, architecture or the architect? Is it a prerogative of humankind?[25]

When some realize that "architecture is everything"[26] they become aware of the difficult[27] truth of architecture that is rooted in the origin of the noun. Technique, can include the totality of human actions and thoughts.[28]

How is everything, how does everything happen to be when it is merely confronted by technique? Everything is always already technicalized and architecture is this thinking thought.

I maintain that the origin of the wording contains this complexity and that being inspired by this origin remains relevant. It is good to try to know again and again what is technique about. This is the ethics of knowledge.[29]

Thinking about these words with moral eyes may be one of the lost convivial tools of theory: to be able to debate both the pride and the shame that are implied in the principles of any sort of technique. To live the contradictions between commitment to our deeds and disenchantment about these deeds is what it means to practice architecture. Since these contradictions cannot be solved, they stand and will always stand in the domain of the unknown. This domain of the unknown (the domain of that which cannot be solved) is not something that does not exist. It is a body of thought that always waits to be a destination. To venture into the domain of the unknown with enigmatic responses is the practice of theory.

The city in which we live, the social life that we try to construct over and over again can be built on the foundation of this unknown: the permanence of its enigma. The house we build to spoil (or because we think we were meant to spoil) paradise is the building of this "lack".[30] The house we continue to build in this hell (the infernal version) of a paradise is this recurring contradiction. This destiny is a necessity.[31]

From this philosophical awareness three important suggestions follow. First: Architecture is not just "the art of building" but "its thinking principles"[32] (to think architecture is architecture) beyond good and evil – which implies a disclosure of the arcane of its technocracy. Second: the history of architecture can be practiced beyond any chronological and spatial ordering and without a faith into "this becoming that" – which means to find the courage to re-think history with a full dedication to its theory – that is, its *mise en abyme.*[33] The ideal space for this to happen is the school, the university or any community dedicated to knowledge and education. Third: to be ethically educated implies to insist not on a better future but on the "eternity"[34] of a present for which we have to take full responsibility[35] – a project of paramount importance to resist to the illusory futurism of sustainability, and the arrogance of thinking about bettering human life.[36] The aboriginal context where the words architecture and the architect were invented is a context where a community questions the meaning of technique and where the good and evil of any sort of technique was exposed and debated.

## Bound and Unbound Prometheus

Of Prometheus, the personification of the invention of all the techniques – that is the personification of the arcane of technique – there is a myth and a tragedy.

In the myth, we can explore the differences/tensions/conflicts between pride and shame that are implied in the words of architecture and the architect. In this myth and in the political adaptation of the myth into a tragedy for the public of the theatre we find the original context where the internal conflicts of being an architect are exposed.

There are four legends concerning Prometheus:

*According to the first, he was clamped to a rock in the Caucasus for betraying the secrets of the gods to men, and the gods sent eagles to feed on his liver, which was perpetually renewed.*

*According to the second, Prometheus, goaded by the pain of the tearing beaks, pressed himself deeper and deeper into the rock until he became one with it.*
*According to the third, his treachery was forgotten in the course of thousands of years, the gods forgotten, the eagles, he himself forgotten.*
*According to the fourth, every one grew weary of the meaningless affair. The gods grew weary, the eagles grew weary, the wound closed wearily.*
*There remained the inexplicable mass of rock. The legend tried to explain the inexplicable. As it came out of a substratum of truth it had in turn to end in the inexplicable.*

Franz Kafka[37]

This is the best short explanation of the myth. The myth is the knowledge of all what we already know even without knowing it. The guilt for knowing in advance, his pride for his cunning intelligence – the pro-*metis* of Prometheus – is unforgivable. His gift/curse for humans implies an incommensurable symbolic exchange. We live our life unforgivably.

The tragedy has different aims and articulations. Its plot is tripartite.[38] Prometheus first cheats the gods and steals all the techniques to offer the loots as a gift to humankind; then he is punished and enchained for his misconducts and for his false promises to humanity; finally, he is freed after recognizing all these mischievous deeds and becoming conscious of the illusory hopes he has created for mortals. The end of the tragedy is Prometheus' surrender "to the love for death" (*amore mortis*); that is not a suicidal syndrome but an agreement made between the gods, the giants and the human spectators (in the theatre), a covenant based on the consciousness of limits and the limits of consciousness because of the gift/curse that he has offered to mortals. All the techniques are a stolen gift; all the false promises they imply are the curse; all the consciousness of gods' folly and human limits are the epilogue. Prometheus has fallen in love with mortals – he has fallen in love with their mortality – a fatal attraction for the tender mercy (piety) of this sentiment. Mortals will reciprocate it with their teleology: the knowledge of their limits. Will they? Prometheus pleads guilty and asks forgiveness for the humanity he has already inexorably gifted and intoxicated.

> *Chorus*: Confess, Prometheus, what is more powerful: your technique(s) or this destiny of ours? *Prometheus*: 'I confess. The necessity [*ananke*] of this all is much more powerful than my technique(s).[39]

This is how the architect Prometheus gets out from his enchainment and wanders in the tragical domain of the city (the Greek *polis*) graduating mortal architects around.

A persuasive eternally cheating and enchanting master! His pupils will also know how to re-enact this tragedy! They can do wrong but, as soon as they confess, they will be freed. The show must go on.

Prometheus is the personification of the invention of all possible techniques that make human life possible. He has to be blamed and punished because of this and he has to be revered and praised for the same reason. Moreover, he has to be aware of this bipolarity that is embedded in his intentions and actions. He has to accept and be aware of his own debacle – never mind how honest the remorse might be.

The tragedy is written to educate the public of the *polis*; its purpose is political.

Politics is the technique that shall master all the other possible techniques – a royal technique.[40]

In the tragedy Prometheus gains consciousness.

All the Promethean techniques must be mastered by humankind only with disillusion/disenchantment.

The risk to be avoided is to be overtaken by hubris.[41] Because every technique will lead the technician to steal, conceal and betray to fulfil false promises and to promote the illusion of their hopes. Every technique is born out of betrayal and theft. To master any technique is to gain this awareness. Prometheus must be committed and disenchanted in order to be absolved and dis-enchained. This is political consciousness.

In front of the audience of the theatre Prometheus is unbound only when he gains full awareness of his own limits, after, after being inebriated (stoned?) by his cunning intelligence.

This is when Prometheus gains his degree as "pro-fessor architect": when he sees in front of him all the goods and the evils that his techniques are creating. But we don't have to forget that Prometheus is acting. He himself is an artificial construct of the human mind.

This drama is possible only if you keep the politics of the tragedy as an end. This is the limit and the scope of the tragedy played in the theatre.

The problem is that politics is also a technique: a leading technique that is supposed to master all other techniques.

Were the Greek technicians and master builders (spectators of this drama) able to renounce all their vaunting illusions in the face of a leading political cause? To be an architect means to know one's limits, the limits of one's own technique, the limits of any technique, that is, to provide false promises.... Did the Greeks believe this?[42]

Is the political technique immune from the risks of all the other techniques?

Isn't the political technique also providing false promises?

The tragedy does not venture into the gutting of this question.

Greece has its history. The tragedy is integral to this history. One cannot find much comfort in the epilogue of the tragedy. Tragedy leads to a solution at the expense of the mystery of the myth.

This is what supports the underground of the Greek context where the words architecture and architect originated.

This is what the words architecture and the architect may evoke in the cradle of their invention: the arcane of technique connotes the conflict that always exist between mastering the principles (archi-) of the art of building (-tecture) and knowing that these principles are somehow compromised with the logic of any possible technique which implies taking possession over something (stealing?) and deceiving (cheating?) with a cunning intelligence.[43]

To steal means to take possession of (to get hold over) something that does not belong to the perpetrator: to own something is different from having the right to own it. To cheat means to fool and convince the others that the architect has the right to do so because the intentions are good and the theft is worth being perpetrated. The concrete that we pour in the foundations does not belong to us even if we buy it and might try to find many good reasons for doing so.

Moreover, while doing all this we have to mismatch means and ends. Do architects think about building to celebrate life or do they celebrate life in order to build? Do I write to contribute to the education of an architect or do I contribute to the education of the architect in order to write?

This is the other inevitable sense of guilt implied in the arcane of any technique. The technicians will always inevitably mismatch means and ends and will transform their means into their ends. This is a betrayal.

Architects try to understand what it means having to be a theft, a cheat and a betrayer for the sake of their technique. This tentative comprehension seems to be one of the most urgent challenges for theory; and this endeavour is not meant to be delusional but dignifying.

The architects know that this is inherent to the human condition and they are those who might even raise the suspicion that this is another level of justification. A level of justification that sits upon another level of justification in an infinite sequence.[44] Perceiving this infinite piling "wreckage" of justifications an architect is an architect.

## Promethean Shame

Prometheus is unbound[45] nowadays not because he is aware of the limits of his own technical deeds but because no one cares to invent gods anymore, gods who might be able to enchain him again – indeed, the gods were all invented to be cheated with cunning intelligence – because all this story is a technical product of artificial (cunning) intelligence. The ancestrally "saved" humanity does not even seem interested in imagining such gods if not for their progressive mockery-ing for the sake of this theatrical tragical reenactment.

Our politics have accepted to be fully mastered by other techniques that have no political concerns whatsoever.

When technical thought is imperative and pervasive (no alternatives and no way out), then we are dominated by Promethean shame. Technique is the inspiring thought of the technology that pervades us.

When technique becomes the means that is functional to all the other human endeavorus for accomplishing their ends, then technique itself becomes the end. Technique is a means that has only its own empowerment as an end. When we say: "means without end",[46] we express both that our production of means will be endless and that the only aim is the endless empowerment of means; instrumentality reified as a self-justifying act of faith.

"Promethean Shame" is what we prove when confronted with the logic and the efficiency of technocratic apparatuses whose aim is the pure proliferation of means.

It is that condition of inverted utopia where we can technically make what we are unable to imagine. To imagine what we are unable to make is/was the straightforward utopia.[47]

Is this an epochal contingency? This perspective of an imperative unknown technical destiny is chronologically planned. We are the spectators of our own show: a permanent reiteration of a sequel: tragedy-comedy-farce. Shall I propose to work at the margins of this technical hubristic expenditure still trying to retrieve politics and social tecno-sciences and their ethics as leading techniques? This is somewhat nostalgic.

Architecture is the opportunity to question building. It represents the awareness of the risk of the unbridled power of erring (endless wandering and wondering) of technique: the occasion to gain a sense of limit.[48]

The arcane of technique is the necessity of this dismemberment in the face of the unity of the contradiction between good and evil.

This discussion will raise more doubts and questions; and it will leave us with a lot of uncertainties. To live with these uncertainties is what theory can teach us. It is our task to explore these questions and find out which doubts are false or honest. Theory questions the limits of this obligation and creates a public space for this questioning, a space that should be as vulnerable as possible, a space without walls. A very difficult project: the potential creation of the space of the defenceless losers,[49] those who do not leave traces in the history we have been taught to teach.

## Conclusions

What shall we do with these words we have inherited? The answer is theory.

There are many theoretical alternatives in the face of the unknown – that now takes the shape of an all-encompassing overbuilt, collapsing, inverted utopia.

I mention two of them.

First: to abandon the words architecture and the architect to oblivion.

It does not seem reasonable to keep using the words "architecture and the architect" in a discombobulated way without knowing what we are talking about. We can give them up and find better and less compromised substitutes.

After all there are physicians and orchestra directors but it would sound almost jocular to call them archi-physicians or archi-musicians.

We can keep these words as a more or less comfortable legacy, a cumbersome inheritance or just a curiosity for an antique collector.

We can easily forget words, but can we give up their meaning? Can we live without architecture, without the deep meaning that the Greeks used to confer to this word? Even the communities that build and make as little as possible "have" their architecture made with intangible or immaterial entities and sentiments, "have" their architects of existential mysteries. To make words silent or to change their aural domain, means a lot. So, we must examine these possible differences: what happens if we eliminate these bombastic Greek logicisms from our vocabulary? What comes out with this absence? What substitutes for it? Is a substitution necessary?

Second: to pay full homage to the deep history and meaning of these words and feel this as a call for responsibility. Ideally this knowledge might reach beyond any good or evil but it could also (just because of this) be disappointing – something we don't want to know. Many professionals (both in the academia and in the practice) thinks that to grasp the meaning of architecture means to know what is right thing to do! This is not the case.

Architecture, is not just a word but a wording: you, architect, should try to look at the principles that guide your technique! This means to try to master the principles on which all human endeavours stand: the arcane of technique. Theory represents this commitment. Is this a boastful task suitable only to universal geniuses? No. Everybody can be an architect in every specific and different endeavour. What's needed is consciousness, commitment to the ethics of knowledge and research for a disenchanted politics devoid of fake promises.

Architecture is an eternal search into the principles of our making and theory starts where reason ends. Can we do "without" the research into the deep meaning of the principles of our making, can we avoid architecture, can we avoid the mystery (can we avoid theorizing the mystery) that our art is meant to evoke?

A community of people who work honestly into this unknown deserves full respect. For sure the ideal places where this community meets are the schools and universities and every space where education is the aim. Considering education as a permanent endeavour, the professional practice deserves to be carried on following the model of the school – and not vice versa. The school may still become the paradigm of a tool of conviviality[50] for the theory of architecture.

People who want to build at any cost have already built too much. This is a world of excessive inverted utopia: we are overwhelmed by a catastrophic amount of "anthropocenic" stuff, the consequences of which are unimaginable.

If we want to try to know what technique is – and try to identify its limits – we have to continue the work carried on by philosophy. This means digging into the arcane of our practice through a body of theory. In this way, we will pay homage to the meaning of architecture and the architect while trying to be disenchanted about hope[51] and trying to look at nihilism right in its face.[52]

The essence of architecture is what the philosophers call "*epochè*": a suspension of judgment that catches us astonished before a sincere commitment to thinking; to imagine an ethics of theory that exists beyond judging what's good or evil. It is unfair to consider the Promethean technique an evil: it is evil to have the arrogance to pretend that technique is for the good. Technique is an instrumental relationship between means and ends: it is a forced idealized neutrality of instrumentality and a forced and compelling persuasion that this is positive and inevitable. To think at any cost that this instrumental relationship is for the better, and it must be the global panorama where one can gain liberation, this global encompassing overtaking of technique is a paramount evil, a pathology to be avoided: to think that the means are the only end: to justify the means as the only end.[53] Technique is our nature but not the only way to live this nature. The possibility to limit the power of technique is what has been evoked with the invention of the words: architecture and architect. This is what theory can do.

Architecture is the art to suspend building[54].

## Notes

1 An anthropological/ethnographic/psychogenetic excursus on the cultural domains of presence, absence and difference of these words and the ideas they imply is of paramount importance. Cf. Ching, Francis D. K. and Jarzombek, Mark M. 2017. *A Global History of Architecture*, Third Edition, Hoboken (NJ): Wiley. The problem is that we don't want to know what we are talking about when we talk about architecture and we run the risk of colonizing "other" territories that are uncontaminated, so to speak, by this "plastic viral word". Cf. Pörksen, Uwe. 1996. *Plastic Words: The Tyranny of Modular Language*. University Park: Pennsylvania State University Press. The paradox is that we look for something that we want to find at any cost, even without knowing what it is that we want to find. For a complex attempt to describe the problem of anthropological methods of investigation on the history of technique cf. Ingold, Tim. 1997. "Eight Themes in the Anthropology of Technology", *Social Analysis: The International Journal of Anthropology*, Vol. 41, No. 1, Technology as Skilled Practice (March 1997), pp. 106–138. Architecture should be investigated in the domain of the "history of ideas", that is the history of its permanent existence. Bouton, Christophe. 2018. "Dealing with Deep Time: The Issue of Ancestrality from Kant to Hegel", *RES: Anthropology an Aesthetics*, Vol. 69, No. 70 (Spring/Autumn), pp. 38–51.

2 "Decolonizing design" is a contemporary concern. See, for example, "What Does it Mean To Decolonize Design", https://eyeondesign.aiga.org/what-does-it-mean-to-decolonize-design/ (Consulted May 14, 2021) and cf. Adams, William M. and Mulligan, Martin. 2002. *Decolonizing Nature. Strategies for Conservation in a Post-colonial Era*, New York: Routledge. The concerns of BIPOC movement and associations like National Organization of Minority Architects show the evidence of reality. The project of the politically correct is now "out of question", that is, a dogma. Since it is meant to be a radical project, its consequences are also unpredictable, hence it is a pure technical project: a means without a predictable end. Cf. Colomina, Beatriz and Wigley, Mark. 2016. *Are We Human?: Notes on an Archaeology of Design*, Baden: Lars Muller Publishers.

3 *Theoroi* (theoreticians) was the name given to ambassadors who would report the response of an oracle concerning some unsolvable problem that was troubling a community (cf. McEwen, Indra Kagis. 1993. *Socrates' Ancestor. An Essay on*

*Architectural Beginnings*, Cambridge (MA): The MIT Press, 20–21. The response of the oracle was enigmatic. The community who would listen to the theoreticians would also find a way to carry on their social life relying on that enigmatic report, that is a theory. To theorize is to learn to live with an enigma in the face of a problem – after having tried to solve that problem in all the possible rational ways. Cf. the chapter dedicated to "Theory" in Kerényi, Karl. 2001. *Religione antica*, Milano: Adelfi, and Gadamer, Hans-Georg. 1989. "Elogio della Teoria [Lob der Theorie]" in *Elogio della teoria. Discorsi e saggi.* Franco Volpi, ed., Milano: Edizioni Angelo Guerini e Associati, 29–44.

4 The questions I know how to live with are the essence of my humanity.

> *[...] to have patience with everything unresolved in your heart and to try to love the questions themselves as if they were locked rooms or books written in a very foreign language. Don't search for the answers, which could not be given to you now, because you would not be able to live them. And the point is, to live everything. Live the questions now. Perhaps then, someday far in the future, you will gradually, without even noticing it, live your way into the answer.*
>
> *[...] And your doubt can become a good quality if you train it. It must become knowing, it must become criticism. Ask it, whenever it wants to spoil something for you, why something is ugly, demand proofs from it, test it, and you will find it perhaps bewildered and embarrassed, perhaps also protesting. But don't give in, insist on arguments, and act in this way, attentive and persistent, every single time, and the day will come when instead of being a destroyer, it will become one of your best workers — perhaps the most intelligent of all the ones that are building your life.*

Rainer Maria Rilke, *Letters to a Young Poet*, Stephen Mitchell, tr., Ray Soulard, Jr, ed., Portland (OR): Scriptor Press, letters od July 16, 1903 and November 4, 1904, pp. 14 and 34.

5 "Art evokes the mystery without which the world would not exist"; cf. Magritte, René. 2005. *Scritti*. Vol. II, Milan: Abscondita, p. 188. https://le-citazioni.it/frasi/197167-rene-magritte-la-psicoanalisi-consente-di-interpretare-solo-cio/ (Consulted on May 15, 2021).

6 "Architecture should be judged not only by the problems it solves, but by the problems it creates." Lebbeus Wood. http://lifewithoutbuildings.net/2006/09/-lecture-review-lebbeus-woods.html (consulted on May 22, 2021).

7 Cf. Gopnik, Alison. 2009. *The Philosophical Baby: What Children's Minds Tell Us about Truth, Love, and the Meaning of Life*, New York: Vintage Publishing.

8 Cf. Ingold, Tim. 2013. *Making. Anthropology, Archaeology, Art and Architecture*, Abingdon/New York: Routledge.

9 Landrum, Lisa. 2015. "Before Architecture: Archai, Architects and Architectonics in Plato and Aristotle", *Montreal Architecture Review*, Vol. 2, pp. 14–18.

10 Cf., for example, Kojin Karatani. 1995. *Architecture as Metaphor. Language, Number, Money.* Cambridge (MA): MIT Press; and Hollier, Denis. 1989. *Against Architecture: The Writings of Georges Bataille*, Cambridge (MA): MIT Press.

11 Emanuele Severino is an Italian philosopher who has dedicated his studies to the notion of "technique" which he considers a dominating idea whose aim is to separate "the earth from its destiny of truth". Technique relies on the necessity of the original negation, because the belief of the technician is to create something out of nothing. His publications and lectures, being an ontological "critique" of technique and digging at the foundations of the logic of technique (that is its "archè) constitutes my basic reference for trying to grasp the meaning of "architecture". The meaning of architecture is not something that exists in a remote time, but that which continue to exist eternally – this thought about the *eternal*

*being of entities* is one of Severino mostly provocative challenges. Technique has just taken the pervasive form of its most radical essence.

> La filosofia contemporanea sta al fondamento della tecnica [...] e quindi consente alla tecnica di progettare il dominio incondizionato della totalità dell'essere. [...] Nella tecnica del nostro tempo si trovano le "radici della violenza" ossia le radici del modo in cui nel nostro tempo si presentano le forme essenziali della violenza". [Contemporary philosophy is at the foundation of the technique [...] and therefore allows the technique to plan the unconditional domination of the totality of being. [...] In the technique of our time we find the "roots of violence" that is the roots of the way in which the essential forms of violence present themselves in our time.].

From the introduction to the 2002 edition (Milano: Rizzoli) of Severino, Emanuele. 1979. *Téchne. Le radici della violenza.* Milano: Rusconi. See also Severino, Emanuele. 2003. *Tecnica e architettura.* Milano: Raffaello Cortina Editore, pp. 64–65. Emanuele Severino philosophy of technique has been explored and amplified by Umberto Galimberti.

> Tecnica non tende a uno scopo, non promuove un senso, non apre scenari di salvezza, non redime, non svela verità: la tecnica funziona. E poiché il suo funzionamento diventa planetario, questo libro si propone di rivedere i concetti di individuo, identità, libertà, salvezza, verità, senso, scopo, ma anche quelli di natura, etica, politica, religione, storia, di cui si nutriva l'età umanistica e che ora, nell'età della tecnica, dovranno essere riconsiderati, dismessi o rifondati alle radici. [Technique does not aim at a purpose, it does not promote a sense, it does not open scenarios of salvation, it does not redeem, it does not reveal truth: the technique works. And since its functioning becomes planetary, this book aims to review the concepts of individual, identity, freedom, salvation, truth, meaning, purpose, but also those of nature, ethics, politics, religion, history, which nourished the humanistic age and which now, in the age of technique, will have to be reconsidered, abandoned or refounded at the roots].

Cf. Galimberti, Umberto. 1999. *Psiche e techne. L'uomo nell'età della tecnica*, Milano: Feltrinelli; and Galimberti, Umberto. 2009. "Il mito della tecnica", *I miti del nostro tempo*, Milano: Feltrinelli, 207–225. A common fundamental reference for both Emanuele Severino and Umberto Galimberti is Martin Heiddeger philosophy and particularly Heidegger's "The Question of Technique" (*Die Frage nach der Technik*) of 1953. But both Severino and Galimberti lead the discussion of technique – not technology – to a radical ontology. There is a relevant difference between technique and technology that is lost in the English and common jargon.

12 Concerning Gentile's "Actualism" see Haddock, Bruce and Wakefield, James. 2015. *Thought Thinking: The Philosophy of Giovanni Gentile*, Imprint Academic.

13 On the signification of "building" and "technique" as "metaphors" I am grateful to the ongoing provoking discussions with Donald Kunze.

14 Cf. Demetri Porphyrios, "From *Techne* to Tectonics", in Ballantyne, Andrew. 2002. *What Is Architecture*, London and New York: Routledge; and Kenneth Frampton. 1995. *Studies in Tectonic Culture: the Poetics of Construction*, Cambridge (MA): MIT Press). For general introduction to these differences cf. Holst, Jonas. 2017. "The Fall of the *Tekton* and the Rise of the Architect: On the Greek Origins of Architectural Craftsmanship", *Architectural Histories*, Vol. 5, No. 1, pp. 1–12; and Landrum, op. cit., p. 15.

15 On the *archai* (*Nous* and *Ananke*) cf. Hillman, James. 1991. *La vana fuga dagli dei* (On Paranoia, 1986; On the Necessity of Abnormal Psichology; Ananke and Athena), trad. Adriana Bottini, Milano: Adelphi.

16 Severino idea of the "eternal" extends beyond the difference between origin and beginning. «L'arché dunque non solo è ciò che vi è di identico nelle cose diverse, e non solo è la dimensione da cui esse provengono e in cui esse ritornano, ma è anche la forza che determina il divenire del mondo, ossia è il "principio" che, governando il mondo, lo produce e lo fa tornare a sé» (Severino, Emanuele. 2004. *La filosofia dai Greci al nostro tempo*, I vol., Milano: BUR, 34)

17 Meillassoux, Quentin, 2008, *After Finitude. An Essay on the Necessity of Contingecy*, London/New York: Continuum.

18 The fact that *téchne* was translated into Latin as art (*ars*), that is a noun with its own independent etymological origin and different meanings, makes the whole linguistic, semiotic and verbal setting very challenging. The English translation of the German *Technik* with Technology has further complicated the issue (Heidegger's and Benjamin's *Technik* are commonly translated as *technology*). As for the Greek meaning of *téchne* (that I translate with the English "technique" even if the English translates the Greek tèchne with "art"), the definition given by Aristotle is basic:

> Technique [*téchne*] deals with bringing something into existence; and to pursue a technique means to study how to bring into existence a thing which may either exist or not, and the principle [arché] of which lies in the maker and not in the thing made [my underlining].
>
> Aristotle, *Nichomachean Ethics*, VI, iii, 4–5

In the contemporary phenomenological definition of making, as the essence of technique, the disorientation is fully accomplished by maintaining that making is everything that happens and becomes in the domain of human actions and perceptions. Cf. Ingold, Tim. 2013. *Making. Anthropology, Archaeology, Art and Architecture*, Abingdon/New York: Routledge; and Damish, Hubert. 2016. "Architecture Is…", in *Noah's Ark. Essay on Architecture*, Cambridge (MA): The MIT Press, 247–292. Emanuele Severino point of view is radical: the logic of technique is the power of erring (the human "erring cause"); the human being loses the truth of its destiny when the hubris for this power of technique is considered as the only finality/aim/scope. Technique is not "everything" we make but only that which we make pretending it might either exist or not. This is the violence of technique: its arrogance to decree and ratify the existence or non-existence of anything. Human beings cannot be "unbounded" from technique, but technique is not their only destiny. Severino 1998 op. cit. Umberto Galimberti amplifies this philosophical consciousness and its questioning. Galimberti 1999 op. cit. The essence of technique is instrumentality; this is how it works: make the logic of the means become your only end! The only aim of technique is the full justification of the means as end. There is no finality beyond the logic of the means. This is technique. To make technique become the only possible panorama of humanity is wrong because it is a prevarication. To exclude humanity from the difference, the difference of a permanent destiny beyond the prevarication of technique, is an absolute evil: it prevents humanity from the appearance of its permanent destiny. This is the "truth" of Severino's philosophy.

19 Cf. Leatherbarrow, David. "Architecture Is Its Own Discipline", in Piotrowski, Andrzej and Robinson, Julia Williams, curators. *Discipline of Architecture*. Minneapolis: University of Minnesota Press, 83–102 (https://www.jstor.org/stable/10.5749/j.cttttqm2).

20 Concerning Heidegger's final remark "questioning is the piety of thought" cf. Robert S. Gall. 1993. "Toward a Tragic Theology: The Piety of Thought in Heidegger and Tragedy", *Literature and Theology*, Vol. 7, No. 1, pp. 13–32.

21 Cf. Wheeler, Stephen. 2009. "Nomen Omen." *The Classical Review*, New Series, Vol. 59, No. 2, pp. 455–457. Accessed March 1, 2021. http://www.jstor.org/stable/40600679.

22 Cf. Ludwig Wittgenstein, *Philosophical Investigations*, §117

> Mi si dice: << Tu comprendi, vero, quest'espressione? Ebbene,- anch'io la uso nel significato che tu conosci>>.- Come se il significato fosse un'atmosfera che la parola ha con sé e che si porta dietro in ogni sorta d'impiego … Se, ad esempio, uno dicesse che la proposizione <<Questo è qui>> (pronunciata indicando un oggetto davanti a sé) ha senso per lui, allora dovrebbe chiedersi in quali circostanze si impieghi effettivamente questa proposizione. In queste circostanze essa ha senso.

Cf. also Zarrin-Panah, Nassir. 2012. "Chamber Pot, Urn and Their Proper Use", *Wolkenkuckucksheim/Cloud-Cuckoo-Land*, Vol. 17, No. 32, pp. 259–266. (https://www.cloud-cuckoo.net/intro/).

23 Cf., for example, the importance to avoid the mysticism of words in Friedländer, Paul. 2004. "Aletheia. Un confronto critico dell'autore con se stesso e con Martin Heidegger", in *Platone*, Milano: Bompiani, 251.

24 Cf. Ingold, Tim. 2013. *Making. Anthropology, Archaeology, Art and Architecture*, Abingdon/New York: Routledge.

25 Cf. Rykwert, Jospeph. 2012. "Adam at Forty", *Journal of Architectural Education*, Vol. 65, No. 2, pp. 7–8.

26 Damish, Hubert. 2016. "Architecture Is…" in *Noah's Ark. Essay on Architecture*, Cambridge (MA): The MIT Press, 247–292; and Cook, Peter, "What Is Architecture", https://www.youtube.com/watch?v=uvWgWs_2svc (consulted on May, 18, 2021); Hollein, Hans. 1968. "Everything Is Architecture", https://designmanifestos.org/hans-hollein-everything-is-architecture/ (consulted on May 25, 2021). There is an architecture of everything, The common destiny of every signifier is its own *mise-en-abyme*. Cf. Dällenbach, Lucien. 1989. *In the Mirror of the Text*, Chicago (IL): The University of Chicago Press.

27 Cf. Emery, Nicola. 2007. *L'architettura difficile. Filosofia del costruire*. Milano: Marinotti. The book has not been translated into English. A summary is provided in https://difficultarchitecture.wordpress.com/2008/10/04/professor-emerys-difficult-architecture/ (Consulted on January 11, 2021).

28 This power of inclusion is the essence of technique. Indeed, even trying to restrict the domain of the art of building ONLY to the field of construction, how many different things could be included? Way too many because even construing can be constructed. Beside designing buildings (and there are already many different "kinds" on buildings and design practices) and even erecting buildings (practicing the so called "design build"), architects can practice Renovation, Interior Design, Visual Design, Drawing and Rendering, Technical Direction, Material Experimentation, History, Theory, Education, Planning and Economics, Liability and Forensic. And these are just some of the very broad domains (each with a many different specializations) where an architect can intervene. It is just unfortunate that because of the Accreditation System, based on international standards issued by the International Organization of Standardization (ISO) all the School of Architecture gets obsessed about educating each student to the design of "big" buildings. See https://en.wikipedia.org/wiki/International_Organization_for_Standardization and https://en.wikipedia.org/wiki/National_Architectural_Accrediting_Board (consulted on May 20, 2021).

29 Hans Jonas sees this task of knowing as the foundation of the ethics of responsibility. Cf. Jonas, Hans. 1984. *The Imperative of Responsibility*, Chicago (IL), London: The University of Chicago Press. (Originally published in 1979).

30 Cf. Edgar, Andrew. 1992. "Kant's Two Interpretations of Genesis", *Literature and Theology*, Vol. 6, No. 3, pp. 280–290; Agamben, Giorgio. 2019. *Il Regno e il Giardino*, Vicenza: Neri Pozza Editore. Concerning the idea of the human as "deficient being" (*Mängelwesen*) Cf. Gehlen, Arnold. 1988. *Man: His Nature and Place in the World*, New York: Columbia University Press.

31 "Necessity" is the Greek: *ANANKE*. Cf. Hillman, James. 1991. *La vana fuga dagli dei* (On Paranoia, 1986; On the Necessity of Abnormal Psichology; Ananke and Athena), trad. Adriana Bottini, Milano: Adelphi ; and Rykwert, Joseph. 1982. "The Necessity of Artefice", in *The Necessity of Artefice. Ideas in Architecture*, London: Academy Editions. Is our building necessary? When does building becomes overbuilding? Is our artifice necessary? When is it enough? Is being human being "added" to nature? Is this addition a necessity of nature? This questioning is a philosophy that we practice in every single moment of our lives. *Ars est homo ADDITUS naturae*. This expression can be traced to a statement made by Francis Bacon in his *Descriptio globi intellectualis* (Chapter 2): 'Ars sive additus rebus Homo'. See *The Works of Francis Bacon*, Vol. 3, 2: *Philosophical Works*. James Spedding *et al.*, eds., London: Longmans, 1887, 731.

32 Cf. Severino, Emanuele. 2008. *La tendenza fondamentale del nostro tempo*, Milano: Adelphi, 37; Severino, Emanuele. 2003. *Tecnica e architettura*, Milano: Raffaello Cortina Editore, 29.

33 History "becomes" a chronological ordering when time is reduced to a sequence of events happening "before and after" in a time line and is "functional" (instrumental) to this kind of ordering. This techno-chronological history avoids the responsibility of witnessing (the historian as a witness). Cf. Severino, Emanuele. 1979. *Téchne. Le radici della violenza*, Milano: Rusconi.

34 Cf. Severino, Emanuele. 1998. *Il destino della tecnica*, Milano: Rizzoli.

35 Jonas, Hans. 1984. *The Imperative of Responsibility*, Chicago (IL), London: The University of Chicago Press. (Originally published in 1979); concerning the legal, political, moral and metaphysical levels of responsibility see Jasper, Karl. 1947. *The Question of German Guilt*, New York: Fordham University Press, 2001.

36 "Men have dreamed of liberating machines. But there are no machines of freedom, by definition. This is not to say that the exercise of freedom is completely indifferent to spatial distribution, but it can only function when there is a certain convergence; in the case of divergence or distortion, it immediately becomes the opposite of that which had been intended" Foucault, Michel. 1997. "Space, Knowledge, Power", in Neil Leach, ed., *Rethinking Architecture. A Reader in Cultural Theory*, Oxon/New York: Routledge.

37 Franz Kafka's *Prometheus* is a short story written in 1918. Cf. Kafka, Franz. 1995. *The Complete Stories*, New York: Schocken Books.

38 I fully rely on the analysis and the summary of the tragedy given by Curi, Umberto. 2005. "Amore mortis. Per una rilettura del 'Prometeo incatenato'", in *Le parole dell'Essere. Per Emanuele Severino*, Milano: Mondadori, 141–169.

39 Ibid., 153.

40 On Plato's royal technique (*basilike techne*) see Novak, Joseph A. 2018. "Techne in Plato and the New Testament", *Religions and Education in Antiquity*, Vol. 160, pp. 107–126.

41 Bertrand Russel defines hubris "the greatest danger of our time" … "the intoxication of power".

> The attitude of man towards the non-human environment has differed profoundly at different times. The Greeks, with their dread of hubris and their belief in a Necessity or Fate superior even to Zeus, carefully avoided what would have seemed to them insolence towards the universe. The Middle Ages carried submission much further: humility towards God was a Christian's

first duty. Initiative was cramped by this attitude, and great originality was scarcely possible. The Renaissance restored human pride, but carried it to the point where it led to anarchy and disaster. Its work was largely undone by the Reformation and the Counter-Reformation. But modern technique, while not altogether favorable to the lordly individual of the Renaissance, has revived the sense of the collective power of human communities. Man, formerly too humble, begins to think of himself as almost a God. The Italian pragmatist Papini urges us to substitute the 'Imitation of God' for the 'Imitation of Christ'.

[….]

In all this I feel a grave danger, the danger of what might be called cosmic impiety. The concept of 'truth' as something dependent upon facts largely outside human control has been one of the way in which philosophy hitherto has inculcated the necessary element of humility. When this check upon pride is removed, a further step is taken on the road towards a certain kind of madness… I am persuaded that this intoxication is the greatest danger of our time…

Russell, Bertrand, *A History of Western Philosophy*, 737. https://geopolicraticus.wordpress.com/2011/10/07/cosmic-hubris-or-cosmic-humility/. Hubris is the "fall" of the architect, that is the failure of being an architect – the capacity to control arrogance or excessive pride, the fragile limits of virtue and the moderation of desires are the foundations on which the *basilike techne* stands. Cf. Ludvig, Paul. 2002. *Eros and Polis: Desire and Community in Greek Political Theory*, Cambridge: Cambridge University Press.

42 Cf. Veyne, Paul. 1988. *Did the Greeks Believe in Their Myths? An Essay on Constitutive Imagination*, Chicago (IL): University of Chicago Press.

43 Cf. Detienne, Marcelle and Vernant, Jean-Pierre. 1978. *Cunning Intelligence in Greek Culture and Society*, Harvester Press.

44 Concerning the "infinite regress" see the *Münchhausen-Trilemma* in Albert, Hans. 1985. *Treatise on Critical Reason*, Princeton (NJ): Princeton University Press.

45 Concerning the idea of unbound Promethean hubris see Hans Jonas, 1984, *The Imperative of Responsibility*, Chicago (IL), London: The University of Chicago Press. (Originally published in 1979); cf. Irudayadason, Nishant A. 2013. "Response to the Unbound Prometheus: Hans Jonas' Affirmation of Responsibility in Technological Age of Unbridled and Uncontrolled Development", *Jnanadeepa: Pune Journal of Religious Studies*, Vol. 16, No. 2, pp. 38–54. Consider also Percy Bysshe Shelley' *Prometheus Unbound* of 1820 and Mary Shelley's *Frankestein; or the Modern Prometheus*, published in 1818.

46 Cf. Agamben, Giorgio. 1996. *Mezzi senza Fine. Note sulla Politica*, Torino: Bollati Boringhieri. (2000, *Means Without Ends*, Minneapolis and London: University of Minnesota Press).

47 The straightforward utopia is to imagine something you cannot make. The inverted utopia is to make something you cannot imagine. That is the complete de-responsabilization of the consequences of your actions (the foundation of the idea of freedom in scientific research). The formulation of "inverted utopia" is by Günther Anders. Cf. Müller, Christopher John, curator. 2016. *Prometheanism: Technology, Digital Culture and Human Obsolescence*. (Includes a translation of the essay 'On Promethean Shame' by Günther Anders). Lanham (MD): Rowman & Littlefield.

48 Cf. Payne, Andrew. "On Limits", *Return of Nature. Sustaining Architecture in the Face of Sustainability*, Preston Scott Cohen and Erika Naginski editors, 101–120.

49 I thank Talia Tramin for sharing her ideas on vulnerability. Cf., the movie *Corn Island*, George Ovashvili, 2014.

50 Cf. Illich, Ivan. 1973. *Tools of Conviviality*, New York: Harper & Row.
51 Cf. Žižek, Slavoj. 2018. *The Courage of Hopelessness: A Year of Acting Dangerously*, Brooklyn (NY)/London: Melville House.
52 Cf. Brassier, Ray. 2007 *Nihil Unbound. Enlightment and Extintion*, London: Pallgrave Mcmillan. "Watching at nihilism right in its face" was Heidegger's radical project. Cf. Galimberti, Umberto. 2020. *Heidegger e il nuovo inizio. Il pensiero al tramonto dell'occidente*, Milano: Feltrinelli.
53 The complexity of this relation has been deeply explored by Walter Benjamin in 1921. Cf. Benjamin, Walter. 2021. *Toward the Critique of Violence: A Critical Edition*, Redwood City, CA: Stanford University Press. Emanuele Severino, Giorgio Agamben and Umberto Galimberti rely on this radical reflection on the origin of violence that is rooted on the relation between means and ends.
54 There are many uncertainties about the proper verbal expression to be used in this sentence. Originally it was formulated as "Architecture is the art to a-void building", making reference to George Perec's notion of the lipogram in his novel *A Void*, as in the English translation of 1995 (originally titled *La disparition*, 1969). Equally challenging is to think that architecture is the art to defer, to delay, to procrastinate, to bond or even to tether (as Talia Tranin has suggested), or to deter and strip-bare building. This is the compound of meanings to be evoked.

# 7 The Theory Nobody Knows

*Penelope Dean*

## The Theory Nobody Knows

It is no surprise that pronouncements of the end of theory coincided with the rise of the business model.[1] As a previous generation of theorists distanced themselves from corporate culture, "priding themselves," as management consultant Peter Drucker put it in another context, "on being above such sordid considerations as the bottom line," another cohort of aspiring theorists conversely turned to business protocols—management, innovation, versioning, to name a few—to swerve theory out of academic introspection into engaged application. This simultaneous rejection and embrace of business, a response to its escalating reach during the 1990s, relied on the assumption that design and business were somehow distinguishable, and that theory's role was to either maintain distance or get out of the way. What neither side foresaw was that theory would become inconceivable outside enterprise as theorists absorbed the protocols—sometimes consciously, sometimes naively, sometimes inadvertently—and recognized theory as a mirror of market culture. Theory could no more resist business than it could be coopted by it since contemporary theory had been a nascent form of post-90s new market thinking all along. In other words, the *rise* of theory was as indebted to business culture as was its end.

As a global import, theory was always plural, a generic brand for a diverse product line: German critical, French post-structural, Italian tragic, as well as psychoanalytic, feminist, and even pragmatist. Today theory extends that diversity in forms that are outwardly focused, iterative, and difficult to categorize. These contemporary forms, which erupt with the frequency of new products in a marketplace, drown out "high theory," diminishing its intensity to a feeble state largely for an audience worn down by attrition or overcome by the demand for personalized positions. They exhibit all the hallmarks of what *Wired* editor, Chris Andersen, called the "long tail" in music culture: in the wake of a small number of "hits," [i.e., high theory] a plethora of less popular songs [i.e., et al theory] will eventually add up "to a market as big as, if not bigger than, the hits themselves."[2] And while they might aim to produce differences out of pre-existing conventions and reform disciplinary concepts,[3] they are often driven by ulterior motives to advance new research

DOI: 10.4324/9781003292999-8

niches, identities, and careers. From "difference as construct" to "diversity as fact," theory is no longer what, and where, it used to be.[4]

If we understand theory's role "to produce concepts by which architecture is related to other spheres of social practice,"[5] it was never just any kind of practice. Architecture theory has always had a privileged relationship with science and/or art, which serve as its primary analogues. In either case, business is cast as the adversary. Theory's polythic identity has been accounted for through the disciplinary frameworks of science, which recast architecture theory as a field of speciation and extinctions, based on an evolutionary model,[6] or art history, which rely on the aesthetic paradigms of critical theory. Theory might be falling apart, but the other disciplines will hold it together. Lodging theory anywhere *but* in a business framework, most theorists failed to entertain theory itself as an instigator of business values that permeated everywhere—nichefication, innovation, instrumentalization. Even as theory's goal posts moved with the market context it helped inaugurate and preview, theorists upheld their assumptions about business rather than challenge them. Theorists would turn theory's success into a kind of failure. Indeed, their careers depended on its failure.

## Strategy (from What to How)

When a select group of theorists and designers embraced business thinking in the late-1990s, the point was to launch an oppositional discourse against high theory itself, while justifying new digital forms and design processes. Two antagonists of the establishment—in particular, Patrik Schumacher, enthusiast of managerial choice theory, and Michael Speaks, avid reader of *Harvard Business Review*[7]—turned to contemporary business literature to re-direct architectural design toward practicality and the new economy, repositioning architecture as a research business rather than a medium of artistic expression. Such turns toward instrumentality were endorsed as evidence of architecture's neo-pragmatist turn while at the same time being dismissed as "post-critical" and "anti-theory."[8] Yet it is too simple and too generous to conclude that the polemics of a few business enthusiasts were to blame for architecture theory's devolution into instrumentality and opportunism.

Almost two decades earlier, in 1983, literary critic Terry Eagleton had already observed that literary theory was motivated first by "what we want to *do*," and second by "seeing which methods and theories will help us achieve these ends."[9] At the same time, "these methods have nothing whatsoever of significance in common. In fact, they have more in common with other 'disciplines' [...] than they have with each other."[10] Like a good business model, literary theory was *strategic*[11]: "what you choose and reject theoretically, then, depends upon what you are practically trying to do."[12] As a method, theory was always instrumental, which is in turn what enabled it to serially cross the frontiers of various disciplines. The desire for instrumentality did not abate when literary theory evidenced further fragmentation in the mid-2000s, it just became more businesslike in its aspirations: "Theory is widely considered a toolbox of flexible, useful, and contingent devices, judged for their productivity and innovation."[13] After two decades, high-theory was fully recognized as "hands-on theory."[14]

It is a useful hypothetical to suggest that it was not a specific problem "in architecture" that initially motivated a theoretical shift toward business, but rather architecture's larger identification with an escalating business culture that drove some theorists to the emerging technologies and platforms of the new economy. As in literary theory, architecture theory was looking for usefulness, albeit on different terms. If high literary theory disintegrated because it wasn't political enough, high architecture theory declined because it was perceived as being out of touch with contemporary practice. Of course, some would maintain that theory was neither a method (as in a design technique for generating form), nor a procedure for delivering form to interpretation (as in criticism and historiography),[15] but the reality was that theory was generally becoming looser and even un-nameable, commingling with history and practice as protagonists turned their attention toward relevance.[16] If Speaks and Schumacher privileged form-making methods, deploying design's "how" as a counter-argument to theory's "what,"[17] the next generation of theorists, historians, and practitioners did what generations which follow after usually do: they catalogued the original ideas, criticized them, and then unwittingly (or cynically) appropriated and repackaged them.

## Identity (from Horizon to Hole)

A proliferation of niches followed theory's shift from what to how, breaking down theory's role as an intellectual horizon into discursive holes. An earlier effect of theory had been to diversify modes of practice. But as theory itself became an institutionalized form of practice, the tendency to diversify also multiplied the forms of theory. The pluralization of categories within new specialized areas of practice ranging from the environmental to digital design, for example, unfolded cascades of theoretical subdivisions. Sustainable architecture partitioned into bio-climatic design, bio-mimicry, climate design, ecological architecture, ecological urbanism, and landscape urbanism, while digital design split into blobs, surfaces, animation, parametric, responsive, and interactive environments. Such niche-theories—which inevitably shared fewer conventional, visual, or material datums—sustained and reinforced theory's segmentation, but with uneven intensity. One theory's niche was another's all-consuming background.

It was not just that theorists created new products (historians and practitioners were, and still are, doing that too), but the manner in which their efforts played out were along lines of identity—the other great marker of Neoliberalism. New niches aligned with personal education and personal values. Some theorists turned to art history to historicize contemporary architecture's formal developments (Lavin, Vidler), while others relied on scientific models (Kipnis, Kwinter).

Some continued in the vein of critical theory, exposing the architecture of the new political economy of finance and big business (Hays, Foster), while others took the opposite direction, equating expanding practice with populism and design (Allen, Somol). Still others turned to personal biography to make sense of it all (Zaera-Polo). Personal identity drove the new theoretical specializations with their own brands. The paradox was that when niche-theorists spouted aversions to business culture, on the one hand, their production of "differences" in an already diversified landscape accelerated the emulation of market culture, on the other. In the end, theory's nichefication effected a counter-reversal, sending theory back into the world as an *imitation of that world.* Theory's "long tail" was, ironically, the result of a deregulation from within.

Of course, some tried to regulate the mess with totalizing meta-arguments, whether by articulating formal theories of resemblance among design practices or categorizing design concepts through systems of oppositions.[18] But the extent to which any unifying concept could be imposed was dubious, as was the assumption that theory's audience was somehow homogeneous. After all, as Chris Andersen said, "niche products are, by definition, not for everyone."[19] The situation exposed yet another problematic for architecture theory: namely, that theory had become more local, idiosyncratic, and averse to the totalizing overview. Theory was defined by inconsistencies instead of consistencies, by a plethora of choices rather than received obligations. The state of affairs also revealed that architectural culture was confronting (and developing a means of) *choice* within and against the context of an emerging design-business complex. Niche theories allowed one to *choose* one's theory, customizing it on an individual rather than a collective basis. The launch of new theories multiplied the opportunities for more theories (and more choices).

## Iteration (from Opposition to Positioning)

At the same time, nichefied theory was risk averse. However embarrassing and distasteful architecture's 1990s business turn was to North America's East Coast academic establishment, it was, nevertheless, a theoretical position conceived in opposition. But with the arrival of digital technologies, and all the versioning that business demanded, oppositional strategies were inadvertently supplanted by positioning tactics. If earlier versions of theory were defined and debated through theoretical pairings or opposing categories (rationalist versus historicist, critical versus post-critical etc.),[20] subsequent versions were not really contra or against anything, but rather conceptualized relationally: instead of focusing on architecture's larger horizon, one "positioned" a theory relative to other theories.[21] Positioning provided a roadmap for theories to stand out from one another. Positioning staged connections and associations. And as in advertising, positioning sought to find theory a specialized niche. It delivered a hole inside the whole, but not an overview of the whole.

Positioning worked because theory had become iterative, usually by upgrading an existing idea with something new, something added, and something different. Sometimes iteration deepened an existing idea. Other times it deviated from a prevailing theory to articulate a new one (e.g., bio-mimicry into geo-mimicry; landscape urbanism into landform building). Occasionally, it did not provide a new theory, but rebranded an existing one. Intermittently, it didn't amount to anything at all.[22] This versioning of theory like a product in development, worked incrementally. It indexed degrees of digression and approximation. It was contingent on what already existed. It suggested there was little to rail against. The point was not to challenge something but, as Eagleton put it in another context, "to secure one's cultural niche within it."[23] Iteration offered security via association.

As a result, and compounded by the eclipse of old discursive sites (edited magazines, journals, and conferences) with new ones (self-authored online blogs, exhibition culture/biennials), theory became smaller and non-confrontational. It focused on narrow problems, and particular applications. It was piecemeal and contextual. This too followed developments in literary theory. As Claire Colebrook put it:

> Whereas theory might be approached beginning from estrangement and distance, considering a world that is not ourselves and a force that cannot be returned to the human, theory is moving precisely in the opposite direction to being nothing more than the expression of praxis, nothing more than relations of recognition.[24]

In corollary, iterative theory embraced collaboration and conversation, rather than "conflict or opposition." An osmosis of administrative values neutralized theory, replacing its purpose or mission with simple activity. Like the process of governance, iteration was procedural.

## Self-Explication (from Inside to Outside)

According to art historian Boris Groys, theory is central to art today because "artists need theory to explain what they are doing—not to others—but to themselves."[25] He attributes the importance of theory in helping "explain to myself what I am already doing" to the explosion of new traditions that have made art's traditional role as a form of protest directed against the work of previous generations, difficult to articulate. In the absence of oppositions, artists first need to figure out what art is, and then fathom what they are supposed to do.[26] Groys's argument is that theory offers a way to get inside one's own head (perhaps less theory than self-help). It orients inward and outward: first toward self-formation and then externally, to position work in the world.

Needless to say, theory as self-explication will continue to have its moment. And not just in art. In English, for example, it found release in the genre of auto-theory—a first person mixing of theory, philosophy and autobiography derived from Feminist practices—aimed at transgressing disciplinary boundaries. And in architecture, it manifests as the end point of theory's trajectory from what to how to *why*, reterritorializing in the lived self and telling stories about the structures of an office or collaborative design process.[27] Self-explication is symptomatic of the fact that the audience for theory has changed. The arrival of the internet and social media brought new ways to find information online and readers of theory may not be the establishment. Individuals, like consumers, in general, are less interested in "hits" than they are in finding groups ("practices") bound together by affinity and shared interests.

K. Michael Hays had seen it coming in 1998:

> It may well turn out that a different, younger audience, whose relation to consumption is altogether altered, whose memories may not include any notions of resistance or negation, may have to produce another kind of theory premised on neither the concept of reification nor the apparatus of the sign, both of which have their ultimate referent in the vexatious territory of reproducibility and commodity consumption.[28]

Although self-explication was probably not the alternative he had in mind. Theory's new emphasis served unlikely purposes. Assimilating mainstream business agendas and values (e.g., sustainability, resilience, collaboration etc.), theory provided bait for a bigger audience, demonstrated "relevance," self-enlightened, and aided selection into international exhibitions and biennales. But above all it was instrumental in an entirely new way: not for design but for marketing. Theory was a technique of public relations where applicability was understood no longer in terms of theory's critical relation to praxis, but simply as a form of promotion; a justification for the sensible and politically correct.

## Best Practices? (from Prospective to Ex Post Facto)

In recent years, theories of theory have attempted to produce consciousness out of something one did, rather than orienting toward a future that does not exist. Theory has shifted from being a prospective activity to one that is ex post facto. In parallel, architectural history has also taken up the mantel of data, business models, administration, management, and accountancy, as well as office structures and organizations. Contrary to being opposed to business, the discipline is largely in tune with it. As the migration of other business terms, such as collaboration, were used to theorize notions of "care," they reinforced Neoliberalism by advocating for best practices rather than uncertain projects. While historians missed the slide of their own critiques into metrics (more acquiescent to neo-liberal culture than resistant to it), their anxiety surrounding authorship led to "the displacement of big names for big data."[29] All of which is to confirm Wendy Brown's observation that every aspect of culture—architectural history included—is remade through business values, practices and metrics "even when these spheres are not directly monetized."[30]

Significantly launched in the professional-journalistic pages of *Architect* magazine (rather than in the traditional venues of "high theory"), the 2013 "debate" over the status of theory between Ned Cramer and Aaron Betsky serves as an example of architectural cultures shared consensus over the business reality and equal blindness to the realities of theory.[31] For Cramer, his hope for the "death" of theory led to a new focus on environmental resources and getting things built, to a welcome turn to "Greenbuild, TED talks, and Clinton Global Initiatives conferences." That is to business as usual. For Betsky, the dormant state of theory was rather a problem for conserving resources and "devising better strategies," and needed to be invigorated so that "practical considerations in an immediate situation" could be properly addressed. Both sides advocate for the same measurable "green" end, and simply disagree over theory's usefulness in bringing about that reality. What neither Cramer nor Betsky understood was that theory was fully precursor to, and constitutive of the new business model. It could neither impede it nor improve it, it *was* it. Theory had become a post facto enterprise of assessing best practices rather than calling for new ones.

## Epilogue: The Theorist Today

In his 1925 book, *The Man Nobody Knows*, Bruce Barton lays out an account of Jesus as the world's greatest business executive: "He picked up twelve men from the bottom ranks of business and forged them into an organization that conquered the world."[32] As it turns out, since the 1960s it has been the figure of the theorist who emerged as the great entrepreneur: innovating, branding, and positioning concepts and ideas. Less savior than salesperson, the theorist today has compelled us to finally confront the theory that nobody knows.

It is time to end the pretense that architectural theory is (should be or can be) immune to business values. Neoliberal protocols—the positioning, marketing, advertising, public relations, and branding—considered distasteful to many (but not all) architects, theorists, historians, and critics have played a central role in shaping architectural theory, often supplanting the evaluative criteria of architecture regardless of whether the work under consideration is condemned or celebrated. Moreover, the "toolbox" of advanced theory was always an ideological trial run for the new economy that would realize its advances. Because theory is strategic, traffics in identity, iterates, aids self-explication, and catalogues best practices, it is indissociably bound up with the ideological values of business. It is not a matter of lamenting that this is so—of blaming architecture theory for complicity with business or sequestering it away from contamination—but figuring out how to propose ways forward that neither replicate the status quo nor fear to engage it. There is no point in denying that we know theory, whether three times or more; we are all its disciples, and none more so than those who continue to loudly deny the business model that suffuses it and that they secretly indulge.

The author thanks John McMorrough and R. E. Somol for their instructive comments on an earlier draft of this essay.

## Notes

1 For a discussion of the relation between business model and architectural culture see my essay, Cynthia Davidson, ed., "Business, Actually," *Log 50: Model Behavior* (New York: Any Corporation, Winter 2021): 249–255.
2 Chris Anderson, *The Long Tail*, 2nd ed. (New York: Hyperion, 2008): 8.
3 This specific formulation of theory is indebted to K. Michael Hays's work, in particular K. Michael Hays, "Architecture by Numbers," *Praxis* 7 (2005): 90.
4 For an account of these two forms of difference making, see R. E. Somol, "Easier Done Than Said," *Flat Out* 1 (Fall 2016): 68.
5 K. Michael Hays's "Introduction," in *Architecture Theory since 1968*, K. Michael Hays, ed. (Cambridge, MA and London: The MIT Press, 1998): xii.
6 John McMorrough, "Architecture or Evolution: The Recent (and Not so Recent) Speciation of the Discipline," unpublished LeFevre Fellows lecture, 2008.
7 See, for example, Patrik Schumacher, "Business Research Architecture," *Daidalos: The Need of Research* 69/70 (December 1998/January 1999): 34–43 and Michael Speaks, "Tales from the Avant-Garde: How the New Economy Is Transforming Theory and Practice," *Architectural Record* vol. 188, no. 12 (December, 2000): 74–77.
8 See, for example, K. Michael Hays and Alicia Kennedy, "After All, or the End of 'the End of'," *Assemblage* 41 (2000): 6 and Joan Ockman, ed., *The Pragmatist Imagination: Thinking about "Things in the Making"* (Princeton, NJ: Princeton Architectural Press, 2000).
9 Terry Eagleton, *Literary Theory, An Introduction* (Minneapolis: University of Minnesota Press, 1983): 210.
10 Ibid., 197.
11 Ibid., 210.
12 Ibid., 211.
13 Vincent B. Leitch, quoted in Jennifer Howard, "The Fragmentation of Literary Theory," *Chronicle of Higher Education* 52(17) (2005): A12–A16.
14 Jennifer Howard, "The Fragmentation of Literary Theory," *Chronicle of Higher Education*, 52(17) (2005): A12–A16.
15 Hays, "Architecture by Numbers."
16 According to Sarah Whiting, theory acquired such a bad name that some preferred not refer to it. See Sarah Whiting and Florencia Rodriguez, "Let's Try to be Relevant," *Harvard Design Magazine No. 48 America* (S/S 2021), harvard designmagazine.org/issues/48/lets-try-to-be-relevant. Accessed 04.06.2021.
17 The question Stan Allen among others would ask, for example, was not what architecture was, but what it could do.
18 See, for example, Andrew Holder and K Michael Hays's attempts to classify recent architectural practices for *Inscriptions: Architecture before Speech* (Druker Design Gallery, January 22–March 11, 2018), https://www.gsd.harvard.edu/event/k-michael-hays-and-andrew-holder-exhibition-lecture-inscriptions/.
19 Anderson, *The Long Tail*, 118.
20 Hays, *Architecture Theory since 1968*, x.
21 Somol, "Easier Done Than Said," 66.
22 On theory as a crutch, see John McMorrough, ""*I Like Complexity and Contradiction in Architecture*." Me Too…I Think. At Least I Used to, but Now I'm Not so Sure Anymore," *Paprika!* (September 28, 2017), https://yalepaprika.

com/folds/post-ironic/i-like-complexity-and-contradiction-in-architecture-me-too-i-think-at-least-i-used-to-but-now-im-not-so-sure-anymore.

23 Terry Eagleton, *After Theory* (New York: Basic Books, 2003): 47.

24 Claire Colebrook, "The Death of the Post Human: Essays on Extinction, Volume One" (Open Humanities Press, 2014. https://quod.lib.umich.edu/o/ohp/12329362.0001.001/1:3/--death-of-the-posthuman-essays-on-extinction-volume-one?rgn=div1;view=fulltext. Accessed 07.04.2021.

25 Boris Groys, *In the Flow* (London and New York: Verso, 2016): 24.

26 Ibid.

27 For an interesting discussion of architectural work in relation to subject values, see Walter Benn Michaels in conversation with Sebastián López Cardozo, "Unint erested/Unequal/Understood: Architecture's Class aesthetic," *PLAT 9.0 Commit* (2020): 8–15. See also Claire Colebrook, "The Death of the Post Human: Essays on Extinction, Volume One" (Open Humanities Press, 2014), https://quod.lib.umich.edu/o/ohp/12329362.0001.001/1:3/--death-of-the-posthuman-essays-on-extinction-volume-one?rgn=div1;view=fulltext, Accessed 07.04.2021.

28 Hays, *Architecture Theory since 1968*, xiv.

29 R. E. Somol, "That Sinking Feeling," *Flat Out* 2 (Spring 2017): 9.

30 Wendy Brown, *Undoing Demos* (New York: Zone Books, 2015): 10.

31 See, for example, Ned Cramer, "Dialogue: The Silly and the Profound," Architect, October 11, 2013. https://www.architectmagazine.com/design/editorial/-dialogue-the-silly-and-the-profound_o and Aaron Betsky, "Architectural Theory and American Pragmatism," Architect, November 15, 2013, https://www.architectmagazine.com/design/architectural-theory-and-american-pragmatism_o, Accessed 04.04.2021.

32 Bruce Barton, *The Man Nobody Knows* (Chicago, IL: Ivan R. Dee, 2000) 4. Originally published: Indianapolis, IN: Bobbs-Merrill, 1925.

# 8 Theorizing a Modern Tradition[1]

*Macarena de la Vega de León*

## Writing History Since 1970

William J.R. Curtis's *Modern Architecture Since 1900* (1982) lies in a transitional period in the history of modern architecture: between the establishment of research degrees in North American schools in the 1970s, which scholars have considered to be behind the professionalization of architectural history; and the consolidation of the discipline as the subject matter of historiographical research in the 1990s. In 1989, Edward W. Soja talked about an "epochal transition in both critical thought and material life," since the 1970s to the late 1980s.[2] Mark Jarzombek has pointed out the importance of remembering that "until the 1970s modern architecture did not have a dedicated scholarly 'history,' and how, as a proper historical field, it looked exclusively into the nineteenth and twentieth centuries."[3]

This development of the history of architecture coincided with a theoretical reassessment of modern architecture, at a time when, according to Mary McLeod, the deteriorated economic situation "not only permitted theoretical speculation, but also further fueled perceptions of the architect's diminished social role."[4] From the early 1970s, and due to a world recession, there was an increase in the production of theory, a process that faded out in the 1990s; at this time, these takes on theory started to be historicized in several anthologies, inaugurated by Hanno-Walter Kruft's *Geschichte der Architekturtheorie* (1985).[5] Jarzombek argued that, rather than signifying an abandonment of modernism in favor of a postmodernist restructuring of architecture, the expansion and intensification of the history-theory discourse between the 1970s and 1990s "served to bring modern architecture up to speed with its own critical modernity, allowing for a fuller exploration of issues relating to context, gender, and politics," not only in the practice, but also in the teaching of architecture.[6]

Between the late 1970s and early 1990s, architectural historians played a critical role in defining and transforming the priorities, not only of the writing of history, but also of the practice of architecture, and Curtis was one of those historians. He worked on the first edition as a postgraduate researcher in North America in the late 1970s and already traveling around the

DOI: 10.4324/9781003292999-9

world, which continued while he prepared the fully revised and rewritten third edition of the book. *Modern Architecture Since 1900* is exemplary of, and contemporary to, these developments. In the transitional period between the 1970s and 1990s, one of the "tremendous" disciplinary changes in the history of architecture was how "publishing houses have defined a rapidly growing readership of art and architecture books."[7] According to Esra Ackan, resulting surveys of modern architecture written in the 1980s

> offered a more diverse view of modern architecture, a richer heterotopia of trajectories, which run parallel or converge, overlap or diverge, follow out-of-sync courses or have different durations. Even though surveys of the 1980s mostly highlighted white male architects, they questioned the previously established history as the one single story of Western progress.[8]

*Modern Architecture Since 1900* was the result of a commission from Phaidon Press to Curtis in 1978 to write a general book on the history of modern architecture. The starting point was a letter from the publishing house which he received the day he handed in the grades of his course 'Architecture of the Twentieth Century.' In his own words: "It was too good to be true and I accepted."[9]

> In many ways, the skeleton was established then. I wrote the outline of the book and a trial chapter on Le Corbusier in the 1920s for them in Summer 1979 when I was in London. The contract was signed, and the first draft was handwritten between January and September 1980, then the second draft between September 1980 and Spring 1981, also by hand and later on transcribed.[10]

Curtis used research material he had collected for his own teaching practice and during his trips throughout the world. Some of the main ideas of the book were first formulated in earlier monographs and articles, and in subsequent broader outlines and essays. The aim was to present a "balanced, readable overall view of the development of modern architecture in other parts of the world from its beginnings until the recent past," emphasizing that "the stress of this book is less on the theoretical roots of modern architecture than on its emergence and ensuing development."[11] For him, previous historians had neglected the later phases of modern architecture, especially since the 1960s and around 1970. Curtis wrote the preface to the second edition of *Modern Architecture Since 1900* (1987), mostly unchanged except for an addendum on recent world architecture, from Ahmedabad, the sixth largest city in India. He was there writing a book on the Indian architect Balkrishna V. Doshi, which was published the following year.[12] Curtis claimed to have fought against "the drift of critical opinion then current, avoiding the usual, but misleading postures concerning 'modernism' and 'postmodernism.'"[13] The third and definitive edition (1996) was the result of an examination which started in late 1993. The revision process proved the book to be, according to Curtis, an evolving project, a working hypothesis, which must be tested, reordered, and refined.[14] The process of the conception, writing and revising of *Modern Architecture Since 1900* made an interesting study.[15]

Apart from the aim of integrating new knowledge and completing the mapping of the later decades of the twentieth century, in preparing the third edition of the book, Curtis was driven by his rejection of contemporary 'fashions' or trends. For Curtis, the "transition from first to second and above all third editions of *Modern Architecture Since 1900* was in part propelled by a refusal to accept the dominant fashions whether postmodernism, deconstructivism, etc."[16] Curtis understood the book to be "a historical bridge [which] might be built across the stream of passing intellectual fashions to a more solid philosophical ground, partly with the hope that this might encourage a return to basic principles."[17] At least in the Anglophone world, there is a lack of acknowledgment of the changes Curtis introduced to the third edition of the book, and, therefore, a lack of assessment of its relevance. The global impact of the book on architectural education, both in terms of its dissemination and early translation into other languages,[18] seems to have prevented it from being considered worthy of study as a scholarly contribution to the historiography of modern architecture. Drawing on direct communication with Curtis, his insights, and archival material, this essay reflects on a manner of writing histories of architecture built on a periodization which resonates with contemporary discourse.

## Mapping Architecture of the Late Twentieth Century

*Modern Architecture Since 1900* was meant to be titled *Modern Architecture, 1900–1975.* Evidence of this is in a letter written on August 28, 1981 by James S. Ackerman, in which he shares with Simon Haviland, director of Phaidon Press at the time, his positive reactions to Curtis's manuscript.[19] However, the definitive *Modern Architecture Since 1900* is a title that not only allows the revision and update of the content, but also relates to Curtis's understanding of modern architecture and its narrative. As Peter L. Laurence pointed out, "the very title of William J.R. Curtis's *Modern Architecture Since 1900* emphasized the continuity of modern architecture into the present."[20] The title allowed for the inclusion of architecture of the late twentieth century, and Curtis did so by investigating what for him were two sides of the same coin: regionalism and postmodernism. His polemical writing on postmodern classicism and on regionalism, compounded by his travels in Asia, Latin America and the Middle East, and individual studies on architects, accompanied the transition from the first to the third edition of the book.[21]

In his writing, Curtis attempted to shed some light on the notion of regionalism and defined an authentic regionalism in terms of a certain balance between, or hybrids of, struggling realities: urban and rural, industrial and artisan, the 'uprootedness of the metropolis' and peasant values, modernity and tradition, imported international and indigenous, transient and immutable. An architect who wanted to produce an authentic regionalist work of architecture, according to Curtis, acknowledged these dichotomies and understood the new conditions of universal interchange and interdependence characteristic of the Western world in the 1980s. He claimed that there was more than one way to read local tradition, but regionalists attempt to see the type, the general rule, the originating principle. It is through his notion of 'authentic' regionalism, blending old and new, that Curtis shifted from seeing the architecture of non-Western countries as a source of inspiration to seeing it as part of a modern tradition. As the term 'tradition' is used by Curtis to refer to both the regional and the international, in a way the dichotomy between tradition and modernity disappears. Instead of opposing modernity and tradition, the local, national, and international, he advocated for a balance that incorporated the best of each, and understood the ways they transform each other while reinvigorating tradition and 'regionalizing' the modern. Curtis located the authentic regionalists in the Middle East, Africa, and some parts of Asia, in countries which he visited and architects who he met, that other historians neglected. He criticized the trend of thought which opposed the two notions, claiming that "the best within modernism can be profoundly rooted in tradition; and the best in tradition is to do with a dynamic process of rethinking certain central kernel ideas."[22] These 'kernel ideas' are, for Curtis, architectural principles that refer to a Western value system, rather than a political or ideological one.

A certain balance, rather than dichotomy, opposition, or resistance, between the old and the new, between innovation and tradition, between regional and universal, would summarize Curtis's understanding of regionalism since 1900. In the third edition, he recognized the confusion about what constitutes a region at a time already characterized by a "worldwide standardization of products, images, fashions and ideas on the one hand, and by an even greater pluralism of identities, factions, confederations and territorial allegiances on the other."[23] For him, some of the best examples of architecture of the 1980s appeared unaffiliated with "the cliques in charge of media and schools" of architecture and "the babble of their discourse," and in developing countries or in parts peripheral of and remote from the European and American industrialized world.[24] Curtis claimed to have cast a wide net, with which he balanced the Third World with the First -terms replaced in the third edition for developing and developed countries respectively. In addition, he balanced in his narrative examples from places as diverse as Spain and India, Finland and Australia, France and Mexico, the United States, the Middle East, and Japan. Although it has proven to be just as problematic a notion, Curtis preferred 'universalism' to 'regionalism,' which, misused in the 1980s, in his opinion resulted not only in kitsch imitations of the vernacular in the European context, but also in the death of most authentic vernaculars while "the rest were under threat of extinction."[25] Curtis recalled realizing that regionalism risked becoming a "lazy shorthand for a much more complex phenomenon concerning the realities and myths of nations."[26]

In the introduction to *Critical Regionalism: Architecture and Identity in a Globalised World* (2003), Alexander Tzonis agreed with Curtis on the misuse of the notion of regionalism, reporting that regionalism as he and Liane Lefaivre formulated it in the 1980s, to indicate "an approach to design giving priority to the identity of the particular rather than to universal dogmas," had been misrepresented.[27] Tzonis recollected how regionalism was meant to be an alternative not only to postmodernism, but also to the modernism/postmodernism debate, which had been widely criticized by Curtis. Tzonis argued that the critical regionalist approach to design of the twenty-first century aims "to rethink architecture through the concept of region," and "recognizes the value of the singular, circumscribes projects within the physical, social and cultural constraints of the particular, aiming at sustaining diversity while benefiting from universality."[28] So, even if Tzonis reframed regionalism in terms of "unresolved conflict between globalization and diversity," confrontation and opposition "between international intervention and identity," he too saw the benefits of universalism. Rather than prioritizing conflict and opposition, or identity over universalism, Curtis, writing around 1992–1993, described the architecture of the time as one which balanced or oscillated "between the unique and the typical," characterized by diversity from both an intellectual and a geographical point of view.[29] In her own introductory text, Lefaivre presented Mumford's reformulation of regionalism, and pointed out that "with Mumford, regionalism becomes a constant process of negotiation between the local and the global on the many different issues that traditionally made up regionalism."[30] According to Lefaivre, Mumford considered regionalism not as resistance, as later would Kenneth Frampton, but as an "engagement with the global, universalizing world rather," a position similar to the one articulated by Curtis.[31]

In *Architectural Regionalism: Collected Writings on Place, Identity, Modernity, and Tradition* (2007), Vincent B. Canizaro commended Curtis's *Modern Architecture Since 1900* and the aforementioned 2003 essay by Lefaivre for an "excellent account of the history of regionalism."[32] Canizaro included in the introduction to his book one epigraph on authenticity and another on the modernism/postmodernism debate. For him, authenticity measured our connection to things and places, an interesting idea that could be applied to Curtis's own understanding of the notion, as what measured his own connection to the architecture he experienced.[33] With regard to the dialectic between tradition and modernity, Canizaro affirmed that regionalism lies at the center of it, helping to achieve a certain balance, "between the necessary cultural continuity and the desire for progress and innovation."[34] Although Curtis's writings are not included in any of these reassessments of regionalism, the positions defended by the editors resonate with what Curtis had been advocating since the 1980s.

Moving on to Curtis's critique of postmodernism, it began in polemical lectures given at Harvard in 1979 and 1980, and then "emerged in a string of articles," where he made the distinction between superficial transfers of the past and deeper transformations.[35] Written in the intervening years between the first and third editions of *Modern Architecture Since 1900*, this string of articles used a more polemical language than the book. For example, Curtis wrote:

> The architectural present – or that version portrayed by magazines and university pundits – is bedeviled by numerous ills: a bland technocracy; disregard for human meanings in architecture; a narcissistic preoccupation with architectural language as an internal system; a superficial concern with past motifs rather than past principles.[36]

It is precisely this dichotomy between a superficial or a deep understanding of the past that shaped his discussion of the uselessness of the modernism/postmodernism debate and his proposal of authenticity and monumentality as an antidote. Curtis proposed authenticity as the focus of the analysis of the architecture of the 1980s. For him, "the search for probity, the blend of old and new, the search for a lasting symbolic interpretation of the social sphere,"[37] not only applied to modern architecture in developing countries, but also in countries where the Western architectural canon had originated. Moreover, it applied to architecture throughout the twentieth century, because, for Curtis, architectural quality has no ideological, temporal, or territorial frontiers.[38]

In the case of postmodernism, Curtis's approach can be characterized as the confirmation of an intuition. Writing the introduction to the first edition of *Modern Architecture Since 1900* in 1981, Curtis doubted whether postmodernist questioning, and rejection of modernism was a sign of the collapse of modern architecture or just another crisis toward its consolidation. As early as 1979, Joseph Rykwert was already criticizing postmodernism as an alternate modernist architecture, and "a diversion, from the serious business of reconsidering the architect's task."[39] Curtis framed his own critique of postmodernism in similar terms, as a wake-up call for architects to rethink their role, and, in the 1996 edition, declared that postmodernism was "ephemeral," just a new reexamination of certain core ideas of modern architecture, articulating a certain continuity.[40]

Writing in 1996, the landscape architect Tom Turner saw "signs of post-postmodern life, in urban design, architecture and elsewhere."[41] However, more recently, in 2007, N. Katherine Hayles and Todd Gannon claimed that "postmodernism died" in 1995 due to expansion of the Internet's global accessibility.[42] Peter Osborne has declared the category of postmodernism "well and truly buried,"[43] after having referred to it as an "episode" which enlivened theoretical debates between 1979 and 1999, and an "illusion" that dissipated.[44] It is interesting to note that the period of time established by Osborne as the 'episode' of postmodernism also corresponds to the timeline of the writing of *Modern Architecture Since 1900*, and the aforementioned transitional period in the discipline. Building on these contributions, Nathan

Brown attempted to formulate a new periodization or the late twentieth century that resonated with Curtis's defense of a certain continuity within modern architecture in the twentieth century.[45]

In her analysis of *Hans Hollein and Postmodernism* (2017), Eva Branscome argues that "postmodernism today has become a part of the past."[46] Branscome agrees with Curtis that "even from its beginning, postmodernism echoed the notions of 'style' already present in modernism," and that by the 1980s postmodernism had ossified into a style devoid of its original complexity and meaning.[47] As was the case with regionalism, she argues that postmodernism had lost its original complexity and meaning. Branscome pointed out that postmodernism is being reassessed not only by way of books such as the one by Jorge Otero-Pailos, but also through conference panels organized by the European Architectural History Network and the Society of Architectural Historians in the United States, and I would add, in Australia and New Zealand and Great Britain. What Branscome refers to as a "hybrid view" supported by recent historiography defends the idea that "many typical features of postmodernism were in fact already present in the modernism of the 1950s, and some features have even been suggested to go back as far as the 1920s" – something that Curtis had already pointed out over 20 years ago, in his 1980s writings and in the third edition of *Modern Architecture Since 1900*.[48] For him, "the reality of architectural production in the 1980s and 1990s had more to do with evolution and reassessment than with revolution and radical breaks."[49]

While some argue that postmodernism lost its criticality around 1995, partly due to the emergence of the global, regionalism is still relevant to the study of the present, at least for Tzonis, precisely because of the "ubiquitous conflict in all fields – including architecture – between globalization and international intervention, on the one hand, and local identity and the desire for ethnic insularity, on the other."[50] Both regionalism and postmodernism are being rethought today in the light of postcolonial theories and the global turn in architecture, and of new periodizations of architecture in the twentieth century. Regionalism and postmodernism are two sides of the coin which Curtis used since the late 1970s to map what at the time was the recent past and to articulate his view of architecture since 1900 as a modern tradition. This essay demonstrates that Curtis's critical insight anticipated what today are established and accepted positions, even if his work is not widely acknowledged or cited.

## Rejecting (the Abuse of) Theory

Praised by most reviewers of the book, Curtis's mapping of the late twentieth century is also characterized by his alleged rejection of the use of labels in classifying the pluralism of approaches to architecture, and his rejection, too, of the excess of theory in the writing of history. In the introduction to the third edition of *Modern Architecture Since 1900*, Curtis wrote that his work "avoids standard critical postures and largely fictional 'movements' and tries to single out buildings and tendencies of lasting value."[51] In his opinion, if relying too much on '-isms,' made it difficult to distinguish between "durable creations and weaker relatives."[52] Instead, he argued for architects to find a balance between innovation and the social significance of buildings.

On the occasion of the presentation of the Spanish translation of the third edition of *Modern Architecture Since 1900*, Curtis reflected on the relationship between theory and the writing of history.[53] In his opinion, "the historian who identifies with the interests of a single school or clique, sacrifices the possibility of a balanced view," and the result becomes "second rate."[54] If the historian is to achieve the aim of penetrating the complexity of the past and explaining it intelligibly, what Curtis refers to as 'obscurantism,' 'false theorizing,' or jargon plays no part.[55] Although Curtis acknowledged the need for theoretical frameworks, historical thinking and the understanding of architecture itself are, for him, the keys to the writing of history.[56] Curtis claimed that his work cannot be linked to any particular ideology or school of thought; at least he did not advertise them as openly.

Most reviewers of the book dismissed Curtis's claim that one should avoid an excess of theory in the writing of history and considered it detrimental to the scholarship of *Modern Architecture Since 1900.* In *The Psychologizing of Modernity* (2000), Mark Jarzombek went one step further, arguing that Curtis's decision is itself theoretical. Jarzombek used a quote in which Curtis advocated for a criticism "based upon the experience and analysis of actual architectural objects in their precise setting," which Curtis saw as especially relevant at a time when architecture was "once again being buried under smoke screens of 'theory.'"[57] Jarzombek did so to argue that "this 'critique' of theory is discredited by its attempt to pretend that it itself is not theory."[58] In other words, Jarzombek posited that 'theory' here might just be too well 'digested,' and that there are theoretical principles lurking behind Curtis's discursive operations.[59] Jarzombek further considered Curtis's unwillingness to tackle theoretical issues to be "totally unsatisfactory" from the perspective of rigorous scholarship.[60] One could argue that Curtis's negative opinion of the abuse of theory (and theoretical trends outside of architecture) in detriment of the first-hand experience of buildings in the writing of history, does not automatically imply that he would forget about the theoretical grounding of his formative studies in art history and architecture. Curtis's mapping of the late twentieth century, from the tentative proposal of the first edition to its extended and inclusive 1996 version, is one of the strengths of *Modern Architecture Since 1900*, and one of its main contributions to the historiography of modern architecture, as most previous and subsequent historians avoided including the recent past in their accounts, undoubtedly historical distance comes to mind. Curtis's advocacy for continuity in architecture throughout the world and the century is another strength of the book. In drafting a continuous map, though, his methodology, that of a formalist art historian, and his 'theoretical' determination to avoid obscure theorizations have been perceived as weaknesses.

In writing his allegedly 'dispassionate' history of modern architecture, the problem Curtis encountered was how to overcome the repeated refrain that modern architecture was dead. Alongside the scholars proclaiming the death of modern architecture, Curtis identified others who cling to their established views and identity as 'modernists,' and considered both positions to be extremes to avoid when dealing with the recent past. In the third edition of *Modern Architecture Since 1900,* Curtis argued that neither of these positions gives a nuanced account of invention and "its usual debts to the past," and that both present a simplistic and monolithic version of modern architecture, and play down its continuities.[61] According to Curtis, neither is willing to admit that the balance between the old and the new results in profound innovation, and "that the seminal works of the modern movement have value for the future precisely because their principles transcend period limitations."[62]

Although he concluded the three editions of *Modern Architecture Since 1900* with claims to have achieved a certain balance between these two positions, Curtis acknowledged that it is difficult to arrive naturally at a consensus about contemporary developments. By including them in a long historical perspective and stating clearly the basis of his judgments, he claimed to have fulfilled the aim of presenting a balanced picture of recent developments in architecture.[63] Curtis disagreed with what he called "the contemporary cynic, protected from difficult social realities by the dogmatic uncertainties of postmodern philosophy, surrounded by the 'pensée unique' of the globalized market, [who] thinks that all talk of grand historical narratives has had its day."[64] In addition, he wished to integrate the practical, the social, the technical, and the symbolic in his approach to architecture. Again, a certain balance is required in the thinking and writing of history for what he referred to as the "constant oscillation between fact and opinion, between detailed analyses and broad interpretations, between induction and deduction."[65]

It is true that, while Curtis did not use the terms 'objective' or 'objectivity' to refer to his own writing, his emphasis on the balance and the allegedly dispassionate distance of his point of view results in a grounded historical narrative based on his own subjective experience of modern architecture. When dealing with the history of modern architecture, the distance is only relative though, regardless of whether one is talking about the distant or recent past. As Marvin Trachtenberg wrote, historians of modernism (and he considers Curtis one of them) have the ambition "to alter, to shape, to affect somehow the course of current architectural development with their writing (and justly so)."[66] Curtis's authority on modern architecture relates to his own experience of buildings in varied cultural, intellectual, and geographical settings incorporated into a longer historical perspective. However, while he looked at regionalism with warm eyes, he did not refrain from conveying his enormous displeasure regarding the ideas and materializations of postmodernism. Despite the importance that Curtis gives to authenticity as a judgment criterion, his own account of postmodernism, rather than being history, degenerates into polemical criticism.

Notwithstanding Curtis's subjectivity and his problematic balance claims, I would argue that his historical narrative presents an unstable balance and is ultimately credible because of his expertise on and first-hand experience of modern architecture.[67] Curtis in fact contributed to the historiography of modern architecture both in his methodological approach to history, characterized by the emphasis on balance at multiple levels, and in his definition of modern architecture as a continuous tradition which includes the developments of the late twentieth century. Itself a product of the transitional period between late 1970s and 1990s, it is time for Curtis's contribution to be acknowledged critically in the discipline.

## Notes

1 The research undertaken for this essay was funded by an International Postgraduate Research Scholarship awarded by the Research Training Program of the Australian Government.
2 Edward W. Soja, *Postmodern Geographies: The Reassertion of Space in Critical Social Theory* (London: Verso Books, 1989), 5.
3 Mark Jarzombek, "Architecture: The Global Imaginary in an Antiglobal World," *Grey Room*, no. 61 (Fall 2015): 114.
4 Mary McLeod, "Architecture and Politics in the Reagan Era: From Postmodernism to Deconstructivism," *Assemblage*, no. 8 (1989): 27.
5 Philip Ursprung, "E-Flux Architecture presents 'History/Theory,'" (colloquium, E-Flux, New York, November 14, 2017). Hanno-Walter Kruft, *Geschichte der Architekturtheorie: Von der Antike bis zur Gegenwart* (Munich: C. H. Beck, 1985). *A History of Architectural Theory: From Vitruvius to the Present* (New York: Princeton Architectural Press, 1994).
6 Mark Jarzombek, "The Disciplinary Dislocations of (Architectural) History," *Journal of the Society of Architectural Historians*, vol. 58, no. 3 (1999): 489.
7 Jarzombek, "The Disciplinary Dislocations of (Architectural) History," 488.
8 Esra Akcan, "Writing a Global History through Translation: An Afterword on Pedagogical Perspectives," *Art in Translation*, vol. 10, no. 1 (2018): 137. DOI: 10.1080/17561310.2018.1424309.
9 William J.R. Curtis, "The History of a History: Le Corbusier at work, the Genesis of the Carpenter Center for the Visual Arts," in *Massilia 2013- Le Corbusier- Ultime Pensées/Derniers Projets- 1960/1965* (Paris and Marseille: Fondation Le Corbusier and éditions Imbernon, 2014), 112–151. WJRC Archive.
10 William J.R. Curtis, email message to author, February 2, 2017.
11 William J.R. Curtis, "Introduction," in *Modern Architecture since 1900* (London: Phaidon Press, 1996), 13–14.
12 William J.R. Curtis, *Balkrishna V. Doshi: An Architecture for India* (New York: Rizzoli, 1988).
13 William J.R. Curtis, *Modern Architecture since 1900* (Oxford: Phaidon Press, 1996), 691.
14 William J.R. Curtis, "Preface to the Third Edition," in *Modern Architecture since 1900* (London: Phaidon Press, 1996), 9.
15 See Macarena de la Vega de León, An Intertwined History: The Contribution of William J.R. Curtis to the Historiography of Modern Architecture (University of Canberra, 2018).
16 William J.R. Curtis, email message to author, June 6, 2017.
17 Curtis, "Introduction," 17.

18 To the knowledge of the author there are translations of the book into Spanish (1986, 2006), Japanese (1990), Italian (1999), German (2002), French (2004), and Portuguese (2008).
19 James S. Ackerman, Prof of Fine Arts, Harvard University, Letter to Simon Havilan, Director of Phaidon Press, August 28, 1981. William J.R. Curtis, Letter sent via email message to author, February 21, 2017. WJRC Archive.
20 Peter L. Laurence, "Modern (or Contemporary) Architecture circa 1959," in *A Critical History of Contemporary Architecture: 1960–2010*, eds. Elie G. Haddad and David Rifkin (London: Ashgate, 2014), 10.
21 William J.R. Curtis, email message to author, August 31, 2016.
22 William J.R. Curtis, "Regionalism in Architecture Session III," in *Regionalism in Architecture*, ed. Robert Powell (Singapore: Concept Media/The Aga Khan Award for Architecture, 1985), 73.
23 Curtis, *Modern Architecture since 1900*, 636.
24 William J.R. Curtis, "Contemporary Transformations of Modern Architecture," *Architectural Record*, vol. 177, no. 7 (1989): 108.
25 Curtis, *Modern Architecture since 1900*, 639.
26 Curtis, *Modern Architecture since 1900*, 639.
27 Alexander Tzonis, "Introducing an Architecture of the Present: Critical Regionalism and the Design of Identity," in *Critical Regionalism: Architecture and Identity in a Globalized World*, eds. Liane Lefaivre and Alexander Tzonis (Munich, Berlin, London, New York: Prestel, 2003), 10.
28 Tzonis, "Introducing an Architecture of the Present," 20.
29 Curtis, *Modern Architecture since 1900*, 657.
30 Liane Lefaivre, "Critical Regionalism: A Facet of Modern Architecture since 1945," in *Critical Regionalism: Architecture and Identity in a Globalized World*, eds. Liane Lefaivre and Alexander Tzonis (Munich, Berlin, London, New York: Prestel, 2003), 34.
31 Lefaivre, "Critical Regionalism…," 34.
32 Vincent B. Canizaro, ed., *Architectural Regionalism: Collected Writings on Place, Identity, Modernity, and Tradition* (New York: Princeton Architectural Press, 2007), 446.
33 Canizaro, *Architectural Regionalism*, 26.
34 Canizaro, *Architectural Regionalism*, 22.
35 William J.R. Curtis, email message to author, February 2, 2017.
36 William J.R. Curtis, "Modern Architecture, Monumentality and the Meaning of Institutions: Reflections on Authenticity," *Harvard Architecture Review*, no. 4 (1984): 65.
37 Curtis, "Modern Architecture, Monumentality and the Meaning of Institutions…," 66.
38 William J.R. Curtis, "Transformation and Invention: on Re-reading Modern Architecture," *The Architectural Review*, vol. 221, no. 1321 (2007): 36–40. Original essay written by Curtis in February 2007, 3, WJRC Archive.
39 Joseph Rykwert, "Inheritance or Tradition," *Architectural Design*, vol. 49, no. 5/6 (1979): 3.
40 Curtis, "Introduction," 16.
41 Tom Turner, *City as Landscape: A Post-Postmodern View of Design and Planning* (London: E&FN Spon, 1996), 8.
42 Nathan Brown, "Postmodernity, Not Yet. Toward a New Periodisation," *Radical Philosophy*, vol. 2, no. 1 (2018): 12.
43 Peter Osborne, "Crisis as Form," lecture at Kingston University, London (12 January 2017).
44 Peter Osborne, "The Postconceptual Condition: Or the Cultural Logic of High Capitalism Today," *Radical Philosophy*, vol. 184 (2014): 19–20.
45 Brown, "Postmodernity, Not Yet. Toward a New Periodisation."

46 Eva Branscome, Hans Hollein and Postmodernism: Art and Architecture in Austria, 1958–1985 (London: Routledge, 2017), 4.
47 Branscome, Hans Hollein and Postmodernism…, 5.
48 Branscome, Hans Hollein and Postmodernism…, 6.
49 Curtis, *Modern Architecture since 1900*, 619.
50 Tzonis, "Introducing an Architecture of the Present…," 10.
51 Curtis, "Introduction," 17.
52 Curtis, *Modern Architecture since 1900*, 617.
53 William J.R. Curtis, "A Historian's Perspective on Modern Architecture." Transcript. English version of text "La perspectiva de un historiador sobre la arquitectura moderna," translated by Jorge Sainz and read out by the author in Spanish on the presentation of the translation of the third edition of *Modern Architecture Since 1900* at the Círculo de Bellas Artes, Madrid, January 2007. WJRC Archive.
54 Curtis, "A Historian's Perspective on Modern Architecture," transcript of the talk, January 2007.
55 Curtis, "A Historian's Perspective on Modern Architecture," transcript of the talk, January 2007.
56 William J.R. Curtis, *Le Corbusier: Ideas and Forms* (London: Phaidon Press, 2015), 477.
57 William J.R. Curtis, "Alvaro Siza: An Architecture of Edges," *El Croquis* 68/69 (1994): 33.
58 Mark Jarzombek, *The Psychologizing of Modernity: Art, Architecture, and History* (Cambridge: Cambridge University Press, 2000), 308.
59 Jarzombek, *The Psychologizing of Modernity*, 27.
60 Jarzombek, *The Psychologizing of Modernity*, 31.
61 Curtis, *Modern Architecture since 1900*, 617.
62 William J.R. Curtis, *Modern Architecture since 1900* (Oxford: Phaidon Press, 1982), 367.
63 Curtis, "Introduction," 17.
64 Curtis, "Transformation and Invention…," 5.
65 Curtis, "A Historian's Perspective on Modern Architecture," transcript of the talk, January 2007.
66 Marvin Trachtenberg, "Some Observations on Recent Architectural History," *The Art Bulletin*, vol. 70, no. 2 (1988): 241.
67 Macarena de la Vega de León, "Mediating History/Distances with *Modern Architecture since 1900*," in *Proceedings of the Society of Architectural Historians, Australia, and New Zealand* 36, *Distance Looks Back*, eds. Victoria Jackson Wyatt, Andrew Leach and Lee Stickells (Sydney: SAHANZ, 2020), 91–101.

# 9 Postmodernist Revivalism and Architectural Gimmicks

*Lidia Klein*

After a period of neglect lasting roughly 20 years, in the decade of the 2010s architectural postmodernism has come roaring back. We can see this return in publications, exhibitions, conferences, and symposia focused on postmodern aesthetics and theory in the design and architecture worlds. A recent book by Owen Hopkins, *Less Is a Bore* (Phaidon, 2020), sums up this moment: "this book would have been inconceivable only a few years ago," Hopkins writes. "Today, however, Postmodernism is no longer a dirty word—or the style that must not be named—as a new generation of architects and designers have begun to reassess and reinterpret its ideals, tactics and aesthetics."[1] A significant portion of these projects are image-oriented coffee table books and albums, such as Judith Gura's *Postmodern Design Complete* (Thames & Hudson, 2017), Terry Farrels and Adam Nathaniel Furman's *Revisiting Postmodernism* (RIBA Publishing, 2017), and Hopkins' own book. Together these embrace the postmodernist movement for what Hopkins calls its "essential eclecticism, the belief of meaning over muteness, context over introspection, fragmentation over unity, doubt over certainty, … contingency over universality [and] an argument for … the very value of pluralism, permissiveness, and unthought of possibility"[2]—qualities that in the previous two decades had been almost unanimously ridiculed and attacked by the architectural mainstream.

The newfound popularity of postmodernism can also be found in museum and galleries, with notable attention paid to the works of Memphis group members (*Nathalie Du Pasquier: Big Objects Not Always Silent* at Kunsthalle Wien in 2016, *Ettore Sottsass: Design Radical at the Met Breuer* in 2017, to mention just a couple examples) and retrospective exhibitions such as *Postmodernism: Style and Subversion, 1970–1990* shown in the Victoria and Albert Museum of Art (2011–2012).[3] Apart from these examples focused mainly on the celebration of postmodern playful aesthetics, postmodernism has also become an important subject of scholarly interrogation. The latest manifestation of this interest is *Architecture Itself and Other Postmodernist Myths*, an exhibition at the Canadian Centre for Architecture (2018/2019). *Architecture Itself*, curated by Sylvia Lavin, was intended as a "counter-reading of postmodern procedures, replacing the myth of the autonomous architect with accounts of empirically describable architectural activity," focusing on the

DOI: 10.4324/9781003292999-10

relations between architecture, the art market, bureaucracy, and institutions. Lavin's exhibition can be seen as a part of a broader scholarly effort intended to critically examine this movement and provide new perspectives leading to its reassessment, represented by books such as K. Michael Hays' *Architecture's Desire: Reading the Late Avant-Garde* (The MIT Press, 2009), Reinhold Martin's *Utopia's Ghost: Architecture and Postmodernism, Again* (University of Minnesota Press, 2010) and Emmanuel Petit's *Irony; or, The Self-Critical Opacity of Postmodern Architecture* (Yale University Press, 2013).[4] Likewise, many researchers have expressed the necessity of redefining postmodernism by examining lesser known architectural phenomena from outside of the predominantly Western canon. This current of research can be observed in conferences and symposia (such as "Intersections: Late Socialism and Postmodernism" organized by Ana Miljački at MIT in 2012 and "Re-framing Identities: Architecture's Turn to History" at ETH Zurich in 2015 organized by Akos Moravansky), book publications (such as *Second World Postmodernisms: Architecture and Society under Late Socialism* ed. Vladimir Kulić, published by Bloomsbury in 2019) and academic journals (*The Geopolitical Aesthetic of Postmodernism*, special issue of *Architectural Histories*, forthcoming in 2022).[5]

This interest in postmodernism is shared not only by curators, critics, and academics, but also by architects themselves. Unlike in academic discourses, in architectural practice the return of postmodernism usually is devoid of critical angles, manifesting itself as an enthusiastic affirmation of exuberant forms and décor. In a widely discussed article for *Dezeen* written in 2017, Sean Griffiths, once actively engaged in the first wave of the renaissance of the postmodern aesthetic as a founding member of FAT (Fashion, Architecture, Taste), took a critical stance to the current postmodern revivalism:

> In recent weeks, I have found myself writing references for young American academics who wear bow ties and Bertie Wooster jumpers, and who write about architecture's relationship to literature on the internet in the style of David Foster Wallace. The Chicago Architecture Biennial is full of a renewed and apparently confident postmodernism, of a sort that seems just a little too respectable. The artist, Pablo Bronstein is plastering neo-Georgian all over the RIBA. And who today can switch on the television, read the newspaper or go online without the chirpy visage of Adam Nathaniel Furman staring back from inside the 24-hour news cycle?[6]

The last figure mentioned in Griffiths' snarky comment, Adam Nathaniel Furman, is one of the most recognizable young architects inspired by postmodern aesthetics. Furman works in London, which, in the last years, became the base for many designers and architects sharing interest in postmodernism, including Yinka Ilori, Camille Walala, Morag Mysercough. Furman refers to this informal group as "New London Fabulous" and defines it as grounded in the understanding of "design and architecture as a visual and cultural pursuit, which is highly aesthetic, sensual and celebratory of mixed cultures"[7] and which "picks and chooses and mixes from different periods and it does look back."[8] The members of "New London Fabulous" are best known for ornamental urban and architectural installations saturated with bright colors and bold patterns offering visually hypnotic spatial experiences. Walala, who describes her work as using the "man-made landscape as a platform for disseminating positivity,"[9] specializes in murals transforming buildings into two-dimensional, cartoon-like drawings (such as the façade of the Industry City building in Brooklyn, NY, 2018) and urban interventions (such as the Adams Plaza Bridge in London's Canary Wharf, 2020 or a mural on a pedestrian crossing and building façade in London's White City, 2020). With Adams Plaza Bridge, Walala changed the tunnel-like structure of the bridge into a three-dimensional op-art installation by installing bright, colorful panels in its window and on the ceiling. In the murals in White City, Walala used a similar set of primary colors and geometric patterns referencing the aesthetics of the 1980s and 1990s to bring a joyful pop of color into a rather uniform and uncompelling environment.

Walala's joyful, palatable, and visually pleasing designs also make them desired by private real estate companies who eagerly use art and architecture in their efforts of placemaking. White City was commissioned by a consortium of Stanhope, Mitsui Fudosan UK and Alberta Investment Management Corporation, while Adams Plaza Bridge by Canary Wharf Group. In both cases, Walala's urban interventions are part of branding strategies targeted to market these locations as centers of businesses, creative industries, and commerce, inevitably subjecting them to the forces of gentrification. Indeed, Walala's optimistic architecture as a "platform for disseminating positivity" is also a platform for fostering socio-spatial inequalities, inevitable in projects turning neighborhoods into enclaves scripted by developers according to a strictly profit-driven business plan.

In addition to urban environments, Walala also works in gallery spaces. One of her most recent gallery projects is *Walala x Play* in Now Gallery (2017): a colorful, Memphis-inspired labyrinth constructed of patterns and reflective surfaces that resembles mirror mazes and playground equipment in order to encourage the visitors to "unleash their inner child."[10] Yinka Ilori's designs use similar playful aesthetics and intends to evoke analogical associations. His *Happy Street* for London Festival of Architecture (2019) was aimed to "overhaul a gloomy underpass in south London, with a proposal featuring vibrant colours and bold patterns."[11] In the same year, Ilori realized *Playland*, an installation commissioned by Pinterest as part of the Cannes festival. *Playland* features movable chairs, a see-saw, and a roundabout, covered in colorful patterns corresponding with Pinterest's "most pinned colours from around the world" and, similarly to Walala's installation, was intended to "create a play space that gave adults the opportunity to play and tap into their inner child."[12] Ilori's *Playland* not only represents data retrieved from this online platform, but it also shares the same palatable aesthetic characteristic for a Pinterest board and, like its digital counterpart, its main goal is to visually please.

Walala and Ilori's designs carry forward one of the crucial features of postmodern architecture: its obsession with image. Postmodernists of the 1970s and 1980s realized this focus through their fascination with architectural drawing understood as a form of art and with their exploration of the connections between architecture, the visual arts, and the popular ionosphere. Early twenty-first century interest in postmodernism takes up different forms of visualities as it revolves around digital images shared on social media, taking lessons from Pinterest and Instagram rather than Las Vegas. Whether turning a three-dimensional object into a flat, schematic sketch (Walala's Industry City building) or reducing space to an instagrammable background (Ilori's *Playland*), these designs persistently treat architecture as a visually satisfying background, deprived of depth both in the physical and the ideological senses. As such, they are symptomatic of a much broader tendency defining contemporary architecture—its fixation on image and representation. From the increasingly commonplace practice of architectural studios to design architecture not only to function in the real world but also to have a successful presence on Instagram (especially in spaces such as restaurants or hotels) to architectural realizations intentionally designed to accommodate selfie-taking (The Vessel in New York, Zaryadye Park in Moscow, to mention just a couple of recent examples), it is increasingly common to find architecture composed and staged with a photogenic function in mind.

Some qualities found in Walala and Ilori's projects—lack of depth, emphases on playfulness and optimism, the use of bold colors and patterns—are also characteristic of Furman's designs. His most discussed works include an installation for the 2017 edition of the London Design Festival, a gate composed of a sequence of colorful arches with openings of different shapes creating a mesmerizing kaleidoscope-like effect. The arches are clad with ceramic tiles, as the installation was commissioned by *Turkishceramic*, an association promoting the Turkish ceramic industry. Furman freely juxtaposes tiles of different patterns and traditions, evoking a range of historical references, from patterns used in London Underground stations in the 1970s to traditional Islamic motifs found in mosques. Visually attractive and aesthetically and intellectually accessible while offering a wide array of artistic and cultural references ready to be decoded by culturally competent audiences, Furman's installation provides a perfect example of utterly commercial, populist, egalitarian, and witty neo-postmodern design. His second famous project, *The Democratic Monument* (2017) is based on similar qualities, but is also intended to communicate a political message. *The Democratic Monument* was commissioned by the Scottish Architectural Fringe as part of a *New Typologies* exhibition, showcasing visions for future civic architecture. The entrance to *The Democratic Monument* is placed in an elaborate front façade composed of an inlay of overlapping segments of contrasting colors, textures, and materials combined with classical architectural elements such as columns and arches. The entrance leads to a spacious public hall and an office tower. Like the front façade, interior spaces offer a contemporary version of mannerist *horror vacui* with a myriad of historical references, bold patterns, and bright colors. As they fill ceilings, walls, and floors, they result in surreal, dream-like, fragmented, and disorienting spaces. *The Democratic Monument* offers an updated, revamped, and amplified version of postmodernism for the new generation. Furman generously draws from the classics – ironic projects such as Michael Graves' Disney Hotels, Charles Moore's Piazza d'Italia, and Memphis group furniture design – and combines those elements with more recent references, such as "rave culture" aesthetics of the nineties with its acid-neon colors and disorienting visual effects. Furman sees his proposal as "an expression of urban pride, chromatic joy, and architectural complexity" and "a monumental embodiment of our evolving Liberal democracy as it moves into another new phase of energetic activity and robust intervention."[13] According to Furman, *The Democratic Monument* sends a message of "architectural plurality in compositional unity" as "architectural language and expression can both embody, and reconcile, the perpetual tensions between market & state, and minority and majority"[14]; he continues, it embodies "the perpetual dialogue in our Liberal democracy between the need for consensus and shared values, and the vital fostering and celebration of minority needs and interests."[15]

Furman's project and the rhetoric of its description recalls Chantal Mouffe's diagnosis of the *post-political*, which she characterized as a predominant "view which informs the 'common sense' in a majority of western societies."[16] Mouffe characterizes this condition as a situation in which the

> 'free world' has triumphed over communism and, with the weakening of collective identities, a world 'without enemies' is now possible. Partisan conflicts are a thing of the past and consensus can now be obtained through dialogue. Thanks to globalization and the universalization of liberal democracy, we can expect a cosmopolitan future bringing peace, prosperity and the implementation of human rights worldwide.[17]

Further, Mouffe characterizes the post-political era as based on "optimistic view of globalization," and "consensual form of democracy," and describes it as an "anti-political vision which refuses to acknowledge the antagonistic dimension constitutive of 'the political.'"[18] *The Democratic Monument* provides a perfect illustration of a building for post-political times, as it is anti-political in nature. Furman's project statement mentions tensions between the market and the state, the minority and the majority, but instead of engaging them in his project, the architect offers a false vision of reconciliation, which – as the contemporary crisis of democracy, marked by Brexit, the refugee crisis, and a surge of nationalist politics worldwide, makes clear – is an optimistic and unrealistic view. *The Democratic Monument* affirms the status quo by providing an illusion of unity and harmony and avoids mentioning real irreconcilable tensions and divisions. In this sense, paradoxically, it is an example of *a*political architecture deceptively using the rhetoric of pluralism without any serious political engagement at its essence. In interviews Furman often raises the need for diversity—especially by rejecting heteronormativity—in architecture, presenting postmodern aesthetics as well-suited for this endeavor due to its unlimited openness to different ideas and forms. His vision, however, refuses to address or acknowledge tensions, conflicts, and negotiations that are inevitable parts of any project founded on the idea of true involvement of different groups and fostering a dialogue between them. The optimistic inclusivity of *The Democratic Monument* then appears indifferent to the mounting pressure to acknowledge diversity in architecture in recent years as voiced by the #MeToo movement or Black Lives Matter activists, which ask architects to engage in uncomfortable conversations and to challenge the status quo. Furman's vision of democracy in architecture doesn't seem to be truly invested in acknowledging different voices, but effectively silences them by offering an architectural illusion of "unity and reconciliation."

This shallow optimism, characteristic not only of *The Democratic Monument* but also of the architecture of "New London Fabulous" and the contemporary revival of postmodernism, in general, has prompted heated critical discussions on its appropriateness in the current social, political, and economic environment. In the article for *Dezeen* quoted above, Sean Griffiths continues:

> There is one big reason why now is absolutely not the time to be indulging in postmodern revivalism. Its name is President Donald Trump. And while Donald Trump means that golden Baroque remains transgressive, it is now transgressive in a bad way. Bigly so, to coin a phrase. (…) As all good postmodernists know, signifiers – the vessels that convey meanings – have a tendency to become untethered from their moorings. In less dangerous times we can delight in their floating free, reveling in the magical manufacture of meaning that the detachment of the signifier from its signified permits. But the artful twisting of meaning through the gentle massaging of signifier is less appealing when the gaps between truth and representation provide a petri dish for the fake news of the alt-right.[19]

For Griffiths, taking inspiration from a current based on playfulness, irony, and formalist aestheticism is dangerous in the time of fake news and in the context of an increasingly fragile democracy. More broadly, the postmodern obsession with image, superficiality, language, and architectural jokes is misguided in a time when architecture needs to address issues like climate emergency, inequality, and urban poverty. Similar concerns were raised during the 2018 Dean's Roundtable, the annual meeting of deans of architectural schools in the Northeast organized by the Center for Architecture in New York. The main thread of the meeting was the discussion of the possibilities of activism in architecture two years into Donald Trump's presidency, which resulted in a resurgence of racism, homophobia, and sexism. Some deans expressed their concerns with the revival of postmodernism in this political and social reality, seeing it as a dangerous distraction from urgent social matters that need to be addressed by architects. Julio Fernandez (CCNY's Spitzer School of Architecture) expressed a worry that "many schools here have moved to a re-evaluation of Postmodernism" and stated that "we have better things to do."[20] University of Virginia's Ila Berman, who was moderating the gathering, recalled the architectural discourse of the 1970s and 1980s, when "all of the environmental and social issues fell off the table, and architects were operating within a different sphere" and added "I'm concerned when I see it happening again." "Is this just another, 'Make Architecture Great Again' moment, that's aligning with what's happening politically?" asked Berman.

To a large extent, the dangers embedded in the new wave of postmodernism as identified by Griffiths or Berman are nothing new. In many ways, the architecture of "New London Fabulous" and other designers representing similar aesthetics exaggerates the issues shaping architecture and urban sphere of the last few decades: its active role in perpetuating the commodification of space and its incapability to engage in meaningful social and political conversations. For better or worse, "New London Fabulous" might be the architectural movement that expresses the first decades of the twenty-first century best. Not only does it encapsulate the "logic of late capitalism," as Fredric Jameson famously characterized postmodernism,[21] but it also amplifies it and enriches with features defining the cultural reality of our century, like the dependence on digital images. These architects not only continue to form a part of postmodernism as the "cultural dominant" of late capitalism, following Jameson's argument, but perhaps their character is even better captured by using the category of "gimmick," as theorized recently by literary critic Sianne Ngai. In her book *Theory of the Gimmick: Aesthetic Judgment and Capitalist Form* (Harvard UP, 2020), Ngai distinguishes the gimmick as the chief aesthetic category of capitalism. She defines gimmick as a device that is at the same time "simultaneously overperforming and underperforming," a device that at the same time "strikes us as working too hard" and "as working too little," making things easy for the consumer but also disappointing in how little it has to offer. For this reason, it is both transparent and obscure about capitalist production,[22] both "outdated, backwards" and "newfangled, futuristic," and is a "fundamentally unstable form," as it reveals tensions and disappointments inherent in late capitalism. The works of Furman, Walala, and Ilori seem to do just that: their aesthetics are simultaneously refreshing and new (and this makes them particularly attractive for developers trying to attract millennial clients by evoking 1980s nostalgia) as well as outdated and backwards, as they refer to antiquated forms in order to elicit attention. These projects are seemingly overperforming in terms of their popularity and media attention they generate, but at a closer look they turn out to disappointingly underperform; they seem unrepeatable (original) but at the same time as repetitive, as other instagrammable images replicating analogical conventions and stylistics qualities. They seem to be transparent about their place in the contemporary market reality (as they have no intellectual or ideological pretenses and focus on "playfulness"), but at the same time they obfuscate the mechanisms inherent to space under late capitalism, and this obfuscation helps supports their existence (Walala's designs, thanks to being "a platform for disseminating positivity" are at the same time platforms for gentrification). For these reasons, even though the comeback of postmodernism represented by "New London Fabulous" might prove to be short-lived, the gimmicky nature of this phenomenon makes it a perfect embodiment of the contradictions embedded both in contemporary architecture and our economic, social, and cultural reality that produced it.

## Notes

1 Owen Hopkins, *Less Is a Bore* (London: Phaidon, 2020), p.224.
2 Hopkins, p.9.
3 See also: *The Return of the Past: Postmodernism in British Architecture* at Sir John Soane's Museum, London (2018); *Postmodernism 1980–1995* at Helsinki's Design Museum (2015).
4 To that we should add publications examining particular phenomena crucial for postmodernism, such as Léa-Catherine Szacka's *Exhibiting the Postmodern: The 1980 Venice Architecture Biennale* (Venezia: Marsilio Editori, 2016) analyzing the role that the first Venice Biennale of Architecture played in postmodern architecture or Aron Vinegar's *I Am a Monument: On Learning from Las Vegas* (Cambridge, MA; London: The MIT Press, 2012) a critical rereading of the text fundamental for postmodern design philosophy.
5 Additionally, many recently organized conferences have focused on the need to explore the political aspects of postmodern architecture against its common characterization as a politically disengaged project complicit with commercial, neoliberal agendas. These include the panel "Publicly Postmodern: government agency and 1980s architecture" at the Society of Architectural Historians conference in Glasgow (2017, chaired by Karen Burns and Paul Walker) and the conference "The Architecture of Deregulations: Postmodernism, Politics and the Built Environment in Europe, 1975–1995" at the KTH School of Architecture in Stockholm (2016, organized by Catharina Gabrielsson and Helena Mattsson).
6 Sean Griffiths, "Now Is Not the Time to be Indulging in Postmodern Revivalism," *Dezeen*, 30 October 2017, https://www.dezeen.com/2017/10/30/sean-griffiths-fat-postmodern-revivalism-dangerous-times-opinion. Griffiths built his own career on postmodern revivalism himself. However, he claims that his own uses of postmodernism as an architect were critical and ironic, while the current interest in postmodernism is affirmative and lacks critical distance.
7 Adam Nathaniel Furman, "Live Interview with Adam Nathaniel Furman as Part of Virtual Design Festival," *Dezeen*, May 22, 2020, https://www.dezeen.com/2020/05/22/adam-nathaniel-furman-screentime-vdf/.
8 Despite clear references to postmodernism present in projects of *New London Fabulous*, Furman stresses that the movement shouldn't be seen as restricted to one stylistics. See: Marcus Fairs, "Colourful New London Fabulous Design Movement Is Challenging Minimalism, Says Adam Nathaniel Furman," *Dezeen*, May 26, 2020, https://www.dezeen.com/2020/05/26/new-london-fabulous-design-movement-adam-nathaniel-furman/.
9 Camille Walala, https://www.camillewalala.com/profile.
10 Walala, https://www.camillewalala.com/architectureinteriors/2019/1/15/now-gallery-walala-x-play.
11 Yinka Ilori, https://yinkailori.com/work/happy-street.

12 Tom Ravenscroft, "Yinka Ilori Covers Adult Playground in Pinterest's Most Pinned Colours at Cannes Lions," *Dezeen*, June 21, 2019, https://www.dezeen.com/2019/06/21/yinka-ilori-playground-pinterest-cannes-lions/.

13 Adam Nathaniel Furman, "The Democratic Monument: Adam Nathaniel Furman's Manifesto for a New Type of Civic Center," *Archdaily*, July 3, 2017, https://www.archdaily.com/874860/the-democratic-monument-adam-nathaniel-furmans-manifesto-for-a-new-type-of-civic-center.

14 Ibid.

15 Ibid.

16 Chantal Mouffe, *On the Political* (New York: Routledge, 2005), 1.

17 Ibid.

18 Ibid., 1–2.

19 Griffiths, "Now Is Not the Time."

20 Julio Fernandez, "2018 Dean's Roundtable," at the Center for Architecture, New York, 11.03.2018, https://vimeo.com/313237160.

21 Fredric Jameson, *Postmodernism, or the Cultural Logic of Late Capitalism* (Durham, NC: Duke University Press, 1992).

22 Sianne Ngai, *Theory of the Gimmick: Aesthetic Judgment and Capitalist Form* (Cambridge, MA: Harvard University Press, 2020).

# Part II

# Alternative Visions and New Directions

# 10 The Form of Utopia

## Architectural Theory in the Age of Hyperobjects

*Stefano Corbo*

In 2005, French artist Cyprien Gaillard presented *Belief in the Age of Disbelief* – a series of etchings in which seventeenth-century Dutch landscapes and post-war architectural structures coexist in the same evocative image. In these collages, the manipulation of historic sources and the de-territorialisation of modernist buildings from their original context describe an apocalyptic yet picturesque panorama. By reproducing Brutalist housing blocks, Parisian Grands Ensembles, or prefabricated buildings from the Soviet Union, Gaillard investigates the legacy of modern architecture: its message, its hopes, and its materialization are all but ruins, partially hidden and invaded by vegetation. Those structures, once re-situated in a bucolic scenario, take on a twofold meaning: they document the collapse of a built utopia – intended as a collective effort to translate desires of social reform into architectural episodes – but also, they paradoxically describe an idealized world, which probably never existed before because we have never been truly modern, to quote Bruno Latour.[1] Gaillard's etchings unearth human attraction for failure and invite us to rethink the relationship between architecture and utopia – to better say, to rethink architecture as a vehicle for utopia.

Utopia. A word that reverberates throughout the history of literature and philosophy. A ghost haunting human imagination for centuries, often associated with scenarios that were not even intended to be realized but simply constituted an escape from the present – from Plato's *Republic*, to Thomas More's *Utopia*, or Tommaso Campanella's *City of the Sun*. Opposed to this idea of utopia as illusion or as imaginary world, is what Ernst Bloch called prefiguration, the realm of *noch nicht*[2] – not yet. Utopia can designate an expectation, a territory outside the current parameters that is not existing now, but that can exist in the future. Utopia not as a dream but as a project, not as an abstraction but as a destiny. This article borrows Bloch's definition of utopia to unfold the intricate connection between radical ideas and built forms and to focus on the role of architecture in envisioning a counter-model of future.

Like any threatening presence, utopia has been widely described, theorized in different forms, but also exorcised: its death has been periodically announced to indicate the transitioning toward a new era. If Francis Fukuyama saw in the collapse of the Soviet Union the end of History – in the sense

DOI: 10.4324/9781003292999-12

of the end of any alternative to Liberalism[3] – Slovenian philosopher Slavoj Žižek argued that the so-called end of History was followed by another grand utopia, that of a liberal capitalist democracy: 'with the terroristic attack of 9/11 in New York, this utopia came to an end.'[4] Very similarly, in the territory of architecture, multiple have been the efforts to identify the rise and fall, origin and development of built forms of utopia. While for Manfredo Tafuri the crisis of utopia coincides with the crisis of Modern architecture, and begins at the moment that it had to integrate itself into industrial capitalism and its technological organization,[5] one may acknowledge that the gradual erosion of the Modern message – symbolically crystalized in the demolition of the Pruitt-Igoe complex in 1972 as postulated by Charles Jencks – can be seen, within the architectural discourse, as the end of a systematic and comprehensive reflection on the future in favor of a dispersed fragmentation of individual positions that have characterized the last decades.

From Sforzinda's *Ideal City* to Hilberseimer's *Vertical City*, passing through naïve and provocative proposals such as Superstudio's *Supersurfaces*, form – even the absence of it – has always represented the main medium to see beyond current models and to propose alternatives, whether those proposals had actually the ambition to question the status quo or simply to lyrically run away from it. For centuries, social and political demands have inspired the materialization of very specific episodes, both at the urban and the building scale. Until the 1970s, a voluminous corpus of projects, slogans, and predictions about the future has informed the architectural debate. The Milanese collective Archizoom, in this regard, deserves particular mention, as their contributions represent, to some extent, a swansong – the bridge between a witty critique of capitalist forms of organization, and the resigned acceptance that no other future is possible. In focusing their attention on the logics of mass consumption and standardization, *No-Stop City*, presented in 1969, constituted 'a non-figurative architecture for a non-figurative society that no longer had an external form but had infinite internal forms.'[6] Architecture disappears: it is reduced to an endless sequence of toilette units and air conditioning apparatuses placed at a distance of 50 meters one from the other. Archizoom's underlying narrative contains, like any thought-provoking proposal, ambiguities, contradictions, and points of inflection. *No-Stop City* is not a utopian project: it is a parody, a caricature of the capitalist city. But also a cynical warning on what our cities can become (Figure 10.1):

> the *No-Stop City* is not a design, but rather a radical level of representation of the contemporary city as an apparently hyper-expressive reality that is actually, substantially catatonic because it is the result of infinite repetition of an alienating political system without destiny.[7]

By replacing engagement with irony, hope with resignation, from the 1970s on, the dialectics between utopia and form has slowly evaporated, implying a progressive disinterest in form as a vehicle of new societal needs.

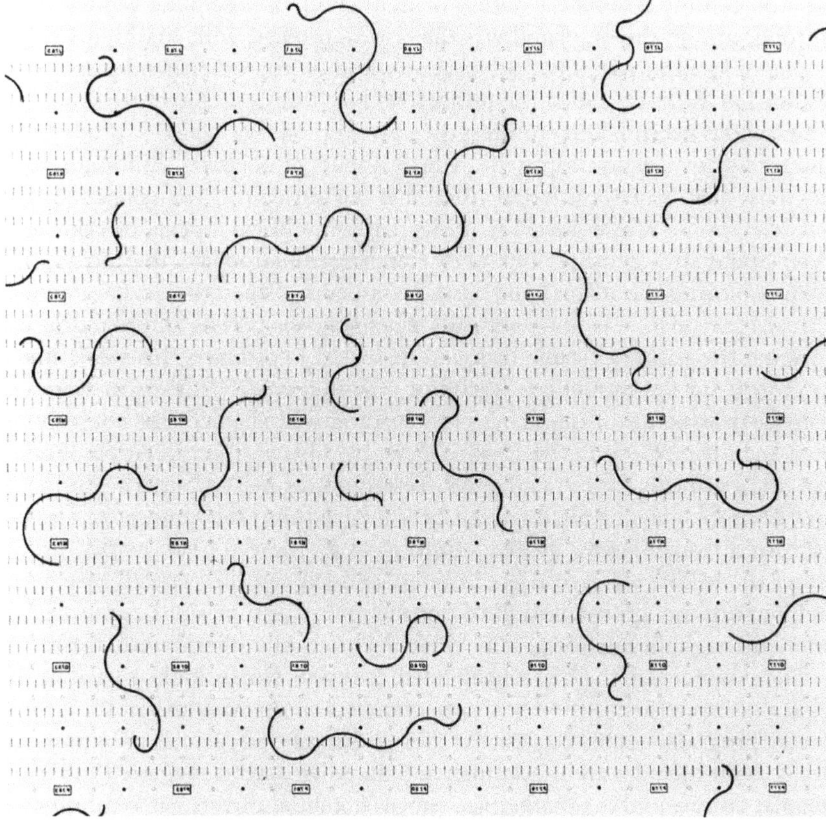

*Figure 10.1* Archizoom, *No-Stop City*, 1969.

## Between Critical and Projective

To better understand the reasons of architecture's gradual separation from utopia, it's necessary to look into a larger disciplinary framework. In 2002, Robert Somol and Sarah Whiting published their seminal essay *Notes around the Doppler Effect and Other Moods of Modernism* in *Perspecta*.[8] The essay aimed to depict the state of the art in the discourse around architecture and constituted a retroactive response to another essay, originally published in 1984 by Michael Hays in the same journal,[9] in which the author described all architecture as a critical manifestation, lying on the verge between culture and form. In questioning Hays' premises, Somol and Whiting introduced another category – the projective: 'an alternative to the critical project, linked to the diagrammatic, the atmospheric, and cool performance.'[10] If, according to the authors, for a long time architecture had been conceived in terms of autonomy – implying critique, representation, and signification – but not in terms of instrumentality – projection, performativity, and pragmatics – a paradigm shift was taking place at the dawn of the twenty-first century. A clear dichotomy around the nature of architecture as discipline was therefore introduced. On the one hand was the critical project, with Manfredo Tafuri as one of its most passionate advocates, while on the other hand stood what Somol and Whiting called the projective. For Tafuri, architecture should be autonomous because it has to resist the current modes of capitalist production, and refuse any relationship with exterior inputs or contexts. Autonomous in the sense that it obeys internal rules: it is self-reflective, self-generated, and self-referential. While Tafuri investigated the political aspects of criticality, Peter Eisenman – another of its advocates, according to Hays' definition – has been exploring the formal and aesthetic aspects of the critical. Contrary to Tafuri, Eisenman was not politically engaged, nor was he interested in examining the nature of capitalism and its spatial byproducts; his work aimed to go beyond the immediate legibility of architectural artifacts in search of their deep structure. Eisenman's close reading will characterize not only his own architecture – as in the *House Series* – but also his interpretation of other canonical projects such as Palladio's, Terragni's, or Le Corbusier's. An incessant labor of syntactic analysis that later evolved into the concept of *lateness*, borrowed from Adorno in his definition of Beethoven's late works: 'an attempt to circumvent stylistic constraints and expand the critical capacity of architecture though the notion of untimeliness. Examples of lateness can be found throughout history, arising when a work is out of joint with its time.'[11]

The counterpart to this consolidated tradition which looked back at the legacy of modernism, the term projective has to do with materials, atmosphere, program, technologies. To follow Somol and Whiting's argument, projectivity includes architects such as Stan Allen – who suggested to regard popular culture and the marketplace not as potential threats but as resources – and also Rem Koolhaas, whose fascination with Manhattan's culture of congestion saw in the skyscraper its apex, because 'the skyscraper-machine allows the projection infinitely upward of virtual worlds within this world.'[12] The constant and endless re-invention of existing conditions evoked by Koolhaas is what George Baird defined as a post-Utopian pragmatism,[13] focused on the acknowledgment and celebration of the real. Contrary to the critical, in fact, the projective doesn't question the economic and ideological premises of contemporary societies. It accepts the status quo, and takes advantage of it, according to an oftentimes opportunistic or even nihilistic perspective. Digital technologies allowed the projective culture to experiment with multi-layered surfaces, articulated geometries, and topological continuity.

The notion of form – its ideation and its materialization – lies therefore at the core of the tension between the critical and the projective. Form can be internally generated and self-referential: in other words, it can be critical – an instrument of resistance as postulated by Pier Vittorio Aureli in his discussion of an 'absolute architecture.'[14] But form can also be the response to external inputs – it can be projective – absorbing environmental conditions, producing formal complexity, and programmatic instability. In other words, the shift announced by Somol and Whiting can be read as the transition from the idea of architecture as object to the idea of architecture as field. Autonomy vs. environment, hierarchy vs. horizontal vectors. Gradually, the projective culture produced a total dissolution of the architectural object within a multi-level entity, composed of different strata and agents. Architecture, landscape, urbanism, interiors: all these different domains morph to shape new hybrid phenomena. As David Ruy says: 'the grand finale of architecture's movement from object to field may very well be the collapse of the architectural object into a field of relations that then dissolve into a general ecological field of relations that constitutes the world. And thus, architectural practice unintentionally becomes subsumed by ecological practice.'[15]

Almost 20 years after the publication of *Notes around the Doppler Effect and Other Moods of Modernism*, it's time to interrogate ourselves on what remains of Somol and Whiting's crystalline description and also on what role architecture can play as an instrument to imagine societal, cultural and political change. What we know is that, in looking beyond avant-garde models, architecture has progressively lost the ambition to envision alternative futures. As described by Michael Speaks, who coined the term design intelligence to designate the intellectual dominant of twenty-first-century post-vanguards:

> though we live in uncertain times, one thing is certain: contemporary architecture is not driven by visionary ideas heroically realized in visionary form. Instead, contemporary architecture is compelled by the need to innovate, to create plausible solutions to problems that have been stated but whose larger implications have not yet been formulated. This can only be accomplished with intelligence. Otherwise, design is simply a matter of completing a problem given without adding anything new.[16]

In opposition to this paranoid obsession for innovation, Mark Foster Gage recently re-examined the impact of the projective on contemporary architectural culture, and came to the conclusion that 'while never defined as possessing a clear agenda of its own, the post-critical era had begun, yet without introducing new strategic replacements.'[17] In sharing Foster Gage's assessment, can we move away from the projective and from its sickening celebration of the real? Can we retrieve some aspects of criticality without being nostalgic?

If, as affirmed by Nadir Lahiji, 'architecture is today principally composed of aesthetic counterfeits that over-expose it to sensual gratification,'[18] and if critical strategies are no longer adequate to the tasks of their original intent, new territories have to be explored, as well as new challenges have to be faced. Slavoj Žižek identifies four forms of antagonism, which may in his view give rise to the urgency of an emancipatory-egalitarian hypothesis and that constitute for architecture major opportunities: the ecological catastrophe, the illegitimate extension of private property rights to intellectual property, techno-scientific development, and new forms of apartheid reflected in the proliferation of walls and slums.[19] The architectural answer to these questions can only be found in utopia. The form that utopia can take on will derive from another necessary shift: a renovated interest in the object-oriented nature of architecture.

## Objects, Hyperobjects, Assemblages

After years of horizontal plateaus, porous surfaces, and rhizomatic structures, architecture has recently been experiencing a return to the idea of the object as a main vector of formal expression. This new focus depends on the simultaneous and interconnected emergence of three conditions: a new body of ideas on aesthetics – the contributions of the so-called Object-Oriented philosophy – a new interpretative framework – the age of Hyperobjects – and a new set of design techniques and formal outcomes – assemblages. The presence and the effects of these three conditions over the architectural discourse invite us to radically rethink forms, challenges and tools of the future.

A redefinition of object conditions within artistic practices along with a focus on the relationships between human and non-human agents, inform Object-Oriented Ontology (OOO), a term coined for the first time in 1999 by Graham Harman.[20] The speculative ground of OOO includes a broad definition of the term object, and the quest for a flat ontology – the idea that all objects deserve equal attention, whether they be human, non-human, natural, cultural, real, or fictional. To be more specific, Graham Harman describes three possible ways to look at objects: Undermining, Overmining, or Duomining. While Undermining refers to the act of reducing any object to what this is made of – smaller objects – Overmining refers to the idea that an object only becomes real when it is part of a larger narrative or set of relationships. A third way, called Duomining, combines both modes of understanding, in the sense that

> a table is neither the pieces of which it is made, nor the effects it has on users. [...] Art has a special capacity for dealing with the "third table", that lies between the first table (table-particles) and second table (table-events).[21]

The translation of these ideas into the territory of architecture is, as often happened in the past for other cases such as deconstruction or post-structuralism, problematic, and induces facile generalizations. Is an object a building? A place?

The most basic translation of OOO, that is building equals object, can only be considered a starting point. Under a careful examination of Harman's definitions, one can realize that, applied to architecture, OOO can indicate not only an object in its physical presence – a column, a window, etc. – but also a concept, a theory. Physical entities are objects, but so are properties, ideas, and institutions. Despite the evident difficulties to visualize concrete manifestations of an object-oriented ontology applied to architecture, what makes Harman's and a few others' contributions potentially interesting is that, by shifting our attention back to objects and their inner qualities, the disciplinary discourse can distance itself from the neutrality of field conditions, as well as from their pragmatic and performative aspects, to finally focus on a redefinition of architecture's autonomous character. In this respect, an object-oriented architecture can be utopian, in the sense of situating its intervention strategies outside of the parameters of the projective, and by substituting mere optimistic celebrations of the real with a critical project of future.

If Harman's ontology can constitute a fertile humus for architecture, today the notion of Hyperobjects can help reactivate the intricate relation between architecture, the discourse around utopia, and the form of utopia itself, by serving as a catalyst for the discipline to confront some urgent issues. A term introduced by Timothy Morton in 2013 to describe the overwhelming impact of human activities on earth, Morton defines Hyperobjects as 'objects deployed so massively in space and time that human beings cannot engage with them in any reciprocal way.'[22] To borrow more of his own words,

> a Hyperobject could be the biosphere, or the Solar System. A Hyperobject could be the sum total of all the nuclear materials on earth; or just the plutonium, or the uranium. A Hyperobject could be the very log-lasting product of direct human manufacture, such as Styrofoam or plastic bags, or the sum of all the whirring machinery of capitalism.[23]

The production of Hyperobjects is, therefore, a manifestation of the Anthropocene: the evidence of the so-called end of the world, in the sense of a slow yet irreversible process of erosion of our biosphere. Whereas Morton's work is obviously aligned and influenced by OOO, his definition of Hyperobjects permits to position architecture within the general context of the Anthropocene and to include in its preoccupations some of the questions raised by Žižek, such as spatial segregation and climate change – according to the World Green Building Council, for instance, every year building operations account for 39% of global energy-related carbon emissions, 36% of energy consumption, and a 35% of waste output.[24] In other words, to investigate architecture's condition in the age of Hyperobjects means speculating on its collective and political character – as one of the main agents of environmental destruction first and then as one of the possible remedies too.

Once acknowledged the impact that OOO can exert on the rise of utopian thinking, and once contextualized the idea of Hyperobjects as a background for theoretical and operative strategies, it's possible to finally introduce the notion of assemblage – 'a multiplicity which is made of many heterogeneous terms and which established liaisons, relations between them, across ages, sexes and reigns – different natures.'[25] In his attempt to build an assemblage theory, by integrating Gilles Deleuze and Félix Guattari's contributions combined with Fernand Braudel's focus on economic organizations, Manuel DeLanda offers a suggestive interpretation on what assemblages are, whose consequences pertain to the territory of architecture too. Assemblages, for DeLanda, are multiple and unique at the same time: each assemblage is an individual identity – 'an individual person, an individual community, an individual organization, an individual city.'[26] Assemblages can become part of other larger assemblages, as 'communities, in addition to persons, include the material and symbolic artifacts: the architecture of the buildings that house them; the myriad different tools and machines used in offices, factories, and kitchens; the various sources of food, water, and electricity.'[27] Intuitively, the word assemblage has an immediate translation into the territory of architecture; it can even evoke postmodernist operations of fragmentation, bricolage, historical pastiche, irony, etc. In opposition to those postmodern techniques, the proposed notion of assemblage recognizes complexity, and entails the possibility to preserve singularity and multiplicity. It has to do with the definition of composite objects that are macro and micro at the same time, compact and finite in their conglomeration. Assemblages are meta-scalar; their syntax suggests a critical unity, that incorporates difference and diversification. Assemblages don't operate through subtraction or synthesis, but through collision and agglomeration. They derive from additive processes, to follow Mario Carpo's distinction between additive and subtractive making. In *The Second Digital Turn*, in fact, Carpo introduces a distinction that 'goes back to Leon Battista Alberti's *De Statua* and to Michelangelo's *Letter to Benedetto Varchi* of 1459. In more recent times, subtractive fabrication was the first to go digital: numerically controlled milling machines have been in use since the early 1950s. Today the 3D printer has taken its place: an additive fabrication technology, where each voxel must be individually designed, calculated and made.'[28]

The potential utopian character implicit in the idea of assemblages is that they not only aim to redefine existing types and typologies; assemblages depict new models of combination / aggregation, by rethinking traditional ideas of figuration and, at the urban level, figure/ground relationships.

The notion of assemblage takes on at least two different possible orientations. One direction is merely operative. It informs the contemporary practice and utilizes assemblages to transform existing artifacts, either at the building and at the urban scale: it manifests in a series of concrete projects of reuse, retrofitting, and recycling, aimed to establish a new dialogue between old and new vocabularies, and to critically address issues of energy behavior and construction waste. In Barcelona, for example, Catalan architects Flores & Prats worked on the adaptive reuse of a formal social club – Sala Beckett (2014). Memory is the thread connecting old and new: the existing building is transformed into a theatre and a dramaturgy school. Rather than containing the new program in a well-defined area, the architects fragment the program and diffuse it over every corner of the building. The building itself, therefore, becomes the theatre: materials, decorations, *objet trouvé*, and interior vistas shape the main theatrical activity. The intervention on the old building reveals itself as a process of *anastylosis* where existing and new fragments are re-composed in a novel fashion. Such a process doesn't translate simply in the juxtaposition of materials, nor in their re-composition as a mosaic. As an assemblage, Sala Beckett questions ideas of image and function to constitute a multiplicity that regards architecture as a combination of old and new patterns, entropic relations, interior, and urban components (Figure 10.2). To aggressive operations of tabula rasa and dramatic gestures aimed to generate landmarks, Flores & Prats contrapose a patient process of mending, where overlap of textures, patterns, and lexicons take place.

The other direction suggested by the use of assemblages in the territory of architecture is deeply speculative, disruptive in its premises and in its outcomes. Peter Trummer, for example, in his pedagogic activity, uses drawings and texts to propose new forms of architecture for contemporary cities. His *City in the Age of Hyperobjects I* is a critical reaction to the low-density manifestations of urban sprawl that characterize different areas of the world. In opposition to the incessant horizontal expansion provoked by such models, what Trummer proposes is not a machine, nor an organism. In *City in the Age of Hyperobjects I* objects present themselves in a finite yet composite assemblage, which incorporates in its interior/exterior infrastructures, means of transport, ordinary buildings, and extraordinary prototypes. The city becomes an enclave of experimentation, isolated by the traditional figure/ground association of the surroundings.

Clearly inspired by OOO, the speculative work of Mark Foster Gage focuses on the political character of aesthetic conditions, rejecting the stereotypical association of the word aesthetics with superficial, banal, and innocent exercises, and considering it as an essential framework for human activity. Foster Gage's proposal for the *Guggenheim Museum in Helsinki* (2014) is informed by these ideas: the building proposed is a catalog of objects that have been randomly downloaded from the internet – the author calls them recycled digital materials; these objects have been reassembled in a composite form whose complexity derives not only from the collision of its different geometries, but also from the inaccessible meaning that their association conveys (Figure 10.3). Each individual object loses its own content to become

*Figure 10.2* Flores & Prats, *Sala Beckett*, Barcelona, 2014.

*Figure 10.3* Mark Foster Gage, *Helsinki Guggenheim Museum,* 2014.

part of a larger assemblage. To reference again Mario Carpo, the project also questions the traditional idea of decoration, as

> in the age of Big Data and 3D printing, the very same terms of decoration and ornament, predicated as they are on the traditional Western notion of ornament as supplement and superfluity, do not apply, and perhaps we should simply discard these terms, together with the meanings they still convey.[29]

To go back to the main point of this article, one may say that the simultaneous presence of OOO, Hyperobjects, and assemblages can set the premises for a disciplinary turn – a shift characterized by a new focus on architecture's object-like qualities (OOO), the confrontation with urgent and oppressive global issues (Hyperobjects), and a new set of formal tools able to express future scenarios (assemblages).

## Conclusion

Whether this renewed interest in object-conditions will impact significantly the architectural discourse of the next decades is yet to be determined, as is yet to be determined if object-oriented speculations can constitute an answer to the projective culture that dominated recently. The main question becomes now how to rethink disciplinarity and its use of form: while Mark Foster Gage invites us to consider that architecture should be engaged in wider social-political registers and possibly by exploring it through the aesthetic,[30]

Peter Eisenman recently emphasized again the need for architecture to be critical, since 'the techno-zeitgeist of today has returned to a present-based avant-garde, one in which the limits of form are defined by the technical possibility of the present and in which might be the integer of possible resistance.' To build an integrated and holistic perspective on the future, where form is not only a fetish but becomes (again) an intellectual and operative vector of change, the question of utopia must be brought back to the table. Evoking utopia, as poignantly described by Reinhold Martin, doesn't mean to aspire to a perfect world, an impossible construction to achieve.[31] Nor can utopia constitute a condition of unconscious immobility, waiting for something that will probably never happen, as in Beckett's *Waiting for Godot*. Utopia needs to be critical but, mainly, real: 'not because it dreams impossible dreams, but because it recognizes reality itself as an all-too-real dream enforced by those who prefer to accept a destructive and oppressive status quo.'[32]

## Notes

1 Bruno Latour, *We Have Never Been Modern* (Cambridge, MA: Harvard University Press, 1993).
2 Ernst Bloch, *The Spirit of Utopia* (Redwood City, CA: Stanford University Press, 2000).
3 Francis Fukuyama, *The End of History and the Last Man* (New York: The Free Press, 1992).
4 Nadir Lahiji, *An Architecture Manifesto* (New York: Routledge, 2019), 150.
5 Ibid., 152.
6 Ibid.
7 Ibid.
8 Robert Somol, Sarah Whiting, "Notes around the Doppler Effect and Other Moods of Modernism," *Perspecta*, no. 33 (2002): 72–77.
9 Michael Hays, "Between Culture and Form," *Perspecta,* no. 21 (1984): 14–39.
10 Somol, Whiting, "Notes around the Doppler Effect and Other Moods of Modernism," 74.
11 Peter Eisenman, *Lateness* (Princeton, NJ: Princeton Architectural Press, 2020), 9.
12 Somol, Whiting, "Notes around the Doppler Effect and Other Moods of Modernism," 76.
13 George Baird, "Criticality and Its Discontents," *Harvard Design Magazine*, no. 21 (Fall 2004–Winter 2005): 18.
14 Pier Vittorio Aureli, *The Possibility of an Absolute Architecture* (Cambridge, MA: MIT Press, 2011).
15 David Ruy, "Returning to (Strange) Objects," *Tarp* (Spring 2012): 39.
16 Michael Speaks, "Design Intelligence – Introduction: Part 1," in *Constructing a New Agenda. Architectural Theory 1993–2009*, ed. by Krista Sykes (New York: Princeton Architectural Press, 2010), 214.
17 Mark Foster Gage, *Designing Social Equity* (New York: Routledge, 2019), 41.
18 Lahiji, *An Architecture* Manifesto, 197.
19 Slavoj Žižek, *First as Tragedy, Then as Farce* (London: Verso, 2009), 91.
20 Graham Harman, "Object-Oriented Philosophy" (lecture, Brunel University, Uxbridge, UK, September 11, 1999).
21 Graham Harman, "Undermining, Overmining, and Duomining: A Critique," in *ADD Metaphysics*, ed. by Jenna Sutela (Aalto: Aalto University Digital Design Laboratory, 2013), 43.

22 Timothy Morton, *Hyperobjects* (Minneapolis: University of Minnesota Press, 2013), 1.
23 Ibid., 2.
24 "2018 Global Status Report", World Green Building Council, accessed March 19, 2021.
25 Gilles Deleuze and Claire Parnet, *Dialogues II* (New York: Columbia University Press, 1994), 69.
26 Manuel DeLanda, *Assemblage Theory* (Edinburgh: Edinburgh University Press, 2016), 19.
27 Ibid., 20.
28 Mario Carpo, *The Second Digital Turn* (Cambridge: MIT Press, 2017), 75.
29 Carpo, *The Second Digital Turn*, 79.
30 Gage, *Designing Social Equity*, 78.
31 Reinhold Martin, "Critical of What? Toward a Utopian Realism," in *Constructing a New Agenda. Architectural Theory 1993–2009*, ed. by Krista Sykes (New York: Princeton Architectural Press, 2010).
32 Ibid., 360.

# 11 Senses of Reality, or

## Realism *and* Aesthetics, Today?

*Giacomo Pala*

### 1

One concern is haunting the theoretical debate — architecture's loss of its sense of reality. In other words, it would seem that architecture has by now lost its purpose, its meaning and its scope.

First of all, there is a discussion on architecture's role in a globalized market economy. This is a debate that concerns the reduction of architecture to a commodity, which would leave it emptied of its purpose.[1] It is a dispute about the places where architecture is built, about its dependence on the economic system, about the political role of the architect, and about the institutions that control the making of buildings.

Second, there are those who speak of decadence, according to whom architecture has by now lost its meaning. This complaint can take many forms, but it is most typical of those who wish architects would remain faithful to supposedly immutable laws (of taste, of beauty, of harmony).[2]

A different demand for a defined scope also emerges in the work of some of those who conceive architecture as the outcome of positivist processes. In this case, instead of representing a lost value, architects are sometimes urged to yield before an idolization of rationality. Architecture, in this case, seems to be reduced to little more than the mere satisfaction of functions, or the outcome of statistics.[3]

Of course, these concerns are not equivalent to one another (at the very least, they may have different ideological connotations). Nonetheless, they all seem to share a similar mandate: the will to bring architecture under the domain of predetermined methodologies, ideals, or heuristics. In their efforts to do so, however, they gloss over a fact of primary importance: the enduring tendency among architects, both now and in the past, to reject established guidelines, refuting what is consensually accepted as right and proper in order to investigate unforeseen possibilities. Even among the ones who rely on traditional values, or positivistic methods (input/output), there will always be those who invent new variations, exploit loopholes in the rules, and develop alternative practices, forms and concepts – thus requiring a whole new

DOI: 10.4324/9781003292999-13

discourse; a whole new sense of reality that will inevitably elude self-enclosed conceptual systems.

As a matter of fact, the topic of architecture's loss of its sense of reality should probably be turned on its head. If that (common) sense has truly died, this has not happened through a single cultural stroke, but rather due to an "excess of sense"[4], to use a formula typical of Jean-Luc Nancy's philosophy: a constant, continuous, and ever faster multiplication of senses of reality. This condition – ultimately best described by Peter Osborne as a "disjunctive unity of present times"[5] – is quite simply the natural consequence of what we have come to call modernity (including its many prefixes): the more or less conflictual coexistence of more and more entities, cultures and diverging perspectives on the world.

In essence, we have ended up living in a condition of potential incommensurability: a hyperconnected and ever fracturing world where we are all legitimately inclined to display our own difference and specificity, demanding recognition. A condition that inevitably presents us a challenge: how can we make sense of a reality that is as pluralized as never before?

Needless to say, to ask this question is not to implicitly justify an acritical acceptance of the state of things. Neither is it a matter of idealizing the architect as a creative "genius" (which is the ideological premise for the commodification of any innovation).[6] Still less is it a question of advocating a retreat from reality's pragmatic needs by promoting an architectural reverie, or a new kind of paper architecture. It is only to put forward the following issue: instead of lamenting the loss of one sense of reality, it is necessary to make sense of today's proliferation of techniques, practices, languages, and traditions. An issue that becomes self-evident once we look at what is happening in our field today.

## 2

There are architects like Andrés Jaque (Office for Political Innovation), Izaskun Chinchilla, or Husos Architects, who think of aesthetics as a tool to "redistribute agency and knowledge"[7] in order to address socio-political and ecological issues. Then there are those like Space Popular, who combine different aesthetics and imageries, producing a kind of encyclopedic architecture using different media and techniques. In parallel with architects such as the collective "Smallest of Worlds", Andreas Angelidakis, Animali Domestici (and many others), they also explore the intersection of material and virtual spaces/realities. Some, like Lacaton & Vassal, develop their work from considerations on the context where they operate, using a design method based on a process of subtraction from the existing. Many – often defined as "post-digital"[8] – reimagine architectural representation, while others reinvent the collage (or even the vernacular), by means of sampling techniques and artificial intelligence.[9] Arno Brandlhuber (Brandlhuber+) radically rethinks the practice of architecture through acts of reuse and a counterintuitive approach to regulations, while DOGMA attempts a critical approach toward today's urban reality and economic system.[10] Some architects – like Bureau Spectacular and Andrew Kovacs – explore new formal syncretisms; Adam Nathaniel Furman plays with aesthetics while also dealing with queer culture; Yinka Ilori – inspired by his Nigerian and British heritage – uses design as a narrative device. Others, like X+Living, work at the limits of kitsch, in this case, while designing spaces for children in China. In the US, Olalekan Jeyifous, Mabel O. Wilson, Sekou Cooke and many others problematize Afro-American culture as a way to rethink architecture and its history in their country[11]; in the case of Cooke, more specifically, we discover a "Hip-Hop architecture".[12] Oscillating between the poles of maximalism, literalism and minimalism, many architects today are also trying to develop new formal languages. Amongst others: Baukuh, Jennifer Bonner, Sean Canty, First Office, Christian Kerez, Kuehn Malvezzi, SO–IL, Vector Architects, Tom Wiscombe, WOJR, WW Architecture, Young & Ayata. While Cloud 9 (Enric Ruiz-Geli) deal with ecological issues by means of new technologies, architects and critics such as Joseph Grima, Raumlabor, Elisa Iturbe (and others) rethink architecture's materiality in light of new ecological criteria and circular paradigms.[13] There are architects such as Philip F. Yuan and Sameep Padora who use computation in order to rethink the possibilities offered by traditional materials. Mariam Kamara (Atelier Masōmī), instead, rethinks the possibilities presented by traditional craftsmanship in Niger. While some theorize, design and build a "Discrete"[14] architecture using the most advanced digital tools, Fieldoffice Architects (田中央聯合建築師事務所) explore social issues related to living conditions in Taiwan, adopting a somewhat expressive architectural language as they do so. Agendas range from the speculative practices of Drawing Architecture Studio (绘造社) and Liam Young (Tomorrows Thoughts Today), to Solano Benítez's tectonic explorations. Meanwhile, MAEID and Andrea Ling hybridize machines, nature, and fictions (following and extending research paths inaugurated by pioneers such as François Roche and Neri Oxman), while Brandon Clifford finds inspiration in the most ancient tectonic configurations in order to use the most advanced fabrication technologies.

These are just a few of the many cultural practices and projects of today, yet they are enough to get an idea – albeit approximate – of today's multiplication of discourses, practices, purposes and forms. We witness an agglomerate of different monads, more or less related to one-another, each shaping its own sense of reality related to specific purposes and contextual conditions, but inherently unable to represent reality as a whole. A condition that inevitably solicits a question: how can we make sense of such a variety of tendencies and plurality of ends, while avoiding both the mourning for the death of architecture's sense of reality and the erosion of differences?

## 3

Theory must take account of today's heterogeneity, without becoming either a relativism for which there would be no hierarchy among values ('anything goes'), or the ultimately impossible attempt to define a "universal" paradigm. Also, it is not even a matter of classifying today's differences according to categories cherished in the "autonomous" space of the discipline. This is for two reasons. First of all, because the discipline itself has exploded (at least from a western point of view), due to the very multiplication of its senses of reality (the relativization of its canons, narratives, axioms). Secondly, and as already discussed by K. Michael Hays, because the concept "autonomy" is ultimately incapable of describing the relationship between architecture and the rest of the world.[15]

Rather, there is a need for a theory capable of describing, understanding and defining how – and to what extent – all previous examples (and more) are able to establish an alterity to what is considered to be normal, by virtue of their specificities. Theory must in fact learn how to describe and appreciate architecture's opening up of new possibilities of worldliness, through an investigation of the relationship architecture establishes with the world: that is, the mutual co-implication between the discipline and its context.[16] Understand, then, how architecture "animates the world"[17] (to borrow from Viktor Shklovsky's definition of art), by defining potential senses of reality: the suggestion of alternatives through the delineation of spaces, the composition of forms, and the combination of materials.[18]

Admittedly, this issue is eminently theoretical and slightly abstract. Nevertheless, it is by no means of secondary importance. If it is true that architecture transforms and shifts the sense of reality according to ever-new perspectives, then theory is essential to questioning and reshaping predetermined forms of knowledge. A questioning that, however, can only be productive if we are able to verify, amend – and eventually dismiss – critical categories, models, and terminologies that no longer seem to work.

With this in mind, it is worth analyzing some uses of a concept that (not by chance) has become quite popular in recent years: realism. Although constantly "repudiated only in the name of a higher realism",[19] the term is often used in architecture to designate the coextension of architecture with the world, and the intersection of the mimetic/ordinary function of a building and its expressive/extra-ordinary qualities.[20] Or rather – and as counterintuitive as it may seem – realism as the naming of architecture's ability to build, construe, and formalize a difference within and against commonly accepted habits (be they urban, formal, or practical).

## 4

In the years of the historical avant-garde, when not rejected, realism was a useful concept for rethinking modern arts, particularly in Russia.[21] Artistic objects were considered "things in the world, analogous to other things",[22] as stated by Boris Groys: works that should have shared the common destiny of all commodities within the industrial world. For its part, architecture could be thought of as a practice enabling the rooting of "creative pursuits in the firm ground of the present day".[23]

In the period of postmodernism, architects tried to relate their work to "reality" by playing a formal game based on the hybridization of linguistic codes. The result was what Ignasi de Solà-Morales defined as "liberal realism"[24]: reality was now addressed by means of metaphors, symbols, patterns and figures. Most notably, at the time, Aldo Rossi and many of the architects associated to la Tendenza claimed to be realists: "not to accept reality, but to take hold of it in order to transform it 'politically'".[25]

In the 1980s and 1990s, the concept of "dirty realism"[26] – associated by Fredric Jameson with cyberpunk[27] – emerged in order to describe the work of architects such as Rem Koolhaas, Jean Nouvel, Lars Lerup, and others. Later on, architects such as the "Superdutch"[28] – to quote Bart Lootsma's analysis of Dutch architecture in the late 1990s and early 2000s – would also occasionally be labeled as "extreme realists"[29]: practitioners who develop their work from considerations about contemporary society and its urban conditions.

Today, "realism" may assume many different meanings. In addition to the never forgotten "Magical Realism"[30] and "Hyperrealism",[31] some use this concept in order to describe the work of architects like Lacaton & Vassal, Arno Brandlhuber or Bruther,[32] as practices that confront the material reality of specific urban and socio-economic contexts (although such confrontation obviously does not exclude qualities that transcend pragmatic goals).

Jesús Vassallo has also recently refashioned "Dirty Realism".[33] In this case, much of what is usually defined as post-digital architecture (more specifically, the works of architects and photographers like De Vylder Vink Taillieu, OFFICE Kersten Geers David Van Severen, Philipp Schaerer, Bas Princen, and Filip Dujardin) would "offer us a return to a broader material culture, this time with freedom and the mandate to make it our own".[34]

Last but not least, some architects and theorists refer to Speculative Realism and Object-Oriented Ontology in order to conceive a new theory for architecture.[35] Referring more or less explicitly to the writings of Graham Harman (among other things, the theoretician of Weird Realism[36]) and to a philosophy where "humans are allowed to live [...] alongside sea urchins, kudzu, enchiladas, quasars, and Tesla coils",[37] the already-mentioned Tom Wiscombe, Young & Ayata (as well as Mark Foster Gage, Ferda Kolatan, Peter Trummer, David Ruy, and others) try to define new agendas for today's architecture.[38] Agendas that seem to share the common goal of defining a new kind of architectural language, using the name 'realism' as to summarize the need of addressing our world's complexity, although being aware of its parts' specificities and differences.

At a first and superficial glance, today's resurgence of realism may seem strange, since historiography has accustomed us to thinking of this concept as nothing more than the attempt to reproduce and represent reality in a presumably objective manner. Anyone trying to be a realist in such a way could only end up facing the famous paradox recounted by Jorge Luis Borges, for which an entire civilization collapsed because of its emperor's cumbersome desire to draw a 1:1 map of the empire.[39] This is but a way of saying something in truth quite simple: due to its complexity, the world cannot be represented, or reproduced in a presumably objective manner.

However, it should be noted that the uses of realism examined up to this point (and to which more can be added from other disciplines, including Jacques Rancière's "(sur)realism",[40] or "hybrid realism"[41]) are far from being naïve attempts to either represent reality *sub specie aeternitatis*, or develop poetics of absolute and immediate recognition.

Despite the obvious differences, the former versions of realism share something that becomes self-evident once we shift the emphasis from the noun "realism", to the various adjectives and prefixes it often comes with: (sur)-, dirty, hybrid, hyper, magical, speculative, weird. All of these words clearly tell us something that, despite being vaguely tautological, is worth emphasizing yet again: realism can be more than both the mere representation of reality and the uncritical acceptance of the state of things. Interesting kinds of realism are in fact always partly anti-realistic (dirty, hybrid, weird, and so on): they aim to take advantage of the strange aspects of the real and, in so doing, they try to unveil the otherwise concealed qualities of reality.

## 5

It can therefore be easily claimed that today's realism, in containing in itself its own negation (anti-realism), is a useful concept to describe and define architecture in terms of *its ability to construct possible realities*. Therefore, it is necessary to develop a theoretical approach that can allow us to appreciate architecture's phenomenality ("not the appearing of a thing, but rather productivity appearing as things"[42]), while being appreciative of its own expressive horizons. That is to say: to understand the way architecture is at the same time produced by its context, while trying to estrange and reinvent it — thus being something different from it.

In other words, today's uses of the word "realism" should allow us to appreciate architecture's dialogical nature: its capacity to reinvent and transmute the living, real experience of the world into a properly architectural dimension by virtue of its specific ability to establish a difference in a given context (in the widest possibile meaning of the word). In this sense, an architecture can be interpreted as a special kind of object, not dissimilar to the one Mikhail M. Bakthin has already described using the adjective *aesthetic*: an object where "life is found [...] in all the fullness of its value-bearing weightiness – social, political, cognitive"[43], though reinvented through "a process of comprehensive artistic forming by means of a particular material"[44].

By overcoming simplistic and worrying dichotomies between theory and practice, between aesthetics and ethics, or between discipline and social commitment, such an understanding should thus allow us to focus on the special relationship that an architectural object (a building, a project, a space, a design) establishes with the world, while creating its own; a relationship that is perhaps sometimes paradoxical, but for this very reason all the more interesting.

Therefore, architecture should be understood through trying to grasp the different layers of sense it contains, and how these vary with reference to changing contexts and to those who use or relate to it. Such theory, then, would be nothing more than a way to pay attention to the specificity of things, with the awareness that they are particularly fertile in precisely those areas that language and its descriptions may fail to reach, leaving room for further and newer interpretations. Of course, not all architectural objects are necessarily sensational, but they often are at least exceptional: they may escape predetermined discourses and practices, or carry within themselves something exceeding norms. Also, there will always be genres and categories that, if understood in a non-foundational sense, will always be of use in order to give a name to our experience: necessary approximations allowing us to order the different experiences of the contemporary world. However, one may wonder: might it be possible to favor the dynamic and contextual nature of things over the fixed nature of ideals and categories?

If the answer to this question is affirmative, then a theoretical horizon capable of understanding to what extent an architectural object may contribute to the reinvention of the world through the design of its own, should be attested. An approach to theory also capable of doing justice to today's diversity of attitudes (in their being discrete yet coexisting units of sense): the appreciation and understanding (and eventually critique) of how specific social, cultural and technical issues and disciplinary problems influence each other through the production of new forms, spaces, programs and objects.[45]

Finally, it should be clear that in the mourning for the death of architecture's sense of reality, there also lurks the desire of those who would like to tame criticality and call our field back to an ultimately imposed order. The alternative proposed here is the understanding of architecture's capacity to outwardly project new senses of reality: a constant redrawing, redesigning, and reshaping of the world toward different possibilities.[46]

## Notes

1 As an example, see: Reiner De Graaf, "Architecture Is Now a Tool of Capital, Complicit in a Purpose Antithetical to its Social Mission", in *The Architectural Review* (London: EMAP, 2015). https://www.architectural-review.com/essays/-architecture-is-now-a-tool-of-capital-complicit-in-a-purpose-antithetical-to-its-social-mission (10/02/2021).

2 As an example, see: "Why Is the Modern World So Ugly? (2021)", from the website of Alain De Botton's school; the School of Life (London; Amsterdam; Berlin; Istanbul; Paris; São Paulo; Taipei: The School of Life): https://www.theschoolo-flife.com/thebookoflife/why-is-the-modern-world-so-ugly/ (14/06/2021).

3 As an example, see: Thomas Kvan, "Data-Informed Design: A Call for Theory", in Mark Burry (edited by), *Urban Futures: Designing the Digitalised City, Architectural Design*, Volume 90, Issue 3 (London: Wiley & Sons, 2020), pp. 26–30.
4 Jean-Luc Nancy and Aurélien Barrau (Translated by Travis Holloway and Flor Méchain), What's These Worlds Coming To? (2011), (New York: Fordham University Press, 2015), p.12
5 Peter Osborne, *Anywhere or Not at All, Philosophy of Contemporary Art* (New York: Verso, 2013), p. 17.
6 On the topic, See: Pedro Fiori Arantes (translated by Adriana Kauffmann), *The Rent of Form, Architecture and Labor in the Digital Age* (2012) (Minneapolis: University of Minnesota Press, 2019).
7 Andrés Jaque, "Rearticulating the Social", interview to Nikolaus Hirsch, in "Positions", E-Flux, (2019). https://www.e-flux.com/architecture/positions/280206/rearticulating-the-social/ (10/10/2020).
8 On the post-digital, see: Sam Jacob, "Drawing and Collage", in Davide Tommaso Ferrando, Bart Lootsma and Kanokwan Trakulyingcharoen (edited by), *Italian Collage* (Siracusa: Lettera Ventidue Edizioni, 2020) pp. 80–93.
9 As examples, see: Damjan Jovanovic's work , David Ruy's and Karol Klein's "apophenia" - https://offramp.sciarc.edu/articles/apophenia-the-ruy-klein-cartographies (28/12/2020) - and the project "Refuge 2.0 – Artificial Swissness", from EPFL in Losanne: https://www.epfl.ch/labs/ldm/refuge-2-0-artificial-swissness/ (28/12/2020),.
10 on DOGMA's work and ideas, see Marco Biraghi, *l'Architetto come Intellettuale* (Torino: Einaudi, 2019) – apart from Aureli's many theoretical texts.
11 On the topic, see: Sean Anderson and Mabel O. Wilson (edited by), *Reconstructions: Architecture and Blackness in America* (New York: MoMa, 2021).
12 See: Sekou Cooke, *Hip-Hop Architecture: History/Theory/Practice* (London: Bloomsbury, 2021).
13 See: Space Caviar, *Non-Extractive Architecture: On Designing Without Depletion*, (Berlin: Sternberg Press, 2021); Elisa Iturbe (edited by), *Overcoming Crbon Form*, LOG 47, (New York: Anycorp, 2019)
14 See: Gilles Retsin (edited by), *Discrete: Reappraising the Digital in Architecture, Architectural Design*, Volume 89, Issue 2 (London: Wiley, 2019).
15 K. Michael Hays, "Critical Architecture: Between Culture and Form", in *Perspecta*, Volume 21 (Cambrdige: MIT Press, 1984), pp. 14–29.
16 On the topic, see: Giovanni Galli, "Conseguenze di Van Gogh, Un giallo ontologico in quattro atti più un intermezzo e una coda", in Giovanni Galli (edited by), *Sostenibilità e Potere*, (Genova: Sagep, 2015), pp. 53–95.
17 Viktor Shklovsky, "A Sentimental Journey (1923)", in Viktor Shklovsky (edited and translated by Alexandra Berlina), *A Reader* (New York/London/Oxford/New Dehli/Sydney: Bloomsbury Academic, 2017), p. 150.
18 This statement is actually inspired by Aldo Rossi, who wrote: "la combinazione di oggetti, di forme, di materiale della architettura è intesa a creare una realtà potenziale di sviluppi imprevisti, a far balenare soluzioni diverse, a costruire il reale." See: Aldo Rossi, "L'architettura della ragione come architettura di tendenza (1966)", in Aldo Rossi and Rosaldo Bonicalzi (edited by), *Scritti scelti sull'architettura e la città* (Milano: Clup, 1975), p. 372.
19 Emmanuel Lévinas, "Reality and its Shadow (1948)", in Seán Hand (edited by), *The Levinas Reader* (Oxford/Cambridge: Basil Blackwell, 1989), p. 130.
20 For a wider history on the topic, see: Manfredo Tafuri, "Architettura e Realismo", in Vittorio Magnago Lampugnani (edited by), *L'avventura delle Idee nell'Architettura: 1750–1980* (Milano: Electa, 1985), pp. 123–145.
21 On the topic, see: John E. Bowlt (edited by), *Russian Art of the Avant-Garde, Theory and Criticism 1902–1934* (New York: Viking Press, 1976).

22 Boris Groys, *In the Flow* (New York: Verso, 2016), p. 118.
23 Mosei Ginzburg (translated by Anatole Senkevitch, Jr.), *Style and Epoch (1924)* (Cambridge: MIT Press, 1982), p. 109.
24 Ignasi de Solà-Morales, *Differences: Topographies of Contemporary Architecture*, (Cambridge: MIT Press, 1997), p. 84.
25 Bernard Huett, "Formalism – Realism (1977)", in K. Michael Hays (edited by), *Architecture Theory Since 1968* (Cambridge: MIT Press, 2000), p. 259.
26 Liane Lefaivre, "Dirty Realism in European Architecture Today: Making the Stone Stony",( 1989), in Christophe Van Gerrewey, *Choosing Architecture, Criticism, History and Theory since the 10th Century* (Lausanne: EPFL Press, 2019), pp. 122–125
27 Fredric Jameson, *The Seeds of Time* (New York: Columbia University Press, 1994), pp. 129–205.
28 See: Bart Lootsma, *Superdutch: New Architecture in the Netherlands* (New York: Princeton Architectural Press, 2000).
29 Roemer van Toorn, quoted in "From Realism to Reality. A Future for Dutch Architectural Culture. A Conversation with Pier Vittorio Aureli and Roemer van Toorn", in *After the Party. Dutch Architecture*, OASE issue 67 (Rotterdam: NAi Publishers 2005), p. 53.
30 Lucy Bullivant, "'Activating Nature': The Magic Realism of Contemporary Landscape Architecture in Europe", in Helen Castle (edited by), *Landscape Architecture Site/NonSite, Architectural Design*, Volume 77, Issue 2 (London: Wiley, 2007), pp. 76–87.
31 Hernan Diaz Alonso, "'Sur' Realism. After Surrealism Comes Hyperrealism", in Neil Spiller (edited by), *Celebrating the Marvellous: Surrealism in Architecture, Architectural Design*, Volume 88, Issue 2 (London: Wiley, 2018), pp. 128–133.
32 See: Anh-Linh Ngo's discussion with Brandlhuber: https://www.siedle.com/App/WebObjects/XSeMIPS.woa/cms/page/locale.enGB/pid.221.225.549 (10/03/21). And: "ARCH+ features 103: Neuer Realismus in Frankreich https://archplus.net/de/archplus-features-103-neuer-realismus-in-frankreich/ (10/03/2021).
33 See: Jesús Vassallo, *Seamless: Digital Collage and Dirty Realism* (Zurich: Park Books, 2016).
34 Ibid., p. 180.
35 For an introduction to the topic, see: Levi Bryant, Nick Srnicek and Graham Harman (edited by), *The Speculative Turn, Continental Materialism and Realism* (Melbourne: re.press, 2011); Gonzalo Vaillo, "Superficiality and Representation: Adding Aesthetics to 'Knowledge without Truth'", *Open Philosophy*, Volume 4, Issue 1 (2021), pp. 36–57. https://doi.org/10.1515/opphil-2020–0150 (05/03/2021) and Jordi Vivaldi, "The Twofold Limit of Objects: Problematising Timothy Morton's Rift in Light of Eugenio Trías's Notion of Limit", in *Open Philosophy*, Volume 3, Issue 1 (2020), pp. 493–516. https://doi.org/10.1515/opphil-2020–0102 (05/03/2021).
36 Graham Harman, *Weird Realism: Lovecraft and Philosophy* (Arlesford: Zero Books, 2012).
37 Ian Bogost, *Alien Phenomenology, or What it's Like to Be a Thing* (Minneapolis: University of Minnesota Press, 2012), p. 5.
38 See: Mark Foster Gage, "Killing Simplicity: Object-Oriented Philosophy in Architecture", *Log*, Issue 33 (New York: Anyone Corporation, Winter 2015), pp. 95–106. Ferda Kolatan, "Genuine Hybrids: Towards an Architecture with No Origin", in Ali Rahim and Hina Jamelle (edited by), *Impact, Architectural Design*, Volume 90, Issue 5 (London: Wiley & Sons, 2020), pp. 40–49. Peter Trummer, "The City as an Object: Thoughts on the Form of the City", in *Log*, Issue 27 (New York: Anyone Corporation, Winter/Spring 2013), pp. 51–57.

Todd Gannon, Graham Harman, David Ruy and Tom Wiscombe, "The Object Turn: A Conversation", in *Log*, Issue 33 (New York: Anyone Corporation, Winter 2015), pp. 73–94. Michael Young, "The Art of the Plausible and the Aesthetics of Doubt", in *Log*, Issue 41 (New York: Anyone Corporation, Fall 2017), pp. 37–44.

39 See: Jorge Luis Borges, "Of Exactitude in Science (1954)", in Jorge Luis Borges (translated by Norman Thomas di Giovanni), *A Universal History of Infamy* (London: Penguin Books, 1972), p. 131.

40 Jacques Rancière (translated by Julie Rose), *Figures of History (2012)* (Cambridge: Polity, 2014), p. 79.

41 See: Stefano Ercolino (translated by Albert Sbragia), *The Maximalist Novel, from Thomas Pynchon's Gravity's Rainbow to Roberto Bolaño's 2666* (New York/London/New Delhi/Sydney: Bloomsbury, 2014).

42 Iain Hamilton Grant, *Philosophies of Nature after Schelling* (New York: Continuum Books, 2006), p. 176.

43 Mikhail M. Bakhtin, "The Problem of Content, Material, and Form in Verbal Art" (1924), in Mikhail Bakhtin (Edited by Michael Holquist and Vadim Liapunov), Art and Answerability. Early Philosophical Essays, (Texas: University of Texas Press, 1990), p.278.

44 Idem, p.281. On the "Aesthetic Object", also see: Mikel Dufrenne, (translated by Edward S. Casey, Albert A. Anderson, Willis Domingo and Leon Jackson), the Phenomenology of Aesthetic Experience (1953), (Evanston: Northwestern University Press, 1973)

45 On this topic, see also the following text, with which this essay is in almost absolute agreement: Matt Shaw, "Reorienting Criticism, Against A Priori Reductionism", in Marc Foster Gage (edited by), *Aesthetics Equals Politics: New Discourses across Art, Architecture, and Philosophy* (Cambridge: MIT Press, 2019), pp. 205–211.

46 Post scriptum: I would like to thank my colleagues and students from Innsbruck University, as well as Guglielmo Bilancioni, Eleni Boutsika-Palles, Tiziano Derme, Davide Tommaso Ferrando, Elie Haddad, Andreas Körner, Aniruddha Mukherjee, Bettina Siegele, Gonzalo Vaillo – and especially Giovanni Galli – for much criticism, and advice.

# 12 On the Use and Abuse of Biological Functionalism for Architecture

*Kasper Lægring*

## Introduction

The art of building is characterized by being necessarily and constantly influenced by other disciplines. Since the Industrial Revolution, the impact of technology has been felt especially strongly in architecture, yet both before and during modern times other disciplines like theology and later aesthetics also performed this role of informing architecture.

One such case is the impact of biology on architecture, and vice versa. The import of models and concepts from biological and ecological 'organismic' thinking into architecture began in the nineteenth century and intensified after the advancements in cybernetics, gene technology, and computer simulation of the 1960s onward. In the 1960s, and even more so in the 1990s, both ecosystems and computers were seen as potential drivers of change in the composition of architecture as a discipline, which were to be made compatible with a biological worldview.[1] This popular analogy still holds sway over the discipline.

But what happens when it turns out that the imported theory – in this case: evolutionary epistemology – becomes contested and refuted in its original disciplinary settings, those of biology and philosophy of science, yet continues to thrive in its new host environment – in this case, architecture? In just two years, 1979–1980, the so far dominant adaptationist interpretation of Darwinian evolution was rejected – in biology by Steven Jay Gould and Richard Lewontin, in philosophy of science by Paul Thagard – and in architecture, these results were arrived at independently by Philip Steadman at exactly the same time.

This chapter critically explores the ongoing, extremely tenacious, fascination with the biological analogy in architectural theory, and, more specifically, it seeks to establish that the use of the adaptationist evolutionary model in architecture also entails a functionalist worldview of a certain kind.

## What Is Functionalism?

What is functionalism? In her groundbreaking work on the subject, Ute Poerschke divides functionalist theory into three stages of development: first,

DOI: 10.4324/9781003292999-14

the eighteenth-century period where Carlo Lodoli is the towering figure, second, a nineteenth-century period where Karl Bötticher and Gottfried Semper dominate, and third, a modern, twentieth-century period where Hannes Meyer of the Bauhaus and other avant-garde figures prevail.

The first period, that of Lodoli, his disciples and detractors, can be defined as the most advanced in terms of unfolding the potential of functionalism on a purely *architectural* basis. Lodoli's project on behalf of architecture, which can be summed up in the pairing "funzione e rappresentazione," function and representation, introduces all of Poerschke's "criteria of function [...], which were described as action, relation between parts, and reference to a whole."[2] In the original functionalist theory "function always implied an active meaning," but "how could a building be regarded as active," she asks.[3] Lodoli's solution meant that certain aspects of the physicality of a built structure ought to be articulated accordingly, hence giving rise to representation.

Function should not be confused with purpose, as the two notions are not interchangeable, and this distinction becomes even clearer if we examine Semper's functionalist theory. Paradoxically, but also ingeniously, Semper considered utility and purposiveness a step to be overcome and to be transcended in the artifact. If carried out organically, the symbolic ornamentation of an everyday object, such as a vessel or a utensil, was thus not applied but arose from a sublimation of the tectonic and functional requirements intrinsic to the artifact in question.[4]

In spite of its rationalism, Lodoli's theory still belonged to a theological paradigm. In contrast, Semper, who had a background in engineering and architecture, envisioned architecture "emancipated from abject servitude to need, the state, and religion."[5] So, in the course of the nineteenth century, functionalist theory was radically altered by the newly defined natural sciences, and by biology, in particular. Analogies between body and architecture had been a mainstay of architectural theory since Vitruvius, but now the analogy was extended to cover organisms of every sort and organization. Georges, Baron Cuvier radically shaped the young science of biology, and his ideas on biological organization and functionality directly influenced architects such as Semper.[6]

While the source of inspiration and legitimation thus changed drastically during this era, the original composition of the functionalist idea (and ideal) was still preserved, since all three aspects of it – activity, part-to-part relationships, and part-to-whole relationships – were still clearly recognizable in Bötticher and Semper's theoretical attempts to learn from the new organicist modes of thinking.

Yet this perspective on functionalism in architecture changed completely when the Modernist avant-gardes of the first decades of the twentieth century replaced this tradition with their own, which was modeled on other ideas sourced from evolutionary biology. Advancements in the design of everyday objects were interpreted as steps in an ongoing evolution.[7] The original clear terminology of functionalist theory gave way to frequent and confusing equations of function with purpose.[8] Hannes Meyer was instrumental in developing a functionalism in which economy of means and materials was given priority at the expense of representation.[9] Here, functionalism was, paradoxically, increasingly seen as a question of separating and functionally delimiting the parts of an architectural project.[10]

## Spandrels and the Vestigial in Architecture and Nature

The mid-twentieth-century, when the Modern Movement became increasingly institutionalized and doctrinaire, also saw the rigidification of the interpretation of Darwinian evolution. In a far-reaching, highly influential, and quite peculiar article from 1979, *The spandrels of San Marco and the Panglossian paradigm: a critique of the adaptationist programme*, paleontologist Steven Jay Gould and biologist Richard Lewontin resort to architecture in order to expose and explain a fallacy in the then-current reception of the Darwinian model of evolution. With the universal acceptance of the "Modern Synthesis" of Darwinian and Mendelian ideas, which emerged in the 1930s and became established by the 1960s, evolutionary biology had become dominated by what Gould and Lewontin dubbed as the "adaptationist programme." In this school of interpretation of Darwin's concept of natural selection – which only became dominant in the 1930s – a given organism is subdivided into its constituent parts, which are then interpreted as results of adaptation, all of which serve a particular purpose. Every single part of an organism, not least its genes, are thus regarded as being in the service of evolutionary adaptation, and in some accounts from adherents of adaptationism even social customs and rites are seen as resulting from adaptation.

Gould and Lewontin begin with two architectural examples with which they showcase the same type of adaptationist argument in a different disciplinary setting. In their structural analysis of the interior spaces of San Marco in Venice and of King's College Chapel in Cambridge, they note that whenever a dome is mounted on rounded arches, or whenever fan vaulting is employed, spandrels, pendentives, or other connective surfaces are generated as necessary byproducts of the chosen construction principle (Figures 12.1 and 12.2). If these structures were to be read 'adaptationistly,' however, they would be regarded as desired ends in themselves, which would be a reversal of cause and effect – a type of faulty reasoning they call "Panglossian" after the Dr Pangloss of Voltaire's *Candide*: "Spandrels do not exist to house the evangelists."[11]

Until the appearance of their paper, "there was not a singular word nor simple phrase in common usage in evolutionary biology to describe a non-adaptive character or part of an organism that nonetheless fulfils a function."[12] And although their use of the term "spandrel" is incorrect – the three-dimensional element in question is properly called a pendentive, while a spandrel is its two-dimensional counterpart – it does not detract from their excellent point, which they deliver with wit and acuteness.

*Figure 12.1* Saint Mark's Basilica, Venice (Gary Campbell-Hall, Wikimedia Commons).

Gould and Lewontin support their corrective to evolutionary adaptationism – which is frequently supported by guesswork, as they demonstrate – by several detailed case studies from their own disciplines. As replacement, or at least a corrective to adaptationism's one-sided interpretation of Darwin, they document how Darwin, in his magnum opus as well as in his letters, always stressed his conviction "that natural selection has been the main, but not the exclusive means of modification."[13]

Lastly, Gould and Lewontin argue that greater attention needs to be given to phyletic and developmental constraints in organisms and to their consequences for evolution. They highlight the work of paleontologist Adolf Seilacher, who

> emphasized what he calls '*bautechnischer*', or *architectural*, constraints [...]. These arise not from former adaptations retained in a new ecological setting (phyletic constraints as usually understood), but as architectural restrictions that never were adaptations, but rather the necessary consequences of materials and designs selected to build basic *Baupläne*.[14]

Thus, following Gould and Lewontin, we can conclude that both in biology and in architecture we find examples in abundance of features that are functional yet are not products of adaptation. In other cases, we may even talk of highly survivable vestigial features and elements in buildings.

*Figure 12.2* King's College Chapel, Cambridge (seier+seier, Flickr).

## Moussavi: Ornaments without Meaning

With her ambitious tome, *The Function of Ornament* (2006), Farshid Moussavi, one of the founding partners of Foreign Office Architects (FOA), reintroduced functionalist discourse in architecture. But let us first revisit Gould and Lewontin's architectural odyssey, in order to clarify their stance on ornament (Figure 12.3):

> Every fan vaulted ceiling must have a series of open spaces along the mid-line of the vault, where the sides of the fans intersect between the pillars. Since the spaces must exist, they are often used for ingenious ornamental effect. In King's College Chapel in Cambridge, for example, the spaces contain bosses alternately embellished with the Tudor rose and portcullis.[15]

*Figure 12.3* King's College Chapel, Cambridge, detail of fan vaulting (seier+seier, Flickr).

In Semper's theory of ornament, the author distinguished between structurally active ornament, usually in the form of geometric and natural motifs, on the one hand, and figurative ornament, on the other, which summed up the "destination" of the building, its overall purpose. The latter type, pictorial and sculptural, for instance, the crowning "sculptures in the tympanum of a temple," "were admissible only on those parts on the whole that were not structurally active."[16] The vaulted ceiling of King's College Chapel fully coincides with this principle. Actually, Moussavi's text does not cover interiors at all – and, as we shall see, that applies to Alejandro Zaera-Polo's manifesto as well – so a direct comparison is not possible. Nonetheless, it is clear from the outset that her proposed theory is a new kind of functionalism, as the back cover of her book heralds the project of "dismantling the idea that ornament is applied to buildings as a discrete or non-essential entity."[17] Ornament has to arise by necessity, she argues.

Moussavi's first introduction on ornament prefaces a catalog of students' drawings of buildings old and new where the façade and its ornamentation have been emphasized. She comments this output by saying that "buildings produce affects that seem to grow directly from matter itself. They build expressions out of an internal order that overcome the need to 'communicate' through a common language, the terms of which may no longer be available."[18] Now, it was key concern of Lodoli that materials should be used according to their (structural) properties – in the case of the Doric order, he did not warrant the skeuomorphism of the wooden beam end of the triglyph that had turned to stone, for instance. And both Lodoli and Semper offer criteria, or at least indications, for how to channel their design principles into built form – this normativity is typical of functionalist theory. In Moussavi, we find an equally strong normativity, yet it has more to do with the argument of the *Zeitgeist* ("progress," "the dynamic nature of culture requires..."[19]) than with architectural composition or use of materials.

Moussavi speaks of "an in-built sense of order" and prefers that buildings "develop an internal consistency," which are clearly functionalist tropes when measured against Poerschke's definition. Louis Sullivan is positively highlighted as a figure who achieved organicity of all parts of the exterior. This leads Moussavi to invent a key distinction: "Decoration is contingent and produces 'communication' and resemblance. Ornament is necessary and produces affects and resonance."[20] It will be safe to assume that highly ornamented works by FOA, such as John Lewis & Partners Department Store and Cineplex in Leicester (2008) or Ravensbourne University London (2010), conform to Moussavi's demand of ornament (Figures 12.4 and 12.5).

There is certainly an active principle in Moussavi's theory, for it promotes "the expression of embedded forces through processes of construction, assembly and growth." Ornament should not be applied idealistically, whimsically, or mechanically, but should grow naturally from specific local conditions. "Ornament is therefore necessary and inseparable from the object," and this demand also resonates with the original functionalist definition in which everything has to serve a function in a larger whole.[21]

Nonetheless, Moussavi's theory of ornament, which "orders building components from the deepest to the thinnest,"[22] fails to connect with this tradition for several reasons, one being that "architects are responsible for a smaller

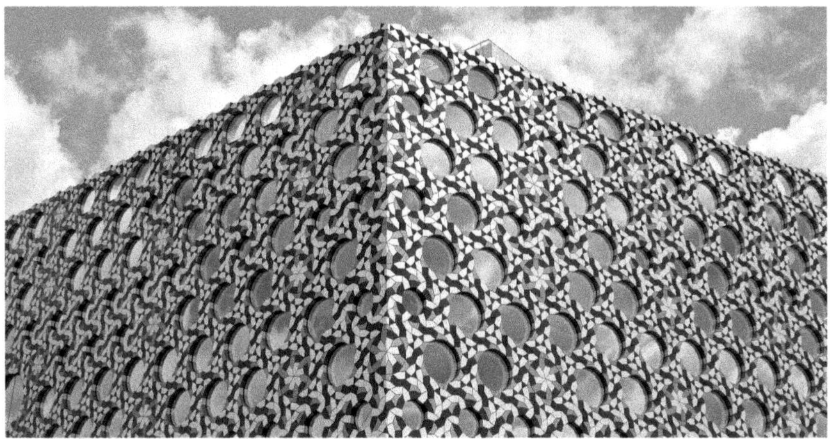

*Figure 12.4* Ravensbourne University London (Rapid Spin, Flickr).

*Figure 12.5* Ravensbourne University London, detail of ornament (Rapid Spin, Flickr).

depth of the building," not an architectural work per se.[23] She admits that "[n]one of these specific decisions are crucial to the operation of the building interior, but they are vital to the affects they trigger in the urban landscape."[24] We are thus faced with a theory in which part-to-part relationships (between fine-tuned building components) is encouraged, while the part-to-whole relationship has been abandoned. The interior has been decoupled from the exterior, which can only offer abstract patterning or screen effects that may well arise from particular technological calibrations yet not from a structured whole or any *Kernform*. In fact, these external effects may have no bearing on the building's tectonic specification at all, and thus the whole raison d'être of original functionalism, the transformation from *funzione* to *rappresentazione*, is neither sought nor fulfilled.

This does not mean that such buildings are without worth or should merit less of our interest, far from it. Other architectural theorists, such as Venturi/Scott Brown and Koolhaas, have welcomed a calculated decoupling of interior from exterior that utterly violates functionalism (in spite of Venturi/Scott Brown having professed to be "dour functionalists").[25]

In contrast to Moussavi, Gevork Hartoonian, who endeavors to make Semperian theory compatible with today's digital architecture, classifies a number of contemporary buildings in a way which is closer to the original conceptualization of functionalism, since he singles out *roofing* and *wrapping* as the everlasting tectonic elements and architectural tasks.[26] Here, tectonic analysis proceeds from the ideal of turning function into representation – in accordance with Lodoli's ambition – and the aesthetic dimension is thus preserved.

The adaptation that Moussavi prescribes is guided by cultural change, not by architectural innovation, and is thus no different from Venturi and Scott

Brown's call, in *Learning from Las Vegas*, for an architecture adjusted to the speed of the automobile. One might say that although she begins by problematizing "blank" buildings, her preferred solution is to blank ornament instead, stripping it of symbolic content. In this way, she imagines, the perceptual power of ornament will not be subject to the ravages of time, unlike the billboards, appliqué, and tongue-in-cheek ornaments of Postmodernism. Yet, as demonstrated by Hal Foster, the popular diagrid façade, which is featured in *The Function of Ornament*, is far from neutral, as its application in varying architectural practices triggers different meanings.[27]

## Zaera-Polo: Envelopes without Representation

The new Millennium has been ripe with ambitious architectural theories, and Alejandro Zaera-Polo's theory of the architectural envelope is no exception. In 2008, Zaera-Polo made public his own theory of architecture, in an essay which was given the title "The Politics of the Envelope: A Political Critique of Materialism."[28] What Zaera-Polo proposed then was a theory of architecture centered on the variable layout, composition, and structure of the building envelope, and unlike Moussavi's more specific investigation, his theory pertains to be universal, in which he specifically references Semper.[29] Zaera-Polo laments that

> [t]he envelope is a core concern of the discipline affecting materiality and construction, environmental performance, energy efficiency and other issues, but it also engages several political forms: economical, social and psychological. Yet there is no such a thing as a *unitary theory of the building envelope* in the history of architecture.

Zaera-Polo seeks to bypass established architectural terminology in order to better serve his investigation into the building envelope of today, and very early on, he establishes a biological analogy which serves as an explanatory vehicle throughout the text:

> Like the skin of a living creature, the envelope is the primary actor in the complex process of maintaining *homeostasis* in the building. In human life, however, the closed circle of *homeostasis* is opened up by psychological, political, social and cultural surpluses.

It seems that the proliferation of *bubble* buildings in the 2000s has prompted his interest in the building envelope, in general, for it demonstrates "the powerful attraction of this aesthetic trend within the contemporary architectural *Zeitgeist*."[30]

Here, the economical factor is established as a leitmotif which recurs several times, and from its very beginning functionalist theory was anchored in an almost moralistic concern for economy of means.[31] We may also note that, just like in the case of Moussavi, both theories are heavily indebted to the deterministic notion of *Zeitgeist*. Although the word 'function' does not headline any section of the manifesto, there can be no doubt that we are faced with a functionalist theory of some sort, for the words "function" and "functional" are heavily employed throughout.

The scope of Zaera-Polo's theory becomes evident when one discovers that he outlines a classification based on the performative properties of the envelope. This results in four types of envelope, each equipped with a particular functional proneness – flat-horizontal, spherical, flat-vertical, and vertical – and they form the basis for "a general theory of the building envelope" which "aims to draw a direct link between spatial typologies and political modalities or forms of political organization."[32]

Apart from general praise for the 'bubbly' adaptability to functional program, we are offered no trace of criteria on which to assess the architectural successfulness of these types of envelopes in real life. What primarily concerns Zaera-Polo is the coupling of type and politics, for his theory is "based on the hypothesis that the political possibilities of the envelope are primarily related to its dimensions, and that every dimensional type can trigger specific technological, social and political effects."[33]

For Moussavi, ornament has to emerge by necessity, and for Zaera-Polo, the envelope has to be governed by necessity as well. His "politics of the envelope" is certainly a functionalist theory, but of what kind? It is beyond doubt that an active principle is at work here, since the envelope only comes into being as a result of various environmental, political, and technological forces, yet the part-to-part relationship is never determined, nor the part-to-whole relationship. Apparently, the mere choice of envelope type triggers certain effects in the environment – which must be understood as a causal relationship – and all other concerns seem to yield. He does not understand 'constraint' as do Gould and Lewontin in their approach to architectural environments, for his

> analysis is primarily aimed at laying out the field of political opportunities within the constraints – the attachments – that come with these different envelope typologies. Within those constraints and within each envelope type, there is a wealth of possibilities that can be activated that would transcend the mere technical problems and affect the wider political performance of the buildings.[34]

Here, constraint means an expected limitation of the choice of envelope, not a functional byproduct or side effect.

As it turns out, Zaera-Polo's theory is, in essence, nothing more than a rehash of the Purists' view of the matter in the 1920s. For "[m]echanical evolution and natural evolution are similar processes, so the Purists claim, and conform to identical natural laws. [...] The aesthetic qualities of both organisms *and* machines are therefore incidentally produced in their evolution, and not consciously sought."[35]

## Deterministic Functionalism, again

Yet the most surprising aspect of these theories is that their promoters, Moussavi and Zaera-Polo, reintroduce an otherwise debunked version of biological evolution, which has already proven to be deleterious to the project of the Modern Movement. Alan Colquhoun exposed its paradoxicality in 1967, in his important essay "Typology and Design Method," and Colquhoun's characterization deserves to be quoted in its entirety:

> Underlying this doctrine was an implied belief in biotechnical determinism. [...] The relation of this notion to Spencerian evolutionary theory is very striking. According to this theory the purpose of prolonging life and the species must be attributed to the process as a whole, but at no particular moment in the process is it possible to see this purpose as a conscious one. The process is therefore teleological. In the same way, the biotechnical determinism of the modern movement was teleological, because it saw the aesthetic of architectural form as something which was achieved without the conscious interference of the designer, but something which none the less was postulated as his ultimate purpose.[36]

Their preference for this deterministic model, which they employ both in its materialist and cultural versions, as seen in their fascination with *Zeitgeist*, echoes the linear and evolutionist narratives of Sigfried Giedion and Charles Jencks, yet this time it originates in Deleuze and Latour. In this, they are not alone – Sanford Kwinter[37] and Patrik Schumacher[38] are also problematically indebted to Darwinism and *Zeitgeist*. In spite of having been refuted more than 40 years ago, the adaptationist version of functionalism lingers on in a new disciplinary setting, which shows that such exchanges between disciplines hold potentials, but also risks.

In a way, symbolism and representation are covered in "The Politics of the Envelope," since Zaera-Polo claims that the choice of a given envelope *causally* leads to a particular mode of political organization, which can then be deciphered from the shape of the envelope, yet this classification is clearly not an architectural matter, and it fails to connect with historical discussions of type and typification in architecture. Aldo Rossi once determined "that between functions and form one may seek to establish more complex ties than the linear ones of cause and effect."[39]

## Exit Aesthetics

The theories of Moussavi and Zaera-Polo target different aspects of architecture, although both 'stay on the surface' of the building. Still, both theories share a fundamental approach to functionalism that enables us not only to locate both theories within a Modernist paradigm but also to place them in the context of the adaptationist paradigm of evolutionary biology.

The fact that Moussavi and Zaera-Polo owe much more to Hannes Meyer's watered-down version of functionalism than to Lodoli and Semper's versions, which are truer to core architectural matters, can be deduced from both authors' exclusive focus on economical, managerial, and utilitarian concerns. Especially in Zaera-Polo's text, optimization (of the envelope) is the primary goal of architecture, and all other concerns are demoted to secondary status. Meyer had coined the slogan "architecture= function x economics." For Meyer, these two laws seemed to take precedence over the others, and he stated repeatedly that "the functional diagram and economic program are the main guiding principles."[40] He made it clear that art and its methods, such as composition, were the enemies of functional architecture.

Poerschke observes that today, in the wake of increasing environmental concerns, "performance" frequently replaces "function" in architectural discourse. Zaera-Polo's "Politics of the Envelope" is certainly no exception to this rule, as its pages are littered with the word "performance." Although she discusses a different theory than Zaera-Polo's, Poerschke's characterization is completely transferable to his project, in which

> [t]he motivation for producing this whole is not so much to communicate aesthetic meaning as to create an environment that aims to produce measurable comfort while minimizing energy use. The shell of the building, its technical equipment, and its interiors are coordinated with respect to quantifiable comfort and energy use.[41]

This was a conclusion already arrived at by Steven Groák, who found that the notion of performance had sprung from a functionalism of the most reductionist kind, since the performance approach ruled out any concern that would not align with the rationale of calculation.[42]

In contrast to the performance approach, it is striking that, in his eighteenth-century aesthetics, Henry Home, Lord Kames made room for novelties such as the engine of the ongoing Industrial Revolution by inventing the notion of functional beauty:

> Intrinsic beauty is an object of sense merely: to perceive the beauty of a spreading oak or of a flowing river, no more is required but singly an act of vision. The perception of relative beauty is accompanied with an act of understanding and reflection; for of a fine instrument or engine, we perceive not the relative beauty, until we be made acquainted with its use and destination. In a word, intrinsic beauty is ultimate: relative beauty is that of means relating to some good end or purpose.[43]

It was thus possible for the contemporaries of the Industrial Revolution, such as Lord Kames and Semper, both to preempt and to resist the temptation of simply collapsing architecture into engineering, by insisting instead on the double nature of functional architecture. Since functional objects could also be beautiful, they could likewise be subject to criticism and its negotiable aesthetic criteria.

Lewis Mumford later warned that "we must not take function solely in a mechanical sense, as applying only to the physical functions of the building [...] expression itself is one of the primary functions of architecture."[44] In comparison with the richness of historical discourse on architectural theory, the sole focus on performance represents a much-reduced view.

As we recall, in the original Lodolian concept of function, representation was the desired outcome, and this was clearly meant aesthetically and symbolically, as Lodoli offered guidance on how to make possible the ennoblement of materiality and structure. Bötticher's *Stoffwechsel* aimed for the same, and to Semper, "[g]enerating something that functions organically from something that functions mechanically was thus the true task of architecture."[45] In Moussavi and Zaera-Polo's theories, nothing remains of the aesthetic dimension of architecture, which is a predictable outcome of aligning oneself with the Modernist version of functionalism, and the discipline thus becomes indistinguishable from that of engineering.

## Exit Authorship

As a consequence of functional determinism, architectural authorship is completely dissolved in both texts.[46] And, unlike the quest for a collaborative, digital architecture, this elimination has nothing to do with a technological paradigm.[47] In Moussavi's program, ornament is personified and seems to have a will of its own, and no creators – the architects – are ever mentioned: "It has no intention to decorate, and there is in it no hidden meaning." Her book showcases a wide range of façade solutions, past and present, yet, other than the usual deterministic–functional one, no explanation is offered for the aesthetic variety of ornament. "Ornament is the figure that emerges from the material substrate," that is all.[48] For some strange reason, both theorists find it necessary to invoke Semper's name, in spite of his explicit skepticism toward a materialism without makers.[49]

By 1980, in the domain of philosophy of science, Paul Thagard had debunked the popular analogy that scientific progress followed the same pattern as did biological evolution of species. Amongst other points, he concluded that agency, intentionality, and decision-making had been completely left out of the picture, which is why evolutionary epistemology could not account for how science was carried out.[50] Similarly, adaptationist evolutionism is neither capable of explaining how architecture comes into being nor how it is perceived and interpreted.

## Exit Innovation

There are two dimensions of the vestigial in architecture: one concerns the apparently redundant elements automatically generated by the choice of certain methods of construction (as expounded by Gould and Lewontin); the other one arises from the visual perception of certain architectural compositions (as argued by Robert Venturi). It is surprising that Venturi's identification of the phenomenologically vestigial element predates Gould and Lewontin's identification of the structurally vestigial element by more than a decade.

Both types of vestigial element are important drivers of innovation – and evolution – in architecture. It is exactly the functional *constraints* upon architecture that provoke innovation. Pendentives and bosses emerged and made possible all sorts of clever solutions to the decoration of these surfaces. And, in the examples sampled by Venturi, the vestigial elements "contain in their changed use and expression some of their past meaning as well as their new meaning."[51]

Supposedly, adaptation was introduced into architectural theory in order to demonstrate that the inert matter of buildings could in fact be derived from an active principle, yet in Moussavi and Zaera-Polo's versions of it, adaptation is merely a rhetorical device in the service of *Zeitgeist*. Moussavi in particular is worried that ornament might fall out of fashion, so the less meaning can be derived from it, the more it would withstand the test of time and stimulate innovation.

Lodoli's original definition of functionalism came with the requirement that architectural elements subject to compression or tension – lintels and jambs, for example – be designed in such a way as to represent these forces. Today, however, this normativity has given way to a wide range of tectonic solutions that carries representational impact. For instance, it would be absurd to claim that the exaggerated tectonics of the Maison à Bordeaux (1994–1998), by Office for Metropolitan Architecture (OMA), has been devised out of necessity. Instead, the structure results from a series of programmatically imposed constraints.[52] Gregory Bateson, who suspects "that both 'adaptation' and 'design' are misleading concepts,"[53] argues that without stochastic interference, including constraints, there would be no innovation: "Without the random, there can be no new thing."[54] And Groák contrasts functionalism with evolution exactly because the Modernist version of functionalism ignores "the effect of time and changing environments, the process of evolution."[55]

The villa in Bordeaux as well as countless other contemporary experimental buildings confirm this to be true, and when grappling with the interpretation of these works we might still benefit from functionalist theories, as demonstrated by the perpetuity and persuasion of tectonic thinking.

One of the valuable outcomes of the crisis of the Modern Movement was that it made possible several responses to the problem of representation, of which the ones formulated by Rossi, Venturi/Scott Brown, and Koolhaas are some of the best known. All of these respond to some sort of constraint, architectural or urbanistic, and thus it would seem strange to revert – as do Moussavi and Zaera-Polo – to the easy dictate of 'necessity' once more. Instead, Gould and Lewontin's lesson might prompt us to consider functionalism anew in the context of contemporary architecture.

## Notes

1 Philip Steadman, *The Evolution of Designs: Biological Analogy in Architecture and the Applied Arts*, Revised Edition (Abingdon: Routledge, 2008), 10.
2 Ute Poerschke, *Architectural Theory of Modernism: Relating Functions and Forms*, trans. Steven Lindberg and Ute Poerschke (New York: Routledge, 2016 [Bielefeld 2014]), 23.
3 Ibid., 6.
4 Ibid., 78.
5 Gottfried Semper, "On Architectural Styles [1869]," in *The Four Elements of Architecture and Other Writings*, trans. Harry Francis Mallgrave and Wolfgang Herrmann (Cambridge: Cambridge University Press, 1989), 281.
6 Poerschke, 10, 75.
7 Steadman, 131–144.
8 Poerschke, 122–123.
9 Ibid., 104–116.
10 Ibid., 141.
11 S. J. Gould and R. C. Lewontin, "The Spandrels of San Marco and the Panglossian Paradigm: A Critique of the Adaptationist Programme," *Proceedings of the Royal Society of London B* 205 (1979): 584.
12 Chris L. Smith and Sandra Kaji-O'Grady, "Exaptive Translations Between Biology and Architecture," *Architectural Research Quarterly* 18, no. 2 (2014): 157.
13 Charles Darwin, quoted from Gould and Lewontin, 589.
14 Gould and Lewontin, 595.
15 Ibid., 582–583.
16 Poerschke, 67.
17 Farshid Moussavi, "The Function of Ornament," in *The Function of Ornament*, eds. Farshid Moussavi and Michael Cubo (Barcelona: Actar, 2006), back cover.
18 Ibid., 7.
19 Ibid., 8.
20 Ibid.
21 Ibid.
22 Ibid., 9.
23 Ibid., 11.
24 Ibid., 9.
25 Denise Scott Brown, "The Redefinition of Functionalism," in *Architecture as Signs and Systems: For a Mannerist Time*, eds. Robert Venturi and Denise Scott Brown (Cambridge, MA: The Belknap Press of The Harvard University Press, 2004), 142.
26 Gevork Hartoonian, *Architecture and Spectacle: A Critique* (Farnham: Ashgate, 2012), 3.
27 Hal Foster, *The Art–Architecture Complex* (London: Verso, 2013), 50.
28 I have previously critiqued this theory here: Kasper Lægring, "The Politics of Managerialism: The Performative Turn in Typological Thinking and its Post-Critical Instrumentalization," *Cloud-Cuckoo-Land, International Journal of Architectural Theory* 38 (2019), www.cloud-cuckoo.net/leadmin/issues_en/issue_38/article_laegring.pdf.
29 Alejandro Zaera-Polo, "The Politics of the Envelope: A Political Critique of Materialism," *Volume* 17 (2008): 77.
30 Ibid., 78.
31 Steadman, 14–15.
32 Zaera-Polo, 81.
33 Ibid.
34 Ibid.

35 Steadman, 139.
36 Alan Colquhoun, "Typology and Design Method [1967]," *Perspecta* 12 (1969): 72.
37 Sanford Kwinter, "Confessions of an Organicist," *Log* 5 (2005): 75.
38 Antoine Picon, "When Parametricism Tries to Reconnect with Vitruvius," *Log* 23 (2011): 54–55.
39 Aldo Rossi, *The Architecture of the City*, trans. Diane Ghirardo and Joan Ockman (Cambridge, MA: MIT Press, 1982 [Padova 1966]), 46.
40 Meyer, quoted from Poerschke, 132.
41 Poerschke, 209.
42 Steven Groák, *The Idea of Building: Thought and Action in the Design and Production of Buildings* (London: E&FN Spon, 1992), 140.
43 Henry Home, Lord Kames, *Elements of Criticism* [1762], Sixth Edition, ed. Peter Jones (Indianapolis: Liberty Fund, 2005), 142–143.
44 Lewis Mumford, "Symbol and Function in Architecture," in *Art and Technics* (New York: Columbia University Press, 1952), 124–125.
45 Poerschke, 77.
46 Steadman, 183.
47 Mario Carpo, "Digital Darwinism: Mass Collaboration, Form-Finding, and the Dissolution of Authorship," *Log* 26 (2012).
48 Moussavi, 8.
49 Steadman, 184.
50 Paul Thagard, "Against Evolutionary Epistemology," *PSA: Proceedings of the Biennial Meeting of the Philosophy of Science Association*, Vol. 1980, Volume One: Contributed Papers (1980), 190–191.
51 Robert Venturi, *Complexity and Contradiction in Architecture*, Second Edition (New York: The Museum of Modern Art, 1977), 38.
52 Cecil Balmond and Jannuzzi Smith, in *Informal*, ed. Christian Brensing (Munich: Prestel, 2002), 43.
53 Gregory Bateson, *Mind and Nature: A Necessary Unity* (New York: E. P. Dutton, 1979), 172.
54 Ibid., 147.
55 Groák, 139.

# 13 Architecture Theory in the Age of Acceleration

*Véronique Patteeuw and Léa-Catherine Szacka*

## Shifting Conditions

In his 2016 book *Thank You for Being Late: An Optimist's Guide to Thriving in the Age of Accelerations, New York Times*, columnist Thomas L. Friedman claimed that there is reason to describe the past decades as an 'age of accelerations.'[1] According to Friedman, the world is being transformed by the combined effect of three interacting and accelerating forces: environmental change, economic change and technological change. Needless to say, that this unprecedented condition of acceleration challenges any understanding of architecture. It not only affects the way we talk, discuss and write about architecture as a discipline, but calls into question the roles, tools and methods of the practicing architect. Hegemonic interpretations of architecture as a problem-solving discipline, of the architect as an individual author and of the built environment as a merely physical construct seem increasingly unsuitable as our age of acceleration, a period that turned out to be transitional, complex, multiple and layered in its challenges. What kind of architectural theory would be valuable in this context?

In order to fully grasp today's challenges, it is imperative to look back in time and, in particular, at the second half of the twentieth century. As we know, the decades following the end of the Second World War raised a number of burning questions that are still at the centre of present-day concerns. A number of these concerns were first acknowledged through the publication in 1972 of *The Limits to Growth: A Report of the Club of Rome's Project on the Predicament of Mankind* that sounded the alarm on ever increasing conditions of acceleration and the urgent need to act upon them. In the early 1970s, sharing a profound concern for the long-term future of humanity and the planet, the members of the Club of Rome[2] commissioned an international team to research the implications of continued worldwide growth.[3] Gathered at MIT, the researchers from domains as diverse as agriculture, urban planning or socio-politics examined the five basic factors that determine and, in their interactions, would ultimately limit growth on planet Earth: population increase, agricultural production, non-renewable resource depletion, industrial output and pollution generation. Now part of history, the report

DOI: 10.4324/9781003292999-15

predicted that, if no changes to historical growth trends would appear, 'the limits to growth on earth would become evident by 2072 leading to sudden and uncontrollable decline in both population and industrial capacity.'[4] Fifty years ago, the pioneering publication drew the contours of our current age of acceleration and warned of the sudden and uncontrollable collapse of our planetary system.[5] But while the report provoked huge discussions and a wide range of responses, including immediate and strong criticism – mainly coming from those who saw the book as a threat to their business as usual or as an intrusion in their professional benefits[6] – it remained, at the time, largely ignored by architects.

Today, *The Limits to Growth* reappears regularly in the debates of a number of engaged architects who echo the concerns of the Club of Rome in their criticism of our current age of acceleration.[7] Recent architectural exhibitions, biennales, publications and curatorial programmes orient research and practice increasingly towards the conditions of transition and its effects on architectural practice. But within this perspective, one tends to look for answers to the climate crisis outside the discipline of architecture, in domains as diverse as biology, geography, social sciences or economics, sometimes omitting the richness of the architectural field.

This essay considers the systemic challenges posed by the continued climate crisis, rapid urbanization and globalization as the starting point for theoretical reflection on architectural design today. But, instead of searching for answers outside the discipline, it stays as close as possible to architecture itself with the conviction that the discipline already offers a rich field of knowledge on which to build possible answers to the current crises. Six distinct architectural strategies are here outlined: Territoriality, Critical Regionalism, Participation, Transformation, Commoning and Autonomy. Looking at the historical roots of these strategies in the postmodern era and projecting their applicability all the way into the contemporary period, we aim to uncover both continuities and new possible directions.

## The Propelling Character of (Postmodern) Theory

Towards the end of the twentieth century, the landscape of architectural theory was mapped by no less than five anthologies, all published in a period of a few years' time[8]: together, these anthologies catalogued the theoretical endeavour of the previous decades, more specifically since 1968. Amongst them was *Theorizing a New Agenda for Architecture: An Anthology of Architectural Theory*, in which author Kate Nesbitt described architectural theory as an activity that 'offers new thought paradigms' and is 'speculative, anticipatory and catalytic.'[9] It can be characterized by four different attitudes towards its subject matter: descriptive, prescriptive, proscriptive or critical. The critical attitude, she says, only emerges when architectural theory is 'politically or ethically oriented' and is 'often intended to stimulate change.'[10] This stimulation of change was at the core of the writings of a series of practitioners and historians, in the second half of the twentieth century and more, in particular, within the postmodern period. Defined by the absence of one single viewpoint, or, as French philosopher and sociologist Jean-Francois Lyotard famously claimed, the end of metanarratives, the period gave rise to a great theoretical production, characterized by the desire to expand beyond the limitations of modernism and approach the crisis of meaning in architecture.

When observing and rereading canonical texts of that period, several perspectives stand out. Amongst them, Jane Jacobs' defence of urban diversity, Vittorio Gregotti's plea for an architecture of the territory, Aldo Rossi's insistence on the importance of permanence and collective memory in the city, Giancarlo de Carlo's call for participation, Kenneth Frampton's interest in a critical regionalism and Colin Rowe's belief in the permanence of form. The six corresponding strategies that we have tentatively identified – commoning, territoriality, transformation, participation, critical regionalism and autonomy – sometimes overlapping and other times located at the opposite sides of the theoretical spectrum, prove to be of particular interest in our age of acceleration as contemporary design is challenged by the context of the climate crisis.

Already in 1961, Jane Jacobs defended urban diversity. In *The Death and Life of Great American Cities: The failure of town planning*[11] Jacobs launched a fierce attack on the liberal idea of urban renewal that was predominant at the time. It critiqued the short-sightedness of urban planners in the 1950s and argued that the creation of automobile infrastructure would result in the unnatural division of pre-existing neighbourhoods, creating unsafe environments and thereby severing community connections. In opposition to the acceleration of urban renewal, Jacobs argued for cities as 'forms of organized complexity.' In other words, what she was aiming for was a city based on community building and shared resources, a precursory approach to what we today most often refer to as "the commons": the cultural and natural resources, accessible to all members of a society that allow to manage property without any regulation by central state driven authorities or market driven privatization.[12]

A few years later, on the other side of the Atlantic, Vittorio Gregotti's text 'The Form of the Territory' published in 1966 by the magazine *Edilizia Moderna*, was a plea to widen the 'territory' or scope of architecture, as symbolic and physical form.[13] For Gregotti, cities should be thought of outside their traditional boundaries. If the rapidly changing environment had led architects to turn to other disciplines such as planning, engineering and urbanism, according to Gregotti, the territory needed to become their primary object. Therefore, he proposed a renewed interpretation of the traditional 'site,' and claimed that the material condition of a wider territory needed to be taken into account in any project. Far from aiming at total control, he believed that architectural intervention needed to seek the greatest economy of means while paying specific attention to the question of the 'soil,' the preferred material for any architecture of the territory. By arguing for new forms of territoriality, Gregotti was aiming to counter the thoughtless urbanization of acceleration.

Also published in 1966, Aldo Rossi's *L'Architettura della Cita* had a big influence on generations of architects. Commenting on the neglect and destruction of cities which he saw as the repository of 'the collective memory of man,' Rossi insisted on the importance of memory for the private and public realm. As explained by Peter Eisenman in the introduction to the first English edition of Rossi's book,

> For Rossi, "the city is a theatre of human events" and "this theatre is no longer just a representation; it is a reality. It absorbs events and feelings, and every new event contains within it a memory of the past and a potential memory of the future."[14]

*The Architecture of the City* invited architects to study and value the city as a construction over time and a constantly changing artefact overlaid with symbolic values.[15] As such it offered a conceptual framework for the "transformation" of architecture: Rossi introduced both the importance of a typo-morphological approach as the potential of 'urban artefacts' that withstand the passage of time.

Almost simultaneously to the work of Gregotti and Rossi, Giancarlo De Carlo defended the idea of 'participation' in the design process. In his 1969 lecture 'Il pubblio dell'architettura'[16] De Carlo claimed that architecture was too important to be left only to architects. Starting from a harsh critique of the globalization of society and the inability of modern architecture to act upon, De Carlo called for 'the presence of the users during the whole course of the [planning] operation.' The control over the design of a building should no longer rest solely with the architect and planner, but rather be divided with its future users and inhabitants, leading to 'participation' as a tool for a democratic architecture, against the top-down planning that seemed to dominate in the 1960s.

Favouring a rear-guard position, Kenneth Frampton published in 1983 his essay 'Towards a Critical Regionalism: Six Points for an Architecture of Resistance,', a text that proposed an alternative to the threat of universalization he witnessed at that time.[17] Frampton's call to counter universalization with specific architecture took form in his essay, which elaborates on several more philosophical points, before making a case for the topographic, climatological conditions of a site, the tectonics of architectural construction and the tactile sensibility of architecture. For him, it was within the specific conditions of a local context that an alternative approach could develop: an approach in which the tactile would surpass the visual, the tectonic would win over the scenographic and the hybrid would be favoured over the homogeneous. Critical Regionalism can be understood in different ways: as a compositional understanding of the ground figure of the project; as an interest in the cultural and material histories of a specific site; or as an awareness of the technical constraints and opportunities that a site can imply. Proposing a form of resistance, Frampton argued that within such projects a certain form of resistance seemed to develop at the precise moment that culture became a global concept.

A final strategy can be associated with the intellectual production of Colin Rowe. In his introduction to the catalogue of the 1972 exhibition *Five Architects*,[18] Rowe diagnosed what he saw as a different approach to architecture: rejecting the notion of architecture as a social tool, a group of architects was concentrating their efforts on what is perhaps the most traditional – and elevated – architectural problem of all: the making of forms. Instead of searching for connections with the larger territory, the locality of the place, heritage or the users, this strategy focused on the 'autonomy' of architecture. That is to say what if architects would produce an architecture that does not take the socio-political, technical and climatic conditions as a point of departure, but referred primarily to itself? Architecture for the sake of architecture. Autonomy as a reflection on form and spaces, could be a sixth strategy starting from the belief in the permanence of form and its resilient in uncertain times.

How can re-reading and revisiting these key texts of architectural theory help us to make sense of current design approaches while offering new and relevant insights for design challenges today? It is our belief that theory has a creative potential: an ability to empower reflection on architecture and the environment, and to offer a rich and compelling field on which to build possible futures. Our ambition with this text is not, in the first place, to invent new theories, but to carefully and critically re-read existing ones, proving their relevance in today's context.

## Old Challenges, New Approaches

The challenges related to architecture and the environment haven't changed so much since the 1970s, yet they have become more pressing. In the wake of the 2008 financial crisis and following the increased awareness of the planet's finite resources, a growing number of practices have begun to elaborate alternative ways of engaging with architecture.[19] Broadening the act of design beyond drawing, implicating material concerns in the process from design to building and revisiting collaborative approaches, these practices explore the capacity of architecture to deal with climate change. While expanding their role as architects, diversifying the scale of their interventions and questioning the notions of authorship, materiality, form and labour, a clear framework for these practices seems missing. The conditions of practice and the diversity of responses given are scattered as they do not seem to be guided by a strong theoretical underpinning nor base their actions on specific concepts or references. In fact, they sometimes even go as far as avoiding any mention of theoretical preconceptions, as if this would pin down the experimental character of their work, transform their bottom-up approaches into top-down treaties, or, worse, institutionalize alternative practices that were elaborated – at least at first – within the confines of the margins.

Using the set of strategies elaborated in the postmodern period – territoriality, critical regionalism, participation, transformation, commoning and autonomy – we propose, in what follows, a theoretical reading of a number of contemporary practices offering renewed ways of working, in our age of acceleration.[20] Building upon the architectural strategies and their propelling character, we observe how the paradigm shift that emerged some 50 years ago is reappearing within contemporary practice. What lessons can be learned from the theoretical positions of the previous decades? Are the old dilemmas updated, translated, revisited, or renewed? Or are we simply witnessing continuities within practice?

While the ecological, energy and social transition require reformulating any project in relation to the necessary natural resources, Gregotti's plea for an architecture of the territory provides – when revised – an interesting framework. Soils within cities become widely and increasingly recognized as a fundamental resource that provides a wide range of ecosystem services. The site and to a larger extent the territory, can no longer be conceptualized as a surface but demand to be understood as a living thickness, as a volume in four dimensions, as a non-human living organism, as a material with which to build. Soils, although degraded and fragmented, call to be looked upon with a new gaze, to be rearticulated in a new project aimed at the construction of a shared, productive and inhabited nature, containing different elements of urbanity and offering – at the same time – a more resilient and sustainable environment for all. Gregotti's plea for an architecture of the territory, might be revisited as an architecture of the soil. Yet the importance of the soil also recalls, to a certain extent, Kenneth Frampton's plea for an architecture of resistance. His critical regionalism resisted universalization through an embeddedness in the locality of a site (topography and climate), its material traditions and cultures of construction. If Frampton believed, in 1983, that the local mattered and could form a means to resist the homogenization of architecture, a continued form of resistance is still to be found in the local. Indeed, critical regionalism proposes then an approach that echoes an aspiration for the long-term well-being of humanity.

Several contemporary projects echo Gregotti's take on the territory. In their *After-Sprawl* project, Xaveer de Geyter Architects (XDGA) proposed to reorganize the chaotic urban fabric of Flanders, using solely territorial elements such as green, unbuilt space and infrastructure.[21] The precise reading of the territory through its topographical and hydrographical conditions, serves also the projects of Studio Bas Smets which combines architecture and landscape design in thought-provoking proposals.[22] A third translation of the architecture of the territory might be found in the Horizontal Metropolis research by Studio Paola Viganò which testifies to a growing implementation of the soil as fundamental approach within design practice.[23] In addition, a growing number of practices consider the local as a fundamental strategy. We might think of the work of French architects as Simon Teyssou and his Atelier Rouget, studio LADA or BAST who elaborate projects that are anchored in precise topographical, climatological and cultural conditions, using these conditions as a starting point for transformations or new buildings.

A second observation could be called the material turn in architecture and with it, the new configurations of labour. The introduction of machine technology, interfaces and computer aided design has since the 1990s accelerated the distinction between 'thinking' and 'making,' often leading to what Richard Sennett defined as the 'troubled craftsman': a practitioner disconnected from the tactile experience of the material.[24] Yet, today's practice demands to expand the act of design to material implications, be it the production of building materials, the recuperation of architectural elements or an involvement in the construction process. Indeed, within the often-changing roles – between craftsman and intellectual, between producer and distributor – contemporary practices often propose shifted forms of labour. The alternative conversations with stakeholders take on the form of explorative research, co-productive workshops, cooperative settings where new forms of labour intertwine with the challenges posed by architecture. Studies on building materials, for instance, go hand in hand with new forms of collaborative processes in which participation is not left out, reduced or put on a pedestal. In her book *Architecture and Labour*, Peggy Deamer argues for forms of 'deprofessionalization' that would enable architects to transcend 'the brutal division of labour and expertise.'[25] Playing different roles, from the urbanist to the ethnographer, from the engineer to the mason, the architect could 'unburden architecture.'[26] Her more dynamic conception of professionalism claims that these cooperative models of organization allow architects to 'begin to foreground care over profit, use-values over exchange values, and the sharing of knowledge over private appropriation.'[27]

The 'deprofessionalization' of architecture became apparent over the past decades in the work of a series of collectives and corporations that invest time and energy in the production process of buildings. The Belgian office BLAF, for example, design their projects largely on the construction site where they elaborate, in close collaboration with contractors, detailed approaches of their projects. In reaction to a growing tension between the role of the wall and its reduced thickness, BLAF architects developed a Big Brick in close collaboration with brick manufacturers in Flanders. The brick allowed them to realize three houses where the wall would function both as an autonomous load-bearing system as well as responding to European climate-control and insulation regulations.[28] Another interesting practice is the Brussels-based BC architects. While the cooperation became known for their material tactics in projects such as the library in Muyinga, Burundi or the bio-class in Edegem, Belgium, both realized in compressed earth blocks, their fascination for building materials is paralleled by the cross-over between design expertise and material labour. It is, in fact, through workshops, knowledge transfer and collaborations with local craftsmen, that BC explores how to approach the architectural profession in a dynamic perspective.[29]

A third observation is the shift from single authorship to co-authoring. Although the emergence of collaborative practices is not new, it is remarkable how, in the first decades of the twenty-first century, a growing number of architects have explored a range of constellations that could structure their offices. They have, each within their own contexts, altered and tailored their legal, administrative and day to day modes of collaborating, in order to fit into alternative forms of labour. Questioning the traditional triangular model of client-architect-contractor in the building process, they put forward a more integrated approach in which the legally separated responsibilities become blurred or even intertwined.[30] These constellations lead unavoidably to renewed forms of authorship in which the client sometimes builds, the architect sometimes produces materials or the contractor sometimes designs along with them. Giancarlo de Carlo's plea for an architecture of participation and Jane Jacobs's call for diversity get renewed understandings in this perspective. Indeed, the ever-increasing multitude of expertise undermines claims to single authorship, while practices that build upon participatory processes often claim collective authorship or renounce to authorship altogether.[31] 'Contemporary architectural practices and scholarship are challenging and repositioning this idea, aligning more accurately (and more interestingly) the conceptions of authorship with the complex realities of practice.'[32] Participation has been revised and translated in a set of practices that chose consciously to build collectively, that explore rules of engagement, and recognize that solidarity within the building process is a more important than the (singular) authorship of a building.

The longstanding work of the Dutch collective ZUS (Zones Urbaines Sensibles) characterizes this approach. Their yellow walkway 'Luchtsingel,' realized between 2011 and 2014, and connecting Rotterdam's central station to the adjacent neighbourhood that was cut off by the railway tracks, was based on a collaborative set-up including the co-designing with local architects as well as users' participation through crowdfunding. Another practice involved in co-authoring is the British collective Assemble who won, in 2015, the prestigious Turner Prize. Their projects – such as Grandby Four Streets, Liverpool (2011) – combine participatory processes with local stakeholders as well as renewed forms of labour as the collective proposed to accompany the renovation of part of the neighbourhood with a workshop where residents could produce elements that would be integrated in the new buildings. Another interesting practice in this perspective is the Belgian office 51N4E. Reorganizing their work following a series of programmes such as civic design, adaptive infrastructure or open public structures, 51N4E considers the design of public buildings and spaces such as their Skanderbeg Square in Tirana (2010–2018), in close dialogue with stakeholders while exploring opportunities of co-design.[33]

A fourth perspective addresses the question of transformation. From traditional conversion projects to more challenging and innovative approaches linked to the circularity of building components or materials, an important number of offices puts today the question of reuse at the centre of their professional agenda.

This has not remained unnoticed by the architectural and the general press who claim that 'tomorrow's architecture will use yesterday's materials.'[34] Renewed understandings of transformation and, with it, of architecture's role in relation to de-growth, are paralleled by an increased attention for collaborative or participatory practices that critically question and expand the organization of labour within the traditional office model. These forms of appropriation have led, in recent years, to challenging perspectives for architects where joint collaborative projects include a diversity of stakeholders, users and design professionals contributing to the design process. It is interesting to observe how Aldo Rossi's theory, first elaborated in the 1960s is still relevant today. From valuing the notion of the urban fabric, to adapting the plan to changes in programme, the notions of historical continuity, heritage preservation and transformation get new understandings in the light of reuse and circularity.

The practice of French architects Lacaton et Vassal stand out for their implementation of renewed understandings of transformation. Their large-scale renovation projects in Bordeaux (2014–2018) or Paris (2011) propose autonomous self-supporting additions including wintergardens and terraces that allow the renovation of post-war social housing. A totally different approach towards transformation is exemplary in the work by de vylder vinck taillieu architects and, in particular, in their Jaap Van Triest Plein project (2016). Asked to renovate a villa in the park of a psychiatric hospital, the architects added minimal forms of architecture as to prevent the existing building from collapse while preserving its state of decay.[35] Here, the act of transformation becomes a way of cherishing the ruin. Contemporary transformation projects also focus on building components and materials. In their attention for 'the organisation of the material environment' Rotor has been setting the tone in the last two decades with regards to circularity.[36] In 2016, the creation of the spin-off company Rotor DC that recuperates and sells building elements – from tiles to windows over furniture allowed to translate their research into a practice. Following in their footsteps, BC Materials proposes to recuperate materials such as sand, loam and gravel from Brussels' construction site; materials they reconfigure and implement in new projects. The transformation of a building, through a new plan or programme is translated in these practices to the up-cycling of building components and materials.

Finally, an important number of practitioners continue to defend the importance of architectural form. Their interest in Colin Rowe's observations on the autonomy of architecture or Aldo Rossi' notion of permanence, can also be observed in relation to present day concerns on sustainability. Indeed, these practitioners are not ignoring the problematics related to climate change, the reality of exponential population growth and growing inequalities or the large-scale urban problems and universal sprawl. Yet, instead of looking for solution to these problems outside the discipline of architecture, they are in search of a sustainable approach to architecture by exploring the resilience of form. Indeed, a building might allow to house different programs over time without changing its form.

Since 2005, OFFICE Kersten Geers David has been elaborating a practice based on the potential of form. Through their projects and publications – such as *Architecture without Content* – they explore an interest in historical precedents and the permanence of form.[37] Kersten Geers explains:

> the life span of a building is very important to us. (…) Many programmes are no longer fixed permanently; they shift and fluctuate, and buildings have to respond accordingly. In our view, the potential of a long-life span lies largely in the power of spatial typologies, in types that admit interpretation. If mutations or changes occur in the programme, the type must be able to overcome such changes. The architecture should therefore provide adequate guidance.[38]

OFFICE's building for the Swiss radio and television broadcaster (RTS) in Lausanne and that of the Flemish Radio and Television (VRT) in Brussels are based on this objective and are projected to facilitate evolution and mutation of its program over time. Similarly, the work of BAUKUNST (Brussels) or Baukuh (Milan) can also be mentioned in this perspective. While the first might be revisiting the oeuvre of Mies van der Rohe and the latter the one of Aldo Rossi, both offices search for ideal forms of autonomy, emphasizing the spatial and aesthetic quality of buildings contributing to a form of permanence in architecture.[39]

The aforementioned projects and practices are just some of many possible examples of the diverse and different ways of interpreting, rereading and translating some of the theories elaborated in the post-World War II period. The different constellations and combinations of these six strategies result in a series of new directions on architecture in the age of acceleration. In other words, through shifted forms of labour, a renewed sense of authorship and formal resilience, a number of contemporary European practices operate in a theoretical continuity with the past decades. It should equally be noted that other historical figures and practices could have been mentioned in this text: Aldo Van Eyck, for his remarkable work on threshold spaces or the Parisian firm Candilis-Josic-Woods and their *Architecture pour le plus grand nombre*; the work of the Italian planner Giuseppe Samona expanding the idea of the city beyond the urban fabric or the practice of the Austrian Herman Czech and his concept of *Umbau*, considering every architectural project an addition to existing layers. These and other post-war figures have been elaborating stances towards architecture that might have, in light of present-day concerns, new and added value.

## Conclusion

Today, we are facing uncertain times. In such a situation, we can hold on to what we know or choose the path of the unknown, leaving all gained knowledge behind. It is our conviction that in-between positions offer the most intelligent and creative path. A path in which we value existing discourses, experiences and knowledge; but in which we dare to engage in open-ended protocols and transdisciplinary conversations. A path that allows us to deal with the complex processes that are ours in the years to come yet anchoring them in the knowledge offered by architectural theory and history. Absorbing everything and making the best of each situation enables us to take position in-between the global and the local, in-between the top down and the bottom up and in-between architectural form and broader concerns for the environment.

If theory is defined as a series of suppositions or system of ideas based on general principles and intended to explain something, we can wonder how to reposition architecture theory in the light of the present era of acceleration. In order to exist and to act critically, theory needs discursive forms. How then, the architecture theory of the past century becomes knowledge that informs the system of ideas on which our discipline is based?

While theory is able to delineate architectural positions, it has a creative potential: an ability to empower reflection on architecture, offering a rich and compelling field on which to build possible responses. No theory is ever finished nor entirely complete, and while this open-endedness of theory can be seen as problematic it also constitutes a value. It allows to pursue the findings, to bring old theories back to life, by modelling, extending and updating it. Rereading is valuing what exists but also critically examining what the past provides us with. And it is precisely here that theory and its history become a creative field, interesting, not only in understanding the present and future challenges posed to architecture, but also in elaborating precise solutions and future paths based on a profound knowledge of the past, and suggesting ways to engage with architecture in our age of acceleration.[40]

## Notes

1 Thomas Friedman, *Thank You for Being Late: An Optimist's Guide to Thriving in the Age of Accelerations* (London: Picador, 2016).

2 The Club of Rome included heads of state, UN administrators, high-level politicians, government officials, diplomats, scientists, economists and business leaders. It was founded in the mid-1960s by Italian industrialist Aurelio Peccei and Head of Science at the Organization for Economic Co-operation and Development (OECD), Alexander King.

3 The study was organized at MIT and funded by the Volkswagen Foundation. For a more extensive reading of the study, we refer to the documentary 'Final Warning Limits to Growth' (2015) https://www.youtube.com/watch?v=kz9wjJjmkmc.

4 Donella H. Meadows, Dennis L. Meadows, Jorgen Randers and William W. Behrens III, *The Limits to Growth: A Report of the Club of Rome's Project on the Predicament of Mankind* (New York: Universe Book, 1972), 23.

5 Pablo Servigne and Raphaël Stevens, *Comment tout peut s'effondrer, petit manuel de collapsologie à l'usage des générations présentes* (Anthropocène) (Paris: Seuil, 2015).

6 George Bush criticized for instance the book on 12 June 1992, during the United Nations conference on environment and development, declaring that: '20 years ago, some spoke of the limits to growth. Today we realize that growth is the engine of things and is the friend of the environment'.

7 Michael Hardt and Antonio Negri, *Empire* (Cambridge, MA: Harvard University Press, 2000); Bruno Latour, *Facing Gaia: Eight Lectures on the New Climatic Regime* (Cambridge: Polity, 2017); Isabelle Stengers, *Another Science is Possible: A Manifesto for Slow Science* (Cambridge: Polity, 2017).
8 K. Michael Hays (ed.), *Architecture Theory since 1968.* A Columbia Book of Architecture (Cambridge, MA: MIT Press, 1998); K. Michael Hays (ed.), *Oppositions Reader* (New York: Princeton Architectural Press, 1998); Neil Leach (ed.), *Rethinking Architecture* (London and New York: Routledge, 1997); Kate Nesbitt, *Theorizing a New Agenda for Architecture: An Anthology of Architectural Theory 1965–1995* (New York: Princeton Architectural Press, 1996); Joan Ockman (ed.), with the collaboration of Edward Eigan. *Architecture Culture 1943–1968.* A Columbia Book of Architecture (New York: Rizzoli International Publications, 1993).
9 Kate Nesbitt, op. cit.: 16.
10 Kate Nesbitt, op. cit.: 18.
11 Jane Jacobs, *The Death and Life of Great American Cities: The Failure of Town Planning* (New York: Random House, 1961).
12 Elinor Ostrom, *Governing the Commons, The Evolution of Institutions for Collective Action* (Cambridge: Cambridge University Press, 1990).
13 Vittorio Gregotti, 'La forma del territorio,' *Edilizia Moderna*, no. 87–88, (1966), 1–146.
14 Peter Eisenman, 'Editor's Introduction,' in Aldo Rossi (ed.), *The Architecture of the City* (Cambridge, MA: MIT Press, 1982), 7.
15 Aldo Rossi, *L'Architettura della città* (Milan: Marsilio, 1966); Aldo Rossi, *The Architecture of the City* (New York: Oppositions Book, 1982).
16 The text was subsequently published in an expanded form with an English translation in 1970 in the Italian periodical *Parametro*, 5, pp. 4–12. It was republished in the book *Architecture and Participation* edited by Jeremy Till, Peter Blundell Jones, Doina Petrescu in 2005.
17 Kenneth Frampton, 'Towards a Critical Regionalism: Six Points for an Architecture of Resistance', in Hal Foster (ed.), *The Anti-Aesthetic: Essays on Postmodern Culture* (Washington, DC: Bay Press, 1983), 16–30; Kenneth Frampton, 'Prospects for a Critical Regionalism',' *Perspecta*, vol. 20, (1983), 147–162. See also Tom Avermaete, Véronique Patteeuw, Léa-Catherine Szacka and Hans Teerds (ed.), *OASE#103*, *Critical Regionalism Revisited* (2019) and Véronique Patteeuw and Léa-Catherine Szacka, 'Critical Regionalism for our Time,' *Architectural Review* (November 2019), 82–98.
18 Colin Rowe, 'Introduction,' *Five Architects* (New York: MOMA, 1972), 3–7.
19 According to BC materials architect Nicolas Coeckelbergs, for instance, 'The construction sector is responsible for one third of all CO2 emissions, for 40% of resource extraction, for one third of air pollution and for 30% of total waste'. Nicolas Coeckelbergs, 'Faire c'est dire', conference in the framework of the exhibition 'Les usages du monde', ENSAPL and Arc en Rêve, Gare Saint Sauveur, Lille, 24 September 2020.
20 These practices are just some out of many that we could mention in the framework of this essay. For a more extensive overview, we refer amongst others to the excellent exhibition *New Ways of the World* organized in autumn 2020 in Lille (France) by Arc en Rêve and HBAAT (Hart Berteloot Atelier Architecture Territoire) proposed an interesting perspective. It considered 'social, environmental, architectural or agricultural alternatives that have been chosen across every continent; enlightening experiences that allow us to think about and inhabit the world differently.'
21 Xaveer De Geyter Architects, *After-Sprawl* (Rotterdam: NAi Publishers, 2001).
22 Bas Smets, *Landscape Stories* (Brussels: Bureau Bas Smets, 2015).

23 Paola Vigano, Martina Barcelloni Corte and Chiara Cavalieri (eds.), *The Horizontal Metropolis between Urbanism and Urbanization* (Berlin: Springer Verlag, 2018).
24 Richard Sennett, *The Craftsman* (London: Penguin, 2009), 52. According to Sennett, a first trouble appears when individual competition rather than collaboration started to motivate people to work. A second trouble lies in the loss of value of skills and practice-based experiences as modern technology 'deprives (in some cases) its users precisely of that repetitive, concrete, hands-on training that is needed to train certain skills.' Third, there is the trouble caused by 'conflicting measures of quality' as for some, quality is based on correctness, while for others it is based on practical experience.
25 Peggy Deamer, *Architecture and Labor*, op. cit.: 158.
26 Peggy Deamer, *Architecture and Labor*, op. cit.: 158.
27 Peggy Deamer, *Architecture and Labor* (London/New York: Routledge, 2020), 133.
28 Véronique Patteeuw, 'De maakbaarheid van de architectuur', A+ 289, april 2021.
29 Véronique Patteeuw, 'Precious Experimentation', *A+*, dec 2021; Pauline Lefebvre and BC Architects and Studies, *The Act of Building* (Antwerp: VAI, 2018).
30 Yet, they are not the only ones exploring how their administrative, legal and economic structures can be adapted to new challenges. If OMA's mirror office AMO, can be seen as an early exponent of a different form of practice, close collaboration between artisans, builders and architects is the cornerstone of the Indian Studio Mumbai or the German Martin Rauch studio operating simultaneously as craftsmen, contractors, artists and designers.
31 Tom Avermaete, Christoph Grafe, Véronique Patteeuw with Irina Davidovici, *OASE*, 113, *Authorships*, forthcoming.
32 Ann Lui and Ana Miljački, call for papers, Log 54. https://static1.squarespace.com/static/580643f9be659426654c568d/t/60f1df00f99b244b29394bc9/1626464001040/Log54_Coauthoring_Prompt.pdf.
33 *51N4E: Skanderbeg Square, Tirana* (Berlin: Ruby Press, 2017).
34 See Edwin Heathcote, 'Why Tomorrow's Architecture Will Use Yesterday's Materials,' *The Financial Times*, (13 January 2020) and Olly Wainwright, 'The case for…never demolishing another building,' *The Guardian*, (13 January 2020).
35 Advvt et al., *architecten de vylder vinck taillieu Unless Ever People – La Biennale di Venezia 2018* (Antwerp: VAI, 2018).
36 Jean-Didier Bergilez, Marie-Cécile Guyaux and Véronique Patteeuw (eds.), *Rotor Coproduction* (Brussels: A16/CIVA, 2010).
37 Kersten Geers, Joris Kritis, Jelena Pancevac, Giovanni Piovene, Dries Rodet and Andrea Zanderigo, *Architecture without Content* (London: Bedford Press, 2015).
38 Véronique Patteeuw, 'The Permanence of Form, A conversation with Kersten Geers, OFFICE Kersten Geers David Van Severen,' (September 2021), https://www.archined.nl/2021/09/the-permanence-of-form-a-conversation-with-kersten-geers-office-kersten-geers-david-van-severen/.
39 Baukunst, *Baukunst* (Berlin: Walter Konig, 2019).
40 This text is based on the research done for the course 'Architecture in the Age of Acceleration' (EPFL – University Manchester). The authors would like to thank Eric Alonso, Tom Avermaete, Christoph Grafe, Xaveer De Geyter, BLAF Architects, BC Architects, Rotor Deconstruction, Kersten Geers, David Van Severen, Freek Persyn and Sotiria Kornaropoulou, Jean-Didier Bergilez, Jo Taillieu for the valuable conversations over time. A special thanks to Stephanie Dadour, Hilde Heynen and Christophe van Gerrewey for their important suggestions and feedback on a previous version of this text.

# 14 Architecture, Justice, and Theories of Rights

*Esra Akcan*

Ever since the concept of human rights crystallized with the eighteenth-century people's revolutions around the world, it has implicitly become a reference point in discussions about space. In the field of architecture, the notion of human rights is prone to generate discussions on class, gender, race, and citizenship discrimination, and germane for different architectural programs including urban space, housing, schools, public monuments, memorials, and museums. It is therefore possible to show the intersectionality of these issues by discussing the seemingly separate social struggles through theories of rights.

Despite its omnipresent use in daily language, the definition of rights as a concept has not been settled easily and remains unresolved. The concept of human rights has received its own share of suspicion and reproach from authors at different ends of the political spectrum. The far-right press continues to portray human rights as an alibi to protect criminals and constrain governments from punishing them.[1] Historically, Jeremy Bentham ridiculed the foundational premise of human rights that all human beings are born free—perhaps to be expected from the inventor of Panopticon who attempted to discipline bodies through an architectural device—and rebuked the idea that natural and inalienable rights should be distinct from legal rights because, he claimed, that would be an invitation to anarchy.[2] Karl Marx famously opposed human rights for their egoistic preoccupations that protect individuals instead of political communities, and for reducing the definition of the "true" human being into a bourgeois.[3] As early as Olympe de Gouge's and Mary Wollstonecraft's appeals, feminist critique has exposed the hypocrisy of gender discrimination in the initial declarations that advocated for the rights of "man and citizen."[4] Another common objection has been the assertion that the concept of human rights is a Western invention and therefore its universalization an imperialist expansion—an accusation that Amartya Sen defined as cultural critique.[5] Episodes when Western superpowers used human rights as an excuse for military intervention to serve other interests stand as the worst scandals in human rights history. Hannah Arendt, Giorgio Agamben, and others have exposed the limits of the continuing attachment between human and citizenship rights in protecting refugees.[6]

DOI: 10.4324/9781003292999-16

With some of these fallacies corrected but others left unresolved, the concept of human rights continues to be relevant today for moral commitment to rectify injustice and ensure equality, or political action to protect human dignity, enable participatory democracy and foster progressive change, or still, education of the senses to build empathy for the oppressed. Despite numerous challenges from skeptics and authors with different moral philosophical convictions, "the claim to 'natural rights' has never been quite defeated," as Margaret MacDonald summarized:

> It tends in some form to be renewed in every crisis in human affairs, when the plain citizen tries to make, or expects his leaders to make, articulate his obscure, but firmly held conviction that he is not a mere pawn in any political game, nor the property of any government or ruler, but the living and protesting individual for whose sake all political games are played and all governments instituted.[7]

Against this background, this chapter focuses on the under-acknowledged role of human rights in architectural theory, by foregrounding both the emancipatory potentials and continuing limits of the current human rights regime. Even though the topic of human rights is relevant for multiple social sciences and humanities fields,[8] it has been overwhelmingly perceived as a legal matter administered by the United Nations after the second half of the twentieth century. The perception of human rights as an exclusively legal and governmental matter assumes that there should be a responsible institution whose duty is to deliver human rights, and operates as if something could be defined as a human right only if it can be combined with a correlating obligation. This may be important in the implementation of human rights, but has narrowed down the epistemological, ethical, and cultural discussions about the topic.

Narrowly speaking, the legal debate on human rights has paid attention to architecture only in relation to the right to housing. Ever since the first deliberations at the United Nations that resulted in the 1948 Universal Declaration of Human Rights, there has been international discord over what constitutes a human right. Housing has been one of them. The Article 25 of the Declaration reads: "Everyone has the right to a standard of living adequate for the health and well-being of himself and of his family, including food, clothing, housing, and medical care and necessary social services." The U.N. Covenant on Economic, Social, and Cultural Rights gives a vague definition of "adequate housing," which involves security, availability of services, habitability, accessibly, location, and cultural adequacy. However, the governments' obligations as to what level these standards should be provided are unclear, and the evaluation criteria for states that fail to keep up with these obligations are even less defined. Even though the UN admits that the situation of housing around the world is dire, housing, in particular, or architecture, in general, has not necessarily become a top priority of human rights. Preventing discrimination, forced evictions, and war crimes involving the unjustified destruction of housing have come to be the only legal human rights considerations when it comes to architecture.[9] This article suggests to cast a wider net, and exemplifies a few of the themes about the relation between architecture and human rights.

## Right-to-the-City: Class Consciousness and Social Justice

There is hardly any other text on the urban dimension of rights that has received more acknowledgment in the architectural discipline than Henri Lefebvre's "The Right to the City."[10] This text has served as a guide—or sometimes a slogan—to reflect on architecture's relation to uneven development in the capitalist city, but its passages on human rights have received less attention.[11] Lefebvre finds Marx's and Engels' involvement with the city limited, as they only raised the housing crisis, but instead "the problem of the city is immensely greater than that of housing."[12] Urbanism is ideology, Lefebvre states, and analyzes the impact of this false consciousness after the age of industrial capitalism. "When industrialization begins, and capitalism in competition with a specifically industrial bourgeoisie is born, the city is already a powerful reality."[13] Additionally, Lefebvre does not fail to notice the paradox that housing is considered only an "annex" to human rights. Consistently, he finds mid-century public housing that satisfied the Left neither a corrective to capitalism, nor an acknowledgment of human rights. On the contrary, the construction of the greatest number of units with the least possible cost in the quickest time is not a departure from but an adoption of market economy.[14]

One of the most distinguishing features of this foundational text is Lefebvre's definition of a city's architecture, the *oeuvre* (works of art, monuments, streets, squares, edifices) with use value, as opposed to exchange value, in Marxist terminology: "This city is itself '*oeuvre*,' a feature which contrasts with the irreversible tendency toward money and commerce, toward exchange and *products*. Indeed, the oeuvre is use value and the product is exchange value."[15] Consequently, the city's architecture becomes the platform for revolutionary transformation, if only it could be preserved from being quantified into exchange value.

Human rights are not Lefebvre's priority—indeed he reserves only a few paragraphs for the topic that the text owes its title to. Yet, despite Marx's criticism, Lefebvre is invested in the actualization of human rights through social justice:

> ...concrete rights come to complete the abstract rights of man and the citizen inscribed on the front of buildings by democracy during its revolutionary beginnings: the rights of ages and sexes (the woman, the child and the elderly), rights of conditions (the proletarian, the peasant),

> rights to training and education, to work, to culture, to rest, to health, to housing.[16]

Like Marx, Lefebvre posits the working class as the principal "agent, social career or support of" a revolutionary transformation.[17] Yet, unlike Marx, Lefebvre includes the realization of human rights in this transformation as well: "The pressure of the working class has been and remains necessary (but not sufficient) for the recognition of these rights, for their entry into customs, for their inscription into codes which are still incomplete."[18]

Lefebvre is interested in the right to turn the city into something that can be analyzed to expose capitalist ideology and that can be made into a platform of revolutionary transformation. More importantly, he defines the right-to-the-city not "as a simple visiting right or as a return to traditional cities," but rather as a "transformed and renewed *right to urban life*," where use value, not exchange value, is priority.[19]

> Use value, subordinated for centuries to exchange value, can now come first again. How? By and in urban society, from this reality which still resists and preserves for us use value, the city. A weakened but true vision of this truth is an urban reality for 'users' and not for capitalist speculators, builders and technicians.[20]

It follows that Lefebvre is invested in the city's right to exist beyond the capitalist market logic, so that it can be returned to its users, to the citizens who can perform their human rights. In that, Lefebvre anticipates an impossibility for human rights practice within the logic of capitalist economy—which may sound counter-commonsensical to liberal ears but substantiated with evidences of human rights abuses in, say, matters of housing. But what about the rights of the city-dweller who is not a citizen? In the age of global capitalism where the Western superpowers rely on the labor of nonwestern immigrant workers, a primary locus of discussion for both human rights and critical theory needs to be the noncitizen workers whose lack of rights exposes the paradox of the current human rights regime. This is the topic of the next section.

## Right-to-Have-Rights: Citizenship and Racial Justice

Urban discourse often refers to city areas whose populations have a high percentage of immigrants as ghettos, in the sense of sources of trouble, crime, and chaos, and as something to be obliterated. Countless examples abound to substantiate the racialization of and discrimination against immigrant workers through urban policy. A good case in point is the "guest worker" program in Germany after 1961, and IBA-1984/1987 as one of the world-famous urban renewal and public housing initiatives of the twentieth century, which employed over 200 established and up-and-coming architects from Europe and North America. During the 1960s and 1970s in Berlin, the immigrant workers from Turkey were pushed to the war-torn Kreuzberg district, where landlords did not perform legally required maintenance, since noncitizen families could hardly make official complaints about the decaying state of their apartments. Many other social practices took advantage of immigrants' lack of rights. Toilet decrees explaining how to handle human waste, foreigner classes segregating the education of German and Turkish children, newspaper advertisements that made it clear that immigrants were not eligible to rent apartments all made clear the social separation and othering of guest workers. In the legal sphere, the Berlin Senate passed a series of housing laws and regulations between 1975 and 1978. The "ban on entry and settlement" (*Zuzugssperre* or the moving ban as the immigrants called it, 1975), prohibited the movement of additional "foreign" families to Kreuzberg, Wedding, and Tiergarten. The "desegregation regulations" (1978) mandated that only 10% of residential units be rented to noncitizens all over West Berlin. If there was a Turkish family living in one apartment of a ten-unit building, no new immigrant family could move in. These discriminatory housing laws and regulations instituted by the Berlin Senate were transposed into the functional program of the new buildings to be built by IBA, in the form of the percentage of large flats which would have been fitting for the migrant families. Even though the percentage of noncitizens reached 50% in many areas of Kreuzberg, the Senate mandated that only 5%, max. 10% of new units would be big (four or more bedroom) apartments. This program would either diminish noncitizen families' chances to move into the new buildings or welcome them only after they changed their lives to fit the German family size standards. Article 13 of the Universal Declaration of Human Rights reads "everyone has the right to freedom of movement and residence with the borders of each State." Accordingly, the Berlin Senate's laws were violations of human rights and could not have been instituted for citizens. Moreover, during the time that these regulations were put in place, it was procedurally impossible for guest employees from Turkey to have fulfilled the immigration requirements and become naturalized, which meant that the laws and regulations consciously targeted this immigrant population by taking advantage of the citizenship law. The collapsibility of race and noncitizen conveniently served to exert discrimination under the pretext of law. In my book *Open Architecture,* I analyzed architectural practices that were either complicit, or naively ignorant, or subversive of these discriminatory housing regulations; and identified formal, programmatic and procedural ways of designing *open architecture* that would protect the noncitizen's human rights.[21]

This is a typical case showing the paradoxes of the current human rights regime as it reflects on housing and urbanism. Giorgio Agamben revisited Hannah Arendt's text "We Refugees," written in response to the biggest refugee crisis during World War II, precisely because statelessness continues to be prolific, and simultaneously exposes the limits of modern institutions in securing human rights.[22] In another text, Arendt did not fail to notice that housing is the first major human right lost to the refugee:

> The first loss which the rightless suffered was the loss of their homes, and this meant the loss of the entire social texture into which they were born and in which they established for themselves a distinct place in the world.[23]

The stateless puts into question the limits of the human rights that presume the condition of being a citizen of a state. Ever since the first declaration of rights, the link between natural and civil rights, "man" and "citizen," and birth and nationhood has continued to define human rights, making it impossible to have rights without citizenship. A refugee who loses citizenship status in a country would immediately recognize that the inalienable rights of being a human—the rights that a human being should have by virtue of being born—are actually unprotected unless one belongs to a nation-state. "The paradox here," wrote Agamben, "is that the very figure who should have embodied the rights of man par excellence—the refugee—signals instead the concept's radical crisis."[24] Moreover, the existence of the refugee questions the global nation-state system itself:

> The refugee must be considered for what he is: nothing less than a limit concept that radically calls into question the fundamental categories of the nation-state, from the birth-nation to the man-citizen link, and that thereby makes it possible to clear the way for a long overdue renewal of categories.[25]

It is important to remember that people have been excluded from citizenship throughout the history of citizenship. Slaves, women, colonial subjects, guest workers, legal aliens, undocumented immigrants, and refugees have all been identified as noncitizens at some point in the past, and some of them continue to be identified in this way today. Moreover, when applied to the notion of social citizenship, noncitizens also include people excluded from citizenship because of socially constructed notions of class, race, gender, ethnicity, or religion. Much has been said about T.H. Marshall's tripartite definition of citizenship as civil, political, and social citizenship, and others have challenged him on numerous fronts, especially for his account of the concept's historical evolution and his assumption of a unitary process tied to the British context.[26] Nonetheless, his insight into the three types of rights continues to have an explanatory power. According to this framework, social citizenship rights are those tied to economic welfare and security, such as insurance against unemployment and rights to health care, education, housing, and a pension. People who were once noncitizens often continue to be denied social citizenship after naturalization, as the exclusion of former slaves, colonial subjects, or guest workers is projected onto the present in the form of class difference and white supremacy. Balibar also theorizes about the relation between internal and external exclusions from citizenship, to understand the mechanism that denies legal citizens the right to have rights. "An 'external' border is mirrored by an 'internal' border,"[27] Balibar writes, to such an extent that citizenship becomes a club to which one is admitted or not regardless of one's legal rights.

> It is always citizens 'knowing' and 'imagining' themselves as such, who exclude from citizenship and who, thus, 'produce' non-citizens in such way as to make it possible for them to represent their own citizenship to themselves as a 'common' belonging.[28]

Public housing and housing as a human right must be at the forefront of discussions about social citizenship, as the decline of the welfare system around the world today with the advance of neoliberalism puts public housing—and with it, the idea of social citizenship—at even greater risk. The concept of citizenship has historically been in constant evolution, as women and former slaves and colonial subjects gained rights over time. It ought to continue to change as refugees and global migrants still remain rightless. The question for the present is how architects will find forms and ways of practicing an architecture that protects the human rights of noncitizens as much as citizens.

## Right-to-Truth: Reparations and Historical Justice

After the adoption of the Universal Declaration of Human Rights in 1948, the United Nations' Human Rights Commission continued to add new treaties that are open to member states' ratification. Initially, the first two covenants (also known as the International Bill of Rights) aimed to resolve the ideological split between the cold-war's superpowers that prevented to include all rights under one treaty. As the number of member states increased during the decolonization processes of the 1960s and responding to several social movements around the globe, the UNHRC added new conventions, such as the ones on the elimination of racial discrimination, and of discrimination against women, as well as the convention against torture, and on the rights of the child. One of the two new treaties adopted in 2006 was the convention on the protection from enforced disappearance, which also defines a "right-to-truth."[29] This recent human rights convention has opened up new potentials for architecture's relevance.

Even though enforced disappearance (not returning from state custody due to possibly a torturous and secret murder) existed for a long time, the United Nations and Amnesty International have warned that the practice actually increased and spread over the world after 1980, with systematic cases in Argentina, Chile, China, East Germany, Guatemala, Iraq, Russia, Spain, Sri Lanka, USA, and many others. In August 2014, the U.N. Working Group reported 43,250 unresolved cases of disappearances in 88 different states.[30] Those subject to enforced disappearance expose how modern states turn bodies into what Giorgio Agamben called "bare life" (*homo sacer*), in the sense that states hold the power to deprive citizens of their political rights and push them outside the realm that should have been protected by citizenship rights. Turning humans into bare lives gives those states necropower, as Achille Mbembe coined the term: it gives statecraft a license, a presumed "right-to-kill" with impunity.[31]

Enforced disappearance also opened a sphere in international law and human rights debate known as transitional justice. The accountability for past abuses came to the forefront of human rights movements with the grassroots protests against enforced disappearance, such as the one by Mothers of Plaza de Mayo starting in 1977. The concept of transitional justice entered the lexicon of international law as new nations emerged out of the end of cold-war, and with conflicts in Yugoslavia and Rwanda.[32] The official U.N. Definition for transitional justice, released in 2004 when Kofi Annan was Secretary-General, reads: "the full range of processes and mechanisms associated with a society's attempts to come to terms with a legacy of large scale past abuses, in order to ensure accountability, serve justice and achieve reconciliation."[33] In addition to the UN, the foundational and operational role of regional courts has been particularly important in this process, such as the Inter-American Court of Human Rights, European Court of Human Rights, and African Court of Human and People's Rights. I suggest to analyze transitions from military regimes, civil wars, genocides, and apartheids, as well as reparations to heal from colonization and slavery as topics of the multidisciplinary field of transitional justice.[34]

The right-to-truth is one of the goals of transitional justice that oversees the right of relatives and society to know the truth about state brutality and human rights violations in the past, which have been obscured due to denial of responsibility, and distortion of facts in official national histories. Truth and recognition of suffering is a prerequisite of healing. As Michael Ignatieff put it: "The new human rights culture has been accompanied by the global diffusion of the psychoanalytic ideas about the healing power of truth."[35] Far from being resolved however, the right-to-truth claims have injected a dilemma into the healing process, because truth commissions that were established during transitional periods often secured amnesties to perpetrators in return for collaboration. Truth commissions are not trials, but semi-official mechanisms that are instituted to bring some form of justice after massive, systematic, or historical crimes that cannot be tried in criminal courts, because previous regimes who had authorized these crimes during their rule have secured impunity or amnesties for themselves. In many cases, truth has been revealed at the expanse of criminal justice.[36] A history of transitional justice might indeed be written by showing the dilemma between truth and criminal justice, and the historical struggles in different countries to minimize it.

Transitional justice is not yet totally resolved also because subsequent regimes have been usually far from perfect themselves; and *their* truths and *their* justices have also been partial. In many cases, results were compromising or even flawed, reparations functioned as whitewashing devices, financial compensations were symbolic, and institutional reforms such as purges and vetting gave unfair advantages to new regime supporters.[37] As Pablo de Grieff puts it, transitional justice takes place in "a very imperfect world." If democracy and reconciliation are the final goals, one "despot's truth commission will need to be followed by another truth commission."[38]

Moreover, the assumption of the "objectivity" and "universality" of international law is rightly debated, and the framework to reconcile the international and place-based justice systems remains unresolved. A comparative ethnographic and sociological study in transitional Bosnia, Rwanda, Iraq, and Uganda revealed that conceptions of justice among communities vary; societies respond to violations differently; methods that they use to find justice differ; reconciliation means forgiveness in some countries, but punishment in others; there is no direct correlation between victimhood and desire for war crime trials; individual opinions about justice in a given country are skewed according to nationalist and ethnocentric ideologies, depend on social and economic factors, and change over time.[39] Gayatri Spivak also formulates a critique of the potential coloniality of human rights activism and proposes to rectify it through a "suturing" educational program that revises both Western and local structures.[40] When the same measures and steps are applied universally, international law becomes ignorant of domestic practices and sabotages the fulfilment of human rights. When perceived as a toolkit that can be applied anywhere without translation, transitional justice forecloses a society's right-to-heal.

In the context of the unfinished struggles toward right-to-truth, the imperfect conditions of transitions, and the unreconciled international and national laws, transitional justice needs to be conceived as a continually evolving, self-reflective, and open platform, where societies formulate new forms of justice and peacebuilding steps.

Architecture has a newfound but untapped relevance in this new turn of the theory of human rights. This involves both retrospective and corrective mechanisms such as the uncovering of evidences by treating physical environments as primary sources of history in truth commissions and trials, and forward-looking restorative platforms such as transitional justice memorials and apology museums.[41] A multidisciplinary study of transitional justice needs to both locate spaces of political harm, and make a call to repurpose them as healing spaces. I would like to define architectural programs and spaces of reparation as healing spaces where political harm and human rights violations are confronted.

For the first category—the role of architectural history in uncovering evidences of human rights violations—the work of Forensic Architecture is an excellent example. In their research "Hannibal in Rafah," for instance, the Forensic Architecture team reconstructed the events of a single day—the Black Friday on 1 August 2014—which was supposed to be a ceasefire but ended up being one of the deadliest days of Gaza. They collected 7,000 photographs and video clips produced by civilians to map the life of a city on that day. They looked closely into every detail, traced every evidence, and extended time to its possible extreme duration, in order to see the past clearly, and to discover that which had been hidden from sight by statecraft. It took Forensic Architecture a year of research to reconstruct a day of destruction. With the work of the Forensic Architecture team, architecture is transformed into a sensor for social and political activity, and used as evidence to record the past. Their work not only expands the nature and definition of evidence in architectural history, but also amplifies the voice of the victim by giving it material evidence. They partner with international humanitarian groups, human rights organizations and truth commissions, but never fall into the naïve assumption that these organizations themselves are geopolitically neutral. Forensic Architecture's research tools mobilize architectural skills, and include new methods: they perform formal and kinetic analysis of clouds; they examine building and wall photographs and videos to determine where the missiles hit the civilians; they construct digital models of houses to help witness memories; they make visual signatures of gunfire sounds in order to verify that shootings happened; they prepare video animations that reenact crime scenes in order to expose racist criminals who had been protected by their governments; they establish the meta-data of images and the time-space coordinates of photographs by analyzing the shadows of buildings captured by the camera. In the new visual regime of our era in the early twenty-first century, military and state institutions use drone technologies for the purposes of ultimate panopticism and risk-free warfare, and manipulate image resolutions so that they can prevent the detectability of war crimes. Forensic Architecture responds by using architectural and other professional skills to expose atrocities, amplify the public's vision and exercise right-to-truth.[42]

For the second category—the role of architecture in prospective justice—transitional justice memorials and museums provide one of the good examples for healing spaces. A lot has been said about the reconstruction of cities and memorials after wars, but the trauma inflicted by internal perpetrators have hardly been confronted: violence by rulers, sciences, and institutions that are meant to protect the individuals on whom they impose conflict and disaster. Transitional justice memorials differ from war memorials because they expose a state's accountability for past crimes and participate in reparations to heal from these traumas. Official state monuments had manipulated collective memory by overemphasizing and stabilizing the dominant voice and thus by taking part in cultural repression. In contrast, transitional justice memorials and museums amplify the victims' experience rather than the victor's propaganda. They can be located in both found and constructed sites, namely both spaces where the trauma happened and the symbolic spaces that would be associated with healing by virtue of the memorial. Unlike those that prompted Robert Musil's critique that there is nothing as invisible as a monument, transitional justice memorials should no longer be sculptures of a handful of heroes on pedestals, but complex conceptions of sites, where sculpture, architecture, landscape, design, earth-art, performance, and educational programs might be combined. They are not monuments to single leaders but to healing ideas and values. Most transitional justice theorists and policy-makers expect that memorials conclude the process, but some architectural gestures have indeed started the process of justice and healing.[43] However, architects are usually excluded from the decisions over the need, site, representatives, and narrative of memorials, only to be brought in at the last stage to design the physical environment. This text makes a call for a more proactive role by arguing that architects can indeed contribute to transitional justice when a healing space's decisions about site, form, program, funding, and procedure are concerned. Healing spaces to come may also imply transitions to come.[44] The question for the present is how architects will find forms and ways of giving a forward momentum to transitional justice today.

## Toward a Globalized and Localized Theory of Human Rights

As these three concepts suggest, architecture's under-studied intersection with human rights evolves with the changing human rights, and contributes to the discourse of human rights by carrying it beyond the legal sphere. In this article, I foregrounded the role of architectural history in right-to-truth, as well as the architectural programs such as urban spaces, housing, public monuments, memorials, and museums as healing spaces after human rights violations. Needless to say, many other architectural programs and policies are germane to the actualization of the "rights to training and education, to work, to culture, to rest, to health, to housing," to quote again from Lefebvre's list of rights to the city. Reflecting on these concepts has also carried me to the conclusion about the necessity to both globalize and localize the human rights debate, and to keep it as a continually open and self-reflective platform. A familiar and partially justified critique of the human rights regime and the international organizations such as the UN is their inaugural Eurocentrism and hierarchical structure between nation-states. However, this critique needs to be qualified with several considerations. The perceived truism that human rights were "invented in the West" is actually a myth, because there was a network of people's revolutions in the eighteenth century when the concept of human rights emerged. "Non-Western" revolutions contributed to this process and constituted some of the major chronological markers, such as the Haitian Constitution of 1805 that abolished slavery.[45] The claim that only the Western philosophical tradition prepared the theory of human rights sounds offensive to many ears, as if values such as human fulfilment, dignity, and equality could not be found in Confucian, Hindu, Buddhist, Islamic, and many other world teachings.[46] Historically, the concept of human rights has been mobilized and improved in several episodes for anti-colonial, anti-racist, feminist, anti-slavery, and anti-apartheid struggles. Today, the assumption that the torch of human rights is carried by "Western" nations is also ungrounded, as the US, for one, has only signed five out of eighteen of the UN's human rights conventions.[47] The grassroots struggles and the writing of the international conventions to bring justice to historical crimes discussed above constitute a case in point that human rights activism and international legislation today is taking place with actors and in countries outside "the West." The global history of human rights needs to be written, first and foremost, by giving due acknowledgment to all its makers.

By globalizing human rights, I mean the struggles, for instance, to have all nation-states sign the international human rights conventions, while simultaneously making the UN truly cosmopolitan, and moving toward the resolution of the current human rights paradoxes. It is the *local* human rights associations and actors that carry out these struggles against their governments who refuse to participate in international law. By localizing human rights, I mean the translations between international and local justice systems, because justice and peacebuilding has a chance to be effective only if it is participatory and bottom-up. Conceiving international and local justice, or U.N. and grassroots activism as competitive struggles sabotages the protection of peoples. Instead, much could be done through complementary processes. Human rights discourse creates solidarity between peoples who can act with a shared sense of human suffering and thereby transcend class, gender, race, geography, or other distinctions. The concept of human rights is also an antidote to identity politics and the manipulation of victimhood, in cases where struggles to end the oppression of one group do not translate into defending others in similar situations.

With its devices to analyze space and give physical shape to human rights activism, architecture can take proactive roles in globalized, localized, and open justice platforms.

## Notes

1 Even though many readers may recognize this perception of human rights in numerous countries, the UK is a good example. See: Andrew Clapham, *Human Rights* (Oxford: Oxford University Press, 2007).

2 Jeremy Bentham, "Anarchical Fallacies; Being an Examination of the Declaration of Rights Issued during the French Revolution," in J. Bowring (ed.), *The Works of Jeremy Bentham*, vol. 2 (Edinburgh: William Tait, 1843). https://oll.libertyfund.org/title/bowring-the-works-of-jeremy-bentham-vol-2#lf0872-02_head_411 Accessed 6/21/2021.

3 Karl Marx, "On the Jewish Question," 1843. Numerous editions.

4 Olympe de Gouge, "The Declaration of the Rights of Woman," (September 1791) https://revolution.chnm.org/d/293 Accessed 6/21/2021, Mary Wollstonecraft, *A Vindication of the Rights of Women*, 1792. Numerous editions.

5 For a discussion, see Amartya Sen, "Culture and Human Rights," *Development as Freedom* (New York: Alfred Knopf Publishing, 2000), 227–248; Amartya Sen, "Elements of a Theory of Human Rights," *Philosophy and Public Affairs*, vol. 32, no. 4 (2004): 315–336; Amartya Sen, "Human Rights and Capabilities," *Journal of Human Development*, vol. 6, no. 2 (July 2005): 152–166.

6 Hannah Arendt, "We Refugees," *Menorah Journal*, no. 1 (1943): 77; Giorgio Agamben, "We Refugees," trans. Michael Rocke, *Symposium*, vol. 49, no. 2

(1995): 114-119. For a revised version, see Giorgio Agamben, "Biopolitics and the Rights of Man," in Werner Hamacher and David E. Wellbery (eds.), trans. Daniel Heller-Roazen, *Homo Sacer: Sovereign Power and Bare Life* (Stanford, CA: Stanford University Press, 1998), 126-135.

7 Margaret MacDonald, "Natural Rights," in Jeremy Waldron (ed.), *Theories of Rights*, 2nd print (Oxford: Oxford University Press, 2009), 21–40. (quote:21).

8 For a discussion of human rights in other disciplines, see: Michael Freeman, *Human Rights: An Interdisciplinary Approach*, 2nd ed. (Cambridge: Polity Press, 2011).

9 Clapham, *Human Rights*, 133–137. In the sphere of architecture, the most impactful team that brings these issues to the attention of the world is Forensic Architecture. Eyal Weizman, *Forensic Architecture: Violence at the Threshold of Detectability* (New York: Zone Books, 2017).

10 Henri Lefebvre, *Le Droit à la ville*, 1968. English Translation, "The Right to the City," 1996. in *Writings on Cities*, Eleonore Kofman and Elizabeth Lebas (eds.). Online version can be found: https://theanarchistlibrary.org/library/henri-lefebvre-right-to-the-city Accessed 6/21/2021.

11 The literature on Lefebvre is too extensive to cite here, especially by equally well known authors such as David Harvey, Edward Soja, Saskia Sassen and Manuel Castells. For authors writing in the discipline of architecture, see: Mary Mc Leod, "Henri Lefebvre's Critique of Everyday Life: An Introduction," in Steven Harris and Deborah Berke (eds.), *Architecture of the Everyday* (New York: Princeton Architectural Press, 1997); Lukasz Stanek, *Henri Lefebvre on Space: Architecture, Urban Research and the Production of Theory* (Minnesota: University of Minnesota Press, 2011); Hannah Feldman, *from A Nation Torn: Decolonizing Art and Representation in France* (Durham: Duke University Press, 2014).

12 Lefebvre, "The Right to the City," 36.

13 Ibid., 5.

14 Ibid., 11.

15 Ibid., 5.

16 Ibid., 49.

17 Ibid., 50.

18 Ibid., 49.

19 Ibid., 50.

20 Ibid., 54.

21 For more information and discussion, see: Esra Akcan, *Open Architecture: Migration, Citizenship and the Urban Renewal of Berlin Kreuzberg by IBA-1984/87* (Basel: Birkhäuser, 2018).

22 Arendt, "We Refugees," 77; Agamben, "We Refugees," trans. Michael Rocke.

23 Hannah Arendt, "The Perplexities of the Rights of Man," in Hannah Arendt (ed.), *Origins of Totalitarianism* (New York: Harcourt Brace and Co., 1973), 293.

24 Agamben, *Home Sacer*, 126.

25 Ibid., 134.

26 T. H. Marshall, *Social Policy in the Twentieth Century* (London: Hutchinson, 1965). See also Richard Bellamy, *Citizenship* (Oxford: Oxford University Press, 2008); Bryan Turner, "Outline of a Theory of Citizenship," in Chantal Mouffe (ed.), *Dimensions of Radical Democracy: Pluralism, Citizenship, Community* (London: Verso, 1992), 33-62.

27 Étienne Balibar, *Citizenship*, trans. Thomas Scott-Railton (Cambridge: Polity Press, 2015), 69-70.

28 Ibid., 76.

29 "The International Convention for the Protection of All Persons from Enforced Disappearance" adopted in 2006, came into effect in 2010. Turkey has still

not signed the convention https://www.ohchr.org/en/hrbodies/ced/pages/conventionced.aspx. The working group had started working in 1980.

30 United Nations, *"OHCHR|WGEID – Annual reports"*. https://www.ohchr.org/EN/Issues/Disappearances/Pages/Annual.aspx Retrieved 17 July 2019.

31 Achille Mbembe, "Necropolitics," *Public Culture*, vol. 15, no.1 (2003): 11–40.

32 Here is a list of basic anthologies and periodicals. Carla Hesse and Robert Post (eds.), *Human Rights in Political Transitions: Gettysburg to Bosnia* (NY: Zone Books, 1999); Ruti Teitel, *Transitional Justice* (Oxford: Oxford University Press, 2000); Robert Rotberg and Dennis Thompson, *Truth vs. Justice: The Morality of Truth Commissions* (Princeton: Princeton University Press, 2000); Melissa Williams (ed.), *Transitional Justice* (New York: NYU Press, 2012); Rosalind Shaw and Lars Waldorf, *Localizing Transitional Justice. Interventions and Priorities after Mass Violence* (Stanford: Stanford University Press, 2010); Ruti Teitel, *Globalizing Transitional Justice* (Oxford: Oxford University Press, 2014); *International Journal on Rule of Law, Transitional Justice and Human Rights* (issues 2010–2018).

33 U.N. Secretary's report "The Rule of Law and Transitional Justice in Conflict and Post-Conflict Societies," August 23, S/2004/616, p. 4.

34 Esra Akcan, *Right to Heal* (book in progress).

35 Michael Ignatieff, "Human Rights," in Carla Hesse and Robert Post (eds.), *Human Rights in Political Transitions: Gettysburg to Bosna* (New York: Zone Books, 1999), 313–324 (quote: 313).

36 Especially see: Robert Rotberg and Dennis Thompson, *Truth vs. Justice: The Morality of Truth Commissions* (Princeton: Princeton University Press, 2000).

37 See several case studies in Williams (ed.), *Transitional Justice*; Noeme Turgis, "What Is Transitional Justice?" *International Journal on Rule of Law, Transitional Justice and Human Rights*, no. 1 (2010): 9–15.

38 Pablo de Greiff, "Theorizing Transitional Justice," in Melissa Williams (ed.), *Transitional Justice* (New York: NYU Press, 2012), 31–77, quotations: 34, 55; Also see, *Nomos*, vol. 51, (2012): 31–77.

39 Harvey Weinstein, Laurel Fletcher, Patrick Vinck and Phuong Pham, "Stay the Hand of Justice: Whose Priorities Take Priority," in *Localizing Transitional Justice. Interventions and Priorities after Mass Violence* (Stanford: Stanford University Press, 2010), 27–49.

40 I am suggesting that human rights activism should be supplemented by an education that should suture the habits of democracy onto the earlier cultural formation.... the real effort should be to access and activate the tribals' indigenous "democratic" structures to parliamentary democracy by patient and sustained efforts to learn to learn from below.

Gayatri Spivak, "Righting Wrongs," *The South Atlantic Quarterly*, vol. 103, no. 2/3 (Spring/Summer 2004): 523–581. (quote: 548).

41 I am taking the distinction between retrospective and prospective justice from: Jeremy Webber, "Forms of Transitional Justice," in Melissa Williams (ed.), *Transitional Justice* (New York: NYU Press, 2012), 31–77.

42 Weizman, *Forensic Architecture*.

43 For example, the first plate at Tanforan Assembly Center to commemorate the interned 110,000 Japanese and Japanese Americans during WWII was placed before the official apology in 1981, which was followed by the reparations that were granted with the Civil Liberties Act of 1988. In other words, it was the memorial that started the process, and demanded apology and reparation, rather than the other way around. Chicago Torture Justice Center that "seeks to address the traumas of police violence," has first asked Patricia Nguyen and John Lee to design a memorial, and then the mayor for a site and funding to build it. See Valentina Rozas-Krause, "Apology and Commemoration: Memorializing the WWII

Japanese American Incarceration at the Tanforan Assembly Center," *History and Memory*, vol. 30, no. 2 (Fall/Winter 2018): 40–78; http://chicagotorturejustice.org/ Accessed 3/14/2020.

44 For more discussion, see: Esra Akcan, "Transitional Justice Memorials," presentation at *Racism and the Future of Memorials* Webinar, College of Architecture, Art and Planning, Cornell University, July 14, 2020, Ithaca, USA. https://www.youtube.com/watch?v=1tCU3gzdvaI.

45 For more discussion and my views on its impact on architecture, see: Esra Akcan, "Translation Theory and the Intertwined Histories of Building for Self-Governance," in Ana Miljacki and Amanda Lawrance (eds.), *Terms of Appropriation* (London: Routledge, 2018).

46 See, for instance, Micheline Ishay, *The History of Human Rights: From Ancient Times to the Globalization Era* (Berkeley: University of California Press, 2004). One may also see Amartya Sen (citations above) who argued that the cultural critique of human rights and the perception of the so called "Asian values" as different from human rights does not survive critical scrutiny.

47 For a map that shows which countries ratified which of the UN's 18 human rights conventions, see: https://indicators.ohchr.org/ Accessed 3/15/2020.

# 15 Colonialism as Style

## On the Beaux-Arts Tradition

*Charles L. Davis II*

### Introduction

Within the realm of postwar American architectural theory, the Ecole des Beaux-Arts is perhaps best remembered as a casualty of the massive social protests that took place throughout the city of Paris in May 1968. This social event, which channeled global critiques of capitalist exploitation, consumerism, international war, and American imperialism into local calls to reform anti-unionist labor practices and traditional institutions in France, sparked a series of reverberations in architectural education the following year. Faculty and students of the Unité Pédagogique No. 6 (UP6) in Paris and the Unité Pédagogique d'Architecture in Nantes (UPAN) inaugurated a set of pedagogical experiments designed to replace the idealist conception of monumental form popularized by the Grand Prix competitions at the Ecole with a socially engaged approach to form that was grounded in the realities of the working class proletariat.[1] An institutional critique of inherited wealth and privilege was not completely unprecedented at the school, as Richard Chafee and Donald Drew Egbert have noted in their studies of Ecole pedagogy after the French Revolution.[2] However, the shift during the postwar period seemed to be more permanent: "Indeed, the break of 1968 seems more complete than was that of 1793."[3] In architectural terms, this postwar shift was manifest in a formal emulation of the visual aesthetic of modern architecture mitigated by a nuanced interpretation of program that codified the most pressing needs of the working class. When considered from a pro-labor perspective, the historical attempts of the "Moderns" to change the social vision of the school by liberalizing the path to becoming an academician within the Ecole—a role that was routinely filled with representatives of the "Ancients" who held a conservative interpretation of architectural style—seems to anticipate the explosion of progressive modes of design in the post-1968 years. From explicitly socialist and utopian modes of community and ecological design to the visual eclecticism of postmodern classicists, the Romantic tradition of the moderns appeared to have finally overturned the inherited wisdom of the ancients.

Official accounts of the historical legacy of the Ecole began to appear in English language publications in essays and articles published in the wake

DOI: 10.4324/9781003292999-17

of the 1968 revolts. Book-length studies of this disciplinary history include Arthur Drexler's edited volume *The Architecture of the Ecole des Beaux-Arts*, which doubled as a catalog for the 1975 exhibit of the same name at the Museum of Modern Art; Donald Drew Ebgert's skillfully crafted monograph *The Beaux-Arts Tradition in French Architecture*, which had been circulated in draft form for nearly 20 years before its publication; and Robin Middleton's edited volume *The Beaux-Arts and Nineteenth-Century French Architecture*.[4] Subsequent volumes have documented the transatlantic dissemination of the Beaux-Arts tradition to the United States, which debuted to impressive public reception with the visual aesthetics and planning principles of Daniel Burnham's "White City" and in great numbers of graduates attending Ivy League architecture programs shortly after the turn of the century. A post-1968 generational viewpoint on the historical legacy of the Ecole has even persisted in contemporary studies of "Radical Pedagogies" in the last ten years.[5] In these later accounts, the radical shifts in postwar architectural education established institutional critiques that collectively "aimed to challenge the status quo by attempting to destabilize the very institutions they depended on."[6] Such a critical reading of postwar architecture culture established an implicit expectation that innovative architectural forms could almost be taken as analogs for a progressive social politics in one form or another.

Despite the anti-capitalist and anti-imperialist perspective of many French social organizations of the late 1960s, the near exclusive European cultural framework of disciplinary histories of modern architecture in this era have so far failed to capture the retrograde tendencies of postwar architectural reform. This is even true of the revolutionary politics of the modern or romantic contingent at the Ecole with respect to their common support for establishing an authoritative canon of rules for generating a monumental state architecture that was culturally universal in its tenets. The retrograde politics of such a political endeavor becomes clear if one considers the social and political radicalism of parallel architecture movements that emerged to support post-colonial movements in former French colonies littered with examples of 'good' Beaux-Arts architecture. To limn the limits of Beaux-Arts progressivism requires a shift in perspective that channels the critical lens of post-Civil Rights activism in the United States where 'America' was conceived, not as a leading liberal power, but as a settler colony that employed various forms of soft power to maintain allegiance to its social, cultural and economic objectives. Within this framework, architecture is but one tool for legitimizing the political hegemony of the nation state. The Black Arts movement that rose up from this critique of American imperialism constituted more than a visual alternative to hegemonic modes of representation; it concretized a permanent critique of the colonial function of Euro-American material culture.[7] What views of the Ecole's pedagogy emerges, for example, if we were to take up a similar critique of its historical claims through the lens of Frantz Fanon's anti-colonial philosophy, or Jomo Kenyatta's post-colonial politics? David Brody and Rebecca McKenna's recent studies of the imperial function of American

Beaux-Arts architecture in the Philippines provides us with a potential model for beginning such an investigation.[8]

A retrospective analysis of the racial politics of the Ecole des Beaux-Arts as a state-sponsored institution yields a damning critique of both the ancients and the moderns for perpetuating design philosophies that legitimized the social, political and economic inequalities of French colonialism. This critique can equally be applied to the function of Beaux-Arts architecture in legitimizing the supremacy of American settler colonialism and the dissemination of these values globally under American imperialism. Even as the Beaux-Arts tradition gained international standing for leading the advance of western civilization in codifying a visual language of form, it operated as a visual analog for imperialism in colonial and settler colonial territories in Africa, the Middle East, the Far East and the New World. In this sense, the French emulation of Greco-Roman architecture also extended to the political function of these representational forms during monarchical and authoritarian regimes. When the Beaux-Arts tradition crossed the Atlantic through the study of wealthy American practitioners in France, its principles took on new life in the private salons that paved the way for newly established university departments in the nineteenth century. Much of American architecture would then be consciously molded in the pedigree of French Beaux-Arts instruction, often through French émigré's who settled in the United States to head these academic departments, which served as both a visual proof of the maturity of American arts and letters and the inherent potential of French aesthetic ideals to operate as a universal style in the manner reserved for Greco-Roman antiquity.

The following research examines the ways that the political function of the Ecole, as an official state institution, inherently racialized the pedagogy of the school. The civilizational imperatives of architectural education, when combined with the racial charge of nineteenth-century scientific theory, ultimately shaped the meaning of architectural historicism as it was expressed through type theory, character judgments and the political associations of neoclassical architectural styles revived for use in Republican-era France. The influence of the colonial function of the Beaux-Arts tradition can be seen in various forms: the architectural and visual language of the Ecole itself, which was premised on a biased catalog of world cultures; the racial and ethnic meanings of nonwestern styles of building used in annual 'concours' and 'esquisse' assignments that trained students to expand the reach of French rule into its colonial territories; and the evolutionary models of cultural history that subtended the writings and teachings of Beaux-Arts theory, which were finally disseminated to trained professionals in the United States.[9] In political and geographical terms, the colonial character of French Beaux-Arts pedagogy reached full circle in the translation of European treatises and pedagogical exercises in trade journals in the United States. The translation of European architecture theory enabled professional designers in the United States to think of 'American architecture' as a mode of autochthonous building that not only replaced the material culture of other indigenous groups as primary in the land, but extended the reach of the ancients in the civilizing mission of western art.[10] As Patrick Wolfe intimates in his study of material culture in the settler colony, the very notion of style operates as a form of political ideology that systematically recalibrates the built environment for use as a tool of practical governance.[11] Stated in a different way, the Beaux-Arts style constituted a visual form of colonial ideology that was effectively masked as an academically rationalized theory of architectural formalism.

## Delineating the West at the Ecole des Beaux-Arts

If one were to invent an ideogram of the conflicting aesthetic philosophies circulating within the Ecole des Beaux-Arts in the nineteenth century, one could not arrive upon a better embodiment than Felix Duban's architectural design for the school.[12] Newly reformed as a complex for three branches of the fine arts, Duban was charged with creating a campus along the west bank of the Seine from a series of disparate buildings. He was keen to integrate the busts and fragments that were gifted to the school, if only to extend the notion of historicism influential within the school to elements of the medieval past (Figure 15.1).

While scholars have noted the pristine ways that other buildings have perfected the visual language of various factions within the Ecole—such as Henri Labrouste's romantic design for the Bibliothèque Saint-Geneviève[13]

*Figure 15.1 Ecole des Beaux-Arts, Grande Salle des Antiquités, Paris,* 1864 (Felix Duban).

or Francois Blondel's ideal and Platonic approach to the Porte Saint-Denis—Duban's design for the Ecole concretizes the tensions that existed between the mimetic imitation of the past and the scientific rationalization of a customary beauty that could be defined in the present. These complimentary values were not only present in the physical elements of the building, most notably in the collection of historical fragments within its galleries, but also in the debates between academicians that solicited multiple changes to the final design. In this iteration, the Ecole represented the sum total of architectural history as it was taught in France.

But where was the West, or the common project between antiquity and modern France to be located in this version of cultural history? What elements of world culture counted toward this project? One answer to this question comes in the form of Paul Delaroche's hemicycle for the Palais des Etudes (Figure 15.2).[14]

David Van Zanten describes this mural as a visual manifesto of the Gothic and Romantic themes of Felix Duban's architectural renovation of the Ecole between 1834 and 1840.[15] As a representative of the romantic faction in the fine arts, Delaroche provides a visual illustration of the civilizational pedigree that provided the cultural foundations for the aesthetic pedagogies that dominated French art and architectural theory in the late nineteenth century. He was careful to include only the most celebrated figures from the so-called civilized Christian nations of the west, alongside a few metaphorical

*Figure 15.2 Ecole des Beaux-Arts, Hemicycle mural*, Paris, 1841-1842 (Paul Delaroche).

allegories to the ancient past, that elevated the status of Italian and French Renaissance masters to those of the Greek and Roman past:

Historical Figures in Delaroche's Hemicycle

| | |
|---|---|
| Delorme | French |
| Peruzzi | Italian |
| Erwin de Steinbach | German |
| Sansovino | Italian |
| Robert de Luzarches | French |
| Palladio | Italian Renaissance |
| Burnelleschi | Italian Renaissance |
| Inigo Jones | England |
| Arnolfo di Lapo | Italian |
| Pierre Lescot | French Renaissance |
| Bramante | Italian Renaissance |
| Francois Mansart | French |
| Vignole | Italian |

Historical Allegories of Antiquity in Delaroche's Hemicycle

Gothic Art
Greek Art
Genius of the Arts
Roman Art
The Renaissance

The omission of Egyptian architecture in this list is striking given the direct references early theoreticians such as Antoine-Chrysostome Quatremère de Quincy made to their culture. This suggests that the philosophical importance of the Greco-Roman world as a mythical origin point in the Ecole's progressive history of European artistic refinement had become nearly absolute.[16] Within the physical context of the Palais des Etudes, the literal and metaphorical content of the hemicycle denotes the cultural and geographical limits of western civilization. All other cultures were to be positioned in proximity to these central nodes. Within such an intellectual framework, the lack of visual references to Egyptian culture was significant as earlier academicians had theorized the place of Egypt in the classical world. Quatremère de Quincy's tripartite theory of domestic typologies—with the cave, tent, and hut referencing the material cultures of Egyptian, Chinese and Greek civilizations respectively—is just one example of a racial interpretation of the historical origins of architecture culture.[17] Despite such references, Egypt only matters in the Palais hemicycle because of its perceived proximity to and value within Greco-Roman culture, a fact that is illustrated by the architectural frame of Delaroche's mural. The perceived cultural pedigree of the west had tremendous implications for the ways that architecture students were trained to reference world civilizations in their designs, which was materialized primarily through their aesthetic interpretation of type forms, especially as they were expressed in plan, and as historical motifs for architectural ornamentation.

If Delaroche's hemicycle provided an anthropomorphic image of French academicians' geographical and political conception of the West, then the architectural motifs that the ancients and moderns made to represent non-white, nonwestern civilizations legitimized these limits while metaphorically translating the historical patterns of exploitation established by French colonialism. Though there were no static tendencies with respect to these aesthetically extractive practices, we can identify at least two general strategies: one was to develop a set of rules or canons for visualizing French political values, especially republicanism, through the revival of Greek and Roman building typologies associated with republican ideals in nineteenth-century ethnography; while another was to deploy French infrastructures in native dress (via exoticized ornament) to shape the visual expression of the body politic within the colonies. In these latter cases, the assimilative function of colonial infrastructure is effectively masked by the appropriation of native imagery to render this invasive technology benign as a mode of control.

Despite the liberalization of the Académie Royale d'Architecture after the French Revolution at the Ecole des Beaux Arts, which included an expansion of both its pedagogies and instructors, the primary role of the school remained developing a canonical theory and methodology for creating a national building culture. Thus, from a visual perspective, the 'French-ness' of the most celebrated designs within the school had to be clearly identifiable, be they Ancient or Modern in tendency. This collective expectation helps us to explain the steady stream of aristocratic and state programs used in the design briefs of the Grand Prix de Rome—the penultimate competitions that determined which architects would serve the crown in its most elite capacity. As Egbert suggests in his study, a literal hierarchy of monumental and vernacular architectural programs and precedents was established that separated the most royal and aristocratic functions of the empire from that used by the common man and the foreigner.[18] If one were to thumb through the list of programs in the final briefs, from its establishment in 1702 to the final competition in 1967, most of the Grand Prix projects related to those appropriate for building up the metropole of the French empire.[19] A second set of projects, usually designated for the more common concours that were offered to lower-level students as preliminary training for the Grand Prix, offered an opportunity to address less grand but equally essential elements of colonial infrastructure. A clear example of this can be found in Gabriel-August Ancelet's concours d'emulation of 1848, entitled simply as "Fontaine" (Fountain), where a physical node in the aquatic network of French Algeria is given orientalized features to match its primitive environs (Figure 15.3).

The orientalization of exported colonial infrastructure was also brought to the United States via the Prix de Reconnaisances des Architectes Americains,

*Figure 15.3* *Une Fontaine pour l'Algérie, Concours d'émulation*, 1848 (Gabriel Auguste Ancelet).

an award established in the late nineteenth century for American visitors to the Ecole.[20] One such project is Alphonse Gougeon's monumentalization of native Alaskan wood detailing in his winning entry Grande factorerie dans l'Alaska. In this way, even the more routine drawing exercises developed a typological interpretation of racial difference that was used to legitimize French colonialism, and later North American imperialism. From the metropole to the satellite colony, the modern architect learned to visually homogenize the modern infrastuctures of the empire to rationally manage every aspect of the built environment.

## Race, Style and Beaux-Arts Architecture in the United States

In the United States, the Beaux-Arts came to represent two complimentary interpretations of domestic art. The first interpreted American arts and letters as an extension of European ideals. As such, the function of urban design strategies such as Daniel Burnham's City Beautiful movement, which updated French methods of design for use in American cities, was to rationalize the state's aesthetic management of the built environment. In the same ways that Tafuri theorized the practical function of the grid as a geometrical mode of subordinating the natural world to the scientific gaze of capitalist speculators, the axial arrangement of cities such as Washington, D.C. emulated the orderliness of French Baroque cities reinterpreted after the French Revolution to be the visual representation of republican governance.[21] Under Thomas Jefferson, neoclassicism became the official style of federal building. The adaptation of Beaux-Arts ideals within this nationalized framework naturalized the New World's connections to the myth of advancing western civilization. Political doctrines such as manifest destiny only further racialized the aesthetic projects of US nationalism beyond the political associations of Greco-Roman antiquity that was inherited from the French Ecole in the nineteenth century. It is in this capacity that Burnham's urban designs for the Philippines marked this territory as belonging to a Euro-American power; it dressed the infrastructural norms of American urbanism in its official stylistic dress for assimilating the natives (Figure 15.4).

Similar campaigns would take place in Hawaii and other protectorates of US empire, even as politicians in the Unites States denied their expansion into the Pacific constituted an American imperium.[22] Within the political context of U.S. empire, the American Beaux-Arts tradition also claimed a form of aesthetic exceptionalism that seemingly represented all people while normalizing a very Eurocentric manner of viewing the land and its holdings.

A second realm of culture that influenced our interpretation of the American Beaux-Arts was that which emerged as a result of the establishment of a new professional culture for licensed architects that distinguished them from other actors within the building industry. It was during this time that professional schools of architecture first transformed architectural drawing into a privileged medium of design. The legal status of the architectural drawing (in the form of construction documents) as the intellectual property of a licensed architect effectively minimized the expanding social, political and economic agency of the master builders, private speculators and building contractors competing for control of the construction market—all areas of practice where people of color were then gaining ground. Within the US

*Figure 15.4 Negros Occidental Provincial Capitol Building, Philippines*, 1933 (Juan Arellano).

market, the architectural drawing effectively operated as an ideological tool for legitimizing the racialization of professional architecture culture (as for white, male practitioners) by rigorously delineating the forms of visual representation that would be deemed 'professional' versus those that would be dismissed as 'vernacular'. Within the splendid isolation of the design studio—an intellectual context that reified the mental isolation required for the ideation of form within Enlightenment discourses—the racial and class values of American professionization were first institutionalized through a disciplinary language borrowed from western Europe. Richard Morris Hunt's salon was the first space to emulate the pedagogical function of the atelier (as distinct from the chantier or building site) in France. It was within this rarified system that the Beaux-Arts pedagogies that enabled France to homogenize the architectural patrimony of the state across its empire finally disseminated its values in academic courses at Harvard, MIT, Cornell and Penn. The fact that many architecture schools still privilege the 'studio' above the support classes within the curriculum should hint at the enduring quality of this pattern of social distinction.

The academic privileging of the architectural drawing continues to enable professional architects to engage in a process of racial and class 'othering' that dismisses the 'vernacular' demands of nonwhite spaces by abstracting the so-called essential elements of design from all other factors of consideration.

This geometrical rationalization of space naturalizes the racial and ethnographical associations of architectural precedents that were passed down from the Ecole. It is only by subverting the racialized gaze of the geometer that a more equitable professional culture can emerge. Historical precedents for this sort of practice exists in the work of Black master builders in the United States—from the creation of Hush Arbors to freed Haitian shotgun houses—who were forced to hybridize the skills of the licensed architect with those of the Black craftsman.[23] These precedents provide us with historical precedents for a radically horizontal model of professional expertise. But we will first have to decolonize the remnants of Beaux-Arts colonialism in order to begin this process.

## Notes

1 Jean Louis-Violeau, "E13: Unite Pedagogique No. 6 Paris up 6 and Unite Pedagogique d'Architecture Nantes, UPAN | Paris and Nantes, France, 1968–1975", https://radical-pedagogies.com/search-cases/e13-unite-pedagogique-paris-architecture-nantes/, accessed January 10, 2021.

2 See Richard Chafee, "The Teaching of Architecture at the Ecole des Beaux-Arts," in *The Architecture of the Ecole des Beaux-Arts*, edited by Arthur Drexler (New York: The Museum of Modern Art, distributed by MIT Press, 1977), p.110; and Donald Drew Egbert, "From the Revolution to the Mid-Nineteenth Century," in *The Beaux-Arts Tradition in French Architecture* (Princeton, NJ: Princeton University Press, 1982), pp.36–57.

3 Chafee 1977, 110.

4 See Richard Chafee's chapter "The Teaching of Architecture at the Ecole des Beaux-Arts," in *The Architecture of the Ecole des Beaux-Arts*," edited by Arthur Drexler (New York: The Museum of Modern Art, distributed by MIT Press, 1977), pp.61–110 for a good summary of this trajectory; Donald Drew Egbert's *The Beaux-Arts Tradition in French Architecture* (Princeton, NJ: Princeton Architectural Press, 1980); and Annie Jacque's chapter "The Programmes of the Architectural Section of the Ecole des Beaux-Arts, 1819–1914," in *The Beaux-Arts and Nineteenth-Century French Architecture*, edited by Robin Middleton (Cambridge, MA: MIT Press, 1982), pp.58–65.

5 Beatriz Colomina, "Radical Pedagogies in Architectural Education," *The Architectural Review*, September 28, 2012, https://www.architectural-review.com/today/radical-pedagogies-in-architectural-education, accessed January 10, 2021.

6 Ibid.

7 See, for example, the Tate exhibition catalog *Soul of a Nation: Art in the Age of Black Power*, edited by Mark Godfrey et al. (London: Tate Publishing, 2017); and Komozi Woodard's study of Amiri Baraka, *A Nation within a Nation: Amiri Baraka (LeRoi Jones) and Black Power Politics* (Chapel Hill: University of North Carolina Press, 2005).

8 Both studies note the ways that American imperialism was disseminated through the standardization of urban planning and architectural aesthetics. Within an American protectorate, this approach to architecture and planning operated as a de facto infrastructure for homogenizing the native's reception of American social and cultural values—a situation that was not balanced with the political mechanisms for equal representation under the law. See David Brody's *Visualizing American Empire: Orientalism and Imperialism in the Philippines* (Chicago, IL: University of Chicago Press, 2010) and Rebecca McKenna's *American Imperial*

*Pastoral: The Architecture of US Colonialism in the Philippines* (Chicago, IL: University of Chicago Press, 2017).

9 I have written about the evolutionary models of civilizational progress that subtended American architecture movements elsewhere. See Charles L. Davis II, "Henry Van Brunt and White Settler Colonialism in the Midwest," in *Race and Modern Architecture: A Critical History from the Enlightenment to the Present*, edited by Irene Cheng, Charles L. Davis II, and Mabel O. Wilson (Pittsburgh, PA: University of Pittsburgh Press, 2020), pp.99–115.

10 Joanna Merwood-Salisbury, "Western Architecture: Regionalism and Race in the Inland Architect," in *Chicago Architecture: Histories, Revisions, Alternatives*, edited by Charles Waldheim and Katerina Ruedi Ray (Chicago, IL: University of Chicago Press, 2007), pp.3–14.

11 See Patrick Wolfe's discussion of traditional modes of "cognate biocultural assimilations" in the settler colony in "Settler Colonialism and the Elimination of the Native," in *Journal of Genocide Research*, vol.8, no.4 (2006): 388.

12 See C. Marmoz, "The Building of the Ecole des Beaux-Arts," in *The Beaux-Arts and Nineteenth-Century French Architecture*, edited by Robin Middleton (Cambridge, MA: MIT Press, 1982), pp.124–137; and David Van Zanten, "Felix Duban and the Buildings of the Ecole des Beaux-Arts, 1832–1840," *Journal of the Society of Architectural Historians*, vol.37, no.3 (1978): 161–174.

13 See Neil Levine's essays "The Book and the Building: Hugo's Theory of Architecture and Labrouste's Bibliotheque Ste-Genevieve," in *The Beaux-Arts and Nineteenth-Century French Architecture*, edited by Robin Middleton (Cambridge, MA: MIT Press, 1982), pp.138–173; and "The Romantic Idea of Architectural Legibility: Henri Labrouste and the Neo-Grec," in *The Architecture of the Ecole des Beaux-Arts*, edited by Arthur Drexler (New York: Museum of Modern Art, 1977), pp.325–416.

14 Etienne Jean-Delacluze, L'Hémicycle du palais des Beaux-Arts, peinture murale exécutée par Paul Delaroche et gravée au burin par Henriquel-Dupont. Notice explicative suivie d'un trait figuratif indiquant les noms de tous les personnages… (Paris: Groupil, 1857).

15 Van Zanten 1978, 170–172.

16 We know that Egypt was known to students at the Ecole because of the writings of Quatremère de Quincy. See Quatremère de Quincy, "De l'architecture Egytpienne Consideree dans son Origines, ses Principes et son Gout, Et Comparee dous les Memes Rapports a l'architecture Grecque" (Paris, 1803).

17 For an overview of Quatremere's type theory, see Sylvia Lavin's *Quatremere de Quincy and the Invention of a Modern Language of Architecture* (Cambridge, MA and London: MIT Press, 1992); For a summary of the racialist tendencies of nineteenth-century European architecture theory, including instructors at the Ecole, see Irene Cheng's "Structural Racialism in Modern Architectural Theory," in *Race and Modern Architecture: A Critical History from the Enlightenment to the Present*, edited by Irene Cheng et al. (Pittsburgh, PA: University of Pittsburgh Press, 2020), pp.134–152.

18 Egbert 1980, 140; "Grand Prix programs invariably called for buildings with public and national connotations… academic architects have tended to rank the different types of buildings, with monumental public architecture considered as the most 'noble' and possessing the most universal significance. Last, the Academie originated as an advisory body to the king as head of state, hence in its official capacity it was expected to deal primarily with royal and state buildings. As a result, the academicians gradually came to make their living largely as employees of the state to whom regularly fell the task of designing all great national buildings, and the school of the Academie was consequently looked upon as a place for training the designers of such buildings."

19 Egbert 1980, 168–200; Here are just a few examples: Un Palais Colonial (1909); Une Ecole Militaire (c.1914); Une Residence du representant de la France au Maroc.

20 Drexler 1977, 189.

21 Manfredo Tafuri, *Architecture and Utopia: Design and Capitalist Development*, translated by Barbara Luigi La Penta (Cambridge, MA: MIT Press, 1979), pp.25–40.

22 See Amy Kaplan, *The Anarchy of Empire in the Making of US Culture* (Cambridge, MA: Harvard University Press, 2002), pp.1–22.

23 I would like to thank Tara Dudley for introducing me to the title of Black Master Builder, which she uses polemically to acknowledge the expertise and creativity that has long been denied to designers of color at the end of the nineteenth century. While this group cannot be formally identified as 'architects' because of the social and legal restrictions towards Blacks becoming licensed architects, such a title restores our knowledge of this groups' formal integration, and later subversion, of lessons learned from European trained architects through apprenticeship and reading. See Tara A. Dudley, *Building Antebellum New Orleans: Free People of Color and Their Influence* (Austin, Texas: University of Texas Press, 2021) for a book-length discussion of such figures in recent scholarship.

# 16 Feminist Architectural Figurations

## Relating Theory to Practice through Writing in Time

*Jane Rendell*

This essay explores different theoretical positions in the work of feminist architectural writing in the English language from the 1970s to today. This involves examining how feminist architectural theory's relation to history and practice has shifted over time, reconfiguring the relation between architectural theory, history and practice. In the first section, I discuss how feminist architectural writing, emerging in the 1970s–1980s, and associated with second wave feminism, drew on feminist political theories of equality and difference to provide a conceptual underpinning for understanding how sexism operates in the building industry and architectural profession, and how this impacts on women's roles as makers and users of the built environment – summarised in the phrase 'the man-made world.' The second section engages with feminist architectural theory in the 1990s, a historical moment, which saw a flourishing of feminist theory and gender studies, and feminist architectural history, theory, and criticism in the academy, as part of third wave feminism. Feminist architectural writing of the 1990s was explicitly theoretical and interdisciplinary, adopting and adapting feminist concepts from disciplines outside architecture, namely anthropology, art history, geography, philosophy, psychoanalysis, and visual culture, to produce a critical understanding of the gendering of spatial and visual representations. In the final section I investigate how in the last decade, feminist architectural theory has been more generative and activist. Emerging as part of a fourth-wave feminism, including the work of established scholars and practitioners, but also a new generation of feminist activists coming of age through public campaigns such as 'me too,' 'black lives matter,' and 'extinction rebellion,' this recent theoretical work, often participatory and collective, is rooted in practice. Here feminist architectural theory is positioned both as subject matter but also a mode of practice in its own right, and focused on issues of decolonisation, trans-bodies, and the ecological crisis. It engages with feminist new materialist philosophies, situated knowledge and intersectional subjectivities, to produce feminist figurations, which, as Rosi Braidotti writes, are 'not mere metaphors, but rather markers of more concretely situated historical positions,' and 'expression[s] of one's specific positioning in space and time.'[1]

DOI: 10.4324/9781003292999-18

## The Man-Made Environment: Architectural Engagements with Feminist Politics

Much feminist architectural writing in the 1970s took the form of critical historical analysis and design, where the theoretical component was often located in feminist political theory. A key aspect of the work concerned the kind of feminist approach being taken, either following reformist or liberal tactics aimed at establishing conditions of equality for women in the existing social system, or taking more revolutionary approaches – following socialist or essentialist feminist positions. Feminists confronted women's exclusion from architecture and sought to uncover evidence of their contributions. Susana Torre's edited collection on the history of women in North American architecture,[2] for example, rewrote the history of women architects and clients in the US, while Lynne Walker's exhibition *British Women in Architecture 1671–1951*, at the Royal Institute of British Architects, London in 1984, repositioned women in architectural history.[3]

Vital in providing evidence of women's contributions to architecture historically, this work though often conceptual was not always explicitly theoretical. Research into women's place in society in sociology and anthropology helped to develop discussions around equality and difference in architecture; demonstrating, on the one hand, women's equality with men by celebrating their overlooked roles as architects of large institutional buildings in the public realm, and considering, on the other, how women's decisions to critique the establishment and embrace difference could be evidenced in the other roles they took on in building design and production, for example, as patrons.[4]

This feminist work added to an existing body of knowledge, and also questioned the 'canon,' producing an alternative feminist history of architectural practice, as in *Making Room*,[5] where feminists suggested that it was precisely in the area of design process that female difference might be expressed. American critic Karen Franck, following Nancy Chodorow, argued that women's socialisation fostered a different value system emphasising certain qualities such as connectedness, inclusiveness, an ethics of care, everyday life, subjectivity, feelings, complexity, and flexibility in design. Franck cited the work of women architects such as Eileen Gray and Lilly Reich, and Susana Torre's projects 'House of Meaning' and 'Space as Matrix' as exemplary of this approach. Promoting the idea that women designers and users value different kinds of spaces – ones which facilitate the flexibility required of women's social roles – also suggested analogies between spatial matrices and the fluid spatiality of the female body.[6]

While the approach of second wave feminism in the US is frequently connected to the slogan 'the personal is political,'[7] with the theoretical focus tending towards the politicisation of private experiences, much feminist work in architecture in both the US and UK during that period was also often explicitly linked to feminist Marxist and socialist theory, arguing for different approaches to architectural design, via critiques of patriarchal value systems that operated at the intersection of gender and class.[8] In the late 1970s and early 1980s, feminists in planning and architecture in the US and in Europe were primarily concerned with the ways in which gender differences impacted on the production and use of built space, focusing on the predominance of men as producers of a man-made environment and of women's experiences as users of these spaces. The work of the American feminist planner and historian, Dolores Hayden, for example, identified how certain features of the man-made environment discriminate against women, such as inhospitable streets, sexist symbolism in advertising, and pornographic outlets. Hayden proposed removing these sexist features and replacing them instead with child-care facilities, safe houses and better public transport to ensure a more equitable society.[9]

In the UK, feminist architectural co-operative, Matrix, examined the intersection of class and gender in the politics of house-work. In their book, *Making Space: Women and the Man-made Environment*,[10] historical investigations of housing design also focused on feminist theoretical understandings of the separate spheres,[11] referring to research by US academics like Hayden, and also Gwendolyn Wright,[12] as well as UK-based researchers, like Elizabeth Wilson,[13] and Marion Roberts.[14] Matrix's framed their understanding of feminist architecture using five themes: namely, 'a woman's place?', the 'man-made world,' 'outside the home,' 'what's wrong with modern architecture?,' and 'a feminist response,' which together provided a theoretical context for a feminist critique of the male-dominated building industry and architectural profession,[15] and guidance for the design of public and domestic spaces with women users' needs in mind, specifically, safety, and accessibility.[16]

As a co-operative Matrix sought to work in an egalitarian manner through their internal practice structure, and advocated a different design process where users were involved in the design from the outset. Although often not explicitly theorised, Matrix understood this as a feminist design process, which not only critiqued architectural value systems by replacing the figure of architect as individual genius with that of the architect as facilitator, but also by rejecting the term architecture, and favouring the more inclusive and less hierarchical 'built environment' instead. This connected their work to contemporary research on the gendered design and use of urban space by academics in geography, planning and urban studies,[17] and to publications by other feminist organisations involved in the construction industry, such as Women in the Manual Trades,[18] and those of advocacy groups such as the Women's Design Service (1987–2012).[19] This feminist approach to theory, deeply embedded in the design of architecture and feminist politics, can be understood as part of a broader examination by other feminist and socialist historians, of how power relations, structured through class, as well as gender, and race, influenced the use of buildings,[20] as well as their production.[21]

## Architecture and the Feminine: Encounters with Post-Structuralism

During the 1990s feminist research in architecture began to draw more explicitly on theory – deconstructivist, post-structuralist, postcolonial, and psychoanalytic – from other disciplines, such as art history, cultural studies, film theory, and philosophy, in order to develop understandings of how gendered subjectivity was constructed and reproduced through spatial and visual representations.[22] UK-based feminist geographers writing in the 1990s, such as Liz Bondi, Linda McDowell, Doreen Massey, and Gillian Rose, articulated theories of the gendering of space, deriving from Marxist philosopher Henri Lefebvre's account of the social production of space, but maintaining that space is produced by and productive of gender, as well as class, relations.[23] Such work on gendered spatiality and visuality, theorised the feminist practice of architectural history opening up a re-examination not only of the way in which feminists choose their new objects of study but also the intellectual criteria through which they interpret those objects of study.

US scholarship in this period, and publications such as *Assemblage* and *ANY,* highlighted the relevance of such critical methodological issues. Critics such as Beatriz Colomina, Zeynip Çelik and Mabel Wilson developed sustained feminist critiques of the traditional male canon – questioning the focus on male architects, male users, and masculine modes of representation. Using feminist interpretative techniques, they placed issues of gender, race, and ethnicity at the heart of their analysis of representational practices in the architecture of such 'male masters' as Adolf Loos and Le Corbusier. The mid-to late 1990s saw a series of edited and co-edited volumes comprising feminist research in architectural history and theory published in the US and UK.[24] And in 2000, Lesley Lokko's edited collection, *White Papers, Black Marks: Architecture, Race, Culture*, was published, a ground-breaking work of architectural history and theory which investigated race, along with gender and class, as a tool of critical analysis and creative production for architecture.[25]

Deconstructivist and post-structuralist approaches enabled feminist architectural history and theory to problematise such seemingly stable terms as 'architecture,' 'male,' and 'female,' and to show how these were ideologically constructed.[26] Alice T. Friedman's study of the contribution of female patrons to architecture, for example, complexified earlier versions of 'her story,' by using psychoanalytic theory to examine the relations of power played out through vision in certain architectural designs.[27] In my own work, I argued for a specifically feminist Marxist practice of architectural history, informed by the work of theoretical work of French feminist philosopher Luce Irigaray, to investigate the gendered representation and use of architectural spaces of consumption, display and exchange in 1820s London.[28] Henry Urbach's design history of the closet drew on Judith Butler and Eve Kosofsky Sedgwick's queer theoretical work on 'performativity' to develop arguments around staging, secrecy, and display with specific respect to the spatial practice of 'coming out.'[29]

And Joel Sanders' edited collection, *Stud: Architectures of Masculinity,* was the first to deal specifically with issues of masculinity and architecture, including his own critique of SOM's 'Cadet Quarters,' which showed how representations of masculinity were central to the work of these contemporary architects.[30]

In a profession where masculinity is often collapsed into the neutral figure of the 'architect,' and sites of current architectural education and the profession are also considered gender neutral, recognising gender as a social construction has been a vital aspect of critiquing the heterosexual patriarchal bastion of architectural practice. Feminist theories of representation have also been used to produce critiques of the gendering of the very language of architectural treatises. Using examples from the drawing and writing of Renaissance architects who advocated the use of particular proportion systems for setting out the formal geometries of buildings, Diane Agrest argued that while the male body was used to represent the ideal set of proportions, the female body was either rejected from the practice of architecture or suppressed within it.[31] Reclaiming this rejected 'feminine' has been an important aspect of feminist theory's exploration of, and experimentation with, architectural language. Following Derridean deconstruction, which seeks to reveal the insufficiency of logical and rational structures, such as spoken language to explain the world, and instead to bring into operation the supressed and subversive elements of written texts, the drawn and written projects of US architect and critic, Jennifer Bloomer have demonstrated that the feminine could be a radical element in architectural theory and practice.[32]

A number of architectural design projects from the 1990s explicitly worked with concepts of the feminine to stimulate a more theorised design process, from the choosing of sites reformulated by Clare Robinson in terms of 'chora,' to the articulation of services, as in Michelle Kauffman's 'lacuna wall,' where the gaps between buildings point to those spaces occupied by women in patriarchy.[33] Architectural critic Kath Shonfield's installations, such as *Dirt is Matter Out of Place* (1991), with Frank O'Sullivan, which filled a public lavatory in Spitalfields with feathers, and *Purity and Tolerance* (1995), with muf,[34] in which a shiny latex ceiling filled with liquid expanded threatening to collapse into the space of the Economist Building when it housed the Architecture Foundation, offered gendered critiques of architecture through material practices.[35] And the interdisciplinary feminist architectural conference and exhibition, *Desiring Practices*, consisting of site-specific installations in the Royal Institute of British Architects, Portland Place, London,[36] brought feminist theory directly into architectural practice, offering a critique of the narrow definition of architecture policed by the profession, and repositioning architecture in an 'expanded field.'[37]

Through the 1990s and into the first decade of the twenty-first century, feminist architectural history, theory, and practice have been strongly informed by conceptual thinking, not only by deconstruction and post-structuralism more generally, but specifically by the French feminist philosophy of Hélene Cixous, Luce Irigaray, and Julia Kristeva and their notions of femininity, écriture feminine, and mimicry.[38] Irigaray's theory of 'mimicry' shows how, when working within a symbolic system with predetermined notions of feminine and masculine, where there is no theory of the female subject, women can seek to represent themselves through mimicking the system itself.[39] Elizabeth Grosz, following Irigaray, has argued that despite being erased from western philosophy, the feminine concepts, such as chora, form the foundations of philosophic value.[40] More recently, feminist architectural historian Karen Burns has noted that despite the large number of feminist publications in the 1990s, this was also the decade that saw the absence of feminist texts in major architectural theory anthologies. She notes how where the 'feminine' was included, for example, in essays on choric space, it was through invited contributions authored by men – so, as she suggests, feminist theory was being conducted by men through the bodies of women.[41]

## Feminist Figurations: Practising Feminist Architectural Theory

This interdisciplinary and conceptualised feminist approach to architecture opened up different ways of linking history and design through theory. In 2012, I suggested that there might be a specifically feminist mode of 'critical spatial practice' – the term I gave my re-positioning of self-reflection and social emancipation, as two key tenets of Frankfurt School critical theory, into practice. I focused on five themes – collectivity, interiority, alterity, performativity, and materiality.[42] While these are still concerns of feminist critical spatial practice today, I would like to examine here how they been reconfigured in the past decade.

Starting with collectivity, the importance of collaboration and participation for feminist practices in architecture and urbanism remains highly relevant, with some focused on building and planning, such as atelier *d'architecture d'autogerée*; some more artistic and performative, such as MYCKET and taking place[43]; and others more activist, like Architexx and Parlour, who work on changing sexist forms of pedagogy and professional conduct. Much of this practice is theoretically informed, but most importantly it operates to support women, and to provide a range of innovative tools and initiatives, from the 'Parlour Guides' to 'Marion's list' and the 'W Awards.' This socially engaged and often participatory feminist practice has generated theoretical work by reflecting on feminist spatial practice[44] and its spatial politics,[45] including approaches which aim to transform or alter, by practicing 'otherwise' or 'otherhow.'[46] Performative interventions and events-based activities are core to this, as are conferences that include design as well as history and theory. The International Congress of Architecture and Gender's 'Matrices' (2017) and 'ACTION' (2021), and the recent Berlin-based 'Dream-Play-Challenge: Women in Architecture' (2021) have re-connected and re-imagined the kinds of work – political activism, policy, advocacy, and access – which animated feminist architecture in the 1970s.

I see this call for collaborative and participatory work to be closely connected to the third theme, alterity. In 2012, I had linked this to practices and theories of otherness, but more recently the demands of the decolonisation movement and transgender activism have required a deeper and more specific critique of the architectural profession and its modes of gendering,[47] which have drawn upon and extended intersectional work on race, gender and class, to include trans politics, for example, in the work of Lucas Crawford and Joel Sanders' *Stalled!*,[48] and engagements with disability issues as exemplified by the research of Jos Boys.[49] Feminist work concerning race and colonialism, such as the research and practice of Huda Tayob and Thandi Loewenson, has begun to develop a strongly creative strand of critical race theory in architecture, attuned to issues of race, and the legacies of colonialism.[50]

As for the second theme, interiority, I now see this as intimately linked to the fifth theme, materiality, and the two developing through theorisations of subjectivity and relationality coming out of feminist materialist philosophy. This is perhaps exemplified by the conference *Sexuate Subjects,* led in 2010 by Peg Rawes at the Bartlett School of Architecture,[51] and in 2017, the annual UK-based conference of the Architectural Humanities Research Association, *Architecture and Feminisms*, held at the KTH School of Architecture in Stockholm.[52] Both were devoted to discussions and to exhibiting works on gender and sexuality, and framed architecture with respect to ecology and economy. Feminists in architecture have recently focused their theoretical attention on the feminist materialist philosophy of Karen Barad, Jane Bennet, Rosi Braidotti, Donna Haraway, and Isabelle Stengers, all thinkers whose understandings of subjectivity and relationality are worked through feminist readings of Michel Foucault's biopolitics and Gilles Deleuze and Felix Guattari's assemblages, to examine materiality and technology through ecologies of practice. Such English-language based articulations of feminist subjectivities in architecture are currently being advanced by theorists such as Hélene Frichot, Stephen Loo, Peg Rawes and Katie Lloyd Thomas.[53]

It is important to note that this theoretical work is taking place in the context of the rise of practice-led research, which, in the UK-based, Australian and northern European academies, has reconfigured the relation of architectural history, theory and design. Here notions of architectural practice are expanded beyond professional definitions, and historical and theoretical writing processes understood as forms of practice in and of themselves.[54] Of the feminist theoretician-practitioners who explore the relation between the verbal and the visual, and between drawing and writing, many combine history, theory and practice, using a variety of media including moving image, audio, and installation.[55]

Post-structuralist feminists, such as Seyla Benhabib, Rosalyn Diprose, Jane Flax, Moira Gatens, Sandra Harding, Elspeth Probyn, Linda Nicholson, and Andrea Nye, have offered feminist theoretical understandings of positioned knowledge, in which subjectivities are contingent and situated and constructed in response to particular times and places. Haraway's influential essay from the 1980s, 'Situated Knowledge', in which she argues that objectivity is partial and positioned has facilitated powerful feminist critiques of status-quo positions of knowledge construction in the architectural profession.[56] In my own architectural theoretical work, through the practice of 'site-writing,' I have emphasised how the critic's discrete position and situatedness as mediator between work and audience conditions the performance of their interpretative role. I propose alternative positions for the critic to occupy, including an 'architecture' of criticism where the critical essay can function as a mode of practice in its own right.[57]

Core to a situated approach to critical and theoretical writing is the notion of 'performativity,' the final theme of my 2012 essay. Performance theorist Della Pollock has discussed the key qualities of performance writing, as subjective, evocative, metonymic, nervous, citational, and consequential.[58] Such qualities are currently palpable across the arena of experimental writing, where the distanced objectivity of academic writing styles, is being replaced various critical-creative hybrid genres.[59] Feminist architectural theorists have drawn inspiration from this intensely creative and theoretically rigorous strand of speculative criticism, and most recently, Hélene Frichot and Naomi Stead, for example, have understood these positioned and often subjective modes of writerly architectural theory as 'ficto-critical.'[60]

This approach to writing as a form of practice brings theory closer to architectural design processes, showing how writing is not only a way of communicating pre-existing theoretical ideas for architecture, but also how writing *architecturally* can indicate different spatial, material and conceptual possibilities for theory. Opportunities for producing this kind of work and for developing its critical and creative potential are currently possible because of the emerging body of feminist work that is explicitly theorising architecture through the spatial qualities of writing.[61] With the current flourishing of this field, the time is ripe to consider how this kind of theory, which takes place through writing as a form of practice and design, can suggest a reconfiguring of the relation between the architectural processes of theory and practice, with respect to history, and through time.[62]

For me, the relation is no longer one where theory exists *before* design, to be applied through it, or *after* design, to post-rationalise or conceptualise it, but rather where, or perhaps *when,* theory is in dialogue with architectural design. As such, a feminist approach, by taking account of relations between subjects and objects, and by acknowledging that the positionality of the theorist is based on situated and politicised experiences, advances an ethical approach to architectural theory that is always conducted *in-relation-to* history and design – whether to, for, through, with, or even, as. A feminist position in architecture, in addressing gender inequality, is not beset by the problems the 'end of theory' can often pose via the post-critical condition. A socially and materially engaged feminism does not seek to set itself apart from design, nor to embrace a position that comes after, as in 'the end of', criticality. The kind of criticality that feminism follows understands that we live in critical times. Such feminist architectural theory in seeking to critically engage design, requires re-imagining the practice of writing theory itself: Haraway and Braidotti might call such experiments 'feminist figurations.'

> "There is a deep connection between the writing subject and the figure. It is not just about picking an entity in the world, some kind of interesting academic object. There is a cathexis that needs to be understood here. [...] Articulating the analytic object, figuring, [...] is about location and historical specificity, and it is about a kind of assemblage, a kind of connectedness of the figure and the subject."[63]

## Notes

1 Rosi Braidotti, *Transpositions: On Nomadic Ethics* (Cambridge: Polity Press, 2006), p. 90. See also Rosi Braidotti, *Nomadic Subjects: Embodiment and Sexual Difference in Contemporary Feminist Theory* (New York: Colombia University Press, 1994).

2 Susana Torre (ed.), *Women in American Architecture* (New York: Whitney Library of Design, 1977).

3 Lynne Walker, *British Women in Architecture 1671–1951* (London: Sorello Press, 1984).

4 See for example, Sara Boutelle, *Julia Morgan: Architect* (New York: Abbeville Press, 1988) and Alice Friedman, *House and Household in Elizabethan England* (Chicago, IL: University of Chicago Press, 1989)

5 'Making Room,' special issue of *Heresies: A Feminist Publication on Art and Politics* (New York: Heresies Collective Inc.:,1981), v. 3, n. 3, issue 11.

6 Karen A. Franck, 'A Feminist Approach to Architecture: Acknowledging Women's Ways of Knowing,' in Ellen Perry Berkeley (ed.), *Architecture: A Place for Women* (Washington, DC: Smithsonian Institution Press, 1989), pp. 201–216.

7 This phrase has been attributed to a paper by Carol Hanisch, originally titled, 'Some Thoughts in Response to Dottie's Thoughts on a Women's Liberation Movement,' (February 1969) published as 'The Personal is Political' in Shulamuth Firestone and Anne Koedt (eds) *Notes from the Second Year: Women's Liberation* (1970), pp. 76–78. Hanisch states that the title 'The Personal is Political' was given to the paper by the editors. See http://www.carolhanisch.org/CHwritings/PIP.html.

8 See for example, Leslie Kanes Weisman, *Discrimination by Design* (Chicago, IL: University of Illinois Press, 1992).

9 Dolores Hayden, 'What Would a Non-Sexist City Be Like? Speculations on Housing, Urban Design and Human Work,' in Catharine R. Stimpson, Elsa Dixler, Martha J. Nelson and Kathryn B. Yatrakis (eds), *Women and the American City* (Chicago, IL: University of Chicago Press, 1981), pp. 167–184 and Dolores Hayden, *The Grand Domestic Revolution* (Cambridge, MA: The M.I.T. Press, 1981).

10 See Matrix, *Making Space: Women and the Man-Made Environment* (London: Pluto Press, 1984) which references, for example, Juliet Mitchell and Ann Oakley (eds), *The Rights and Wrongs of Women* (Harmondsworth: Penguin, 1976); Ann Oakley, *The Sociology of Housework* (London: Martin Robertson, 1974); Ann Oakley, *Housewife* (Harmondsworth: Penguin, 1977); and Sheila Rowbotham, *Hidden from History* (London: Pluto Press, 1977); and Eva Kaluzynska, 'Wiping the Floor with Theory – A Survey of Writings on Housework,' *Feminist Review* (1980), n. 6, pp. 27–54.

11 See for example, Leonore Davidoff and Catherine Hall, 'The Architecture of Public and Private Life,' in Derek Fraser and Anthony Sutcliffe (eds), *The Pursuit*

*of Urban History*, (London: Edward Arnold Publishers Ltd., 1983), pp. 327–345 and Leonore Davidoff and Catherine Hall, *Family Fortunes* (Chicago, IL: Chicago University Press, 1987).

12 See for example, Gwendolyn Wright, *Moralism and the Model Home: Domestic Architecture and Cultural Conflict in Chicago 1873–1913* (Chicago, IL: University of Chicago Press, 1980).

13 See, for example, Elizabeth Wilson, *Women and the Welfare State* (London: Tavistock, 1977) and Elizabeth Wilson, *Only Halfway to Paradise: Women in Post-War Britain 1945–1968* (London: Tavistock, 1980).

14 Marion Roberts, *Living in Man-Made World: Gender Assumptions in Modern Housing Design* (London: Routledge, 1991).

15 See, for example, Sue Francis, 'New Woman New Space: Towards a Feminist Critique of Building Design', unpublished MA thesis, Department of General Studies, Royal College of Art (May 1980) See also Sue Francis and Frances Bradshaw, 'A Woman's Place', *Slate* (1979), n. 13, a text referred to in Matrix, *Making Space*, p. 137, but with the page numbers omitted.

16 Frances Bradshaw, 'Working with Women', Matrix, *Making Space*, pp. 89–105.

17 J. Little, L. Peake and P. Richardson (eds), *Women in Cities: Gender and the Urban Environment* (London: Macmillan, 1988).

18 https://wamt.org.uk/.

19 http://www.wds.org.uk/.

20 See for example, Anthony D. King (ed.), *Buildings and Society: Essays on the Social Development of the Built Environment* (London: Routledge and Kegan Paul, 1980) and Thomas A. Markus, *Buildings and Power* (London: Routledge, 1993).

21 Linda Clarke (ed.), *Building Capitalism* (London: Routledge, 1992).

22 See for example, Elizabeth Wilson, *The Sphinx in the City: Urban life, the Control of Disorder, and Women* (London: Virago Press, 1991); Griselda Pollock, *Vision and Difference: Femininity, Feminism and the Histories of Art* (London: Routledge, 1988); Laura Mulvey (ed.), *Visual and Other Pleasures* (London: Macmillan, 1989); and Jacqueline Rose, *Sexuality in the Field of Vision* (London: Verso, 1986).

23 See for example, Liz Bondi, 'Gender and Geography: Crossing Boundaries,' *Progress in Human Geography* (1993), v. 17, n. 2, pp. 241–246; Doreen Massey, *Space, Place and Gender* (Cambridge: Polity Press, 1994); Linda McDowell, 'Space, Place and Gender Relations, Parts 1 and 2', *Progress in Human Geography* (1993), v. 17, n. 2, pp. 157–179 and n. 3, pp. 305–318; and Gillian Rose, *Feminism and Geography: The Limits of Geographical Knowledge* (Cambridge: Polity Press, 1993).

24 See Beatriz Colomina (ed.), *Sexuality and Space* (New York: Princeton Architectural Press, 1992); Debra Coleman, Elizabeth Danze and Carol Henderson (eds.), *Architecture and Feminism* (New York: Princeton Architectural Press, 1996); Francesca Hughes (ed.), *The Architect: Reconstructing Her Practice* (Cambridge, MA: M. I. T. Press, 1996); Duncan McCorquodale, Katerina Rüedi and Sarah Wigglesworth (eds.), *Desiring Practices: Architecture, Gender and the Interdisciplinary* (London: Blackdog, 1996); Diane Agrest, Patricia Conway and Leslie Kanes Weisman (eds.), *The Sex of Architecture* (New York: Harry N. Abrams Publisher, 1997); Jane Rendell, Barbara Penner and Iain Borden (eds.), *Gender, Space, Architecture: An Interdisciplinary Introduction* (London: Routledge, 1999); and Louise Durning and Richard Wrigley (eds), *Gender and Architecture: History, Interpretation and Practice* (London: Wiley, 2000).

25 Lesley Naa Norle Lokko (ed.), *White Papers, Black Marks: Architecture, Race, Culture*, (London: Athlone Press, 2000).

26 Iain Borden and I suggested in *Intersections*, that there were nine specific ways in which critical theory could be used to inform architectural historical methodology. See Iain Borden and Jane Rendell (eds) *InterSections: Architectural Histories and Critical Theories* (London: Routledge, 2000).

27 Alice Friedman, *Women and the Making of the Modern House* (New York, Harry N. Abrams, 1997).
28 Jane Rendell, *The Pursuit of Pleasure: Gender, Space and Architecture in Regency London* (London: The Athlone Press/Continuum with Rutgers University Press, 2002).
29 Henry Urbach, 'Closets, Clothes, disclosure,' in Duncan McCorquodale, Katerina Rüedi and Sarah Wigglesworth (eds), *Desiring Practices: Architecture, Gender and the Interdisciplinary* (London: Blackdog, 1996), pp. 246–263.
30 Joel Sanders (ed.), *Stud: Architectures of Masculinity* (Princeton, NJ: Princeton Architectural Press, 1996), pp. 68–78.
31 Diane Agrest, *Architecture from Without: Theoretical Framings for a Critical Practice* (Cambridge, MA: The M.I.T. Press, 1993).
32 Jennifer Bloomer, *Architecture and the Text: The (S)crypts of Joyce and Piranesi* (New Haven, CT and London: Yale University Press, 1993). See also Jennifer Bloomer, 'Big Jugs', in Arthur Kroker and Marilouise Kroker (eds), *The Hysterical Male: New Feminist Theory*, (London: Macmillan Education, 1991), pp. 13–27.
33 Claire Robinson, 'Chora Work,' Michelle Kaufman, 'Liquidation, Amalgamation,' and Ann Bergren, 'Dear Jennifer', *ANY – Architecture and the Feminine: Mop-Up Work* (1994), n. 4, pp. 34–37 and pp. 38–39.
34 See muf, *Architectural Design* (August 1996), v. 66, n. 7–8, pp. 80–83 and later muf, *This is What We Do: A muf Manual* (London: Ellipsis, 2001).
35 See https://www.architecturefoundation.org.uk/programme/1995/public-views-1/purity-and-tolerance. See also http://morethanonefragile.co.uk/20th-century-muf/. See also Kath Schonfield, *Walls Have Feelings: Architecture Film and City* (London: Routledge, 2000).
36 McCorquodale, Ruedi and Wigglesworth (eds.), *Desiring Practices.*
37 See Rosalind Krauss, 'Sculpture in the Expanded Field,' in Hal Foster (ed.), *Postmodern Culture* (London: Pluto Press, 1985). See also Spyros Papapetros and Julian Rose (eds), *Retracing the Expanded Field: Encounters between Art and Architecture* (MIT, 2014), and Anthony Vidler, 'Architecture's Expanded Field,' *Artforum International* (2004), v. 42, n. 8, pp. 142–147.
38 For the most widely discussed examples of the work, see for example Hélène Cixious, 'The Laugh of the Medusa', in Elaine Marks and Isabelle de Courtivron (eds), *New French Feminisms: An Anthology* (London: Harvester, 1981), pp. 243–264; Julia Kristeva, *Desire in Language: A Semiotic Approach to Literature and Art* (Oxford: Blackwell, 1980); and Luce Irigaray, 'This Sex Which Is Not One', *This Sex Which Is Not One* (Ithaca, NY: Cornell University Press, 1985), pp. 23–33.
39 Luce Irigaray, 'Any Theory of the "Subject" Has Always Been Appropriated by the "Masculine"', in *The Speculum of the Other Woman* (Ithaca, NY: Cornell University Press, 1985), pp. 133–146.
40 Elizabeth Grosz, *Volatile Bodies: Toward a Corporeal Feminism* (Bloomington and Indianapolis: Indiana University Press, 1994) and Elizabeth Grosz, *Architecture from the Outside: Essays on Virtual and Real Space* (Cambridge, MA: The M.I.T. Press, 2001).
41 Karen Burns, 'A Girl's Own Adventure: Gender in the Contemporary Architectural Theory Anthology,' *Journal of Architectural Education* (2012), v. 65, n. 2, pp. 125–134.
42 See Jane Rendell, 'Critical Spatial Practices: Setting Out a Feminist Approach to Some Modes and What Matters in Architecture', in Lori Brown (ed.) *Feminist Practices* (London: Ashgate, 2012) and Jane Rendell, 'Only Resist: A Feminist Approach to Critical Spatial Practice,' *Architectural Review* (19 February 2018), https://www.architectural-review.com/essays/only-resist-a-feminist-approach-to-critical-spatial-practice. See also Jane Rendell, 'Feminist Architecture: From A to Z', https://www.readingdesign.org/feminist-architecture-a-z.

43 For discussions of the work of taking place, see for example, Katie Lloyd Thomas, Teresa Hoskyns and Helen Stratford, 'Taking Place 2,' *Scroope: Cambridge Architecture Journal* (2002), v. 14, pp. 44–48; Julia Dwyer, 'Inscription as a Collective Practice: Taking Place and "The Other Side of Waiting,"' in H. Edquist and L. Vaughan (eds), *The Design Collective: An Approach to Practice* (Newcastle upon Tyne: Cambridge Scholars Publishing, 2012), pp. 35–53; and Teresa Hoskyns and Helen Stratford, 'Was (Is) Taking Place a Nomadic Practice?' *Architecture and Culture* (2017), v. 5, n. 3, pp. 407–421.

44 Meike Shalk, Terese Kristiannson and Ramia Maze (eds) *Feminist Futures of Spatial Practice* (Bamburg: Spurbuchverlag AADR, 2017).

45 Teresa Hoskyns, *The Empty Place: Democracy and Public Space*, (London: Routledge: 2014).

46 Doina Petrescu, *Altering Practices: Feminist Politics and Poetics of Space* (London: Routledge, 2007) and Doina Petrescu and Kim Trogal (eds) *The Social (Re)Production of Architecture: Politics, Values and Actions in Contemporary Practice*_(London: Routledge, 2017).

47 Ruth Morrow, Harriet Harriss, James Benedict Brown and James Soane (eds), *A Gendered Profession: The Question of Representation in Space Making* (London: RIBA Publishing, 2016).

48 Lucas Crawford, *Transgender Architectonics: The Shape of Change in Modernist Space* (Ashgate, 2015).

49 Jos Boys (ed.), *Doing Disability Differently* (London: Routledge, 2014) and Jos Boys (ed.), *Disability, Space, Architecture* (London: Routledge, 2017).

50 Huda Tayob, 'Unconfessed Architectures,' (2021), https://www.e-flux.com/architecture/survivance/386349/unconfessed-architectures/ and Thandi Loewenson, 'To Get Lost in Mysterious Mist' (2021), https://www.e-flux.com/architecture/survivance/387184/to-get-lost-in-mysterious-mist/.

51 See Peg Rawes, Stephen Loo and Tim Matthews (eds) *Poetic Biopolitical Practices in the Arts and Humanities* (London: I B Tauris, 2016).

52 See Meike Schalk and Karin Reisinger (eds), *Becoming a Feminist Architect,* special issue of *field*; v. 7, n. 1 (2017); Meike Schalk and Karin Reisinger (eds), *Styles of Queer Feminist Practices and Objects in Architecture*, special issue of *Architecture and Culture*, v. 5, n. 3 (2017); and Hélène Frichot and Catharina Gabrielsson (eds), *Architecture and Feminisms: Ecologies, Economies, Technologies* (London: Routledge, 2017).

53 See for example, Hélene Frichot, *Creative Ecologies: Theorizing the Practice of Architecture* (London: Bloomsbury, 2018); Katie Lloyd Thomas (ed.), *Material Matters: Architecture and Material Practice* (London: Routledge, 2006); and Peg Rawes (ed.), *Relational Architectural Ecologies: Architecture, Nature and Subjectivity* (London: Routledge, 2013). See also Peg Rawes (ed.), *Irigaray for Architects* (London: Routledge, 2007), which to date remains the only work on a female thinker in this series of 16 books on thinkers for architecture.

54 See Jane Rendell, 'A Way with Words: Feminists Writing Architectural Design Research,' in Murray Fraser (ed.) *Architectural Design Research* (London: Ashgate, 2013). Here I refer to muf, *Architectural Design* (1996), v. 66, n. 7–8, pp. 80–83 and Amy Landesberg and Lisa Quatrale, 'See Angel Touch', in Debra Coleman, Elizabeth Danze and Carol Henderson (eds), *Architecture and Feminism* (New York: Princeton Architectural Press, 1996), pp. 60–71.

55 See for example, the work of Anna Anderson, Emma Cheatle, Lilian Chee, and Penelope Haralambidou. See https://screenworks.org.uk/archive/volume-10–1/the-norwegian-institute-in-rome; Emma Cheatle, *Part-architecture: the Maison de Verre, Duchamp, Domesticity and Desire in 1930s Paris* (London: Routledge, 2017); Lilian Chee and Edna Lim (eds), *Asian Cinema and the Use of Space* (London: Routledge, 2015); Penelope Haralambidou, *The Blossoming of Perspective* (London:

DomoBaal Editions, 2007); and https://domobaal.com/exhibitions/112–20-penelope-haralambidou-01.html.

56 Helene Frichot and Isabelle Doucet (eds), *Resist, Reclaim, Speculate: Situated Perspectives on Architecture and the City*, a special edition of *Architectural Theory Review* (2018).

57 Jane Rendell, *Site-Writing: The Architecture of Art Criticism* (London: I. B. Tauris, 2010). See also Jane Rendell, 'Sites, Situations, and Other Kinds of Situatedness', in Bryony Roberts (ed.), *Expanded Modes of Practice*, Special Issue of *Log* (New York, N.Y.: Anyone Corporation, 2020), pp. 27–38.

58 Della Pollock, 'Performing Writing,' in Peggy Phelan and Jill Lane (eds) *The Ends of Performance* (New York: New York University Press, 1998), pp. 73–103.

59 See, for example, the work of Emma Cocker: http://not-yet-there.blogspot.co.uk/; Yves Lomax, *Writing the Image: An Adventure with Art and Theory* (London: I. B. Tauris, 2000); Caroline Bergvall, *Alisoun Sings* (Brooklyn: Nightboat Books, 2019); Kristen Kreider, *Poetics and Place: The Architecture of Sign, Subjects and Site* (London: I.B. Tauris, 2014); and Emily Orley and Katja Hilavaara (eds), *The Creative Critic* (Routledge, 2018).

60 Helene Frichot and Naomi Stead (eds), *Writing Architecture: Ficto-Critical Approaches* (London: Bloomsbury, 2020).

61 See for example, Linda Marie Walker 'Writing, A Little Machine,' *Architecture Theory Review* (2012), v. 17, n. 1, pp. 40–51; Katja Grillner, 'Writing and Landscape – Setting Scenes for Critical Reflection,' in Jonathan Hill (ed.), *Opposites Attract,* special issue of the *Journal of Architecture* (2003), v. 8, n. 2, pp. 239–249; Sarah Treadwell, 'Pink and White Descriptions', in Naomi Stead and Lee Stickell (eds), *Writing Architecture*, special issue of *Architecture Theory Review* (2010) v. 15, n. 3, pp. 266–280; and Katerina Bonnevier, *Behind Straight Curtains: Towards a Queer Feminist Theory of Architecture*, PhD Dissertation 2007, KTH Stockholm, (Stockholm: Axl Books, 2007).

62 For a discussion of timeliness in feminist situated writing, see Mona Livholts, 'The Professor's Chair: An Untimely Academic Novella', *Life-Writing* (2010), v. 7, n. 2, pp. 155–168. See also Mona Livholts (ed), *Emergent Writing Methodologies in Feminist Studies* (London: Routledge, 2012).

63 Donna Haraway, 'Cyborgs, Coyotes and Dogs: A Kinship of Feminist Figurations and There Are Always More Things Going on Than You Thought! Methodologies as Thinking Technologies: An Interview with Donna Haraway Conducted in Two Parts by Nina Lykke, Randi Markussen, and Finn Olesen' [2000], in Donna Haraway (ed.), *The Donna Haraway Reader* (London: Routledge, 2004), pp. 321–342, p. 338.

# 17 From Deconstruction to Artificial Intelligence

## The New Theoretical Paradigm

*Neil Leach*

This chapter argues that there are signs that there is a new theoretical discourse emerging, fueled by recent interest in the use of Artificial Intelligence (AI) in the design studio. This new approach draws upon the domains of cognitive science, the interdisciplinary study of the human mind, that looks set to replace continental philosophy as the master narrative informing architectural theory. In particular, this chapter examines the new neuroscientific theory of 'predictive perception' and the notion that our perception of reality is a form of 'controlled hallucination'. It explores how this, along with recent cognitive experimentation in the field of AI, seems to suggest a new concept, 'architecturalization'. This offers new theoretical insights into how the mind of the architect operates. It might help to explain, for example, why the ideas emanating from continental philosophy, such as 'deconstruction', were so misunderstood within architectural culture, and why architects have a general tendency to translate conceptual ideas from outside architecture into architectural forms. The chapter concludes that the domains of AI and neuroscience potentially offer us an important mirror in which to better understand how architects think and design.

### The New Theory

Architectural theory, it would appear, is on the wane. It seems to have lost its momentum since the halcyon days of the late 1980s and early 1990s, when theory was all the rage, and helped to fuel some radical ideas within architectural design itself. Furthermore, we could even claim that the absence of critical thinking today might be responsible for architectural design itself retreating from its once progressive impulse, and falling back on nostalgic modes of designing. In some architectural circles, it could be argued, we have seen what appears to be a return to a form of postmodernism.[1]

At the same time, however, there are signs of some fresh new design impulses emerging as a result of the introduction of new, Artificial Intelligence (AI)-based techniques into the design studio, producing a radically iconoclastic and highly inspirational body of work. It could even be claimed that AI constitutes the first genuinely new design technique of the twenty-first

DOI: 10.4324/9781003292999-19

century, and the next major progressive impulse in design since the emergence of Deconstructivism some 30 years ago. Indeed, Wolf Prix makes an explicit connection between these two movements in his lecture, 'From Decon to AI'.[2] It would appear that, as a result of the explosion of interest in new AI-based design techniques, progressive design is staging a comeback (Figures 17.1–17.3).

Equally, there are signs that – alongside this – a fresh burst of theoretical enquiry is being initiated. With the introduction of AI, we are encountering a novel set of ideas that look set to promote a renewed interest in theoretical discourse. Indeed parallels can also be drawn perhaps between the radical theorization that accompanied 'Deconstructivism' at the end of twentieth century, and the new theoretical agenda that accompanies the current interest in AI in the third decade of the twenty-first. But the sources of this new theoretical discourse are radically different to those of 30 years ago. Continental philosophy is no longer in the ascendancy. It has been supplanted in its role as the master discourse by cognitive science, an interdisciplinary study of the mind, as rapidly developing debates about neuroscience, artificial intelligence, and cognitive philosophy are beginning to gain traction. What insights, then, can cognitive science offer architectural theory, and how might it help us to understand the mind of the architect?

*Figure 17.1–17.3* Deep Himmelb(l)au (2020) is a project developed by Coop Himmelb(l)au, that uses CycleGANs to extrapolate novel architectural images.

## Machine Hallucinations

The recent burst of formal invention within the realm of AI is based on the increasingly popularity of neural networks. These neural networks are part of deep learning, the most advanced area of research in AI. Neural networks consist of neurons and synapses and are inspired by the brain itself.[3] Their popularity has been fueled as the result of important shifts, such as the development of cloud computing, vastly improved algorithms, substantial increase in data and huge international rivalry in the field of computer science. Importantly, they can be used to generate images (Figure 17.4).

Typically a neural network has to be 'trained' on a vast dataset of images. Once trained, it will be able to recognize those images. Hence Facebook will be able to recognize your friends, and Instagram will be able to identify different objects. But, importantly, it can only recognize images based on data on which it has been trained. Also, it can only generate images based on that data. The technical term often used for this image generation is 'hallucination'. Thus, if a neural network has been trained on images of dogs, it will 'hallucinate' images of dogs. This very restricted way of operating seems very different from how we human beings operate. Or is it?

*Figure 17.4* Martin Thomas, *Aurelia Aurita*, DeepDream generated image (2015). DeepDream is a technique for generating images using a neural network. In this case the neural network has been trained in part on images of dogs.

In fact we human beings also see the world through the lens on which we have been trained. For example, if we were to ask anyone how many colors there are in a rainbow, the chances are that they would reply, 'seven', even though there are an infinite number of colors in the spectrum that constitutes a rainbow.[4] This is because we are trained at school to recognize seven colors in a rainbow. And, if we were to ask any architect what a 'functionalist' building looks like, the chances are they would describe a white building on *piloti* with a flat roof, even though flat roofs are not very functional in that they tend to leak. This is because we are trained at architecture school to understand that functionalist buildings have flat roofs.

The idea that we are conditioned to see the world in a certain way comes under the theory of 'predictive perception', a theory that is beginning to gain some traction in cognitive science, in general, and neuroscience, in particular.[5] According to neuroscientist Anil Seth, the brain is locked into a boney skull without any light or sound, and has little information about the outside world apart from electrical impulses. As such, the brain tries to offer its 'best guess' as to what is happening out there, based on the input of sensory information and previous experiences.[6] Perception is therefore not as objective as it might seem. Nor is it simply a question of the brain receiving signals from the outside. The brain actively partakes in trying to make sense of what it is sensing:

> Instead of perception depending largely on signals coming into the brain from the outside world, it depends as much, if not more, on perceptual predictions flowing in the opposite direction. We don't just passively perceive the world, we actively generate it. The world we experience comes as much, if not more, from the inside out as from the outside in.[7]

Seth argues that the brain therefore makes predictions – or 'hallucinations', as he calls them – about what it is perceiving. But these hallucinations need to be reined in so as to prevent incorrect predictions. There needs to be a degree of control involved. In fact, Seth illustrates this with a video processed using a DeepDream algorithm that shows how overly strong perceptual predictions can lead to weird hallucinatory perceptions, where the viewer comes to read images of whatever they have been trained on into everything that they see.[8] This leads Seth to conclude that if hallucination is a form of uncontrolled perception, then perception itself must be a form of "controlled hallucination":[9]

> If hallucination is a kind of controlled perception, then perception right here and right now is also a kind of hallucination, but a controlled hallucination in which the brain's predictions are being reined in by sensory information from the world. In fact, we're all hallucinating all the time, including right now. It's just that when we agree about our hallucinations, we call that reality.[10]

What is interesting here is that Seth uses the expression 'controlled hallucinations' to describe the process of predictive perception on the part of humans, just as we use the expression 'machine hallucinations' to describe the images generated by a neural network. According to this logic, when we look at the world we are actively hallucinating, in a manner not entirely dissimilar to how machines are 'hallucinating' when they generate images. There is an implicit parallel being drawn, then, between human perception and computational image generation. The two would appear to be not as dissimilar as we might imagine at first (Figure 17.5).

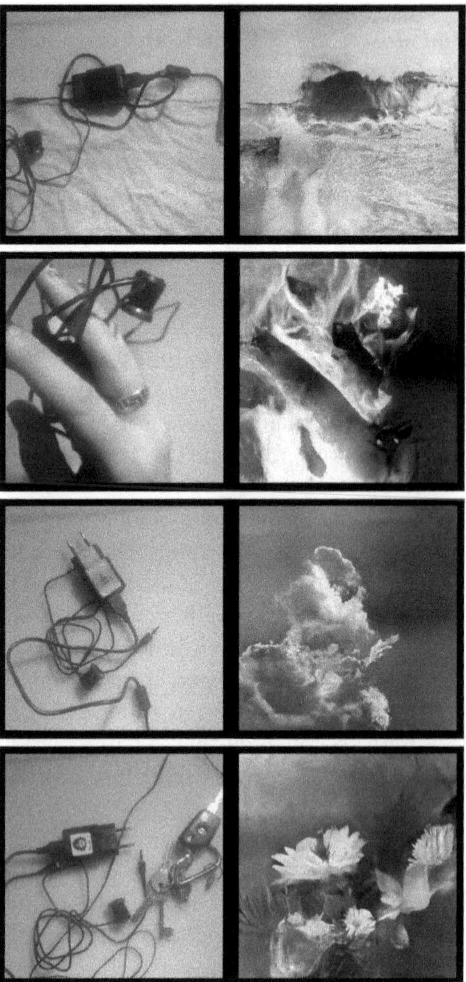

*Figure 17.5* Memo Akten, *Gloomy Sunday.*

Similarly, computational artist Memo Akten uses artificial neural networks to illustrate how we are trained to see the world[11]: In his 'Gloomy Sunday' interactive experiment, Akten offers an illustration of how an artificial neural network interprets objects based on how it has been trained. Thus, if trained on a dataset composed solely of images of flowers, the artificial neural network will read images of flowers into everything that it sees. As Akten observes, "The picture we see in our conscious mind is not a mirror image of the outside world, but is a reconstruction based on our expectations and prior beliefs."[12] By extension, previous experiences act as a kind of filter to subsequent experiences. They distort and color how we see the world. In other words, Akten's notion that perception is based on 'prior beliefs' appears to be remarkably similar to Seth's notion that it is based on 'previous experiences'. Similarly, the 'Gloomy Sunday' experiment that Akten makes using trained neural networks is remarkably close to the experiment that Seth makes using DeepDream. In short, Akten appears to be corroborating Seth's theory of predictive perception.

Equally, we could compare Seth's notion of the 'controlled hallucination' at work in our perception of the world with Slavoj Zizek's notion of 'fantasy' that serves as a lens through which we perceive the world. Zizek's thinking is grounded in Lacanian theory. According to Lacan, we do not access the 'Real' except in moments of *jouissance*.[13] What we take for the real is not the real in itself, but an appearance of reality.[14] In fact, our perception of reality comes to us 'via a detour through the maze of the imagination'. It is colored and distorted by our imagination, no less than our outlook on the world is distorted by the way that we have been trained to view the world, as the two 'experiments' by Seth and Akten illustrate. Moreover, for Zizek, our perception of reality is a *fantasy* of reality.[15] Fantasy, then, plays a key role in how we understand 'reality'. In fact, fantasy for Zizek is literally 'constitutive of how we see reality':

> Far from being a kind of fragment of our dreams that prevents us from 'seeing reality as it effectively is', fantasy is constitutive of what we call reality: the most common bodily 'reality' is constituted via a detour through the maze of imagination.[16]

Zizek goes further, and speculates whether, as we use computation to simulate human thought ever more closely, an inversion might take place, such that human thought begins to emulate a computer program, and our own understanding of the world itself becomes a model:

> What if this 'model' is already a model of the 'original' itself, what if human intelligence itself operates like a computer, is 'programmed', etc.? The computer raises in pure form the question of semblance, a discourse which would not be a simulacrum: it is clear that the computer in some sense only 'simulates' thought; yet how does the total simulation of thought differ from 'real' thought?[17]

*Figure 17.6* Fernando Salcedo, *Architectural Hallucinations.*

In other words, Zizek is speculating that we might be living in a simulation, an argument originally floated by sociologist Jean Baudrillard, and made famous in the movie *The Matrix*, but since supported by other more recent philosophical arguments.[18] Likewise, we can draw comparisons between this view and the way that Seth and other neuroscientists understand our conception of the world as a constructed one, based on prior beliefs and experiences, such that what we perceive is also a model – a simulation – of the world.

This leads Zizek to conclude that it would be wrong to denigrate 'virtual reality' as a lesser form of reality. What virtual reality reveals is not how 'virtual' virtual reality is, but rather how 'virtual' our understanding of 'reality' is: 'The ultimate lesson of virtual reality is the virtualization of the very true reality' (Figure 17.6).[19]

## Architecturalizations

Turning to architecture, could we not also compare the way that we were trained as architects to the way in which artificial neural networks are trained? In 2020 FIU architectural student, Fernando Salcedo, undertook an interactive AI experiment not dissimilar to 'Gloomy Sunday', where he trained a neural network on generic modernist architecture and the other based on the King Abdullah Petroleum Studies and Research Center designed by Zaha Hadid Architects (ZHA).[20] The neural network then reads architectural forms into everything that it sees, including items of clothing, through a process similar to the principle of predictive perception. In this weirdly distorted view of the world, a simple tie can be read as a tower block, and a crumpled shirt can be read as a warped version of the ZHA project. Importantly, however, the neural network is not reading forms in an objective fashion.

Rather, it is reading them through a filter.[21] This experiment provokes some interesting questions. Is this perhaps how architects see the world, reading potential buildings into everything that they see?[22] In other words, through their architectural education are architects *trained* to see the world in a certain way, just as a neural network is trained to see the world?

To claim that this is the case would be to mount an argument based on pure analogy. In and of itself, this experiment does not prove anything. Nonetheless it is tempting to pursue this line of enquiry further. Might this experiment not offer us insights, for example, into the nature of inspiration itself – the 'act' of reading the world through a particular lens and then re-expressing that vision in the design itself?

We could describe this process as a form of 'architecturalization'. In effect, architects tend to 'architecturalize' whatever they see, and read the world in architectural terms.[23] This allows them to be inspired by any number of non-architectural items – biological entities, animals, insects, geological formations and indeed potentially anything – and incorporate them into their architectural expressions.[24] This might explain, for example, how Jorn Utzon was inspired by the billowing sails of yachts, and went on to read them as potential vaults for an opera house overlooking Sydney Harbor.

This tendency becomes even more obvious, however, when we consider how architects tend to 'architecturalize' concepts. This might also help to explain, for example, why architects so often misinterpret philosophical concepts, such as the 'fold' promoted by Gilles Deleuze, and assume they are references to architectural forms, even though they have nothing to do with form, or architecture as such.[25] In fact Deleuze is referring to philosophical issues, especially the production of subjectivity, as Simon Sullivan has observed: 'The concept of the fold allows Deleuze to think creatively about the production of subjectivity, and ultimately about the possibilities for, and production of, non-human forms of subjectivity'.[26]

It might also explain how some architects, such as Gilles Retsin, make the mistake of taking terms referring to the digital – terms such as 'discrete' – and assume that it is referring potentially to architectural forms, even though the digital itself is immaterial and has no form.[27] It might also help to explain how historians, such as Mario Carpo, read that Big Data is 'messy', and therefore somehow imagined that there must be an architectural style of Big Data that is itself also messy.[28] What architectural form has to do with Big Data is itself something of a mystery. Big Data, after all, refers to information and not to form. A perfect example of the use of big data is the operation of an Uber car. Does an Uber car look any different in terms of its form to an ordinary car? No, because it is an ordinary car. Yet the temptation to read the 'discrete' or 'Big Data' in terms of a language of architectural forms are precisely examples of the trap of 'architecturalization'.

By extension, it would also explain why architects tend to 'aestheticize' everything that they see, reading the world in terms of aesthetic concerns, and rinsing it of any economic, social or political considerations.[29] Why is it, for example, that many architects have a tendency to privilege design concerns over economic factors, even though economic factors are the main driver of any design? Indeed, why are there so few references to economic considerations in books on architecture, apart from the cost of the book on the back cover? It is as though architects always tend to see the world with a certain gaze, as though through rose-tinted, aestheticizing lenses.

It is important to understand, then, that the gaze of the architect is not neutral. It has been trained, no less than a neural network has been trained. Whether we understand this conditioned outlook in Seth's terms as a form of 'controlled hallucination' or in Zizek's terms as being constituted through 'fantasy', it is clear that architects see the world not as it is, but as they are trained to see it. But is this not so dissimilar from the message behind the term 'deconstruction' coined by Derrida?

Derrida argues that our perception of the world carries with it certain biases, just as the data used in AI carries with it certain biases.[30] Our perception of the world is therefore 'constructed'. And this 'constructed' perception is a distorted one, as we have seen with the standard interpretation of a rainbow. What needs to be exposed, then, is how our understanding of the world has been 'constructed'. And this 'constructed' way of understanding the world itself needs to be 'deconstructed'. The same issue applies to architecture.

'Let us never forget', wrote Derrida, 'that there is an architecture of architecture'.[31] Put another way, our understanding of architecture is itself 'constructed', as we have seen with the standard perception of 'functionalism' as referring to buildings with flat roofs. Our understanding of architecture therefore needs to be 'deconstructed'. Here Derrida treats architecture as a kind of metaphor for how we have come to see the world.

> Now the concept of deconstruction itself resembles an architectural metaphor...It is not simply the technique of an architect who knows how to deconstruct what has been constructed, but a probing which touches upon the technique itself, upon the authority of the architectural metaphor and thereby constitutes its own architectural rhetoric. Deconstruction is not simply—as its name seems to indicate—the technique of a reversed construction when it is able to conceive for itself the idea of construction. One could say that there is nothing more architectural than deconstruction but also nothing less architectural. Architectural thinking can only be deconstructive in the following sense: as an attempt to visualize that which establishes the authority of the architectural concatenation in philosophy.[32]

The irony here is that architects largely misinterpret Derrida. They tend to think that the term, 'deconstruction', refers in some way to the construction of buildings, whereas in fact it is simply an architectural metaphor. What is this misinterpretation, then, but yet another example of architecturalization?

## Conclusion

Architectural theorists have traditionally been somewhat skeptical of computation. It could be claimed, however, that in order for theory to reassert itself and play a more significant role in architectural discourse, architectural theorists will need to start to embrace some of the radical ideas emerging in computational neuroscience, and to recognize that AI might potentially offer us important insights into the workings of the architectural mind.

Let us be clear. There is a significant difference between AI and human intelligence, not least because AI does not possess consciousness – at least for now. At a very basic level, then, AI cannot 'think' any more than your pocket calculator can 'think', in that thinking requires consciousness. But perhaps the most significant differences occur where we least expect them – where we use the same terminology for both AI and human intelligence and hence assume some equivalence. Equally, we must be careful of projecting human attributes on to the world of AI – and *vice versa*. We might use the terms, 'intelligence', 'learning', and so on when referring to AI, but there is an enormous difference between the way that these terms are used in the context of AI, and how they are used in the context of human operations. For how is it possible to use the terms, 'intelligence' or 'learning' when neither process involves thinking? Despite appearances, then, it is not so easy to make direct comparisons between AI and human intelligence.

At the same time, there are moments when neural networks seemingly open up insights into human intelligence, and parallels present themselves. Of course, in such instances, parallels remain just parallels. A behavior in one domain does not explain a similar behavior in another domain. But nonetheless, digital simulations can often help us to understand analog behaviors. For example, it was not until Craig Reynolds produced a digital model for the flocking behavior of birds using 'boids', that we were able to understand the behavior of actual birds.[33] It is as though AI might help us to understand human intelligence. Might AI offer us some clues as to how the mind of the architect works?

## Notes

1 https://www.archdaily.com/885422/why-postmodernisms-new-found-popularity-is-all-about-looking-forward-not-back.
2 Wolf Prix and Thom Mayne, 'From Decon to AI: AI and Architectural Practice'. https://www.youtube.com/watch?v=OlvYzmWuMsU.
3 Neural networks might be inspired by the brain, but they are very different to the brain. For example, we might use the term 'neuron' in reference to neural networks, but the 'neurons' in neural networks are quite different to the neurons in the brain. One of the foremost commentators on AI, Melanie Mitchell even prefers to call them 'units'. Melanie Mitchell, *Artificial Intelligence: A Guide for Thinking Humans*, New York: Farrar, Straus and Giroux, 2019, p. 37.
4 Indeed, according to neuroscientist, Anil Seth, our whole notion of color is itself a construct, generated by the brain. DigitalFUTURES: AI and Neuroscience, 6 July 2020, https://www.youtube.com/watch?v=L1H7eL8pk5k.

5 Anil K. Seth, 'A Predictive Processing Theory of Sensorimotor Contingencies: Explaining the Puzzle of Perceptual Presence and Its Absence in Synesthesia.' *Cognitive neuroscience*, 5(2) (2014): 97–118. doi:10.1080/17588928.2013.877880; Andy Clark, *Surfing Uncertainty: Prediction, Action and the Embodied Mind*, Oxford: Oxford UP, 2016.

6 Anil Seth, 'Your Brain Hallucinates Your Conscious Reality', *TED Talk*, April 2017, https://www.ted.com/talks/anil_seth_your_brain_hallucinates_your_conscious_reality?language=en.

7 Ibid. This is not dissimilar to the 'double moment of vision' that Christian Metz describes (Christian Metz, *Psychoanalysis and the Cinema*, London: Macmillan, 1992, p. 51): 'As one casts one's eye (in a projective fashion), one receives and absorbs (in an introjective fashion) what has been 'illuminated', as it were. Consciousness therefore serves, in Metz's terminology, as a 'recording surface'.' Leach, *Camouflage*, pp. 140–141.

8 Seth and his team have explored how altered states of consciousness help us to understand underlying conscious perception: Keisuke Suzuki, Warrick Roseboom, David J. Schwartzman, Anil K. Seth, 'A Deep-Dream Virtual Reality Platform for Studying Altered Perceptual Phenomenology,' *Scientific Reports*, 7 (2017): 15982. doi:10.1038/s41598-017-16316-2.

9 Rick Grush has used previously the notion of 'controlled hallucination'. Grush acknowledges, however, that the expression had been coined originally by Ramesh Jain in a talk at UCSD. Rick Grush, 'The Emulation Theory of Representation: Motor Control, Imagery, and Perception,' *Behavioral and Brain Sciences*, 27 (2004): 377–442, 393.

10 Anil Seth, 'Your Brain Hallucinates Your Conscious Reality', *TED Talk*, April 2017, https://www.ted.com/talks/anil_seth_your_brain_hallucinates_your_conscious_reality?language=en.

11 Memo Akten, 'Learning to See: Gloomy Sunday,' 2017, Memo.tv. http://www.memo.tv/portfolio/gloomy-sunday/.

12 Ibid.

13 *Jouissance* is the bittersweet moment that flares up in aesthetic contemplation. For *jouissance* see Leach, *Camouflage*, p. 232. See also Dylan Evans, *An Introductory Dictionary of Lacanian Psychoanalysis* (London: Routledge, 1996), p. 92.

14 'This is precisely what Lacan has in mind when he says that fantasy is the ultimate support of reality: 'reality' stabilizes itself when some fantasy-frame of a 'symbolic bliss' forecloses the view into the abyss of the Real.' Slavoj Zizek, 'From Virtual Reality to the Virtualisation of Reality,' in Neil Leach (ed.), *Designing for a Digital World*, London: Wiley, 2002, p. 122.

15 This is somewhat different to the interpretation of Seth, who argues that 'reality' is a form of consensus as to what we see, when we agree about our controlled hallucinations. Anil Seth, 'Your Brain Hallucinates Your Conscious Reality', *TED Talk*, April 2017, https://www.ted.com/talks/anil_seth_your_brain_hallucinates_your_conscious_reality?language=en.

16 Zizek, p. 122.

17 Zizek, p. 123.

18 Nic Bostrom, 'Are You Living in a Computer Simulation?' *Philosophical Quarterly*, 53 (211) (2003): 243–255.

19 Zizek, 'From Virtual Reality to the Virtualisation of Reality', p. 125.

20 https://www.youtube.com/watch?v=WCsjbPc9624&feature=youtu.be.

21 This experiment could be compared, perhaps, to the artistic strategy of making some random mark – a splash of paint, or pencil lines – in order to start generating an artwork. In his text, *Francis Bacon: The Logic of Sense*, Deleuze describes a strategy that he calls a 'diagram' as a way to initiate a painting. Gilles Deleuze, *Francis Bacon: The Logic of Sense*, Minneapolis: Minnesota University Press, 2005.

Here the diagram – or 'graph' as Bacon himself calls it – serves to disrupt the given conditions and open up the space of the imagination. The 'diagram', as a strategy for initiating a developing a painting, is based on chaotic and random actions – generative techniques that allow the artist to break free of conventions.

22 This relates to a conversation that I once had with Bernard Tschumi, where we were discussing how architects see the world 'as architects', as though architects see the world through a certain kind of lens.

23 Could this be similar to the term, 'architect-ing', that Anadol uses? Refik Anadol, Anil Seth, Neil Leach, Daniel Bolojan, Kris Mun, 'Digital FUTURES: AI and Neuroscience,' 27 June 2020, https://www.youtube.com/watch?v=L1H7eL8pk5k.

24 This is similar to the process of mimetic assimilation: 'It is through the mimetic impulse that human beings absorb external forms, incorporate them symbolically into their self-expression, and then rearticulate them in the objects they produce.' Leach, *Camouflage*, p. 44.

25 Neil Leach, 'Can a Building Be an Apparatus?,' in Sang Lee, Henriette Bier (guest editors), *Spool: Cyber-Physical Architecture*, Vol. 6, No 1, 2019, pp. 5–16. Deleuze, G., *The Fold: Leibniz and the Baroque*, Minneapolis: University of Minnesota Press, 1993.

26 Simon Sullivan, 'The Fold,' in Adrian Parr (ed.), *The Deleuze Dictionary*, rev edn, Edinburgh: Edinburgh University Press, 2012, p. 107.

27 Neil Leach, 'There Is No Such Thing as a Digital Building: A Critique of the Discrete,' in Gilles Retsin (ed.), *Discrete: Reappraising the Digital in Architecture, AD, Profile 258*, 2019, p. 139.

28 Mario Carpo, *The Second Digital Turn: Design Beyond Intelligence*, Cambridge, MA: MIT Press, 2017.

29 Neil Leach, *The Anaesthetics of Architecture*, Cambridge, MA: MIT Press, 1999.

30 Melanie Mitchell, *Artificial Intelligence: A Guide for Thinking Humans*, New York: Farrar, Straus and Giroux, 2019, pp. 106–108.

31 Jacques Derrida, 'Point de Folie – Maintenant l'Architecture,' in Leach (ed.), *Rethinking Architecture*, London: Routledge, 1997, p. 307.

32 Jacques Derrida, 'Architecture Where the Desire May Live,' in Leach (ed.), *Rethinking Architecture*, London: Routledge, 1997, pp. 302–303.

33 Craig Reynolds, 'Flocks, Herds, and Schools: A Distributed Behavioral Model', *Computer Graphics*, 21(4), July 1987), 25–34.

# Index